SLAYING THE BADGER

SLAYING THE BADGER

GREG LEMOND, BERNARD HINAULT, AND THE GREATEST TOUR DE FRANCE

RICHARD MOORE

BOULDER, COLORADO

3002 Sterling Circle, Suite 100
Boulder, Colorado 80301-2338 USA
(303) 440-0601 · Fax (303) 444-6788 · E-mail velopress@competitorgroup.com

Distributed in the United States and Canada by Ingram Publisher Services

Library of Congress Cataloging-in-Publication Data
Moore, Richard.
Slaying the badger: Greg Lemond, Bernard Hinault, and the greatest Tour de France
/ Richard Moore.
p. cm.
ISBN 978-1-934030-87-5 (pbk.)
1. Tour de France (Bicycle race) (1986) 2. LeMond, Greg. 3. Hinault, Bernard, 1954–
4. Cyclists—France—Biography. 5. Cyclists—United States—Biography.
6. Sports rivalries. I. Title.=
GV1049.2.T68M66 2012
796.620944—dc23
2012000701

For information on purchasing VeloPress books, please call (800) 811-4210 ext. 2138 or visit www.velopress.com.

Cover design by Landers Miller Design, LLC
Interior design and composition by Anita Koury
Cover photograph by AP Photo/Lionel Cironneau
Interior photographs by Offside Sports Photography except **first insert**, page 2 (top): Corbis Images UK; page 5 (top): Shelley Verses; **second insert**, page 2 (bottom): Graham Watson; page 8 (top right): Pascal Pavani/AFP/Getty Images; page 8 (bottom): James Startt

Text set in Minion.

12   13   14 / 10   9   8   7   6   5   4   3   2   1

For my ever-supportive dad, Brian,
and brothers, Robin and Peter

CONTENTS

Prologue   1

PART ONE: DÉPART

1. The Badger   15

2. The Cannibal Is Dead, Long Live le Blaireau   31

3. L'Américain   53

4. A Great Champion but a Small Man   73

5. Changing of the Guard   89

6. The Kooky Professor   107

7. The Million-Dollar Man   131

8. The Case of the Broken Ray-Bans   143

PART TWO: ARRIVÉE

9. The Bulldog and the Bird   157

10. Who Is Bernard Tapie?   169

11. The American Invasion   185

12. You Blew It, Bernie   199

13. The Enemy of My Enemy Is My Friend   217

14. A Two-Headed Eagle   237

15. Born in the USA   255

CONTENTS

Epilogue   269

Afterword   275

Acknowledgments   285

Index   287

About the Author   296

PROLOGUE

In the midst of competition, Hinault attempted to snatch victory like a furious, clawing rodent. . . . He acted not only for himself but for a nation horrified that its great race might be hijacked by an American outlaw.

ROLLING STONE, 1986

The stench was overpowering: a putrid smell so bad that several riders looked around, their faces screwing up as though they were sucking on lemons. Glancing back, they saw Greg LeMond, fourth in line, being led up to the peloton—the main pack of riders—by a string of his La Vie Claire teammates.

Up the outside the four-man train continued, the three worker bees escorting their stricken leader back to the front, where, as one of the favorites, LeMond needed to be. But at least one rider, sitting toward the rear of the peloton, saw the brown liquid streaking the insides of the American's legs, running into his shoes.

It was a bad peach, LeMond reckoned. After eating it, his stomach reacted violently. He turned to a teammate. "Pass me your hat."

"What do you want my hat for?"

"Please, just pass me the goddamn hat!"

Taking the small cotton team cap, LeMond shoved it down his shorts, maneuvered it into position, and filled it until it was overflowing. He tried to clean himself up, but it was hopeless. Then he tossed the hat into the hedgerow and began the grim task of getting back into the race, slotting in behind the three teammates who'd dropped back from the peloton to wait for him.

With his stomach churning, LeMond had 60 km of the stage to endure: more than an hour of agony, every second of it spent craving the isolation and privacy of a toilet. As the two hundred riders swarmed across the line in Futuroscope, most eased up, dropped a foot to the road, and reached for a drinking bottle. LeMond didn't. He wove urgently through all the bodies, the riders, soigneurs, and reporters, searching for his team's motor home. He'd never been in it before—it was used mainly for storage—but he knew it had a toilet.

Entering the motor home, LeMond found it packed with boxes, but, tip-toeing awkwardly in his cleated cycling shoes, he negotiated the passage and ripped open the cubicle door. The toilet was gone. Where it had been, there were more boxes. LeMond was desperate. He tore off the lid of the largest box, inside which were thousands upon thousands of postcards. Staring up at him on each of these cards was the smiling, handsome face of his team-mate Bernard Hinault. LeMond didn't hesitate; he yanked at them, pulling out bundles of cards to create a borehole in the middle. Then he dropped his shorts, sat down, and found glorious relief amid—and upon—approximately 40,000 depictions of the great Frenchman.

The common perception is that Greg LeMond was crapped upon by Bernard Hinault at the 1986 Tour de France. What most don't know is that LeMond got there first.

It has been 25 years since Greg LeMond and Bernard Hinault acted out what is arguably the most famous of Tour de France scenes, appearing together at the summit of Alpe d'Huez. So often the race's decisive mountain, on this occasion Alpe d'Huez—a snaking, 14.5-km, 21-hairpinned climb that transforms into an amphitheater for the Tour de France—witnessed something that seemed less dramatic than the usual contest but that was no less sensational, in a different way, for a different reason, for the hundreds of thousands who, according to one writer, formed a "squalid, manic shambles" by the roadside.

LeMond and Hinault, though teammates on the powerful La Vie Claire cycling squad, had fought each other for two weeks. Because they were team-mates, their rivalry was as unusual as it was intense. But there were other explanations for the fact that it was utterly compelling. For one, it pitted cycling's "old world," as represented by the Frenchman Hinault, against the "new," represented by the American LeMond. It saw a clash of radically different cultures, and also of opposing personalities. Hinault, nicknamed "the Badger," was aggressive, surly, and fearless; LeMond was friendly, open, and vulnerable. In football, they talk about "men against boys"; Hinault versus LeMond appeared to be man against boy.

After opening skirmishes on the flat roads of northern and western France in week one of the 1986 Tour, Hinault and LeMond waged all-out war in the Pyrenees in week two. The denouement would come in week three in the Alps. It was here that the LeMond-Hinault duel would be settled, that the battle would be decided.

LeMond and Hinault arrived together at the base of Alpe d'Huez. They had blown everyone else away. LeMond wore the yellow jersey of the race leader for the first time in his career, having wrested it from Hinault's shoulders as the Frenchman had suffered with a leg injury during the previous day's stage. Recriminations followed in the hours after that stage and carried on well into the night. LeMond and Hinault "were at each other's throats," according to their team's owner, the flamboyant Bernard Tapie, who claimed to have convened crisis talks with the pair until four in the morning.

And so it has come down to this day, to this climb. Yet now, as they begin the climb to Alpe d'Huez, there is no visible evidence of their enmity. On the contrary, they appear united. The impression is confirmed as they proceed up in tandem, riding through throngs of supporters, the majority of whom are French and cheering their hero, Hinault, urging him to a record sixth Tour victory. It is as though they don't even see LeMond. They spill into the road, clearing at the last second to leave only a narrow, handlebar-wide passage for the two riders. All the time, Hinault leads and LeMond follows. It seems a truce has been called. For hairpin after hairpin, the order doesn't alter. Neither does the steady pace; theirs is one of the slowest "winning" ascents of Alpe d'Huez in Tour history. Hinault is at the front, pedaling like a metronome; LeMond just behind him, as though the American is hiding in the Frenchman's shadow. Perhaps he is.

And then, through the village at the top, where the road levels, LeMond finally emerges from Hinault's shadow, not to launch an attack within sight of the finish line but to pull alongside his teammate. He reaches out toward Hinault and pats his back. Hinault turns and smiles. There is tenderness between them now. They speak. They smile. They exchange a few more words. They clasp their hands in the air, and then LeMond eases off and seems almost to push Hinault forward, so he can claim the stage win.

On Dutch TV, the commentator is in raptures. "What a gesture! What a gesture! Fantastic! This is fantastic! LeMond putting his arm on that shoulder! That smile! Oh, how beautiful this is. How beautiful sport can be. Oh! How splendid this is! It's fantastic to be seeing this. . . . Oh! It's magnificent!"

For many of those watching, it was indeed a moment of such beauty and poignancy that it seemed to transcend sport. Indeed, it didn't seem fanciful to imagine that what we had just witnessed at the top of Alpe d'Huez might come to be recognized alongside other transcendental sporting moments: Jesse Owens's four gold medals at the 1936 Olympics; Ali and Foreman's Rumble in the Jungle in 1974; Borg and McEnroe's 1980 final at Wimbledon.

Yet the background and aftermath to LeMond and Hinault's all-smiles, hand-in-hand finish at Alpe d'Huez means that, for others, it belongs in a different category, alongside less glorious, though no less memorable, sporting moments: Mike Tyson biting Evander Holyfield's ear during their world-title fight in 1997; Ben Johnson's drug-fueled victory over Carl Lewis at the 1988 Olympics; Diego Maradona's "hand of God" goal at the 1986 World Cup.

LeMond and Hinault were teammates, perhaps even friends, who became bitter rivals in the course of that Tour. Their battle was fascinating for what it revealed of each of them, for what it told us about the sport and the unique event that is the Tour de France. And for many of us in the so-called new world—at least where the sport of cycling was concerned—it provided a first, bewildering introduction to a sport that obviously glorified individuals, yet was organized along team lines, with odd, unwritten rules and etiquette and a rigid hierarchy.

In Greg LeMond and Bernard Hinault, the 1986 Tour had two protagonists who were compelling, and who would also go down in history as two of the most influential riders the sport has ever known. Hinault, as well as being a formidable champion, was, in effect, the riders' trade union leader who helped revolutionize their working conditions; LeMond, the American free marketeer, revolutionized riders' pay. He was a pioneer and a revolutionary in another sense, too. No cyclist from an English-speaking nation had won the Tour de France before 1986; at the time of this writing, 11 of the 25 Tours held since then have been claimed by native English speakers, and the United States has jumped to fourth in the league of nations who have supplied Tour winners, putting the country one ahead of one of cycling's traditional pow-erhouses: Italy.

But the statistics—even the sense that LeMond was making history—fail to explain why I and so many others watched the 1986 Tour with such rapt attention. What captured my imagination was the drama. The intrigue. The subterfuge. Over three weeks, the race became a story with more credulity-stretching plot twists than a dime-store detective novel.

As an introduction to the sport, the 1986 Tour was, in short, mind-blowing. Julys would never be the same.

And it was, even allowing for the inevitably rose-tinted hue of my spec-tacles, a golden period. Watching Hinault at his best, we were able to wit-ness the final bow of one of the all-time greats. Hinault, or Le Blaireau—the Badger—was a proud, stubborn, aggressive Breton whose permanent scowl couldn't detract from his handsome dark looks. The origins of the "Badger" nickname are disputed; its suitability is not, since badgers are ferocious fight-ers, especially when backed into a corner or when they have their prey within their sights. The other thing one should know about badgers is that their jaws *cannot* be dislocated; when a badger gets its prey in its mouth, it is impossible to pry its teeth apart. That is Hinault.

When Hinault was on the attack—as he was a lot in the 1986 Tour, much to LeMond's irritation—his piercing eyes narrowed and his jaw clenched as though he were gripping something in his teeth, like a snarling dog refusing to give up a bone. It had the effect of making him look permanently angry, capable of great violence, and not someone to mess with.

LeMond was the polar opposite: a blond-haired, blue-eyed Californian, as likable and fragile as Hinault was gruff, tough, and self-assured. LeMond was a prodigy—he had to be to defy the odds, and a century of tradition, in becoming the first American to scale the heights of this resolutely European sport. Along the way, he openly questioned conventions, bucked tradition, and acted as a refreshing breath of Californian air through the peloton. He ate Mexican food and American ice cream; he played golf when his team-mates were resting. Yet you didn't feel LeMond was being different for ef-fect, or that there was anything affected about him; he was just being him-self. Though he could appear vulnerable and even endearingly naive at times, it must, paradoxically, have taken a steely kind of confidence to be himself in a world that was not his own, that was so far removed from his own. It left you wondering: Where did it come from? But it helped enormously that

LeMond was, physiologically speaking, something of a freak, the kind of physical specimen that comes along once in a generation.

Hinault and LeMond lined up for the 1986 Tour as teammates, having reached an understanding. With LeMond having acted the loyal teammate to Hinault in 1985, it was Hinault's turn to repay the favor in 1986. That was the deal, even if it meant Hinault, the great French hero, would thereby squander the opportunity to go for a sixth Tour—a record that would have taken him past Jacques Anquetil and Eddy Merckx, the other two five-time winners, in the history books. The question, as the Tour approached, and more particularly as it got under way, was whether he would be willing to honor the deal.

In the background to the Hinault-LeMond duel was a colorful cast of characters. Bernard Tapie, the La Vie Claire team owner, would later earn notoriety for his role, as president of Marseille Football Club, in a match-fixing scandal that led to his imprisonment. Cycling was Tapie's first involvement in sport, and he brought glamour and ambition allied to hardheaded business and commercial sense as well as—in large doses—a sense of showbiz and a charismatic presence such as the sport had rarely seen.

Then there was a man who was in many respects Tapie's opposite: Paul Köchli. Tapie owned the La Vie Claire team, but Köchli was the squad's visionary, science-minded directeur sportif—its director in charge of the entire program. Further in the background was Cyrille Guimard, the early mentor to both Hinault and LeMond. And there were so many other great cyclists of the 1980s—Jean-François Bernard, Laurent Fignon, Andy Hampsten, Steve Bauer, Urs Zimmermann, Stephen Roche, Pedro Delgado, Luis Herrera . . . the list goes on. Almost forgotten was another significant subplot to the 1986 Tour: the debut of an American team, 7-Eleven, a development arguably more influential than LeMond's win in sowing the seeds for the future domination of riders and teams from across the Atlantic.

When I discussed my plans for this book with Samuel Abt, the now semi-retired American journalist for the *International Herald Tribune* and the *New York Times* and veteran of more than thirty Tours, he contested the assertion that the interviews I conducted, and the contemporaneous reports I pored over, constituted "research."

"Really," said Abt, "it's archaeology."

As Abt suggested, the sport has changed so much in the past 25 years that it is almost unrecognizable. And yet many of those changes have their roots in this period, if not specifically in that 1986 Tour.

Still, though, it was the human dimension to the story of the '86 Tour that most interested me—of course it was. The two stars of the race were utterly fascinating, as they still are today. And while their names remain inexorably linked to the sport that made them famous, their legacies are quite different—and surprising. Who would have predicted in 1986 that the stubborn, aggressive Hinault would end up becoming part of the establishment? And that the affable and engaging LeMond would end up being perceived by many as a troublemaker, even a thorn in the sport's flesh?

The motivation for this book was to replay a Tour that, for me, encapsulated all that is so beguiling about the sport and in the process to seek to establish what happened—to separate the truth from the lies and duplicity, a difficulty in a sport of multiple "truths." To do that, it is necessary to fill in the background, and so the first two-thirds of this book are taken up with the stories of the two principal characters as well as the Tours, people, and events that all, in some way or another, act as an extended prelude to 1986.

Another motivation was to revisit Hinault and LeMond, in the process reassessing these two giants of the sport: their impact then, their legacy today. But as well as revisiting these great riders and their legacies in a figurative sense, I wanted to visit them in a literal sense, too. These interviews form the basis of the book. And my visits to each of their homes proved revealing, thrilling, slightly intimidating—and inevitably rather poignant.

And so it seems only right that the story should begin with them.

THE BADGER'S SET, BRITTANY, DECEMBER 2009

In a cheap and uncheerful hotel, one of three adjacent to the railway station in the Breton town of Dinan, the welcome is as warm as this coldest December day in years. It's midafternoon; three bored-looking men sit nursing long glasses of beer, glancing in my direction, though not really at me, as I walk uncertainly toward the bar. The *patron*, polishing glasses, conspicuously fails to meet an inquiring gaze. So I try speaking. "Ahem. *Avez-vous une chambre, s'il vous plaît?*"

"Mmmm." The response is grumbled. I can't even be sure that it's directed at me; Monsieur Patron hasn't lifted his gaze from his glasses. But I linger. Apart from anything else, it's absolutely Baltic outside.

In the past 24 hours, a freeze has abruptly descended on the whole of Europe, and here in the northwest corner of France, the cold claws of the Atlantic are particularly sharp. Even if you don't see the ocean, you feel its proximity;

you can almost taste the spray. Brittany, on the edge of the continent, juts into the sea and receives the worst ravages of its weather. But the residents are used to it, take it in their stride, in some respects define themselves by it. Bretons are famously tough, hardy, stoic. "The wind and the rain forge strong cyclists—those who succeed here are really strong in the head," the region's most famous cyclist, and the man I'm here to see, Bernard Hinault, once said.

The *patron* finishes polishing, wipes his hands on a towel, and wanders out from behind the bar. The briefest of glances in my direction signals that I should follow him. We file through a door that leads out of the bar, and, at the foot of a staircase, there's a chest-high desk: reception. He positions himself behind it; I stand in front. He pulls out a book, licks a finger, leafs through a few pages.

"*Une nuit?*"

"*Oui.*" I hand over my passport.

"*Voilà.*" A key is presented; the book is closed; still no eye contact.

"Oh," I say, "tomorrow, I need a taxi to a village near here. How far is it to Calorguen?"

"Twenty minutes," mumbles Monsieur Patron. Then finally he looks up. "Calorguen?"

"Yes." And then I lob in the conversational grenade, feeling myself stand a little taller: "I'm going to the home of Bernard Hinault."

"*Ha ha! Ha ha! Chez Bernard Hinault? Oui, oui. Ha ha,*" he chuckles, shaking his head. The atmosphere has changed. "*Chez Hinault.*" Then he actually smiles. "*Le Blaireau!*"

Next morning, it's even colder, the kind of coldness that cuts through you like a blade. The taxi heads out of Dinan, through fields coated in a dusting of frost and ice. There's not a breath of wind; the smoke rises from one chimney in a dead-straight line. The roads are empty; the journey is quick, much quicker than predicted by Monsieur Patron.

Which presents a problem. I'm expected at 10 a.m. At 9:35 we reach the smattering of buildings and houses that make up the village of Calorguen, and by 9:37 we are heading out the other side, turning sharply left, along a narrower road, and then slowing as we turn right into an even narrower one, a private drive with a sign, spelling out as much, at the beginning. It's a thin ribbon of tarmac through the fields, a quarter mile long, with a cluster of buildings at the end: a broad, two-story house, barns and outhouses containing, among abandoned machinery, a Massey Ferguson tractor and a Skoda car. The yard is neat, ordered, and very clean for a farm.

At 9:43 a.m. I am standing, freezing, facing the farmhouse. The silence is absolute. It seems too cold even for birds. So this is the Badger's set; like him, it seems handsome, proud, and self-contained. It also seems a bit early to appear at his door, but the alternatives are limited. In fact, there is only one alternative, but the consequences of being caught snooping around by the Badger don't really bear thinking about. Ringing the doorbell early seems preferable. I look up at the house, and at that moment, in a small window on the second floor, a face appears. It's he: the Badger.

He answers the door wearing black, thin-rimmed glasses, which give him an incongruously studious appearance. He is wearing a pale blue Lacoste sweater, indigo blue jeans, and running shoes. He is short and stocky, with thick, dark eyebrows, but the overwhelming impression is of familiarity; his face remains almost spookily recognizable from all those pictures in his heyday of the snarling, aggressive bike rider. Hinault's dark brown hair might be thinning slightly, but his eyes—not blue, as they've been described, but darker—are as penetrating as ever. In those old photos, it was his jaw, really, that defined him; it seemed always to be clenched, as though he were gripping something with his teeth. Now fifty-five, he still looks serious, stern, as though he means business, but his jaw is relaxed. Hinault extends a large hand, gripping mine firmly. And although eye contact is fleeting, he is welcoming.

Which is the first surprise, since I'd been told by a journalist friend not to expect a warm welcome from Le Blaireau. "I did an interview with him in his house in 1985," my friend had told me. "His wife was there. My wife took the pictures. We were there for at least a couple of hours. He never offered us a coffee. My wife said afterward, 'He didn't even offer us a glass of water.' I said, 'I think in his world there are no social graces.' That is just the kind of guy he is. Coarse."

Hinault shows me in through a dark, austere hall and into a vast yet homely kitchen, divided in two by a worktop. In the dining area, he invites me to sit down at a long, banquet-style table surrounded by ten seats. It seems to be the kind of house where there are few distractions or sources of entertainment. Certainly no radio, television, books, magazines, or newspapers are in evidence. There is no sign, either, of Hinault's wife, Martine, the mayor of Calorguen. It is deathly quiet, the only sound that of a clock ticking.

Hinault takes off his glasses and places them on the table, then disappears into the kitchen and returns brandishing a large white plastic coffeepot.

"*Café?*" he asks, and then sits down, rolls up his sleeves an inch, and taps his fingers a little impatiently on the table.

LEMOND TOWERS, MINNESOTA, APRIL 2010

"In ten minutes we'll be arriving at Minneapolis–St. Paul," says the pilot as my U.S. Airways flight passes over what looks from the air like pan-flat ground dotted with hundreds of gray blobs of water. Actually, thousands; not for nothing is Minnesota known as the "Land of 10,000 Lakes." But the first surprise is that from here, I can't see any golf courses.

Beth meets me at the entrance to the airport with an enthusiastic "Hey!" and a warm embrace, along with a dazzling white smile. "Listen, this works very well," says the forty-something blond woman with arguably one of the most challenging jobs in world sport: personal assistant to Greg LeMond. She is alluding to my later-than-expected arrival after a delayed flight. "Greg prefers the afternoons and evenings. He's a real night owl." She smiles warmly. Indeed, she exudes warmth, radiates it, as she continues, "I get e-mails and texts from him sent at all times of the night; that's when he gets his work done."

E-mails and texts? From Greg LeMond? "Greg's probably the most difficult person I know to get hold of," Steve Bauer, a former teammate, had told me with laconic understatement—and didn't I know it. I had been trying for the best part of nine months to fix up this interview. Bauer was not exaggerating: Greg LeMond is—almost certainly—the most difficult person in the world to contact and then to pin down. There were times when I wished that, instead of LeMond, the subject of my book had been someone easier to get hold of. Someone like Osama Bin Laden, say.

I had encountered LeMond on two previous occasions: once at a conference in England, when, with two other journalists and his wife, Kathy, we adjourned to a café, and LeMond ordered coffee. And then changed his mind to beer. And then back again to coffee. And then, finally, to tea. Then, for two hours, he talked (there were, perhaps, three questions), recalling in the most vivid and fascinating detail one of his three Tour de France victories—but not, alas, the one I wanted to talk to him about. Eventually, Kathy, who'd been sitting reading a book in a corner, gently reminded her husband of 30 years that they had another appointment. Still, it took 30 minutes for LeMond to finish his meandering—but never less than engrossing—narrative and another 15 for him to negotiate the short distance from his table to the door, a journey punctuated by friendly exchanges with another customer, then with the staff. "The tea was great!" he said enthusiastically as Kathy grabbed his arm and almost literally dragged him outside.

The second meeting was even more bizarre. While I was standing by the Tom Simpson memorial monument, close to the summit of Mont Ventoux, awaiting the denouement to the 2009 Tour de France, a figure appeared over the brow of the hill, negotiating the loose scree of a white hillside that looks like the surface of the moon. Behind this figure—initially in silhouette on account of the dazzling sunshine—a two-person TV crew followed with even greater difficulty over the uneven surface. As they loomed closer, the figure in front grew more familiar. It was LeMond. At the memorial, he was introduced to Joanne Simpson, Tom's daughter, and the pair chatted for twenty minutes. This time, it was the TV crew who dragged him away, anxious to get off the mountain before the riders appeared, and those of us standing by the Simpson memorial were left scratching our heads, wondering if that had really been Greg LeMond.

Beth drives me past the country's largest shopping mall and then turns off the freeway to head deeper into Minnesota. LeMond's house is just 30 minutes outside Minneapolis yet appears to be set in a wilderness of lush woodland; dense forests; lakes; and small, ranch-style villages that almost resemble Alpine ski towns in their concentration of thick, dark, weathered wood. Not that this should be a surprise; though today is warm and springlike, the climate in winter is harsh, with deep snow and temperatures that dip well below freezing. Other than Alaska, it is the northernmost U.S. state. It seems strange that LeMond, a Californian by birth, should live here.

When we pull into the LeMonds' drive, I can see why he lives in this house, though. A gardener waves as we crawl through immaculately tended grounds toward a redbrick mansion, in front of which is a circular, elevated flower garden that looks like a fountain but is actually a miniroundabout. "They've got forty acres," says Beth approvingly. Garages to the side of the house are the size of medium-sized family homes. A tennis court is situated directly behind.

Beth leads me straight through the front door—yelling "Kathy? Greg?"— past a grand central staircase, into the vast kitchen, toward another huge dining table. This one, unlike Bernard Hinault's, is round—easier for conversation.

"Hiiiiiiiiiiiiii," says Kathy LeMond, appearing suddenly and whirlwind-like in the kitchen with four small, yapping dogs at her heels. "Greg's in the shower—he's been for a bike ride."

"I'm jealous," I say.

"You want a shower?" she asks.

"No, sorry, I meant jealous of the bike ride."

"You want a bike ride? We have loads of bikes in the garage. We could find you one!"

When LeMond appears, the impression is not dissimilar to the entrance of the puppies. Thicker-set than he was 25 years ago, with graying hair but the same sparkling blue eyes, he arrives like a hurricane and slides across the kitchen floor. He's wearing a loose-fitting black T-shirt, and he's still sweating a little from his bike ride; he mops his brow, puts on his socks as he moves, smiles warmly, says, "Hey," extends a meaty hand (Hinault has big hands; LeMond has *huge* hands), still pulling on the socks while at the same time starting to say something before starting to say something else, and then he's sitting in front of me, and—shit, oh, no—he's launching into a discussion of Bernard Hinault's (lack of) tactical ability and how he would have fared in today's racing, when each rider is wired up by radio to his directeur. . . .

"Mind if I turn this on?" I try to interrupt, holding my recorder. But I don't think he hears me.

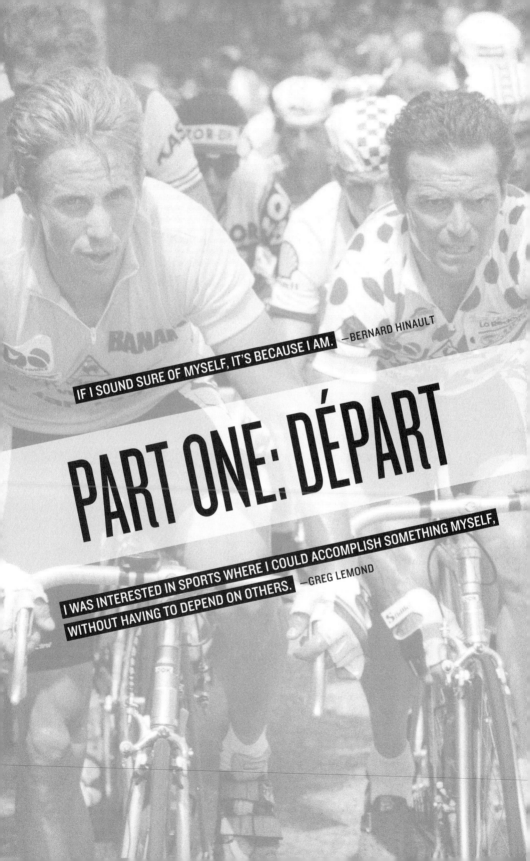

IF I SOUND SURE OF MYSELF, IT'S BECAUSE I AM. —BERNARD HINAULT

PART ONE: DÉPART

I WAS INTERESTED IN SPORTS WHERE I COULD ACCOMPLISH SOMETHING MYSELF, WITHOUT HAVING TO DEPEND ON OTHERS. —GREG LEMOND

1

THE BADGER

I don't really know what kind of a boy I was.
But I imagine that I was pretty stubborn and aggressive. . . .
Life around me was turbulent. It still is.

BERNARD HINAULT

t was early in the morning of July 11, 1978, when spectators began to gather in the streets of the small town of Valence d'Agen. First out was the town's 5,000-strong population, but over the morning the crowd swelled as hundreds poured in from the villages and towns of the surrounding Midi-Pyrénées region.

Valence d'Agen was *en fête*, with shop windows transformed by displays of all manner, style, and vintage of bikes, with bunting hanging from every corner and effigies of cyclists and replica yellow jerseys attached to lampposts and buildings. At the hub of it all was the town's proud mayor, Monsieur Baylet. It was his efforts that had led to this: the visit of the Tour de France. Bringing Le Tour to Valence d'Agen was equivalent to hosting the Olympics.

They gathered early because the stage finished early. Stage 12a of the Tour, 148 km from Tarbes, was expected in Valence at around 11:30 a.m. But that wasn't the end of it. Monsieur Baylet and Valence had won the lottery, for as well as an Arrivée, they would witness a Départ; after two hours' repose, stage 12b, 96 km to Toulouse, would roll out of the town.

However, something strange was going on. At 11:30 a.m. there was no sign of the Tour de France. At midday, still no sign. This kind of thing did happen.

After all, the schedules drawn up by the Tour organizers were based on educated guesswork, but they were at the mercy of the riders' legs and heads, not
to mention the wind. A block headwind could add an hour, easily.

By 1 p.m., with still no sign of the peloton, confusion and the first stirrings
of frustration and annoyance had replaced the excited anticipation that had
galvanized the town not just on the morning of July 11 but in the days and
weeks leading up to that day.

Finally, at 1:15 p.m., the Tour's advance vehicles appeared. The riders
would be just behind them. This was it. Excited anticipation immediately
returned; any questions could be answered later. Roadside vantage points—
effectively "reserved" hours earlier—were reclaimed and defended. A buzz
engulfed the town. In the next ten minutes or so the hundred riders would
appear. Perhaps the peloton would be preceded by a small breakaway playing
cat-and-mouse, or even a lone rider. Or perhaps the peloton would arrive en
masse, swaying, jostling, and heaving into the straight for the most spectacular finish of all: a bunch sprint.

But when the riders did finally arrive, two hours behind schedule, the finish envisaged and fantasized about in the weeks leading up to this moment
did not materialize. The peloton arrived all together, but, far from heaving
into the finishing straight, the riders moved at walking pace. And then, 100
meters before the line, they stopped altogether and climbed off their bikes.

What followed resembled a funeral procession. At the head of the pack
was the rider in the distinctive blue-, white-, and red-striped jersey of the
French national champion. Most people's gaze naturally fell upon him. He
was stern-faced, strong-jawed, and quite clearly full to the brim with righ-
teous anger. He was, of course, Bernard Hinault.

"A little Napoleon" he was immediately dubbed by some, but at 5 feet, 8
inches Bernard Hinault was a veritable giant compared with Napoleon. And
here in Valence he did resemble a giant, his presence and air of authority de-
fying his stature, age, and experience. Hinault was 23. It was his first Tour de
France.

As the crowd's confusion turned to restlessness, Hinault's jaw seemed to
clench tighter. His resolve stiffened. He had struck a deal: "When I move, you
move," Hinault had told the other riders.

Pushing his bicycle, Hinault began walking slowly toward the line, and
the others followed. Howls and whistles began to be heard. The riders
stopped again. Some began talking to each other, joking, laughing, putting

on their caps, perhaps as a response to the crowd's reaction, as a way of hiding. One rider, Jan Raas, unfolded a newspaper and began reading it in a self-conscious gesture.

But Hinault stood motionless, unflinching. His reaction to the crowd's unrest was to tilt his chin marginally upward. In fact, by doing nothing he ensured that he, not Raas, was the center of attention. Though Raas was one of the biggest names in the sport, the cameras lingered instead on this impressive, impervious, audacious, stubborn, statesmanlike . . . Tour de France debutant.

The picture of Hinault standing at the front of the peloton, leading the protest, has become an iconic image. But the frozen snapshot doesn't convey the whole truth; it's the moving footage that tells the full story. It proves that Hinault held that pose for minutes. As well as registering his protest, it is as though he is consciously cultivating his own myth of pride, stubbornness, and strength. His self-assurance and certainty are striking, made more so by the contrast with those around him, who, like children forced to stand in a line and be quiet, seem easily distracted and begin to fidget and talk, joke and laugh, or, like Raas, read the paper.

In that moment, the riders found their leader, despite it being his first Tour, despite the fact that he had yet to win a stage, despite the fact that he had yet to wear the yellow jersey.

When, finally, the riders crossed the line in Valence d'Agen, with the cacophony of boos and whistles ringing in their ears, Hinault was confronted by the irate mayor, Monsieur Baylet.

"We've got nothing against you," Hinault told him. "It's the organizers we are protesting against."

But Monsieur Baylet couldn't hide his anger, and Hinault, as ringleader, was the obvious target for his ire. "He wouldn't let me speak; he kept butting in," recalled Hinault, still indignant, years later. "So I said to the mayor, 'Shut your mouth!'"

"If I have something to say, I'll say it!" responded the mayor, his eyes almost popping out of his skull.

"Not when someone is speaking to you," the 23-year-old Hinault told him. "Then you shut up."

The seeds of Hinault's and the other riders' discontent had been sown the previous evening. That day's stage, the eleventh of the Tour, had finished at Saint-Lary-Soulan, in the Pyrenees, at 5 p.m., following which the riders, and the entire Tour entourage, had had to transfer to Tarbes. To get there, they had to take a cable car back down the mountain to Saint-Lary, then get into buses to travel on to their hotels. One problem was that the spectators were evacuating the mountain at the same time. The result: gridlock, and riders sitting in stationary buses, tired, hungry, and frustrated.

In the end, the riders didn't arrive in Tarbes until 11 p.m. They still hadn't eaten dinner. Nor had they had their nightly massages, administered by the team soigneurs[1] and deemed an essential part of the recovery process, especially midway through a three-week stage race. It was, recalls Hinault, no earlier than 1 a.m. when most finally retired for the night. But the problem of such a late night was exacerbated by the arrangement for the next day's stage—or, rather, stages.

The first, to Valence d'Agen, began at 8 a.m. "Which meant that we had to be up by five a.m. to have breakfast," writes Hinault in his autobiography, *Memories of the Peloton*—three hours being the time it takes to digest the pre-race meal. "We had hardly any sleep. . . . It just wasn't right." What's more, after the second of the two stages, there was another bus transfer scheduled, this one of 150 km. The riders were restless, unhappy. But they'd been that way for years. The problem came in organizing themselves, in speaking with a single voice. To do so, they needed what they didn't have: a leader.

As always, there were other, more immediate priorities. And so a long and exhausting day loomed for the riders as they rubbed their eyes and stifled their yawns over breakfast in Tarbes, while, over 100 km away, Valence d'Agen was waking up to its gala day.

But as the riders rolled out of Tarbes, something extraordinary happened. An agreement was reached. "I remember we had started talking a little about a possible protest," Lucien Van Impe, the great Belgian climber, would later say. "It was yes, no, yes, no [to a strike]. Then Bernard said, 'We are going on strike.' And all the others agreed."

"We were all panicking a little [about the ramifications of a strike]," said Jean-René Bernadeau, another rider. "But Hinault said, 'Do not move before I do.'"

Asked years later if it was true that he was the rider who had instigated the strike, Hinault shrugged. "I was a leader."

---

1. A soigneur is an essential member of the team's backroom staff, responsible for feeding, clothing, escorting, and massaging riders.

"Was it really you who led the strike?" he was asked.

"It was me who ended up leading, but it wasn't just me. Anyway, it was easy. Everyone was tired. We hadn't had enough sleep. There were those two half stages on the same day for no apparent reason. We could have covered the same distance in one stage; it was all about money."

The Tour's deputy director, Félix Lévitan, had for years commanded increasingly large fees from towns wanting to host stage starts and finishes—hence Valence d'Agen and its mayor's sense of having won the lottery by securing both.

"At the start of the stage we called a little strike," Hinault continued. "Everyone was in except for two Spaniards who hadn't understood. They tried to attack from the back of the peloton. But as they drew up beside one cyclist, they were given a bit of a shove."

As he recalled his confrontation with the mayor of Valence d'Agen, Hinault's eyes sparkled with mischief. "I've met the mayor several times since. I told him, 'If I hadn't led the riders' strike, no one would have heard of this place.'"

Hinault put Valence d'Agen on the map, then, if not in the way that the mayor had envisaged. Rather than enjoying its 24 hours' fame courtesy of the Tour de France, it is the place where the Hinault myth began—where Le Blaireau was born.

Or is it? Accounts vary as to the origins of Hinault's nickname. In his autobiography, Hinault claimed that, growing up in Brittany, it was a common form of greeting—an alternative to "mate" or "buddy." However, Maurice Le Guilloux, a teammate and then directeur sportif as well as a fellow Breton and friend (though Le Guilloux is five years older), confirms that it was he and another rider, Georges Talbourdet, who coined the nickname and communicated it to the wider cycling milieu. "We were neighbors," says Le Guilloux, who now works as a driver on the Tour de France and is a gentle-mannered, kindly, almost grandfatherly figure. Quite different from Hinault, in other words. "I first met him as a little guy, his first year [as a professional]; he lived in the next village, and we started training together," continues Le Guilloux. "We'd say, 'Hey, you OK, *blaireau*?'

"It's a common nickname in Brittany—you say, 'Hey, *blaireau*!' But it stuck with Hinault. He could have said, 'Stop,' but he didn't—he was happy with it. So it caught on with the rest of the team, and then the media. It suited him. His personality was like that—aggressive. He hasn't changed; he's the same now."

Le Guilloux is right; Hinault does like it. When I visit him at his Breton farmhouse home on that freezing December morning in 2009, he proudly produces leaflets advertising a new range of cycling clothing, with a black-and-white color scheme and logo both inspired by the creature. Now a 55-year-old retired farmer and aging Badger, he sits at the huge table in his kitchen nursing a mug of coffee, though at various points during our conversation there is evidence that his eyes can still blaze as they did during his racing days. He obviously identifies with the nickname.

"*Mais oui*," he confirms. "It's a bit nasty, like me."

There are stories in Hinault's autobiography that help to paint a picture of him that doesn't so much sail close to caricature as embrace it with open arms. Just after he led the strike in Valence, for example, he recalls, "a few spectators started throwing tomatoes at us, so I put my bike down and jumped over the railings to go and sort them out."

This first autobiography (published in 1989; a second, *Hinault by Hinault*, followed in 2005) opens with a story from his childhood. It concerns an episode from his midteens, when, as Hinault returned from a bike ride, his father "berated me for doing nothing and being good for nothing"—a criticism owing to his concern that his son seemed to be prioritizing cycling over his job as an apprentice sheet-metal worker. Hinault didn't respond. He just walked out, "without a moment's thought." And for the next three days he "lurked in the barns, the haylofts, anywhere I could, sleeping on the straw" while "during the day, I roamed the countryside, free as a bird."

Hinault's elder brother, Gilbert, came to the barn to reason with him. "Gilbert was a bit upset because he liked everything running smoothly, with the family gathered around the table." Bernard, in contrast, "was enjoying myself, roughing it in the barn." Besides, "it was easy for [Gilbert]; he hadn't been accused of being useless."

When, after three days, Hinault returned home, he told his father he would stop cycling and return to his work. "I pointed out that working normal hours didn't give me enough time for training," he writes. "[So] there was no alternative [other than to quit cycling], because I don't like doing things by halves." To this, his father—whom elsewhere Hinault describes as "a hero to me"—"lowered his gaze, and said, 'No, you carry on cycling.' From that day onward it was never questioned again." Hinault had won the confrontation; a pattern had been set.

Most of the later, infamous Hinault moments don't see him taking such a measured approach. Many involve flashes of temper, angry confrontations, and incidents where his rage prevailed, especially in races. Bernard Vallet, a French professional in the 1970s and '80s, speaks of Hinault's "destructive rage," while Sean Yates, a British professional in the 1980s, remembers a stage of the Giro d'Italia in which Hinault was attacked left, right, and center by Italian riders who were keen to wrest the leader's *maglia rosa*, or pink jersey, from the shoulders of the Frenchman.

"You should've seen Hinault the next morning," recalls Yates, almost shuddering at the memory. "He was so angry. He was standing on the start line and there was this area around him where people were afraid to enter. He was so fucking angry, teeth clenched, absolutely raging. When the stage started, he ripped it to pieces. Just rode everyone off his wheel."

There are countless such stories, all of them adding further layers to the myth—or to the caricature. And the Hinault that emerges through these anecdotes, and especially through the pages of his autobiography, is almost laughably one-dimensional. Racing, he writes, "was a kind of game and it hurt sometimes, but when I attacked it hurt others a lot more."

It hurt sometimes? In the course of his career Hinault won five Tours de France, but his most memorable successes involved him overcoming extreme adversity and what must have been excruciating pain. He tumbled into, then climbed out of a ravine to win the 1977 Dauphiné Libéré; he rode through snowstorms, incurring frostbite and long-term damage to his fingers, en route to winning the 1980 Liège-Bastogne-Liège one-day spring classic; he recovered from knackered knees to win the toughest ever world championships, in the French Alps in 1980; he finished the 1984 Paris-Nice with a broken rib after breaking up a dockworkers' protest with his fists; and, most memorably of all, he won the 1985 Tour de France with bronchitis, two black eyes, and a broken nose.

And he can only concede—with extreme reluctance, it would seem—that it hurt sometimes?

True, he did admit on one occasion that there were times when he suffered. But when asked how he responded to physical pain, Hinault replied, "I attack. So the others don't know I'm suffering."

This aspect of the Hinault story—the cartoon Badger, if you like—makes for great stories, great quotes, great "copy," as journalists say (although Hinault was not always popular with the press and often found himself in the running for "*le prix citron*," the lemon prize, symbolically awarded by the photographers on the Tour to the most unapproachable rider). Yet as seductive as the caricature of Hinault as the stiff-jawed, iron-lunged superhero undoubtedly is, it also leads, inevitably, to the question: How real is it? What of the Badger's human side?

I first encountered Bernard Hinault while watching the 1985 Tour de France. I therefore got to witness and enjoy only the twilight, the final two years, of his career, by which time he was well established as the *patron*, the boss, of the peloton. But it was difficult to imagine him as anything else. He was the latest in a recent line of *patrons*; Eddy Merckx and Jacques Anquetil, both five-time Tour winners, as Hinault would become, had been his predecessors. But Hinault was arguably the last, perhaps even the most effective *patron*—the last rider who almost single-handedly (or single-mindedly) could dictate what would happen in a race, who could force his will, his personality, so forcefully on proceedings.

He was made for the role. It wasn't just his strength as a rider that made Hinault such an effective *patron*, it was his aura. A force field seemed to surround him, a bit like that which emanated from him on the morning of the stage of the Giro d'Italia that Sean Yates, a quarter of a century on, recalls so clearly.

Others have equally vivid recollections. Phil Anderson, the Australian rider who became the first non-European to wear the yellow jersey while riding his first Tour in 1981, remembers his first encounter with Le Blaireau.

"It was the day I took the yellow jersey," says Anderson. "We were in the Pyrenees [it was the fifth stage, from Saint-Gaudens to Saint-Lary-Soulan], and we were climbing; I'd never climbed with all these champions before. I was 22, and I looked around at the guys I was climbing with—I had all their pictures in posters on my bedroom walls back in Australia. And now I was surrounded by them. I was certainly spooked by that.

"The field was getting smaller and smaller, until it was quite an elite group at the front," Anderson continues. "It was a warm day, and I'd noticed that the riders would be handed a drink by a spectator, and then they'd pass it to each other across the front of the peloton. I saw someone with a frosty can of Coke by the side, so I reached out and thanked him for it as I grabbed it. I took a swig and looked across at Hinault, who was, like, frothing at the mouth. He wasn't looking very good; he was having a pretty tough day, I think. So I reached out to offer him the can of Coke, and he gave me this look of disgust. . . . I don't think he'd ever seen me before, and he didn't know who I was. So here I am holding out this can of Coke for him. And he takes a swipe and knocks it out of my hands. I think he might even have growled."

Hinault's character is often explained by his birthplace: the French cycling heartland of Brittany. He has lived there all his life.

Usually the description of Hinault as a Breton is prefixed by "proud" or "stubborn" (see also "pugnacious," "tenacious," "obstinate"). As a descendant of Asterix, who also hailed from this rugged northwestern corner of France (or an imagined version of it), Hinault responds to such descriptions with as much satisfaction as he does to the "Badger" nickname. Throughout his career, his Breton roots seemed important to Hinault, to his sense of identity, as was his oft-stated desire to return there when his career was finished. And not just to live there but to return—in a more literal sense—to the land. While many top sportsmen dream of earning enough money to never have to work again, or to retire to some sun-soaked paradise, Hinault's ambition was, he always said, to become a farmer in his native Brittany. And like most of his promises—perhaps with one notable exception—Hinault kept this one.

Hinault was born on November 14, 1954, in his grandparents' house in Saint-Brieuc, the town on the northern coast that is something of a spiritual home for cycling within what is already a cycling heartland. Britain's Tom Simpson, among others, launched his continental career in Saint-Brieuc. Co-incidentally, Hinault was born in the middle of a then record-breaking run of three Tour de France victories by another Breton, Louison Bobet, from the village of Saint-Méen-le-Grand, about 65 km southeast of Saint-Brieuc. In some respects, Bobet was Hinault's polar opposite. He could be fragile, insecure, and was inclined toward the rock-star lifestyle before rock stars had even been invented. His team manager, Jean Bidot, said of Bobet that he lacked confidence. "He is extremely nervous, sensitive, worried, and susceptible . . . some days he shuts himself off, wrapped in his worries," Bidot observed. But Bobet had a quality that was essentially Breton, and that, many observers agreed, was what enabled him to win his three Tours: He was ridiculously stubborn.

Hinault's father, Joseph, was Breton through and through. So was his mother, Lucie. So were their parents, Hinault's grandparents, and his cousins—all 41 of them. By the time Joseph and Lucie's four children—Gilbert, Josiane, Bernard, and Pierre—were born, they had settled in Brittany with Joseph's parents, having briefly tried their luck in Normandy and the Paris suburbs. Back in Brittany, Joseph farmed a single field, growing onions and beans, but that didn't bring in enough money, so he began working as a plate-layer for the SNCF, France's national railway. The family also moved 10 km from Saint-Brieuc toward the coast, to the small village of Yffiniac.

Joseph Hinault "didn't talk much at home, and was strict with his children," Hinault writes in his first autobiography. Not that this stopped young Bernard from becoming "the wild one of the family . . . the one who set the hens free and started the pillow fights." So wild, indeed, that "eventually my parents had to separate me from the others, at least at night. . . . I had a mind of my own, and punishments didn't change me. Already I was the true Breton in our family: stubborn, belligerent, and afraid of nothing."

According to Hinault's own account, he hated school, so much so that in his autobiography, he claims, improbably, that he can't even remember his school's name ("Saint Something or other"). In class, he managed to position himself behind a large black stove out of the teacher's view, where he was able to spend whole days staring out the window "at the passing seasons." The only enjoyment he derived, he claims, was in the fights after class—"Every evening, on the way home, we used to come across the children from the village school [Hinault attended a Catholic school, though these days he has as little time for organized religion as he does for fools], and every evening we had a fight. It used to happen between the church and a garden wall that ran alongside our path, forming a sort of alley which got narrower and lent itself perfectly to skirmishes. There were plenty of other ways home, but I was too fond of fighting to consider taking any of them. I chose that route deliberately. . . . I sometimes wonder whether my only motivation in going to school was the thought of the battles every evening."

When, to his teacher's "great surprise," Hinault gained his graduation certificate on his first attempt, he was given a present by his parents: a bike. By then he had already ridden Gilbert's bike to victory in his first race, against his cousins (or a selection of the 41). Even on Gilbert's bike, on which he initially struggled to reach the pedals, Hinault says he "knew immediately that this bike would change my life . . . it was as if a new landscape had opened

up before me." In fact, however, Hinault initially excelled as a runner, especially in the winter discipline of cross-country. At age 16, he was 10th in the
national championship. But Hinault was led in another sporting direction by
the cousin to whom he was closest, René, two years his senior and already an
accomplished racing cyclist.

Hinault began riding with René, then going on "club runs" with the multi-
sport Club Olympique Briochin of Saint-Brieuc. He acquired his first racing
license on April 27, 1971. And five days later, aged 16½, he entered his first official event, a circuit race in Planguenoual. He did so against the wishes of his
new club's officials, and even of René. He had been on only five club runs—
an activity seen as useful preparation for riding in the company of others but
that doesn't really equip the novice cyclist with the skills needed to ride in a
large peloton of cyclists who are racing, as opposed to training. So it proved
for Hinault, who spent the entire race dangling off the back, afraid to get too
involved in the bunch or too close to other riders.

And yet, while others were dropped and the peloton was whittled down
to about half its original size, Hinault, riding his brother Gilbert's bike, clung
on. With a lap to go, he was still there, still dangling just off the back of the
main pack. And then, on the circuit's main hill, he moved around the outside
of the peloton toward the front and, "petrified with fright" at the proximity of
the other riders, attacked. Only an established rider, Jean-Yves Olivier, could
go with him. Then Hinault accelerated again, 500 meters from the line, and
Olivier was dropped. Hinault won his next three races but didn't place in the
top three in his next eight—"fortunately," says Hinault, "because it brought
me down to earth and made me realize how hard cycling is," a rare public admission from Hinault that cycling can sometimes be tough.

By now Hinault, who from the age of 14 earned pocket money as a garage
hand, was attending the technical college in Saint-Brieuc, where he trained
to be a sheet-metal worker. He cycled there and back, 10 km each way, riding in the slipstream of the delivery trucks. Over the four years he studied at
Saint-Brieuc technical college, he calculates he covered 15,000 km, many of
them tucked in behind a truck, riding at around 50 kph.

The club that Hinault joined, Club Olympique Briochin, was quite an institution. It still is. It was set up in 1947, and a cycling section was created in
1951 under the guidance of Robert Le Roux, a former national champion—
not as a cyclist but as a gymnast. It was Le Roux who was still in charge two
decades later, when Hinault began racing, and whom Hinault credits as

being his first coach and a huge influence. "He was both a sound theoretician and a practical man," says Hinault. "He gave me my education, and I owe him everything."

Le Roux seems to have been an important influence in matters other than cycling, too. Hinault suggests that his first coach provided him with an education that extended, during his formative teenaged years, beyond training and sport. As Hinault explains in his autobiography, "There's always a moment in a young person's life when he's inclined to let himself go a bit and that's exactly the time to make sacrifices and to remain more sensible than ever. Robert Le Roux's talent lay in his ability to make you see this. A race doesn't start on a Sunday morning or afternoon; you have to think about it throughout the week. Eat wisely, sleep, train hard." The key, notes Hinault, is "a life of self-control."

Le Roux also steered his protégé in another direction, toward the military. Le Roux's advice to Hinault was to get his compulsory military service out of the way when he was young so he could return to focus on his cycling career without distraction. Hinault followed the advice, spending a year with the marines, mainly in the south of France, near Marseille, as a gunner in the tank division. His enrollment with the marines came after a snub from the Joinville training center, where France's most accomplished athletes tended to go to complete their year's military service and where they received full support in their sporting endeavors. (This was an oversight, or a snub, that rankled Hinault and may have provided more fuel for the fire.) Instead, in Marseille and then in Sissonne, back in the northeast, Hinault neglected his bike and his training. He put on 10 kg and competed in only one race, the national railway championships, for which he was eligible through his father's employment.

Since it was his first race in some time, he decided to prepare properly, traveling to the circuit near Sissonne the day before. But he struggled as soon as it started and then suffered the humiliation of being dropped. "My grandmother could have done better," he said later. The experience further underlined that, for all that Hinault possessed huge quantities of natural talent, this wasn't a sport where talent alone could suffice; it needed to be allied to hard work, to a "life of self-control."

Hinault returned from military service to hit the 1974 season at full tilt. It was to be his last as an amateur, which means he served a remarkably brief—and interrupted, at that—apprenticeship before joining the professional ranks. But it was an obvious progression and, again, one that was encouraged by Le Roux. By the end of the year, Hinault had claimed regional and national titles on the track, having trained at the Beaufeuillage velodrome in Saint-Brieuc. In June 1974, he was crowned French pursuit champion and selected to go to the world championships in Canada. It was on the road, though, that he began to serve notice of his precocious talent and his equally precocious attitude. He won a stage and finished second overall in the Route de France stage race for amateur riders; then, in October's Étoile des Espoirs, he excelled again against some of the best professionals of the day. It was a race, notes Hinault, in which the amateurs were expected to know their place. "The professionals didn't like it when the amateurs attacked," he says, adding, "Needless to say, I was one of those who attacked."

On one such attack, on the penultimate day, Hinault escaped with Maurice Le Guilloux, the rider who would become his teammate, and later his team director, and who also coined the Badger nickname. Le Guilloux, unhappy that his breakaway companion was a mere 19-year-old amateur, refused to cooperate and do his share of the work, but it was Hinault who brought their escape to a premature end, misjudging a bend and ending up in a wheelbarrow. He climbed out to finish the stage in the peloton. In the afternoon stage, a time trial, he placed second to claim fifth overall, behind the accomplished Roy Schuiten, who won, and trailing Cyrille Guimard, the leading Breton rider of the day, who finished third.

That performance prompted a visit to Brittany from Jean Stablinski, the former French and world champion who had ridden alongside Jacques Anquetil and Raymond Poulidor in the 1960s and who now ran the Gitane professional team. Hinault, encouraged by Le Roux, wanted to turn professional, in part because he feared that he would be roped into the 1976 Olympics if he remained amateur in 1975; his sights were set far higher, on the monuments of the sport, the classics and Grand Tours.

Other than his father, and perhaps Le Roux, the young Hinault was never likely to have heroes, but a rider who certainly made an impression on him was Guimard. In July 1972, a year after his first race, he witnessed his first Tour de France, when stage 1 finished in Saint-Brieuc. It finished, in fact, in the Beaufeuillage velodrome, the 400-meter track where, under Le Roux, Hinault himself was now training, practicing his high-rev pedaling on low gears. With Eddy Merckx in the yellow jersey, having won the previous day's prologue time trial in Angers, the first road stage of the '72 Tour ended in a mass bunch sprint, with one rider emerging on the inside, clipping the grass verge as he came through to claim the win. It was Guimard, winning his first of four stages that year and, in the process, taking over the yellow jersey from Merckx.

Guimard would hold on to the overall lead until stage 8 and would challenge the eventual winner, Merckx, almost all the way to Paris until severe knee pains forced him to withdraw two days before the finish. Guimard, from Bouguenais in the south of Brittany, was to become a teammate of the young Hinault at Gitane and would exercise a significant influence on both Hinault's and Greg LeMond's professional careers. Or phase one of Hinault's professional career, at least.

To underline how "amateur" the world of professional cycling was, and how far removed the teams of the 1970s were from the big-budget, international teams that would come into existence over the next two decades, it is revealing to note that Hinault's salary as a new professional with Gitane was not paid by the team sponsor. Instead his income—which, at 2,500 francs a month, or about $500 then ($2,500 today), was the minimum legal wage—was covered by a Breton supporter of cycling, Paul Tertre, a wholesaler of electrical appliances.

On signing his first professional contract, Hinault also got married. He had met his future wife, Martine, at a cousin's wedding two years earlier. "I admit that I wasn't particularly impressed at the first glance" is his candid, and rather too honest, admission in his autobiography. "But I'd changed my mind by the end of the day." Two years later, in December 1974, Hinault and Martine were married, and they moved into a two-bedroom apartment in Yffiniac, where Martine worked as a secretary for the cooperative dairy. The following June, the couple's first son, Mickael, was born.

By then, a few months into his debut professional season, cracks were appearing in Hinault's relationship with his team director, Stablinski, even though—or perhaps in part because—Hinault's career had got off to a flying start. He finished seventh overall in the first major stage race of the season, Paris-Nice, which seemed to encourage Stablinski to fast-track his prodigy. There was even talk of putting the 20-year-old neopro in that summer's Tour de France. Hinault objected, protesting that he was too young; it would be, he said, "an act of madness."

"I needed a rest," says Hinault. "I hadn't had a break from racing, and I wanted to go home, where Martine was about to have our first baby. Stablinski, Le Roux, and I had agreed that I mustn't race too much." Yet at the Dauphiné Libéré in June, Stablinski suggested adding a couple more races to his program, a suggestion that prompted "a fit of tantrums" from Hinault, during which Stablinski "came very close to going out the window." Hinault packed his bags—actually the suitcase belonging to his mother-in-law, which he'd used since the team's first training camp on the Côte d'Azur in February—and returned home.

For much of the rest of the year, claims Hinault, he raced rarely and trained even less, instead spending a lot of time with baby Mickael and gardening. "I put on 12 kilos," he says. "When I went back to the bike, I weighed 74 kilograms."

This became a theme of Hinault's career—or his so-called first career. His failure to train regularly following the conclusion to the season became notorious: his weight would balloon, and he would endure several weeks of hard graft to lose the weight and rediscover his fitness. It was a process that would have killed many other riders but that Hinault seemed able to handle, though perhaps at a cost, as the coach who masterminded what he called "his second career," Paul Köchli, would tell me.

Ahead of his second pro season, Hinault resumed training in January, by which time, having originally decided to leave Gitane the previous October, he had been persuaded to stay with the team. The reason? Stablinski had been axed, with the newly retired Guimard finally conceding defeat to his long-standing knee problems and, at the age of just 29, appointed directeur sportif in Stablinski's place. "When I resumed training in January, Cyrille made fun of me, puffing out his cheeks whenever he passed me, to imply that I looked like a young pig," says Hinault.

Already, though, Guimard had won over Hinault by promising to allow him to develop at his own pace. Most importantly, he assured him that he wouldn't push him to ride the Tour de France before he was ready. "When we enter the Tour, it will be to win it," Guimard told him. That wouldn't be 1976, their first year together. Or even 1977. Nineteen seventy-eight, reckoned Guimard, was the year that Hinault would first ride the Tour.

But Hinault would not just ride the Tour. He would ride it to win it.

2

THE CANNIBAL IS DEAD; LONG LIVE LE BLAIREAU

"No one else has ever been in the frame with the Badger.
Not even in the frame." "Not even Merckx?"
"Oh, no. Above Merckx. The Badger had the greatest athletic potential
of any rider ever. By far."

CYRILLE GUIMARD ON BERNARD HINAULT

Cyrille Guimard, wearing a freshly laundered white shirt, is sitting behind his desk in his unremarkable, Spartan office. Next door is the Vélo Club (VC) Roubaix shop, and next to that the club bar, in a whitewashed outhouse attached to the famous Roubaix velodrome. On the breast of Guimard's shirt is a logo, offering a clue as to his current occupation: He runs Équipe Roubaix-Lille Métropole, a third-tier professional team affiliated with VC Roubaix.

This could be considered quite a fall from grace for somebody acclaimed as one of the best directeurs sportifs ever to sit behind the wheel of a team car and who, between 1976 and 1984, guided three different riders to no fewer than seven Tours de France—which is to say, every edition of the great race bar two. But his haughty manner and the abrupt way he dismisses those who have taken a wrong turn in the club shop and wandered into his office by mistake show that Guimard should not be counted among those who now doubt his genius. Though his office is modest, the same cannot be said of Guimard.

Perched on his distinctive large nose are his equally distinctive and large 1970s-style spectacles, with his graying mop of unruly hair giving him a vaguely professorial air. In his days as a directeur sportif, Guimard's curly brown bouffant and trademark oversized aviator sunglasses gave him the appearance of a *Boogie Nights*–style 1970s porn star; these days, his hair is grayer and, though it still has plenty of body, straighter, as though the perm is growing out.

A few hours after our meeting, Guimard will begin his other job, commentating for French radio on the famous cobbled classic, Paris-Roubaix. But for now he is casting his 63-year-old mind back 35 years, to his first encounter with Bernard Hinault. Or, rather, the Badger. It is an endearing curiosity that although these two proud Bretons worked together for the best part of a decade, Guimard rarely refers to his former protégé as "Bernard," "Bernie," or "Hinault." Throughout, he is simply "Le Blaireau."

It is said not for comic effect—though Guimard has some funny lines—but with sincerity and even respect. "The first time that I came across the Badger . . . I can't remember," he says initially, searching his impressive mind. "Ah, *si, si, si*, it was the Étoile des Espoirs. He was riding for the French amateur team. I was third and he must have been fourth [in fact, he was fifth]. It must have been . . ." Guimard turns to his computer, launches Google, and after several minutes and countless mouse clicks turns back: "1974! Yes, the Badger's first year as a pro was my last."

Guimard was a good rider—among more than a hundred wins were the French national championship and seven stages of the Tour—but it was as a directeur sportif that he achieved greatness for which he is best remembered today. Like Alex Ferguson, a trade union agitator before he became a footballer and then a great manager, Guimard demonstrated his leadership qualities early in his athletic career. He was appointed president of the professional riders' trade union, the Union Nationale des Coureurs Professionnels, when he was just 23—the same age, coincidentally, at which Hinault would also demonstrate his ability to lead a group of dissatisfied workers in the riders' strike at the 1978 Tour.

But it was as a manager that Guimard transcended his own gifts as a rider, his tactical and strategic genius combining to brilliant effect with his forceful, forthright personality. "Everything Guimard said at the briefing came true by the end of the race," said Lucien Van Impe, the Belgian climber whom Guimard led to the 1976 Tour, in his first year as a directeur. According to the cautious Van Impe, Guimard didn't merely advise; he ordered him when to attack.

"I already knew the Badger when he turned professional," says Guimard now, musing on his early impressions of the rider with whom he would forge such a close and mutually successful relationship until a spectacular falling-out precipitated, in Hinault's words, "three years of war." Guimard explains, "I'd followed his results in races in Brittany, and I was in contact with the people who'd taken care of him around the time he did the Route de France [a major stage race for amateurs in which Hinault placed second]. They'd asked my opinion about whether to pick him for the Route de France, and I'd said no." Typically, Guimard offers no elaboration. "But when I raced with him at the Étoile des Espoirs, that confirmed the impression I had of his physical potential.

"In 1974 he must have been barely 20, he was just out of the army, and I could see straightaway that he was a cut above the others of his age," Guimard continues. "He could already generate enormous power. The only thing he wasn't particularly advanced in was his racing strategy. You know, when you're on a higher [physical] plane, you tend to rely on your strength a bit too much. Later on, he got better in that regard, even if his first line of defense was always his physical superiority." After his competitive encounter with Hinault in the Étoile des Espoirs, Guimard says he "could already see that we had a rider who could scale the highest peaks, without a shadow of a doubt."

On Hinault's physical ability, Guimard is absolutely certain: He was born with it. To emphasize that fact, Guimard twists his wrist as though opening the throttle on a motorbike. "The size of the motor is written in the genes," says Guimard. But in the matter of Hinault's mind-set, of his formidable mental strength, of his ability to lead and the raw aggression he used to such devastating effect in so many races, Guimard is more circumspect.

"You'd have to ask a psychologist about that," he says with a shrug. "There's no satisfactory response to that question. I think there are things in the genes, and that your environment and experience are going to forge your personality. But aggression is also linked to the endocrine system—in other words, to the production of certain hormones."

Guimard agrees that Hinault appeared, from the very start of his career, even from his accounts of relishing fistfights during his school days, to be quite fearless. Moreover, he never came across as someone racked by doubt; he decided on a path and then followed it. Could it be true that the Badger had no hang-ups, insecurities, or complexes? Again, Guimard isn't sure. "To say he had no complexes perhaps isn't totally correct."

Hinault's "destructive rage"—as Bernard Vallet referred to it—could, suggests Guimard, have been a front, an act. "His aggressiveness was maybe a response to a certain number of complexes, or a certain shyness. I'm almost tempted to say that someone who is serene, who is calm, doesn't have this aggressiveness.

"Is aggressiveness not a mask for certain issues, for certain doubts? Is it something someone needs to put them in a kind of trance, this aggressiveness?"

Laughing, Guimard adds, "You know, you can tell the difference between a dog whose training has been all caresses and red meat and one who's been trained with a whip. Anyway, what we can certainly say is that all great champions have a thirst for dominance and, by obligation, a more or less externalized aggression. It's an aggression just underneath the surface, ready to be called upon when they're in difficulty."

Guimard pauses, considers, and offers his conclusion: "I've never met a nice, kind, soft man who's succeeded in sport, whether it be in rugby or in football or in cycling."

It is perhaps surprising that Guimard, who as a directeur gained a reputation in some quarters as abrasive, aloof, and arrogant, should demonstrate so much sensitivity when it came to guiding Hinault through his early professional career. But he felt it was important that his star pupil serve an apprenticeship; he still had to, in Guimard's words, "learn the trade." Guimard also told Hinault, however, that he should "fear nobody, and attack when the stars seem ready to rest."

Hinault took the advice to "fear nobody"—and nothing—to heart. Early in his professional career, in a criterium in Châteaulin, he discovered that the race had been carved up by a mafia comprising some of the sport's biggest names, including Eddy Merckx. Such arrangements were common in what were essentially exhibition races, but Hinault was having none of it. Or, rather, he was furious that he wasn't in on the deal to fix the race and divide the prize money. As Raymond Martin, the French rider, told Sam Abt, "They were willing to cut me in on a share of the prizes, but not Hinault. He got on their nerves too much. So he got mad. He won five or six primes [intermediate sprints, with prize money] in the first laps, making faces at the other riders as he swept past. I told him, 'Cool it,' and he said, 'I don't give a damn.' Eventually Merckx spoke to him. He said, 'OK, you're in on the split, but cut your crap.'"

Van Impe's Tour de France victory, in Guimard's debut year in charge of the Gitane team, eased any pressure on both Guimard and Hinault. Nevertheless, Hinault, after a second year of steady but unspectacular progress, emphatically announced his arrival on the major stage in dramatic fashion in April 1977, winning two classics in a week.

First, Ghent-Wevelgem, the cobbled semiclassic, fell to the 22-year-old, who, in one publication's report of the race, was described as "a wiry little Breton rider." Another magazine trotted out the hoary maxim "In the country of the blind, the one-eyed man is king"—a reference to the stars who were missing. It's fair to say, then, that Hinault's solo victory, after he attacked with 16 km left, was interpreted more as a sign of his potential than an indication of greatness. Interviewed afterward, he said it had been easy and that he was surprised no one had caught him. In Belgium, with a strong cycling culture built entirely around the fabled classics, his victory—the first by a Frenchman since Jacques Anquetil in 1964—and his post-race nonchalance, interpreted by some as arrogance, didn't go down especially well.

Hinault's response to the many who dismissed that win as a fluke—"several journalists denigrated my victory," he noted later—came five days later in Liège-Bastogne-Liège, or "La Doyenne," the oldest one-day race on the calendar and arguably the toughest, with the race's defining feature a series of brief but brutally steep Ardennes climbs on the road back to Liège. It was on one of those climbs, the Côte des Forges, with 15 km to go and Hinault in a small group of favorites, that Dietrich Thurau attacked. At this point, Guimard drove alongside the six-man chasing group. He felt this was the race's decisive moment and wanted Hinault to chase Thurau. But Hinault refused, telling his directeur, "I want to wait a bit longer; have faith in me, because I'm going like a train."

It was Eddy Merckx and Roger De Vlaeminck who led the pursuit, Hinault shadowing the two Belgians, one (Merckx) already acknowledged as the greatest cyclist of all time, the other (De Vlaeminck) known as one of the greatest ever classics specialists. But as Merckx made the bridge with Thurau, André Dierickx counterattacked. Hinault went after him as the others hesitated, looked at each other, and didn't—or couldn't—respond.

Twelve kilometers were left. But, as Guimard might say, the stars clearly needed a rest. Once recovered, the four began chasing, and chasing hard, but

Hinault and Dierickx maintained their advantage, Dierickx initially doing most of the work while Hinault sat on, believing—as Dierickx clearly did, too—that he would be beaten in a sprint.

At the finish in Liège, with the four pursuers bearing down on them, Hinault led out the sprint from 300 meters. Then, as Dierickx countered and came past, Hinault did something that was to become a trademark: He surged a second time, passing Dierickx in the final 20 meters to win his first "Monument." It was a win, he said, "of sheer pride."

"I know it's going to be harder for me now," Hinault told reporters at the finish. "But I'm prepared for that. My win today is just recompense for my hard work, and I'm glad for my family, too. Now I know I have to do more—not just train conscientiously but prepare specifically for the big events. I'll need to, because from now on I'll have a big sign on my back—everyone will be marking me.

"One more thing," continued Hinault, fixing reporters with those dark eyes. "This proves my win in Ghent-Wevelgem was no fluke. Some have said it was worth little because the best Belgians weren't there. Well, they were here today."

Two months later came a race, and an incident, that would come to define Hinault almost as indelibly as his role, just over a year later, in the riders' strike in Valence d'Agen. It remains one of the most dramatic moments in the sport, one that could easily have ended in tragedy and that would prompt Hinault, 32 years later, to acknowledge that he owed his career—and indeed his life—to a tree sprouting improbably out of the steep slopes of the Col de Porte and coming to his rescue as a million watched the 1977 Dauphiné Libéré live on television.

What those viewers witnessed was Hinault, in the yellow jersey of race leader, attacking some of the favorites for that year's Tour—Merckx, Van Impe, Bernard Thévenet, Joop Zoetemelk—and riding alone toward the finish in Grenoble. It was a mountain stage that had started in Romans, and it was long, at 216 km. Yet as the riders tackled the Vercors mountains, Hinault rode away from the best, with the two most recent Tour winners, Van Impe and Thévenet, the last to be dropped on the climb of the Col de Porte. Of his attack, Hinault said later, "It was time for me to go, to see what I had in my belly. . . . Cyrille followed [in the team car] and told me I had 30 seconds, 40 seconds, 1 minute, then 1 minute 20"—his advantage as he crested the summit of the Col de Porte.

The drama comes on the descent. Hinault is flying around the hairpin bends of the mountain, tucking into an aerodynamic position on the straights, arms bent, nose almost touching the handlebars, then making his body a little bigger as he negotiates the bends. But on the fourth bend, with what looks like melted, wet tar in the middle of the road, he appears to be badly positioned. There are small stones scattered across the surface; they force him to take a different, wider line on approach.

As Hinault comes out of the corner, disaster. But it is the frenzied French TV commentator who best conveys the sense of panic that immediately grips those watching, screaming, *"Ooh la la, ooh la la . . . Ooh la la Hinault! Non!"*

It is too late for Hinault to change his line. He is going too fast, and as he hits the small, muddy ridge at the side of the road, his bike tips forward and he is flipped over the side of the mountain. In an instant, he vanishes. The commentator can't believe what he's just seen. The motorcycle-mounted TV camera inches toward what is described, without exaggeration, as a precipice. Beyond the ridge is a sheer drop, and the cameraman isn't brave enough— or stupid enough—to venture too close. As the camera peers into the abyss, Hinault is nowhere to be seen. There is nothing feigned about the panic evident in the live commentary; it's authentic.

Guimard, meanwhile, has jumped out of the team car, which has screeched to a halt as quickly as it could. And now it is Guimard who comes to the rescue. He jogs toward the edge and, in cavalier fashion, throws himself forward, his arm reaching out to a tree to support himself, his body parallel to the road, at 90 degrees to the vertical slope.

Still there is no sign of Hinault. And then, abruptly, an arm appears, and then the yellow-jersey-clad rider, who, as Guimard drops down to help him, is hauled up by another passenger from the car—Hinault's cousin René— along with the team mechanic, André Lama. Guimard, having assisted Hinault with a leg up, attempts to retrieve the bike, though it would be hours before it was recovered, having tumbled a further 10 meters. Hinault's momentum, he explains later, was broken by the branches of other trees until "finally a tree stopped me."

There is a spare bike on the car. And Hinault, without pause and having scrambled back to the road, trots toward it as gracefully as he can in his metal-cleated cycling shoes, running a hand through his hair. He resembles a French James Bond emerging from the sea in his Speedo, though in fact he is checking for blood. His hand afterward is bloody; his head has a nasty gash. But there is no time to worry about that. The bike is handed to him, and Hinault grabs it, leaping aboard and taking off as though the whole potentially fatal incident never happened.

Van Impe and Thévenet are still behind, still chasing, but it seems that Hinault has not only survived but has done so without injury and without consequence. Only that isn't quite true. And what follows, on the final climb of La Bastille, is in some respects even more remarkable. It is here, on a steep, rocky outcrop—with a grade of 18 percent in places—overlooking the city of Grenoble, that the shock of what happened, and what he survived, seems to hit Hinault.

His head drops. His shoulders slump. His legs, he said later, turn to jelly. And he stops. He just stops, midclimb, as hundreds of roadside spectators watch, and climbs off his bike, a look of anguish on his face. It's the trauma, explains the excitable French TV commentator.

But was it? Hinault insisted not. "Bit by bit I feel the pain spreading over my body, especially my back, then my face, my arms," he writes in his second autobiography. "I'm on my own, still ahead of the race, and as I cross Grenoble, then take a turn for the 250-meter climb to the Bastille, which is very steep, the pain becomes more and more violent. I feel I'm hurting everywhere. The first meters of the climb are very painful. I can't do it any more. One hundred meters from the first turn, I put my feet down. That's it; I'm finished. It seems that I'm having a nervous breakdown from the fright I'd had. In fact, it's something else. The bike I've been given doesn't have the gears to go up the Bastille. André, my mechanic, reacts very quickly; he tells me to walk 50 meters, in order to relax my muscles, then get back on my bike. He gives me a strong push and I'm back."

At the time, it was reported a little differently. As well as the mechanic, Guimard also jumped out of the car when Hinault dismounted, and he was said to have exchanged "sharp words" with his rider, though such an exchange is not obvious from the TV footage. All that shows is the strong push and Hinault pulling away, pedaling gingerly at first, then recovering his composure. He survived to win the stage and hold on to the overall lead.

The next day, again in the mountains, his rivals, led by Thévenet, showed no mercy, attacking him relentlessly. Hinault struggled, but he found an unlikely ally—Eddy Merckx, "whose encouragement kept me going [and who said,] 'Come on, stick at it, go on, don't give in' every time he thought I was ready to quit." When the Dauphiné Libéré finished, Hinault had maintained the overall lead, by nine seconds over Thévenet, to claim his first major stage race in an event that usually doubles as the last important tune-up for the favorites of the Tour de France.

But, according to the plan devised by Guimard and Hinault—"a program," said Hinault, "which would allow me to learn the trade without wearing myself out, physically or psychologically [and covering] three or four seasons, up to 1980"—Hinault would not be riding the Tour de France. Despite a media and public clamor for him to make his debut in 1977—a poll organized by Tour director Félix Lévitan in *L'Équipe*, the French daily sports newspaper, revealed a large majority of readers in favor of Hinault's participation—both rider and director were adamant: 1978 would be the year of the Badger. And the dawn, perhaps, of a new era.

Neatly, 1978 also witnessed the end of an era. On March 19, in the Belgian town of Kemzeke, the great Eddy Merckx, known as "the Cannibal" on account of his voracious appetite for gobbling up races, rode his last event. (In another neat coincidence, the Merckx era began in the same year as that of the previous great champion, Jacques Anquetil, ended; the Belgian won his first Tour in 1969, the year Anquetil retired.)

"I am living the most difficult day of my life," said Merckx at a press conference in Brussels, almost two months after his last official event, when the rumors were finally confirmed. After 525 professional wins, including five Tours de France, Merckx conceded defeat to the ill health and poor form that had blighted his final years despite the fact that he was still only 32 years old. It was a relatively young age at which to be bowing out, and yet, with his last significant victory more than two years past, in the 1976 Milan–San Remo one-day classic, some damage had already been inflicted upon his reputation. It was universally recognized that he was leaving the sport not at the summit but on the way down. Hinault, at the other end of his career, perhaps took note.

When Hinault appeared for his first Tour de France, in 1978, he did so having recently ridden and won his first three-week stage race, the Vuelta a España, in which he overcame fierce Spanish opposition. The strength of feeling against foreign "invaders" was often enough to mobilize the "Spanish Armada," though, at this particular time, the country's riders weren't quite as formidable as they would become toward the end of the 1980s.

"You must remember that Spain is the land of the bullfight and of hot-headed anarchists," writes the ever-diplomatic Hinault in his autobiography. He suggests that it was, almost literally, a hard-fought win, during which he came close to thumping one rider, threatened to dump another in a field, grabbed another "by the skin on his back," and on yet another occasion took on 25 angry Spaniards. On the last day, "they were after my skin," he recalls, but "I got to the front and scattered them to the four winds." Again, how much of this is accurate, how much the feverish imagination of Le Blaireau—or his ghostwriter—is anyone's guess. But given the often anarchic state of the sport at that time, it could be closer to reality than many might imagine.

After the Vuelta, Hinault skipped the Dauphiné Libéré to train in the Alps, reconnoitering some of the Tour's mountain stages. By now Guimard's squad had become Renault-Gitane-Campagnolo with the sponsorship of the French car manufacturer—a venerable institution in France—elevating the status of the team, which had previously been regarded in some quarters as second-rate, at least behind teams such as Peugeot. Indeed, the riders on the Renault team, in their distinctive yellow-and-black, wasplike colors, earned a reputation as pioneers, not least thanks to Guimard's willingness to embrace new methods and equipment. It was, for example, the first team to have a fully equipped team bus, an innovation that would become ubiquitous in the 1990s.

Typically, Hinault went into his first Tour with a very precise plan: to claim the yellow jersey on the stage that finished at the summit of the Puy de Dôme on 14 July—Bastille Day (which, as events would transpire, came two days after he led the riders' strike at Valence).

These were interesting times for the sport, for the Tour de France, and for the riders. Some things were changing; others remained the same. By the late 1970s, the Tour generated considerable income, for example. But it had to, with the cost of organizing the event rising to around 10 million francs (more than $2 million). Of that, however, only crumbs fell from the top table and into the mouths of the riders.

At the top table were Jacques Goddet, who had run the Tour since 1936, and Félix Lévitan, who, beginning in 1962, had brought a more commercial focus to the operation. Right at the start of the 1978 Tour was an incident that underlined this. In Leiden, where the prologue time trial was held, Lévitan spotted some "ambush marketing"—advertising billboards and posters on the course for companies that had paid money to the local organizing group but not to the Tour itself. In response to this outrage, Lévitan took the dramatic—not to say heavy-handed—step of "neutralizing" the prologue, though the heavy rain that fell handily provided him with an alternative, more credible explanation: The conditions, he said, made the course "too dangerous."

Goddet and Lévitan argued that increasing revenue—by holding two stages in one day, for example, allowing them to charge two towns for stage starts and two for stage finishes—was essential in the face of increased costs. But fault lines were starting to appear between the organization, on one side, and the riders, on the other. The problem for the riders remained that they hadn't yet established how to stand up for themselves. To do so effectively, they needed to speak with a single voice. For that, they needed a leader. In Hinault—in Valence d'Agen—they found somebody even more effective than the previous *patron*, the great Eddy Merckx, had been.

Samuel Abt, one of the first American journalists to cover the Tour de France, reporting for the *New York Times* in 1978, recalls the Hinault-led strike vividly. "It was something extraordinary," says Abt, who, following his arrival in 1971 in Paris, developed a deep fascination with this most European of sports, covering more than 25 Tours and forming a close friendship with Greg LeMond, the other principal character in this story.

Abt still lives in the French capital, where I meet him. In his stories for the *New York Times* and *International Herald Tribune* (where he was a senior editor, not a sportswriter; he used his holidays to cover the Tour de France), Abt tried always to convey the quirks and foibles, the drama and human interest of his subjects. Despite the friendship he would develop with LeMond, he was not parochial. He would not write about American riders for the sake of writing about American riders (which, besides, was difficult in the 1970s, when there weren't any). But this made the sport a hard sell to his editors. "When I first started, there really wasn't much interest in America," he explains in his languid drawl. Abt specializes in dry, deadpan humor. He has a keen sense of irony and more than a touch of Woody Allen's world-weariness. As Abt explains, "The *New York Times* told me, 'Never again write about any rider whose name ends in "ckx"—we just don't get it.' I said, 'Well, the name of the greatest rider in the sport ends in "ckx," how can I not write it?' They said, 'Well, what is he?' I said, 'He's a Belgian.'"

Abt pauses, but his mournful expression doesn't change as he adds the punch line: "And they said, 'But we don't have any Belgian readers.'"

Of the riders' strike at Valence, Abt recalls, "I mean, Hinault was 23 or something, but he was obviously the leader. He was the *patron*, even then. How extraordinary. Here's a guy in his first Tour. And he was the riders' spokesman. Huh! Says something about him. But you can't understand how badly the riders were treated. They stayed in second-rate, third-rate hotels. They stayed in *maisons des voyageurs*, you know, youth hostels, dormitories. I remember seeing, more than once, Sean Kelly [the great Irish rider] washing out his jersey and shorts in a sink. This is the way it was. The money was nothing. And it was a time of half stages. So a lot of days they'd have two stages. Everything started early. None of these noon starts. It was nine in the morning.

"The strike was . . . justified," concludes Abt, gazing up from his coffee and peering over his small, round spectacles. "They were treated badly, and they'd had enough. What was amazing was that they had the strike. Because in this sport you can't get the riders to do anything together. It's everyone for himself." That it happened was due almost solely to Hinault. As Abt might say, how extraordinary.

As Hinault explained later, radical action proved necessary because the channels of communication between the riders and the organizers were nonexistent. Asked if he'd discussed the issue with Lévitan, Hinault says, "But that was just it. There was no way of getting through to him. It's all so tied up. I was new, [but] I wanted to discuss these things that weren't right. . . . [The Tour organization wasn't] a dictatorship, but no one dared open their mouths. For the first time, there was this brazen young thing prepared to stand up for himself. I said, 'We're here to talk. We're men, we're going to discuss this.' And afterward we had lots of discussion and we achieved a lot. It was important, and I think the fact that we clashed a bit with Mr. Lévitan and Mr. Goddet meant they then engaged with me during the Tour de France, because when we discussed things afterward, I said, 'OK, that's good; that's not good; we can do that; we can't do that.' You have to respect the cyclists' sleep, and we weren't getting enough sleep.

"I was champion of France," continues Hinault. "Someone had to [lead the strike], and it had to be a Frenchman. I didn't ask too many questions. But I don't regret it. I think we helped evolve the conditions of the competitors, and that's not a bad thing."

Yet Hinault also conceded that his role in Valence might have detracted from his efforts two days later, on Bastille Day, when—as he put it—"I had decided I would take the yellow jersey . . . because it was July 14. It was a good way of celebrating." But at the summit of the Puy de Dôme, Hinault could only finish fourth, 1 minute 40 seconds down on Joop Zoetemelk.

Two stages later, the race finished at the summit of Alpe d'Huez, with the winner, Michel Pollentier, also claiming the yellow jersey—until, that is, the ragged, crablike Belgian, arguably the least stylish bike rider ever to grace the higher echelons, was caught trying to cheat the dope control. Beneath his armpit was a bulb of "clean" urine, untainted by drug residue. Tubes strapped to his body were to transport the urine into the drug-testers' container. When the apparatus was discovered, Pollentier was tossed out, and Zoetemelk took over the yellow jersey by 14 seconds from Hinault. The Tour thus came down to the stage 20 time trial, three days from the end, from Metz to Nancy.

Hinault had been so confident before the stage that he slept "the sleep of the just" for three hours in the morning before waking and completing a 10-km warm-up, sitting behind Guimard's car at 70 kph. "I can't explain it, but I knew that I was going to win, and this wasn't conceit on my part." He was right. Hinault slaughtered Zoetemelk, beating him by four minutes.

On the podium after the time trial, still wearing a long-sleeved French national champion's top but waiting to be presented with his first yellow jersey, Hinault beamed, his dark, handsome looks combining with his formidable athleticism to cement his new status as national hero. Unusually, too, he admitted, when interviewed on the podium, to being moved. There were no tears—that would have been very unbadgerlike behavior—but it was as emotional a moment as Hinault would experience. "It's true, because this is the first time and I'm still only 23," he said during his on-podium interview. Asked to whom he dedicated the win, Hinault responded, "To everyone in my team, to all those who have worked for me, and to my wife and child."

In the TV commentary booth, Raymond Poulidor, the popular Frenchman dubbed "the eternal second" after he spent his career finishing runner-up to the aloof, less popular (but five-time winner) Anquetil, paid Hinault the ultimate compliment. Or was it an insult? The Breton reminded him of Anquetil, said Poulidor. He had the same "calm confidence, he knows he is better than the others in the time trials, [he's] a great all-round racer."

Hinault's dedication of his win to his teammates was customary—it remains typical in cycling for leaders to share the prize money equally among their colleagues—but it was genuine. And this is a defining feature of Hinault's career: his commitment to fairness, his democratic principles and willingness to fight for even the lowest of his colleagues. He touches on this in his autobiography in connection with the lucrative post-Tour criteriums. "I've had nearly eighty teammates during my career and I've always tried to help them," he writes. "You don't win races alone; you win because others help you and sacrifice their own chances. If that's their job, mine is to see that they're well paid for their efforts. Fair play for all. . . . We were like a troupe of actors and we had no intention of leaving behind one of our number just because he had only one or two lines."

Future teammates of Hinault's, including LeMond, would attest to this. "He was very confident, a very confident man in his own shoes," says the Canadian Steve Bauer. "But he was willing to share knowledge; he was a good team player. A real team player. I think that's why he was so powerful. He could get people to rally behind him."

Andy Hampsten, the American rider, echoes this: "You know, I don't think he could have been nicer as a teammate. To me, at first at least, he was Mr. Hinault. He was our captain, I wanted to help him, and he saw that I was serious about that, and he helped me help him. He was just so frickin' nice!"

Well, up to a point. On which, more later. Much more.

Hinault became known over the following seasons for his uncanny knack of picking a race—"an appointment," as Hinault always called major targets—and winning it. He wasn't Merckx; he was no cannibal; he couldn't see the point of gobbling up everything and preferred to be more selective. In fact, as those former teammates alluded to, in smaller races he would often help other members of his team to win, in the hope, and expectation, that they would repay him later, when it mattered. Which could explain Bauer's remark about Hinault's ability to get others to "rally behind him."

In 1979, his main "appointment" was once again the Tour—and he crushed the opposition. "*Paris en Fête pour Hinault*," read the front page of *L'Équipe* after his second successive victory, this one far more impressive than the first. Hinault won no fewer than seven stages, including one of his most audacious of all, the final one into Paris, which is normally reserved for the sprinters. But that summed up one of the most commanding overall victories ever: By Paris, Hinault's advantage over Zoetemelk, the runner-up again, was more than 13 minutes.

Yet Hinault's selective approach to racing—an attitude he took to the classics, too, riding and winning Paris-Roubaix, the cobbled "Hell of the North," in 1981 and then summarily declaring it a "*course de cons*" (a dickheads' race) to which he would return only one more time—could also have been a response, especially as his career progressed, to his frailty.

"Frailty" is not a word you'd readily associate with Hinault, but his weakness was his knee. Various explanations have been suggested for what caused this injury to flare up for the first time in 1980, including the idea that he pushed big gears. Footage of him riding the prologue of the 1980 Tour de France lends some weight to this theory; his entire body rocks with the effort of churning a monstrous gear. But another theory is that he did himself permanent damage in the late spring of 1980 in an epic, snowbound Liège-Bastogne-Liège.

The snow began falling not far out of Liège and became progressively heavier. Most riders gave up—by the feeding station in Vielsalm, with 60 miles remaining, a hundred had quit, leaving 74 in the race. Rudy Pevenage was alone in front, just over two minutes ahead of a group containing Hinault, with another rider, Ludo Peeters, caught between the leader and the chasing group. But as the conditions deteriorated and the temperature plummeted, Hinault went on the attack, overhauling Pevenage, and setting out on his own. There were 50 miles left. The snow was becoming so heavy that Hinault "was riding with a hand up to my face to keep the snow out of my eyes."

While Hinault still toyed with the idea of abandoning—in fact, he had earlier made a pact with Maurice Le Guilloux, telling him, "When we arrive at Vielsalm, we'll get off and go back to the hotel"—Guimard urged him on, instructing him to remove his red *cagoule*, his jacket, and telling him "the real race is about to start." Guimard was also concerned that the jacket obscured the sponsors' logos, but Hinault refused to take it off. "I told him to go and get lost, or get on the bike himself." As Hinault later recalled, "My teeth were chattering and I had no protection against the cold, which was getting right inside me. I decided that the only thing to do was ride as hard as I could to keep myself warm."

After catching and dropping both Peeters and Pevenage, he rode alone to Liège, in the process writing another chapter of the Hinault legend. The images of that day show the full extent of the blizzard; riding through it, Hinault resembles not a cyclist but a polar explorer or Everest mountaineer. "When

I reached the Boulevard de la Sauvenière in Liège, I had hardly any feeling left in my limbs, my hands were frozen to the handlebars, but my lead had grown to nearly 10 minutes," recalls Hinault. Only 20 other riders finished; the last one, Jostein Wilmann, was 27 minutes down. But the epic win came at a cost. The index and middle fingers of Hinault's right hand were so badly frozen that it was three weeks before they recovered enough for him to use them properly. "Even now," he says, displaying his large hands for inspection, "they are still affected by cold weather."

Three months later, and after Hinault had completed the triple crown of all three Grand Tours by winning the Giro d'Italia, his bid to emulate his fellow Breton, Louison Bobet, by winning three consecutive Tours de France ended in dramatic failure. It also became one of the most controversial episodes of his career. The Tour started with a prologue in Frankfurt, which Hinault won, then continued with cobbled stages through northern Europe, one of them finishing in Lille. Hinault won there, too, but it was here, he admitted later, that he "started to feel pain in my knees." He wasn't pleased with the cobbles. "My impression of hell was confirmed. I can't understand what inhuman conditions have to do with sport."

The first week of the 1980 Tour also took the riders into Holland, where Hinault was booed, perhaps because he had denied the Dutchman, Zoetemelk, victory in the previous two years. But it was the conditions—cold and rain—that troubled him more and could, as he would later claim, have aggravated his knee problems.

His weakness was underlined, ironically, on the day in the second week when he reclaimed the yellow jersey. A 51-km time trial from Damazan to Laplume—the type of stage that a fit Badger would have dominated—saw him finish only fifth, a minute and 32 seconds down on Zoetemelk. Clearly he was struggling. And yet, presented with the yellow jersey after the following day's 194-km stage to Pau, he was defiant, announcing at the finish not only that he would carry on but that he would win the next day.

Late that night, as the print journalists sat down to dinner, having filed their stories and clocked out for the evening, came the bombshell: Hinault had quit. What's more, he had fled Pau in a perfectly orchestrated escape, designed to cause Hinault minimum fuss but with precisely the opposite consequences for everyone else.

For the man in yellow to abandon the race was extraordinary, almost unprecedented, headline news. For it to be Hinault—*le patron*, the unofficial king of France—was front-page news. Only on this occasion, it was too late: The headlines had been written; the newspapers had gone to the presses. The journalists, who heard about Hinault's withdrawal from the agency that was fed the news by Guimard, were incandescent.

Meanwhile, as Hinault fled to Lourdes in a car with teammate Hubert Arbes, his wife, Martine, and the couple's son, Mickael, Guimard appeared in the hotel lobby. In this vignette—also broadcast on French TV—it is possible to recognize in the then 33-year-old Guimard the same haughty manner that is evident at the Roubaix velodrome 30 years later.

It's 11:30 p.m. in Pau, and Guimard looks tired. His face is sweating, but not, it would seem, out of anxiety. Indeed, he appears to relish the confrontation with the journalists and enjoys goading them. Asked why Hinault announced his decision at 10 p.m., Guimard, in a blue polo shirt and open jacket, responds, "It wasn't 10 p.m., it was 10:30—but let's not split hairs." With a chuckle, he adds, "The reason is simple: At 10:30 p.m., Bernard Hinault left Pau."

Of course he shouldn't keep riding with an injury, one reporter acknowledges, but why keep people guessing until the last moment? Guimard half smiles, then folds his arms, leans back, and peers down his nose. "Bernard wanted to leave without any publicity."

It is put to Guimard that, with journalists "there when things are going well," do Hinault's actions, with the help of Guimard, not amount to "dodging his responsibilities as a champion?"

"No, absolutely not, on the contrary, Bernard didn't want to be hounded by the press," argues Guimard. "When cyclists quit, everyone pounces on them to record the first tears, the first statement, and Bernard didn't want to go through that."

Whom did he tell? "All his teammates. . . . The decision was made a long time ago. As soon as Bernard started having trouble in the stage before the mountains, we knew he wouldn't ride this stage, so pretty much everyone was expecting it. Then, what happened tonight, everyone in the team was told, but no one else."

Hinault contradicts this some years later, saying he had gone to visit the Tour organizers, Jacques Goddet and Félix Lévitan, interrupting their dinner with a senior French politician, to tell them. "They were very decent," says Hinault. He was right to be concerned about the press reaction, though the circumstances of his withdrawal only exacerbated the problem.

After a night in Lourdes, Hinault drove up to Brittany. "When we got home, there were 20 journalists there," he recalls. "They'd tied up the front door with a rope, so we were obliged to stop, and they'd also blocked the road with a car. The way I felt, things could have taken a nasty turn at that moment. I told them to move the car or I'd ram it."

Still, years later, Hinault justifies his clandestine escape and rejects the assertion that it was badly handled. "I just didn't want [journalists] to be bugging me all evening. I already had enough pain in my head; I was too unhappy to put up with people bugging me." As he stood in the yellow jersey on the podium in Pau, Hinault "knew I wouldn't be back next day [but] I wanted to give the impression that everything was fine, I wanted people to leave me alone. I thought that by announcing it at 11 o'clock at night no one could get the information." With apparently more satisfaction than regret, he adds, "It caused a crazy panic."

After gaining access to his house, Hinault visited his doctor, who prescribed a period of rest. That seemed to clear up the problem—at least in the short term. Eight days later, Hinault returned to training.

In the autumn, he returned to the top, winning the world road race championship in Sallanches on a course, nestling in the heart of the French Alps, often claimed to be the toughest of all time. To say that Hinault was fired up for this "appointment" is to gloriously understate his determination to win. He was disgruntled by the suspicion, voiced by some journalists, that his knee injury had been caused by cortisone. Such rumors had swirled around Hinault—as, indeed, they swirled around most successful riders of the era— ever since he had begun winning major races. As far back as June 1977, when he won the Dauphiné Libéré after his spectacular crash into an Alpine ravine, L'Équipe claimed that Hinault, on the stage to Grenoble in which he crashed, was "not in a natural state"—a remark widely interpreted as an insinuation of doping. Six months later, the French sports paper asked Hinault directly about his "reputation, [which] has already raised some reservations [with regard to] the inevitable topic of doping."

"I am aware of that," said Hinault. "You should know that I was tested at the finish [of the Dauphiné stage]. I have been tested two dozen times since I started racing, and I've never tested positive."

Eighteen months later, as Hinault was riding to his second Tour de France, L'Équipe alleged that Hinault was surrounded by an "entourage" containing "characters well known for suspicious activities [and supplying] special products and miracle cures."

"I know who you mean," said Hinault when asked about this. "Yet I swear I only know one way to treat myself; by the methods advocated by Professor Ginet [of Nantes]. I look at literally everything I'm asked to take." (Later, Hinault aligned himself with another doctor, François Bellocq of Bordeaux, who worked with many top cyclists and teams, as well as other sports people, and who in the late 1980s controversially advocated the banned practice of "hormone rebalancing" for Tour de France riders, saying this would improve their health. "I agree with Dr. Bellocq—the doctor I had—on this subject," Hinault told the magazine *Tonus* in December 1988, two years after his retirement. And 11 years later Hinault was asked again, this time by *L'Équipe*, about "hormonal rebalancing." Asked if he was in favor, Hinault said, "Yes, perhaps, but on one condition: that it is strictly controlled.")

After his withdrawal from the 1980 Tour, as Hinault returned to racing in the post-Tour criteriums, he became aware again of the whispers of doping. "One journalist suggested that my knee trouble had been brought about by the use of cortisone," he writes in his autobiography. "I saw this journalist some weeks later, the one who knew more about me than the doctors and specialists did, at the Tour of Germany. He asked me how I was, and I told him that I was as you'd expect someone on cortisone to be."

In Sallanches, Hinault continues in his autobiography, "I would wipe away all the mud that had been slung at me." The Hinault who appeared in Sallanches at the end of August and instructed his French teammates that he would take over after the first 10 laps, or half the race, was the cartoon Badger in all his snarling glory. "I was on the boil," he writes. "I almost struck a woman who wanted my autograph and picked a bad moment to ask me. She insisted, and I gave her a mouthful. If she'd carried on, I don't know what I'd have done."

Oh, dear. The poor woman's sense of timing was almost as lacking as Hinault's self-awareness in so publicly recalling—even boasting about—the incident.

He was certainly on the boil. His performance to win the world title in Sallanches—his only world title—was crushing. On perhaps the toughest course ever used for a world championship, Hinault clenched his teeth and, one by one, rode the rest of the field off his back wheel, finishing over a minute clear of the second-placed Gianbattista Baronchelli of Italy and over 4 minutes ahead of the bronze medalist, Spain's Juan Fernández Martín.

It is fascinating to learn—as I did when I visited Greg LeMond—that as Guimard was looking after his injured star and dealing with the fallout of Hinault's controversial withdrawal from the Tour, he was lining up a possible replacement. Even as he spoke to reporters in Pau, Guimard was thinking ahead, plotting future Tour successes with the most exciting young prospect in the sport. Greg LeMond had somehow splashed out of the cycling backwater of America and landed in the great pool of the sport in Europe, making a big impact on his first visits and catching Guimard's attention.

On the Champs-Elysées, as the 1980 Tour closed with Zoetemelk finally winning for the first—and only—time, LeMond was secretly signing a contract with Guimard to ride for Renault in 1981. Publicly, though, the deal was done in the United States over the winter, with Guimard travelling to LeMond's home in Reno, Nevada.

But Guimard wasn't alone. Intriguingly—given how their careers would be intertwined over the following seasons—he traveled to Reno in the company of his leader, Bernard Hinault. A third member of the traveling party was Jean-Marie Leblanc, the *L'Équipe* journalist and future director of the Tour de France.

"I wanted to go there above all because it was important for me to see how Greg lived in the USA," says Guimard now. "You can bring someone over, put them in an apartment, but it's not just a case of transporting them—you have to integrate them. The best way of doing that was seeing him in his home environment. I didn't know the USA at all. I'd done the Tour of Canada, but that was it. So we went over there, and it was a bit of a publicity stunt; we'd decided to go over and make him sign the contract there. That also gave us the opportunity to go to Washington and meet a few people there, the French ambassador among others.

"Jean-Marie Leblanc also came to cover it for *L'Équipe*. Because there was another problem; even under torture, neither I nor Hinault could speak English. That's why Jean-Marie came, too—I had known him for a long time, he was a friend, and he could speak English."

Hinault, recalls Guimard, was an enthusiastic traveler. "Yes, but you see that's the kind of situation the Badger likes. He's quite an open person, actually. The idea of going to the USA to meet an American was quite *sympa* for him."

Hinault's own recollections of that trip seem more vague. "It was strange, especially Reno," says Hinault, sitting in his kitchen in Brittany, staring into the middle distance. "These big expanses of land . . . it's a lot wilder than Europe." His impressions of the 19-year-old LeMond were similarly hazy. "We went all the way over there because we believed in him," he says with a shrug.

Yet Hinault suggests that, in recruiting LeMond, he and Guimard were already thinking about his succession. "Yes, well, I'd already said in 1980 that I'd stop in 1986," says Hinault, who was just 25 in 1980 and who stated that he would retire on the occasion of his 32nd birthday, on November 14, 1986.

"Also, with Greg we could compete on different fronts," adds Hinault. "That was the idea—that one would win the Giro, another would win the Vuelta. Then we'd both come together, to give us two options at the Tour. *Voilà*!"

3

L'AMÉRICAIN

Yeeeeeeeeehaaaaaaaaaa!

GREG LEMOND

H e doesn't remember it?" yells Greg LeMond, leaning forward until his chest bounces off his kitchen table. "Holy shit!"

LeMond, silver-haired, chunky, almost barrel-chested, but with the familiar sparkling pale blue eyes, has just been told that Bernard Hinault, upon being asked about his visit in November 1980 to the United States, where he, Cyrille Guimard, and Jean-Marie Leblanc stayed in the LeMonds' house, seems to barely remember it.

"That's so funny," chips in LeMond's wife, Kathy.

"I've got photos of it," adds LeMond. "I was looking through them about two months ago; Hinault dressed as a cowboy."

"You do?" says Kathy. "That's cute!"

"Hinault's the first guy who shot me," continues LeMond, almost nostalgically. "Right in the eye. We were shooting . . . I grew up hunting quail, so I took them out quail hunting. And Hinault shot me." Then he adds quickly, "By accident."

Since LeMond had already signed a contract worth $18,000 a year with the Renault team, the stateside trip was essentially a PR exercise, though it also allowed Guimard, as he told me, to see LeMond in his own environment and get to know him better. "I just felt good about Guimard," says LeMond, explaining his decision to join his team. "I didn't speak French, though I took some in high school, but Guimard [contrary to what he now claims] made a big attempt to speak English."

Kathy nods, adding, "Guimard started English lessons when Greg joined the team. A tutor came to his house every week. And every day, even at training camp, he studied English. I thought that was amazing. He was extraordinary to us. I really think that with Greg he went so far beyond the call of duty—I mean, Greg was a neopro. I think he really, truly saw that Greg was going to be his next star—"

"Nooooo, I don't think," LeMond interrupts. "Honey, he—"

"He did things for you he didn't do for your peers."

"I remember being told," adds LeMond, switching tack again, "when I signed that contract, 'Don't tell anybody how much you're getting, because you're the highest paid neopro ever.' Then later, of course, you find out everybody's been told that."

LeMond laughs, but it's clear that Guimard did go to extraordinary lengths to, as he puts it, "integrate" the LeMonds. In this respect he was more enlightened than many others. He understood that in order for LeMond to succeed—and for Renault to get a return on its investment—he would have to do more than simply "transport them from one country to another."[1]

LeMond was born on June 26, 1961, in the suburban city of Lakewood in Los Angeles County. When he was 8, his family moved to Lake Tahoe, in the mountains where California meets Nevada, and three years later, through LeMond's father, Bob's, work as a real estate broker, they were on the move again—this time deeper into Nevada, to the Washoe Valley. With each move, the family—parents Bob and Bertha, Greg, and his two sisters, Kathy and Karen—edged farther away from the metropolis and into the great American wilderness. The Washoe Valley was, in LeMond's description, "ranch country."

---

1. There is a fascinating discussion of the problems inherent in "relocation" in a soccer book, *Why England Lose* by Simon Kuper and Stefan Szymanski. "Relocation is one of the biggest inefficiencies in the transfer market," they point out, because players are told, "Here's a plane ticket, come over, and play brilliantly from day one." They cite the case of Real Madrid's £22 million purchase of Nicolas Anelka. Never mind a house or a phone or a language tutor, "he hadn't even been assigned a locker in the changing room."

The valley sits on the eastern slopes of the Sierra Nevada mountain range; in 6,600 square miles the population is 410,000, though the city of Reno accounts for 75 percent of that total. From the age of 11, LeMond lived in fairly remote places. He had few neighbors; his closest school friends lived three miles away; and he traveled to school by bus, an hour's journey each way. "I was never close enough to school to participate in team sports," LeMond told Sam Abt, with whom he would become friendly after he moved to Europe. "I played football and baseball. But mainly I was interested in sports where I could accomplish something myself, without having to depend on others."

Surrounded by lakes and mountains, LeMond began hiking, hunting, trapshooting, and fishing; there was a stream, with brook trout, behind the LeMonds' house, where he practiced his technique with a fly rod. "I went backpacking almost every weekend when I was 13 and 14," LeMond told Abt. "At one point I was so into it that I bought all these books about it, like *The Complete Walker*, and read them over and over again."

LeMond was restless. He even planned, in the summer of 1975, to walk the John Muir Trail from Yosemite Valley to the summit of Mount Whitney, a 211-mile trek that would have entailed a two-month expedition and would have been an extreme, and perhaps unwise, undertaking for a 14-year-old boy. It hints, though, at LeMond's sense of ambition. It is also clear that, as much as he enjoyed the outdoors, including hunting and fishing—as indeed he still does—these activities did not, and could not, satisfy his latent desire for competition.

Where competitive sport was concerned, LeMond showed promise as a skier, though he never actually competed. And skiing didn't fulfill him, either. "I wanted something more challenging than going up a ski lift and whizzing back down," as he put it, explaining his unlikely switch from downhill to freestyle skiing. Abt has some fun imagining LeMond's dreams of becoming a "champion hot-dog skier." He did want a bike at the time, explained LeMond, but that was because of his isolation and the three-mile commute to his nearest school friends. It had nothing to do with sport.

To save for the bike, LeMond mowed lawns and chopped logs to make pocket money, allowing him to eventually buy a Raleigh Grand Prix. Yet his conversion from skier to competitive cyclist didn't come about through riding his new bike; it began at Wayne Wong's freestyle ski training camp—a 14th birthday present from his parents—in Vancouver in the winter of 1975, when one of the coaches told him that cycling would be good training for his skiing. It was, LeMond admitted, "the first time I thought about my bike as anything other than transportation."

At least two other significant things happened around the same time. In the summer of 1975 the Nevada state cycling championships passed close to the LeMonds' house, and Greg and his father, Bob, went to watch. Both were thrilled by what they witnessed: the color, the speed, the excitement, the sheer spectacle of a road race. And both were inspired to get out into the Nevada countryside on their bikes, even as autumn turned to winter, with the 1975–1976 season producing less snow than normal. That was one reason for LeMond to ski less and ride his bike more.

Bob LeMond, also bitten by the cycling bug and keen to lose a bit of weight in his mid-30s, joined his son on many of his rides, having put behind him a turbulent period in his marriage to Greg's mother, Bertha. They had argued constantly and seemed on the verge of breaking up, but domestic harmony was restored over the summer of 1975. Now, through cycling, relations between Greg and his father also improved. "Up until then he'd tell you that he worked 7 days a week, 14 hours a day," said LeMond of his father. "I didn't really have a dad. He had been drinking beer, putting on weight, and all of a sudden he just stopped. I bought a bike, he bought a bike, and we started riding together." (More than 30 years later, there would be a fascinating parallel as LeMond, after a turbulent period in his life, rediscovered cycling in the company of his own son, in the process mending their fractured relationship.)

When LeMond started going to races, his whole family would go with him: Dad, Mom, and sisters Kathy and Karen. Often it was because his father would also be competing, and competing with distinction. Aged 38 and having been training for only three years, Bob LeMond finished fifth in one of America's toughest stage races, the Red Zinger Classic (which became the Coors Classic in 1979). A talent for cycling was clearly in the LeMond genes.

But there was more to it than that. Through cycling, LeMond junior found an outlet for a hitherto hidden competitive streak and for his apparent desire to push his body. And here there is, perhaps, a revealing contrast between Bernard Hinault and Greg LeMond. While Hinault appears to have been driven by his natural aggression, with his childhood love for playground scraps translating in adulthood into his "destructive rage," or desire to batter opponents into submission, LeMond seemed driven to inflict pain on himself. That urge does not make him unique among endurance athletes—far from it. But it appears to highlight an apparent difference between him and Hinault: Hinault liked to punish others (Guimard describes him as a "boxer . . . he needed an opponent"), whereas LeMond liked to punish himself. LeMond agrees with the analysis. "I don't remember a lot of racers' names," he says, "because I didn't race against people, I raced against myself."

Thus, LeMond's approach to training, from an early age, could border on masochistic. Steve Bauer, the Canadian cyclist and a rider who would play a major role at the 1986 Tour de France, recalls training with LeMond and Phil Anderson in Sacramento in the winter of 1984. "That was where I really learned how to train as a pro," says Bauer now. He admits he was in awe of what LeMond was able to put himself through in training. "He knew how to suffer, that boy. He could hurt himself. Even when he wasn't at his best, he could hang in through suffering, through just wanting to do it. Obviously he had amazing ability as an athlete, too. But his ability to suffer, to not get dropped when he was not at his best, was what made him different to most guys."

At the same time, paradoxically, LeMond could adopt a casual, relaxed approach to training. "We'd always meet at 9 in the morning, usually at his place because he'd always be slow to get out of bed and get going in the mornings," remembers Anderson, a neighbor when he and LeMond lived in Belgium.

"You'd get round there, to his place, and he wouldn't have unpacked his bloody suitcase from the last race, and there'd be shit everywhere in his house," continues Anderson, smiling. "Walking through the garage, there'd just be piles of laundry. I'm not saying Kathy wasn't a domestic person, but it seemed a bit disorganized. So we'd make plans to leave his place at 9, but by the time he bloody got ready and got organized, and found his helmet and shoes, it'd be 9:30 or 10. Then, yeah, he could train hard.

"But the thing about Greg was that he could read his body," continues Anderson. "He was very naturally talented, and I always complained, because I felt I had to go out and work very hard, whereas it seemed that some weeks Greg would sit in the coffee shop all week, then come out and kick everybody's arse at the weekend. He had lots of natural ability. But he really knew what he had to do."

As with any prodigious talent, it was mainly natural ability that saw LeMond—like Hinault—make such an instant impact when he began racing.

In fact, LeMond's record, in his first four races, was identical to Hinault's—
he won all four, the winning streak coming to an end in his fifth race, just as
Hinault's did. He was younger than Hinault when he started racing, just 15,
and within a year he was dominant despite the fact that he was quickly promoted to the junior category. Yet even as a 16-year-old, against riders up to
two years older, he won 30 races, generally events that were quite short. A
year later, he was given dispensation to race with seniors. He also went to the
U.S. team trials for the 1977 junior world championships, where he won two
out of the three selection races, only to be told he was too young to be picked
for the team.

Talent is important, of course, especially among young athletes—and Le-
Mond had talent by the bucketload, scoring exceptionally well in physiologi-
cal tests. At an early testing session at the U.S. Olympic Training Center in
Colorado Springs, his results were staggering—"Jesus, guys, look at this!" the
tester is reported to have said on seeing LeMond's VO_2 results.[2]

Though much is understandably made of LeMond's outsider status, I
thought of LeMond when I read Malcolm Gladwell's book *Outliers*. As well
as explaining the "10,000-hour" rule—that to attain world-class status in
any field requires at least 10,000 hours' dedication, practice, or training—
Gladwell explains away some misconceptions around success, in particular
the myth that it is solely down to "talent." In fact, high achievers, from Roger
Federer to Bill Gates, owe much of their success to what Gladwell calls "accumulative advantages," or a "web of advantages and inheritances" allied to
a strong work ethic.

Though LeMond had talent to burn, it is important not to overlook other
helpful factors—the web of advantages and inheritances that played in Le-
Mond's favor, gently encouraging him along the path to greatness. In this
respect, the American journalist Owen Mulholland offers a description of
LeMond as an outlier in the Gladwell mold: "LeMond had bridges. Paren-
tal help didn't hurt. Loving the activity helped. Being recognized by a small

---

2. Indeed, at 92.5, LeMond's is among the highest VO_2s ever recorded by any athlete. VO_2 is reckoned
to be the most significant measurement in endurance athletes; it refers to the volume of oxygen, in
liters per minute, transported by the athlete during exercise. The Norwegian cross-country skiers
Espen Harald Bjerke and Bjørn Dæhlie are believed to have the highest ever recorded VO_2, at 96.
By way of comparison, Lance Armstrong's has been reported as 85; that of another multiple Tour
winner, Miguel Indurain, was 88. Figures appear to be unavailable for Bernard Hinault. LeMond's
VO_2 of 92.5 could, therefore, be the highest ever recorded by a cyclist. By way of further comparison,
the "normal" VO_2 for a man in his 20s is between 38 and 43.

circle as particularly talented was a boost. All things considered, being in the right place at the right time with that kind of potential put Greg right where he needed to be to break out of the American bubble and onto the stage of world cycling."

As well as enjoying cycling for cycling's sake—as LeMond, the outdoors lover, clearly did—he was seduced by the exotic world of professional cycle racing. Through magazines he learned about the Grand Tours of European racing: Tour de France, Giro d'Italia, Vuelta a España; the single-day classics: Paris-Roubaix, the Tour of Flanders, Milan–San Remo. He read about Eddy Merckx, Bernard Hinault, and the *maillot jaune*, and he began to learn the language of a sport rooted firmly in mainland Europe. As one of LeMond's contemporaries, Kent Gordis, would tell Sam Abt, "At that time cycling in America was like a secret society. . . . You could buy three-month-old copies of *Miroir du Cyclisme* at the French American bookshop in San Francisco. You know how kids find names like 'Bali' or 'Tahiti' exotic? We found all those unpronounceable Flemish names in *Miroir* exotic. We would amuse ourselves by repeating the names to each other."

When LeMond and his young American teammates finally ventured to Europe to race, touching down in Switzerland in 1978, it was "not just a trip abroad; it was attaining some sort of exalted state," said Gordis. On that trip, incidentally, LeMond had his first sight of the Tour de France—the one, of course, that gave Hinault his first victory, on the stage from Grenoble to Morzine, three days before Hinault took yellow. "We rode from Geneva to the Joux-Plane," recalled LeMond. "We were able to watch the Tour go past from [the former champion skier] Jean-Claude Killy's chalet. When I saw it, I thought, that's what I want to do."

In fact, the sight only confirmed his dream. The previous winter, 1977–1978, LeMond had listed a set of goals on a yellow pad of paper (which he still has in his possession, somewhere—he says he remains as domestically disorganized as in the days when he trained with Anderson). The list reads as follows:

1. Place well for experience in the 1978 junior world championships.
2. Win the 1979 junior world championship.
3. Win the 1980 Olympic road race in Moscow.
4. Win the world professional championships by the age of 22 or 23.
5. Win a first Tour de France by the age of 24 or 25.

In spring 1978, with LeMond now old enough to ride the junior world championships, he represented his country on home soil. The championships were staged in Washington, D.C., and LeMond was ninth in the road race, third in the team time trial, results that certainly checked the box marked "place well for experience." LeMond was on his way.

In the same year, he met Kathy Morris at the national championships in Milwaukee, though they didn't start dating until the following year, when LeMond visited Kathy in her hometown of Minneapolis. As with anything Greg LeMond turns his attention to, once he and Kathy were officially a couple, things progressed with remarkable speed. LeMond remains, to this day, a bundle of restless energy, a veritable whirlwind. "Greg's an A-personality, for sure," as Steve Bauer says with a chuckle. "Whatever he does, he does to 100 percent, to exaggeration. That's Greg."

By December, though both were only 18, LeMond had spent $2,000 on an engagement ring and asked Kathy to marry him, much to her parents' alarm. "They were shocked," LeMond admitted to Abt. "They were really upset that she wanted to marry a bike rider. They had no idea what cycling was. . . . I tried to convince them that I was a responsible person, that my physical age might be 19, but that I was really a couple of years older than that mentally. And I was. I'd been to Europe several times. . . . I made about $30,000 that year from prizes and sponsors."

LeMond's eagerness to get married—he and Kathy were married in December 1980 on the eve of his first professional season—and to "settle down" may have been owing to many factors, including his fear that he would suffer homesickness in Europe, but not least to the fact that, in Kathy, he found someone who was willing to support him and his ambitions, who would prove to be a constant companion, almost always by his side, even—in a development that was unheard-of—at races. There is a parallel with Hinault in that he, too, married young, and his marriage to Martine has endured against all the odds (unsurprisingly, there is a high divorce rate among professional cyclists, especially in the years immediately after retirement).

But the differences between the Hinaults and LeMonds are perhaps even more striking. Martine Hinault was a rare visitor to races; she would not have been whisked into the commentary box, as Kathy was at the summit of Alpe d'Huez in 1986. When LeMond talks about his career, he often uses "we," meaning he and Kathy, instead of "I"—something you couldn't imagine Hinault doing.

I asked Sam Abt what he made of Martine Hinault, and his response was as revealing as it was pithy. "Yeah . . . um," he replied thoughtfully, "I would say that she knew her place."

In 1979, the world junior championships—the second objective on Le-Mond's list—were again held across the Atlantic, which seems very odd, looking back now. This was a time when the European hegemony seemed absolute, yet it is interesting that the international governing body decided to award the junior championships to cities, indeed to continents, so far from the sport's heartland: first Washington, D.C., in 1978, and then, in 1979, to Buenos Aires, Argentina. (Even odder, the following year's championships were also held in the Americas, in Mexico City.)

Clearly cycling's world governing body, the Union Cycliste Internationale (UCI), had an eye on the long-term growth and internationalization of the sport. And although it might seem unlikely that these three world junior championships had a material effect on promoting the sport in the countries where they were held, it is interesting to note that, in the decade that followed, the area of most significant growth, in terms of emerging talent and popularity, was the American continents, particularly the United States and Colombia.

Still, the location of the 1979 championships seemed to undermine them a little, to remove a layer of gloss. It was as if an invisible asterisk were placed beside the medalists' names. Which was unfair, because the field that assembled in the Argentine capital was arguably no less strong, and the course certainly no less demanding, than if the championships had been staged in Europe.

LeMond won the road race, though he almost didn't. Andy Hampsten, a colleague in the American junior team, didn't feature at the finish after "a very, very long wheel change" following a puncture, but he recalls what happened. "Greg was actually second across the line, but the Belgian [Kenny De Maerteleire] was hooking him. The race was on a motor-racing circuit, and there were these car tires in the pit lane. Kenny De Maerteleire led the sprint out and hooked Greg into these car tires, repeatedly! Greg was actually riding over the car tires, and he still almost beat him in the sprint."[3]

---

3. Kenny De Maerteleire did finally get a world road race gold medal, at the world masters championship in 2004.

Hampsten spent a lot of time with LeMond on the U.S. junior team that year. "I got on with him really well," he says. "He's a fun guy, and he loved joking around with his buddies. He was welcoming and really good at chit-chatting to everyone. Even though the cycling scene in the U.S. contained hundreds rather than thousands of people to talk to in the late 1970s, Greg was really nice to talk to. He talked to everyone. He liked goofing around, but I could tell, in a group situation, he'd go out of his way to introduce himself and make jokes. He really likes to have fun. He enjoyed life."

With goals number one and two achieved, LeMond could focus on the third item on his yellow pad of paper: winning the Olympic road race. Except that he couldn't—the American boycott of the Moscow Games meant that he wouldn't be going to the Olympics. Instead, with the U.S. national team, he spent much of the year in Europe, serving his apprenticeship and catching the eye of Guimard almost immediately with a stage win and third overall at the early-season Circuit des Ardennes. Missing the Olympics, says LeMond now, hardly mattered. "In my mind the Olympics were just a step-ping stone; I didn't care. I wanted to turn pro.

"In April 1980, I won the Circuit de la Sarthe; then I went to the Ruban Granitier de Breton, a tough stage race for amateurs in Brittany, and I was in a breakaway with the Russians on the last day," LeMond continues. "I had a flat and . . . ah, I tossed my bike away." The U.S. team was sponsored by the French bicycle manufacturer Lejeune, but when LeMond punctured, the Lejeune car was nowhere to be seen. When it did appear, LeMond asked, in no uncertain terms, where it had been. As the mechanic handed him a spare wheel, insisting he finish the race "as if I had some moral or financial obligation to the sponsor," LeMond blew his top. "I got off and threw my Lejeune bike at the car and said, 'I'm done. You just cost me the race.'"

When he was told about LeMond's loss of temper, Guimard was asked if he was still interested in signing him. "Now I want him, yes," he said. "He's got character. But there will be no more nonsense like that."

LeMond—who affects a sheepish look as he recalls this story, though he is clearly unabashed and perhaps even a little proud—says this wasn't his only conflict at that time. He was also in dispute with the national coach. "I ended up getting in a big battle with the coach, because they split the [na-tional] team in two. One lot was down south; our group was in the north of France with no money. The national coach was down south, with the budget, and we had nothing. But we won at the Circuit de la Sarthe, and won some money, and the coach came up to take it! I stood up and said, 'Screw you! It's our money.'"

In Brittany, LeMond encountered Guimard. "I'd met Guimard the day before [the bike-throwing incident], when I was in a break with [Marc] Madiot [a Frenchman who would go on to a successful career, winning Paris-Roubaix twice]. I knew who Guimard was, but I wasn't that big on who the big names in the sport were—it was probably Kent Gordis who told me. And I didn't realize he was there for me until the next day. I thought he was there to see Marc Madiot, but then I heard he was scouting for me.

"He asked me if I wanted to turn pro. But by then I'd had a call from Peugeot, too. I was 18 years old, and I was like, wow! I negotiated in May between Peugeot and Guimard—I played one against the other. And then I went back to France for three weeks, but as soon as I signed my contract we left. We were looking for any excuse we could find to get out of there!"

Though LeMond, talented, ambitious, and already successful, knew that Europe, with its "proper racing . . . proper competition" was "where I wanted to be," he already felt some pangs of homesickness. That was to be a constant battle, and something Guimard was alert to; hence his efforts to learn English and to help with the LeMonds' "integration" into French life. And Guimard took another step; he signed Jonathan Boyer, the only other American in the European peloton, six years older than LeMond, who'd lived and raced, with modest success, in France since 1973.

For LeMond, moving to Europe was a massive step, a huge sacrifice, as it was for Kathy, who, after their marriage on December 21, moved with him. Apart from leaving home, there was also the fact that LeMond—intelligent, articulate—was gambling everything on cycling, giving up the idea of going to college. "Giving up on our education," says Kathy now, "that was a big thing."

"That's what we thought," points out LeMond, "but that's not what most cyclists think. They're not thinking of going to college."

Arriving in Europe on January 9, 1981, the LeMonds picked up the car they'd been promised. Since Greg's new team was a car manufacturer they would have been justified in expecting a reasonable automobile; instead they received the keys to a car with, bizarrely, a warped windshield, seriously affecting visibility. "It was a dud," says LeMond.

Nevertheless, they drove out of Paris and headed west to Brittany. Guimard had wanted the LeMonds to live near him, close to Nantes, and arranged a house in La Chapelle–sur–Erdre, which, he promised, would be fully furnished. But, as with the car, they were to be disappointed. What they found in La Chapelle–sur–Erdre was a shell, a cold house with no furniture, nothing. The couple spent two weeks in a hotel—"It rained every day," says Kathy—before LeMond headed to the south of France for a monthlong training camp. Meanwhile, Kathy temporarily moved into another, furnished house, arranged by Guimard—still trying his best to help the LeMonds settle into French life, but clearly with some difficulty—"with a mattress and a cooking pan." As for the furniture, "they kept saying, 'it'll be here next week,'" says Kathy, "but it was the middle of April when we finally got furniture."

At the training camp, meanwhile, LeMond struggled, because he was seriously overweight. Over the winter, he had followed the advice of Belgian cycling friends who "told me to take six months off and just have fun, because once you turn pro you'll never take six months off again until you're done," says LeMond. "I literally did that, and put on about 10 pounds. When I showed up for the early season, I was so out of shape. Guimard had me do a 110-mile race, then ride another 50 miles afterward. After six weeks of that I was very skinny."

Guimard's program worked. By April, LeMond was going well—well enough to play a strong team role at Paris-Roubaix, which Hinault won. And in May he registered his first win, a triumph vividly recalled by Phil Anderson—not so much for the win as for the victory celebration. It came in a stage of the Tour de l'Oise, north of Paris. "We were in a break," says Anderson. "There were about 10 of us, and, coming round the last corner, Greg just kicked everyone's arse. I got second, but all I remember is Greg, as he crossed the line, yelling out 'Yeeeeeeeeeeehaaaaaaaaaa!' He had his arms above his head, and he just let out this yell. It was so American—he sounded like a cowboy or something. I'd never heard or seen anything like it. That's not what you did at bike races, you know?"

LeMond soon had even more cause to be delighted when Guimard rewarded his protégé's strong performances with a surprising but significant midseason wage increase, upping his pay to around $25,000.

The racing was one thing—LeMond coped admirably with that, his monstrous talent ensuring that he wasn't out of his depth as so many neo-pros are (the average professional career is said to be about three years). But living in France was another matter. Here there were little cultural hurdles to overcome; gaps that LeMond seemed unable, or unwilling, to bridge (to use Owen Mulholland's word). Eating proved a challenge. Not so much the food—though that, too, was testing, and LeMond sought out his favorite Mexican food when he could, which in the early 1980s was with great difficulty—but more the French dining experience. Nothing, LeMond would discover, was allowed to interrupt lunch or dinner. Even long journeys between races would routinely be broken by a lengthy stop for lunch. LeMond, as he told Abt at the time, found the ritual intensely frustrating. "I thought, 'Let's just get there! Then we'll have lunch!'"

Adding to his irritation was the time spent dining—often at least two hours. Unable at first to speak the language—though LeMond did become fluent and would happily give interviews in French later in his career—he found those two-hour lunch breaks with his new teammates to be torture. To alleviate his boredom, LeMond began taking a book to dinner and reading at the table—a heinous social crime in France. "Some dinners were so slow, so long," says LeMond now, "and I was bored. I always liked to read something, anyway. In my first four weeks with the [Renault] team, I read about 12 Robert Ludlum books." Naturally, his teammates—the Francophile Boyer especially—were horrified.

LeMond was aware, of course, that his path would be smoother if he at least gave the impression of adapting and fitting in—which might explain a photograph in a 1981 edition of *Miroir du Cyclisme*. It depicts him in central Paris wearing a beret, nursing a glass of *vin rouge*, with a baguette and a French newspaper tucked under his arm. But it was about as convincing as Hinault's cowboy shtick for *L'Équipe* the previous year. The truth was that while many others, including Boyer, Ireland's Stephen Roche, and even the maverick Scotsman Robert Millar, went to some lengths to fit in—marrying Frenchwomen in the case of Roche and Millar—LeMond made few concessions.

Arguably this highlights a paradoxical aspect of LeMond's personality. For all that he was almost universally liked and lauded for his friendliness and openness, LeMond could also be stubbornly independent, even rebellious. There is, as an example, a story told by Millar from later in his career that constitutes an even more serious breach of French dining etiquette. Finding the restaurant too hot one evening, LeMond is said to have responded by removing his shirt.

I have to ask him: Is this true? LeMond's face takes on an expression of startled indignation—not at the allegation, but at my doubting it. "Oh, yeah. Oh, yeah, it's true. The French riders were all shocked, but I think I was right to do it because your core temperature goes up. We'd be sitting in these ovens. I was like, I can't handle it. You gotta get the heat away from you.

"I loved the heat when I was racing, but I grew up in Nevada, where it's hot during the day, but it drops at night and gets really cool. When it's hot, I can't sleep. Even today, I need it below 68 degrees.

"The best story," LeMond continues, eyes sparkling at the memory, "was when we were staying north of Arles, in the Provence area, in a Club Med–like hotel resort. It was, like, 110 degrees, and this was when there was no air conditioning, nothing. And we had the shittiest rooms. And . . . it was so hot.

"The other riders are fine. They're sleeping. But I can't sleep, so I drag the mattress out, next building's 100 meters this way, and there are other buildings 150 meters the other way, and there's dirt and grass—not grass, but that Provence dirt/grass sort of stuff—and I pull this mattress out there. And I sleep naked. With a sheet and two pillows—one for my head, one between my legs. I always slept with a pillow between my legs. Anyway, I'm out there and . . . I wake up. And there are people walking right past me—families! I'm waking up, it's 7:30, 8 o'clock, a crystal-clear morning, warm and hot, and I'm lying there, butt naked."

GOODWOOD, ENGLAND, AUGUST 1982

Toward the end of the 1982 world road race championship, staged on the Goodwood motor-racing circuit in West Sussex, there's a moment when Greg LeMond looks back, as if he isn't quite sure what he should do next. Ahead of him are three riders, two immediately in front but one with a gap of 10 meters. It's Jonathan Boyer, his long, lean legs pedaling furiously up the final rise to the finish. It is a sight without precedent: a rider in the stars-and-stripes jersey of the American national team, racing toward the world title.

Behind Boyer, the pack, now down to 35 riders, all of them exhausted, mouths wide open, legs flagging at the end of 171 miles, seems to hesitate. LeMond remains third in line. But the fact that he looks around—that he is able to look around—suggests he has something left. He jumps. And as the entire race approaches the final 500 meters, the spectacle is again unprecedented, on two counts. An American rider leading, another American chasing, clear daylight still between them, the rest of the field strung out behind LeMond.

But it isn't so much that two Americans are now at the front of the race that makes this so unusual. It's that one American is chasing the other, a teammate pursuing a teammate, potentially spoiling the front man's chances of victory.

In the final 200 meters, as the gap to Boyer is closed, another rider in blue jumps, coming from behind LeMond and instantly opening a big gap. But this is the more familiar blue of the Azzurri, the Italian national team. The rider is Giuseppe Saronni, a dashing, dark-haired 24-year-old known universally as "Beppe." And known, from this date onward, for *la fucillata di Goodwood*—the Goodwood rifle shot. For Saronni explodes out of the dwindling peloton like a bullet, quickly putting 10, 15 meters between him and LeMond. With Boyer out of the picture completely, LeMond trails Saronni, the rest of the field lagging behind them, but he can't close the gap. The Italian has all the time he likes to sit up and celebrate his world title while LeMond holds on for second before being swamped by team officials and reporters eager to record the historic event of the first-ever world championship medal for an American rider.

In his second year as a professional, still only 21 years old, LeMond has already made waves and headlines. He has a nickname, too, one that acquires more traction—ironically, you could argue—with his silver medal at Goodwood. To the Eurocentric cycling world, he is "L'Américain." The American. Note the definite article—Boyer did.

Why ironic? Because LeMond's ride at Goodwood, and his leading of the peloton in pursuit of Boyer, was felt by some—especially Boyer, of course—to be unpatriotic, and therefore un-American. Boyer thought that LeMond cost him the race.

Others were not so sure. John Wilcockson, the veteran British reporter, said in 2005 that he could "not remember exactly what I wrote at the time . . . but 23 years later, I'm certain that Boyer's chance of turning that attack into a winner was as remote as the South Pole."

Boyer, however, remains convinced that LeMond might have cost him the world title. "Sean Kelly said I had enough time and space that I could have won it," says Boyer, speaking from Rwanda, where, these days, he runs the national cycling team. "During the race, I obviously didn't know what happened. But I saw the tape afterward, and it was pretty evident. I asked Greg why. He said that he didn't care who won, as long as it wasn't me; that I didn't deserve to win, didn't deserve the publicity, that I'd done nothing all year. So, yeah, it was a deliberate move on his part. Who knows what would have happened had I won that race? A victory like that sometimes changes your life for the better, sometimes for the worse."

When Jonathan—or "Jock," as he is known—Boyer and LeMond became professional teammates in 1981, there was a natural assumption that, as Americans, they would get along. Cyrille Guimard, the Renault team's directeur sportif, may even have counted on the older rider, Boyer, taking the 20-year-old neopro under his wing. But it didn't happen. "Greg didn't like the fact that I got any publicity, or anything like that," says Boyer. "He wanted his own publicity; he wanted to do it for himself."

In the case of Boyer and LeMond, it was quite simple: They had very different personalities and didn't get on. "That whole year he acted jealous of me," LeMond says. "I got to not like him, and we had bitter fights." Most people I spoke to seemed to side more naturally with LeMond, finding Boyer to be awkward, difficult, and aloof. Interestingly, too, LeMond is more gracious toward Boyer than Boyer is toward him and says he understood the resentment felt by the older man.

"I hardly ever spoke to Boyer." Sam Abt shrugs. "He was not friendly. Quite prickly. And he never actually did enough to justify writing about him. Years later, I met him at a race in America, and we talked and got along quite well. I said, 'Jesus, you've mellowed.' He said, 'Yes, I have.' Frankly, I'm amazed I never did one story about him. But I didn't much like him. And I didn't witness the 'treachery' at Goodwood—to hear Boyer tell it."

The context of what happened in Goodwood in 1982 is important, and—quite apart from the conclusions of observers such as John Wilcockson—shows Boyer's claims that LeMond cost him the world title in a slightly different light. For one thing, the two Americans were no longer professional teammates; Boyer had moved to another French squad, Sem-France Loire. And in the world championships, for all that the riders represented their national federations, professional team loyalties could often be just as important, if not more so—perhaps not for superpowers such as France, Italy, Holland, or Belgium but certainly for "third-world" cycling nations such as the United States. To illustrate this point, it is interesting to note, for instance, that Boyer cites the Irishman Sean Kelly in support of his claim that he could have won in Goodwood. Kelly, who finished third, was a Sem-France Loire teammate of Boyer's.

Also significant is what happened at the previous year's world championships in Prague. As LeMond told Abt several years later, "It wasn't worth anybody's bother to have a professional championship since most American riders were amateurs. So after the 1980 world championship, Jock had himself declared national champion because he was the best-placed American in the world championships. The whole year he got to race in a star-spangled jersey, just like the American flag, as national champion.

"I had made it clear before going to Prague that I was not going to race the world championship as the national championship and have myself competing against other Americans instead of us all working together. I said absolutely not."

LeMond's rationale was simple. He knew that if the United States was going to develop as a major cycling nation, it had to act as the major cycling nations did, which meant the riders had to work as a team at the world championships. As he put it, "The Dutch team didn't enter the race riding against each other to see who would become the national champion. That's the spirit I wanted."

A vote was proposed by the U.S. officials. "But I didn't want to vote," said LeMond. "My position was firm." He told the U.S. officials, "You can start the race without me if we're racing the national championship. . . . We should be racing with each other and against the Europeans, not against ourselves."

Yet a vote was held. Two riders sided with Boyer, two with LeMond. An official had the casting vote, and he went with Boyer. "'Fine,'" said LeMond, "'but you race without me. . . . If you want me to race, I'm racing for the world championship.' Was I being unfair or acting like a spoiled kid? Was I breaking my word? I don't think so, not at all. Let the majority rule, but don't let them force everybody else to do what they want." He acknowledges his precocity, as a 20-year-old laying down the law, noting that "it's a fine line . . . between being a spoiled kid and respecting your own integrity. But I'm still convinced I had my priorities right. I wasn't saying nobody else should race—just me. The right to decide whether I'll race belongs to me, not to the team."

A year later, before the world championships in Goodwood, the American team held a meeting where it was decided, again, that the race would incorporate the national championship: every man for himself. "We were right back to where we were in Prague," says LeMond, "but this time I wasn't fighting them anymore. If that's what the team wanted, fine. No more fights, no more screaming at each other. We agreed that Greg LeMond was racing for Greg LeMond and that Jock Boyer was racing for Jock Boyer.

"With three or four laps to go, I had made several attacks to get away, and guess who chased me down? Jock Boyer! When it came to the last lap there was a long uphill, and Boyer attacked. I just sat there as he built a pretty good lead. With about 500 or 600 yards to go, I attacked and caught Boyer just like that, absolutely nothing to it, which showed how strong I was and also how much he was weakening. At the same time, Giuseppe Saronni was on me, and I ended up getting second.

"I wasn't going for second; I was going for the victory. But I also wasn't trying to ruin it for Boyer. . . . That was one of the most exciting events in my career. Here I was, the highest-placed American ever! But Boyer cried afterward and complained that he'd have won if I hadn't moved on him. No way!

"Do I have any regrets about Boyer and Goodwood? Absolutely not . . . I trained really hard for two weeks before the worlds. But the week before the race, I got sick, really sick—from bad water, I think—so five or six days before the race, I almost decided to skip it and go to the Alps to train for the Tour de l'Avenir. But my wife's parents were coming to England all the way from Wisconsin, and they had nonrefundable tickets, and my folks were coming, too, so I felt obligated to be there. And I paid for my own trip to England—hotel bills, everything."

For all the mitigating factors and extenuating circumstances surrounding the Goodwood world championship, the assertion by Boyer that LeMond didn't hesitate to put his own interests above his team's interests is interesting, particularly in the context of the Tour de France that is at the heart of this book. It is interesting because there are faint echoes of what Boyer says in the testimonies of one or two others. "He's not the guy who'll call you, you know?" says Steve Bauer. "I like the guy, I got on with him fine, but, to be straight, Greg's a pretty selfish guy."

Then again, a selfish streak is hardly unusual in an elite athlete. Some would say it is mandatory. As Cyrille Guimard said, "I've never met a nice, kind, soft man who's succeeded in sport." But did LeMond cross an invisible line, dividing acceptable and unacceptable selfishness? Stephen Roche, who, as an Irishman, counted as another "outsider" in the professional peloton in the early 1980s, echoes some of Boyer's claims. Asked if he got on with Le-Mond—again, a natural assumption, given their status as English-speaking "pioneers"—the amiable Roche hesitates. "Eh . . . yes and no. He was OK, but, at the same time, he was always moaning about something. That cheesed me off a lot, you know? He rode a lot of the time to be the first English-speaking rider. He didn't ride to win; he rode to not lose, or to be the first English speaker. That was important to him. I don't know why. I couldn't get my head round it, you know?"

Again, though, there is a wider context to Roche's comments, as we shall see later. And more widely, there is also—I discovered as I spoke to some former riders—a current of anti-LeMond feeling that flows through the cycling world, based on his more recent outspokenness on the subject of doping and his public questioning of his countryman Lance Armstrong. It would seem that some prominent figures in the cycling world—even former friends and teammates—have grown suspicious or wary of LeMond on the basis of his rift with Armstrong. It is not universal, though. There are others who perceive him as having stood up to a bully—offering a parallel, perhaps, with what happened at the 1986 Tour de France.

Regardless of their views now, the large majority of LeMond's former associates speak with great warmth of the man they got to know in the 1980s. Abt describes his "friendliness, openness, his . . . pure heart." Andy Hampsten, who recalls LeMond's sense of fun, also knew him as a fierce competitor, though he rejects the assertion that this ever descended into the kind of pettiness that Boyer and, to a lesser extent, Roche accuse LeMond of. "Sure, with Greg, he's a competitor first," says Hampsten. "If we were going head-to-head in different teams, it was business first. That's natural, I think. Would Greg have rather seen another American win the Tour de France if he didn't? I'm not quite sure what the answer is there. But when he relaxed away from the competitive atmosphere, he loved palling around with us. When more Americans came across to Europe, he loved having them there. But at Tour time, it was business. You know, he was there to win the Tour, period."

When he reflects now on the life he chose, LeMond seems to struggle to comprehend the sacrifices, the hardships, the dedication—the extent, in short, to which he was driven to succeed as a cyclist at the cost of a more conventional life. "I can hyper-, hyperfocus," he says. "I either focus like that or not at all—it's one or the other. It was like that in Europe. If I had homesickness, then I needed to go home. I couldn't stay that focused a whole season.

"And I needed to do other stuff than just cycling."

Indeed, almost as controversial as his unconventional dining habits was LeMond's love of golf and his audacity in playing the occasional round midseason. Hinault was among those who scorned such behavior, which flouted a golden rule of being a professional bike rider: Never stand when you can sit; never sit when you can lie down. And never, ever walk.

"I look back now, I don't know how I did it," LeMond continues. "Part of it was, I loved it. Part of me loved the discipline. But it took so much out of you; it required so much dedication. I can't fathom it. It was kind of like that 'eye of the tiger' thing—you can't get too far away from it. I always thought that it would be the worst thing for a young cyclist to sign a 10-year contract— like they do now in U.S. sports. If a cyclist did that, he'd be, like, 'Screw this!' It's too hard. You gotta keep a cyclist hungry. No matter what anybody says, you're not choosing bike racing to make money. It's too hard a sport to do that."

➡ Bernard Hinault, in the French national champion's jersey, on the attack in his debut Tour de France in 1978 during stage 17 from Grenoble to Morzine. Greg LeMond was a roadside spectator catching his first glimpse of the Tour on his first visit to Europe. "When I saw it," said LeMond, "I thought, that's what I want to do."

⬇ Hinault standing defiantly at the head of the peloton in Valence d'Agen, leading the riders' protest against the Tour organizers. "When I move, you move," Hinault told his fellow riders.

A 22-year-old Greg LeMond in the rainbow jersey of the world champion after his victory in the 1983 title race in Switzerland.

Hinault shows off the yellow jersey to an adoring public after his first Tour victory in 1978.

Hinault scrambles out of a ravine after his dramatic crash during the 1977 Critérium du Dauphiné Libéré. He would remount to win the stage and claim overall victory.

➡ Hinault with his mentor and Renault directeur sportif, Cyrille Guimard, the latter looking as if he's just stepped off the set of *Boogie Nights*.

➡ A defiant and intransigent Cyrille Guimard faces the press, and the inquisition, after Hinault's clandestine, late-night withdrawal from the 1980 Tour de France.

⬇ Hinault described Paris-Roubaix, a race whose defining feature is murderous cobbles, as inhumane and "a race for dickheads"—but only after he'd won it while wearing the world champion's jersey in 1981.

⬆ When striking workers blocked the route of the 1984
Paris-Nice race, all the riders stopped except Hinault,
who angrily confronted the protesters amid a flurry
of flying fists.

⬆ Shelley Verses, perhaps the first female soigneur in professional cycling, handing out musettes during the 1986 Tour de France as Greg LeMond leads the peloton through the feed zone.

⬆ Hinault riding through the snow in the 1980 Liège-Bastogne-Liège, which he won by nearly 10 minutes. Three decades later, he still suffers pain in his frostbitten fingers.

Greg LeMond during his debut Tour de France in 1984, talking to the movie star Dustin Hoffman. Hoffman had hoped to star in *The Yellow Jersey*, a movie about the Tour that was never made.

Hinault in his "comeback" Tour goes head to head with Laurent Fignon in 1984.

⬆ A bloody Hinault after the crash in Saint-Étienne during the 1985 Tour, which almost cost him victory.

➡ LeMond in the multicolored combination jersey at the 1985 Tour de France.

◀ Bernard Tapie, the irrepressible La Vie Claire team owner, with his favorite young French rider, Jean-François Bernard.

⬇ LeMond and Hinault share a bottle of water as they begin the climb to the summit of Alpe d'Huez on the decisive stage of the 1986 Tour de France.

4

A GREAT CHAMPION BUT A SMALL MAN

I race to win, not to please people.
BERNARD HINAULT

The 1981 season, Greg LeMond's first with the Renault team, witnessed the emphatic return of Bernard Hinault to the top step of the Tour de France podium, while the following year only confirmed that 1980 had been a blip; that the Badger remained *le patron*, with Tour de France win number four. It no longer seemed possible but probable that Hinault, still just 27, would equal and then surpass Anquetil and Merckx's record of five. He intended to ride four more Tours before he retired, as he had promised in 1980, on his 32nd birthday in 1986.

LeMond's early professional career showed parallels with Hinault's. Guimard appeared to be grooming his young American, allowing him two years to learn his trade before plunging him into the 1984 Tour—just as he had done with Hinault. When LeMond followed his silver medal at the world championships with victory at the 1982 Tour de l'Avenir—the "Tour of the Future" for young riders—by more than 10 minutes over the Scotsman Robert Millar, Guimard was delighted at this apparent proof that his protégé would one day succeed his star. It also rescued LeMond's second pro season after he had crashed and broken his collarbone at Liège-Bastogne-Liège in

April, leaving him sidelined—and recuperating back at his parents' home in Nevada—during one of the most important parts of the season.

Even Hinault was moved to acknowledge his teammate's win at the Tour de l'Avenir and offered what he must have considered the very highest praise for a rider six years his junior. "It doesn't surprise me that LeMond won," said Hinault. "I consider him my potential successor."

Yet Hinault, for all that he was at the summit of the sport and, by some distance, the strongest rider of the era, did not, by the early 1980s, enjoy the popularity you might expect—or that had been predicted in 1978. Instead he had become, in some quarters, something of an antihero, an athlete grudgingly admired rather than universally loved. As Laurent Fignon later put it, Hinault "impressed people, but he was not as popular as Raymond Poulidor or even Bernard Thévenet." Poulidor finished runner-up in the Tour on three occasions; Thévenet was a two-time winner, in 1975 and 1977.

Inevitably Hinault's public image had much to do with his relationship with the media. The manner of his withdrawal from the 1980 Tour contributed to that, still rankling especially with the newspaper journalists, whose reports, on that fateful night, had been rendered out of date before their papers had even finished rolling off the presses. But there were other episodes in which Hinault resolutely refused to play the media game or actively sought to mislead or annoy. More generally, his manner tended to be curt and gruff, for which he offered no apologies. "I race to win," he said, "not to please people."

"Courteous but aloof" is about the kindest description, as offered by Pierre Martin, of *International Cycle Sport* magazine, in 1981. "Not an easy man to talk to," continued Martin, who noted the double standards inherent in Hinault's usually dismissive attitude toward reporters. "A star who uses the press as Hinault occasionally does in order to let off steam must not complain if he is occasionally scalded himself," Martin chided.

When he did talk to reporters, Hinault would often launch withering attacks on opponents, in particular on those from the country in which he was racing—Italians in the Giro d'Italia, Spaniards in the Vuelta, Belgians in the spring classics. A diplomat he was not, and he appeared to court unpopularity outside France despite the potential dangers of antagonizing fans whose proximity to the action means that they effectively share the road with the cyclists.

He, of all riders, knew this. In Brussels, on a stage of the 1979 Tour de France, Hinault was assaulted with, rather strangely, a telephone directory aimed at his head (since leather helmets, or "hairnets," were at the time compulsory in Belgium, he was dazed but OK). In the Belgian classics, he "had beer poured over me, as though that would bother me." And at the Vuelta in 1983, he was spat at by Spanish fans. That treatment prompted Hinault to seek a meeting with the UCI president, Luis Puig, in which he threatened to withdraw. Puig subsequently addressed the Spanish fans on TV, pleading for good behavior.

Naturally Hinault's approach to public relations—which was in sharp contrast to that taken by LeMond, "whose smile and informal way of addressing people in French" was appreciatively noted by *L'Équipe*—mattered less when he was winning. But when he wasn't—especially after the debacle of 1980—there was a queue of reporters, media people, and others waiting to plunge in the knife. Behind them, another queue formed of those wanting to twist it.

After the 1980 Tour, Hinault was, according to Martin again, "pilloried in the Italian and Dutch press, but attacked also in Belgium and even in France." And in 1982, when he retired from the French championship and then, live on national television, slammed all and sundry—public, press, and opponents—*L'Équipe* described his tantrum as "a small masterpiece of the hateful and the stupid. In the eyes of the general public, Bernard Hinault is revealed for what he is: a great champion but a small man."

It wasn't a universal view. The French cycling magazine *Vélo* honored its champion and hero in 1982 with a cartoon depicting Hinault as Superman. Others noted the inevitability of the fame cycle, which so often follows a familiar pattern of the hero being built up and then knocked down, with the very traits and qualities that contributed to and even defined that person's ascendancy—in Hinault's case stubbornness, single-mindedness, the aggressive rage that drove him to so many victories—now perceived as flaws and failings.

It wasn't just Hinault's frostiness toward reporters that rankled. Others grew frustrated at his perceived reluctance to set races alight with daring, swashbuckling attacks, despite the fact that some of his greatest victories—the world road title at Sallanches being just one example—were owed to precisely such a strategy.

In the Grand Tours, Hinault increasingly seemed to rely on his time trialing ability, riding relatively conservatively in the mountains, his priority apparently to limit his losses rather than to make great gains. Gilles Le Roc'h, the respected French cycling journalist, notes that "Bernard Hinault didn't attack once to win his fourth Tour de France—he won the time trials, in the mountains he showed he was the boss, and he won the bunch sprint in Paris. It was spectacular in a way, because he was the first cyclist who could sprint, time trial, and climb mountains. But it wasn't spectacular in the same way as Merckx in '69 in Luchon . . . or Ocaña in '71 in Orcières.

"For me Hinault was great in the big tours," continues Le Roc'h, "but very, very special in the classics. When he won classics, it was always an incredible story. When he won [the 1977] Ghent-Wevelgem, the Belgian press wrote that an unknown rider had won. Then four days after, he wins Liège-Bastogne-Liège. And Paris-Roubaix, and [also in 1981c] Amstel Gold race. He was world champion and he didn't want to ride, but Guimard said, 'Go!' So he said, 'OK, I go, but only with my bike. No massage. Nothing. I will stay the whole day as the last man in the bunch.'

"And at 10 kilometers from the finish, someone tells him, 'You will never win this race.' So he went to the front 1 kilometer from the finish and began the sprint with all the top riders, and he won. Nobody could pass him."

At the memory, Le Roc'h, who has reported every Tour de France since 1987 and these days counts Hinault as a friend—"I hope!"—puffs out his cheeks and blows hard.

"I'm from Brittany, too," Le Roc'h continues. "I was Hinault's fan when I was young; I had his poster in my room. For me, he was a great winner, a champion, a fighter—a killer. Every time he won I was very glad, of course, but when he came to the TV to speak afterward, I was always . . ." Le Roc'h throws up his hands. "*Quelle honte!* It was a shame. Because on the bike, he was honorable, impressive. But off the bike, he didn't have the same . . . style. To work with the media is part of the job of being a professional cyclist, and he didn't do that well. I think it's different for English people, and for American people—for them, to have something to offer the media is natural. And this was another problem for Hinault, later, when LeMond emerged."

In 1982, there was another explanation for Hinault's surliness. Hinault's cousin, René, who had been instrumental in introducing Hinault to cycling and helping him in his early years and who had remained at his side throughout his career, had an abrupt falling-out with Guimard and was fired by the Renault team early in the season. René Hinault's role with the team had been vague—his official title had been "business manager"—but the loss of his cousin hit Hinault hard. They remained close. But when René turned up to see Hinault at the team's hotel in Lorient during that year's Tour de France, Guimard reportedly exploded, threatening to quit the team if René did not leave immediately. The reason for Guimard's rift with René is unclear; neither Hinault nor Guimard has ever elaborated.

Hinault continued his habit of making "appointments"—appearing fired up for certain races, barely turning up at all for others. In one sense, he anticipated future serial Tour winners such as Miguel Indurain and Lance Armstrong—and, for that matter, Greg LeMond—in periodizing his season, but that didn't fully explain or justify his sometimes contemptuous attitude toward some other races.

Hinault himself tells a story from early in his career, of starting the Tour of Flanders, deciding he couldn't face a day of narrow, cobbled climbs made claustrophobic by thousands of (potentially telephone-book-wielding) Belgian fans, and quitting within kilometers of the race start. He located a shortcut back to the start, then jumped into his car and made it home to a startled Martine in time to watch the finish on TV. And in 1981, there was a similar episode during the Midi Libre, traditionally a Tour de France tune-up, in which he simply stopped, turned around halfway up Mont Aigoual in the Massif Central, and rode back to the changing rooms.

During the 1981 Tour, Hinault found himself under attack again in the media, on this occasion for his failure to attack in the Alps. His strategy seemed designed to minimize risk, though he responded in typical Badger fashion on the final Alpine stage, four days from the finish in Paris, winning alone at Le Pleynet. The fact that he won that Tour by almost 15 minutes seemed not to impress Hinault's critics. In fact, it only encouraged them to sharpen their knives since they couldn't fathom why a rider who was so much stronger than his opponents didn't put them to the sword more often. Hinault himself explained it thus: "When I started the Tour, in 1978, I showed a bit of the spirit of youth. Now I'm more calculating, more a thinking rider."

Ever one for the pithy remark—but perhaps also thinking of his fragile knees—Hinault added, "I race to last. Not to finish broken."

By 1982, as Sam Abt wrote at the time, "Hinault's domination reduced the uncertainty about the Tour's outcome to the point where he could say, 'It's a race for second place' and nobody could disagree." Predictability led to boredom. "The crowds came in diminished numbers and enthusiasm, and even in victory, Hinault was criticized. It became difficult to remember by then how fiery the love affair between Hinault and the French people had been when it began." Abt writes that Hinault's early popularity was built around his precocity, his "character." Then, he had represented "*la gloire,* the cornerstone of de Gaullian France." But the Hinault of the early 1980s was different, suggests Abt. Gone was the "bravado, gallantry, flair—panache. Ironically, in many ways Hinault was the Frenchman of the 1980s: practical, efficient and realistic—in short, a pragmatist."

Abt's description of Hinault as a pragmatist will strike some as strange. It struck me as strange, but the Hinault I was most familiar with was the Hinault of his final two years, when, as I now realize, he almost reinvented himself. But taking into account some of Hinault's most notable wins of his earlier years, the characterization of Hinault as pragmatist can jar. After all, what were his victories in the world championships in Sallanches or his seven stage wins, including on the Champs-Elysées, at the 1979 Tour or in the snow-engulfed Liège-Bastogne-Liège if not victories for panache?

And yet, what was the strike at Valence d'Agen in 1978—for all that it might have been justified—if not a victory for pragmatism? Similarly—as Hinault might have seen it—he took a stand in 1982 against "excessive" dope controls during the lucrative post-Tour criteriums. "We are tested every day during the Tour de France," said Hinault, who once again fell naturally into the role of riders' spokesman or trade union leader. "There is no necessity for the tests in criteriums. To honor our contracts, it is sometimes necessary to race twice in a day, with a long journey in between. If we are delayed by tests, it would not be possible to do our jobs. No other sportsmen are harassed like us. The rules should apply equally in all sports, or not at all."

This argument came to a head at a criterium in Callac, in his native Brittany, where Hinault, along with four other French riders—Bernard Vallet, Jean-René Bernadeau, and Patrick and Pierre Le Clerc—refused to take a dope test. Although Hinault raised what could be considered a valid point about drug tests not applying universally, his stance against tests inevitably gave rise to speculation about how he and the other riders coped with the relentless, sometimes twice-a-day races on the post-Tour criterium circuit.

In trying to reconcile these apparent contradictions in Hinault's approach, and in his personality, it is worth acknowledging where he came from. For Hinault, ultimately, the sport wasn't a vocation or a calling or the fulfillment of a childhood dream but a job. In the sport's European heartland, after all, cycling tended not to be a pastime for those with money; it was a blue-collar sport.

For LeMond and others from nontraditional cycling countries, it was perhaps different. A cycling career often did begin with a boyhood dream and could tend to romanticization—recall LeMond's compatriot Kent Gordis being in thrall to the "exotic" names of Flemish riders and races. Hinault's attitude was possibly not uncommon in countries such as France or Belgium, where professional cycling was seen by many as an alternative to working in a factory or on a farm. And for the majority of those who "made it" or "lived the dream"—in other words, the domestiques who made up the vast bulk of the peloton—it proved to be neither glamorous nor lucrative. It was just hard work.

"For me," responded Hinault to criticisms that his approach to racing had become too conservative, or pragmatic, "panache isn't worth anything. If I go all out in the mountains and then have nothing left in the next few days and lose the Tour de France, who really won in the mountains? In the Tour, there are days when you have to know how to help your opponent, the better to beat him tomorrow. I know all this."

François Thomazeau, a journalist with Reuters who began reporting on the Tour in 1986, thinks that the French public's relationship with Hinault was as complicated as Hinault's relationship with his sport. "I think he's rather popular," says Thomazeau hesitantly. "Everyone recognizes him on the street; people are pleased to see him. But, at the same time, he was, in many ways, very un-French.

"Hinault won during a time when France was not used to winning that much," continues Thomazeau. "The 1970s for French sport were appalling. The soccer team was dreadful. Bernard Thévenet won the Tour, but otherwise in cycling we were not doing so well. In tennis there was nobody. In Formula One there was Alain Prost. That was it. Cycling's most popular character was Raymond Poulidor, who was always second.

"There was a real French fondness for losers, runners-up," adds Thomazeau. "I think Hinault was popular to a portion of the population, but there was another portion who hated his . . . not his arrogance but his lack of self-doubt. He was like a French politician—he split the crowd in two. At the same time, he's so French that the French maybe hate him for that. Thévenet had fragility; Anquetil was elegant and drank champagne. Hinault was the

Breton farmer. He appealed a lot to the hard-core cycling fan base in France, the Bretons in particular."

Hinault, concludes Thomazeau, remains widely admired but not universally loved. "Not like Yannick Noah," he says. Noah was a decent tennis player in the 1980s who won the French Open and then became a singer. Presumably Thomazeau means that Noah was more popular than Hinault when both were in their prime. "No!" he says. "Still! It's odd, but Yannick Noah has been the most popular sportsman in France for years. You won't find Hinault in any of these polls, despite the fact that he's the last French winner of the Tour. It's strange."

Mirroring Hinault's strained relationship with the French public and media was his relationship with his mentor, Cyrille Guimard. This was in the midst of the "three years' war" (1981–1983) that Hinault told me about when I visited him in Brittany. The firing of Hinault's cousin René was one source of friction, but in his autobiography, Hinault claims that the catalyst for the breakdown was his use of an agent "to negotiate my terms direct with the company sponsoring the team" rather than going through Guimard, "who normally acted as an intermediary between the employers and riders.

"He seemed to think that he was losing part of his power, that his hold over me had lessened," writes Hinault. "And this was when our relationship began to deteriorate, as I began to question his authority."

Before the 1981 Tour, says Hinault, Guimard "accused me of damaging the morale in the team and I nearly decided not to ride at all. . . . All that I wanted was the right to negotiate my own contract, having always believed in freedom of movement. His attitude and accusations were his way of taking revenge. He looked for any excuse: 'The mechanics are sick of you. You get on their nerves by always having too much to say.' By talking like this, he tried to set the team against me."

Hinault called a meeting of all his teammates prior to the Tour and asked them if Guimard's allegations were true—"If one member of the team had spoken out against me, I'd have packed my bags and been off to Brittany." They didn't, and he stayed, and won, of course. But irreparable damage had been done to the relationship between the two most important people in the team, the directeur sportif and the leader, and—with glorious understatement—Hinault admits that "tension remained."

A witness to this tension was Boyer, who rode alongside Hinault in the Renault team, becoming the first American ever to participate in the Tour de

France. Where Boyer has only ill feeling toward LeMond, he has only praise for Hinault. Indeed, a theme running through the testimonies of most of Hinault's former teammates—and running directly counter to his public image—is of admiration, warmth, and affection.

"It was a pretty amazing experience riding that 1981 Tour alongside Bernard," says Boyer. "But unlike with Greg, my experiences with Bernard were all very good. He didn't communicate a lot during stages, but he wasn't at all dependent. He'd just tell us, 'I need to have the pack intact until this point, then I'm fine'"—this echoes the instruction he issued to the French team prior to the 1980 world title race in Sallanches. "He was," adds Boyer, "an extremely good leader."

But, especially by the early 1980s, there was the suspicion that Hinault didn't act just as the leader of his team but as the man in charge of the whole race. The role of *patron* was a natural one for him to fulfill, of course, but did Hinault abuse the position? There are tales of him ordering go-slow days, or of selecting who could and who could not feature in a break. He seemed to enjoy a level of absolute authority and power that, in any walk of life, could easily lead to corruption. Robert Millar, the Scottish rider, said of Hinault that he admired his ability but not his personality after Hinault "gave me a bollocking for attacking when Hinault didn't want to ride fast."

Such was the strength of Hinault's personality that he seemed able to force his will on proceedings. But that will could act as a dead hand; it may even explain why so many stages of the 1981 and 1982 Tours were described by some observers as stupefyingly boring.

Boyer defends Hinault, saying that his motivation was the same as that which prompted the 1978 riders' strike—namely, concern for the welfare of the group as a whole. Again, there is pragmatism here—as in his comment "I race to last, not to finish broken." (The fans of the sport, needless to say, wanted to see riders, if not broken, then at least very close to collapse.)

"The reason for Hinault wanting some stages to not be run at a fast pace was that he didn't want anyone to get cooked and finish two hours off the back at the finish," says Boyer. But the American admits that Hinault could react aggressively if someone dared to go against his command. "If someone disobeyed, he went to the front and hammered it, and blew everyone away."

Boyer says he wasn't in awe of Hinault. "Awe has its limitations. I respected him, and I respect him to this day—I see him about once a year. But he was one tough rider. I mean, tough: tough on others, tough on himself."

That "tough on others" approach has led to a popular depiction of Hinault as someone capable of intimidation and of instilling fear, of sometimes acting the bully. But even if this capability did form part of his weaponry, he wouldn't have been in a position to instill fear had the rest of the peloton not been in awe of his physical powers; his ability, in Boyer's words, to "blow everyone away." Everything stemmed from Hinault's remarkable physical power.

One of the curiosities about Hinault is that he has rarely spoken of the things that most cyclists acknowledge first: the sheer suffering and pain. For most, these are what define the sport, with the ability to withstand the pain and handle the suffering making heroes of the stars. Yet for Hinault, as he has claimed, it only "hurt sometimes." And when it did, he said he attacked "so the others don't know I'm suffering."

The question is, where did this ability—rated by Guimard as unrivaled even by Merckx—come from? How does Hinault himself explain it?

It was something I was keen to ask Hinault when I visited him at his home in Brittany. But I was also apprehensive since it is generally not a question you ask of top athletes, not if you want to look like you know what you're talking about. I'm not sure why; all I know is that it is so obvious—well, of course so-and-so is good—as to be easily dismissed as irrelevant by the aficionado.

Asking such a question of Hinault could, I speculated, incur the sort of wrath he reserves for ignoramuses, wannabes, or fakes. Take, for example, Hinault's opinion of amateur cyclists who wear replica yellow jerseys: "When I see potbellied cyclists with stomachs like they're pregnant wearing the *maillot jaune*, it appalls me."

And yet this question—whatever variation of "How come you're so good?" you prefer—remains fundamental.

Hinault is sitting opposite me, absentmindedly drumming his fingers on the table, occasionally glancing into the kitchen—checking the time on the clock on the stove, I think. Periodically he leans back, expands his chest, and rubs it hard with his knuckles, a bit like a gorilla. Throughout, though, his gaze is constant—he fixes me with his dark blue eyes and leaves small silences to indicate when he has finished saying what he wants to say. These gaps would ordinarily be filled with small talk, but Hinault doesn't really do small talk. The word that best sums him up is "emphatic," and it strikes me that the Badger nickname is apposite for another reason—he sees everything in black or white.

The time has come to ask him that unaskable, too-obvious question: "How come you were so good? Do you think you felt as much pain as the others, or were you just better at shutting it out?"

"You have to shut it out sometimes," says Hinault with a shrug—an emphatic shrug. "You make the others think that you are stronger than them. So you have to employ a bit of trickery . . . well, not trickery, but you have to deceive them."

As this response suggests, Hinault has a sense of fun, or at least mischief—and perhaps he doesn't take himself as seriously as you might expect. It is something he expands on when asked about his ability to instill fear in opponents—or his ability to intimidate them, if you prefer. Was it learned, or did it come naturally?

"No, you learn," says Hinault before serving up a beautiful contradiction. "You learn, and it's also natural. If you have that natural capacity to play . . . because sport, ultimately, is a game. You mustn't forget that. It's not a job. So if you know how to play, you can do fantastic things. You have fun. I've always compared an elite sportsman with a tiger. He's there, he waits, and as soon as he can pounce on something, he does"—at which point, Hinault imitates a clawing motion. "If you know how to play like that, nothing can beat it."

What Hinault has just said completely contradicts the assertion that he was a pragmatist—and that cycling, for Hinault, was no more than a job. You could argue that in making such a claim, he is indulging in another kind of game. Or, as we shall see, what he says here could perhaps be colored by his last couple of years as a rider—his "second career," as it was described to me by the man who would guide him in his swan song.

But returning to his theory, in order to be able to "play," Hinault points out, "you have to be present. You can be slightly inferior, but you scare them so much that they're scared of moving. One year, in the Giro, we ate ice cream in the valley. It wasn't very smart—my liver was hurting—but instead of saying, 'Oh, I'm in pain,' and taking my foot off the gas, I attacked. That's it. You suffer a bit more than the others for a while, perhaps, but you hang on. I think I won the Giro that day, with that performance."

This harks back to Hinault's claim that when he suffered, he attacked. "Yes," he confirms, "you grit your teeth. You say to yourself that it's hurting, but it won't last. Also, in Italy, I was punished for the mistake I made. I suffered more than I needed to because of that mistake."

Hinault's words also hark back to a very French preoccupation with the liver and the perils of a *crise de foie*. When, later, I tell LeMond about Hinault's tale of eating ice cream in the valley and suffering a *crise de foie* as a result, he can barely contain his mirth. "The French," he says, "were always complaining about their livers. I loved ice cream. I ate bowls of it just to wind them up. But they have these fixed ideas: 'Ice cream is bad, but cheese is good. Wine is good.' Never mind fat content, it was all about tradition."

Phil Anderson tells me, "Greg questioned these traditions, and the wisdom behind them, if there was any. You know, like you can't shave the day of a race, or you can't sleep with your wife the same week as a big race—they had these strange beliefs. But the eating ones were the most extreme. He'd ask, 'What's so bad about having salad to eat?' and they'd say, 'Oh, salad makes you tired. They always feed chickens salad before they chop their heads off, so they're quiet.'"

Hinault's trademark in the Grand Tours that he dominated was to ride at or very near the front, which made him stand out, literally, from other team leaders, who would often be cocooned by teammates offering shelter from the wind. Frequently Hinault would ride so close to the front that he was, in effect, making it much harder for himself. Yet he says that his decision to ride there was because of his status as the boss, *le patron*, and his determination to have total control. "When you ride in the first 30 positions of the peloton, nothing can happen without you letting it happen. You have one line of riders, a second line of riders, and you're in the third line. The riders can't go on either side of you because you'll see them, and if you have four or five teammates around you, as soon as someone attacks, your teammate pounces on them. And the race is shut down.

"Merckx was the same," continues Hinault with another emphatic shrug. "If you ride at the back of the peloton, you can't see what's going on. If you're constantly at the front, the others all see you and say to themselves, 'Shit, if I move, he'll be on me like a flash.' Then you can let a rider go when you want him to go. You say, '*Hup*, yeah, you go can go.' You play."

As Hinault speaks, his eyes occasionally sparkle with mischief. Then, abruptly, he stops—you can almost hear the full stop to the sentence—and his expression turns serious again. And he drums the table, awaiting the next question.

These days, Hinault adopts a more conciliatory tone when he talks of the breakdown in his relationship with Guimard. "You see, when you're young, you don't worry at all about everything that surrounds racing and competition," he explains. "Then a time comes when you want to integrate yourself into the team; in other words, you want to know how the team is managed . . . and Cyrille didn't want that. Also, I'd signed a contract with Renault without his input, bypassing him completely. I'd signed directly with Renault the company. That was the end, as far as he was concerned. He always wanted to be the *patron*, and you were just his executive. And that couldn't work. There comes a point where you start thinking about what's going on."

There was no one particular flash point, says Hinault. "No, there were several. I signed the contract with Renault in 1980, and for three years it was pretty much war." Before the trip to the United States to see LeMond? "No, it started after that. After that."

For his part, Guimard is positively sanguine, barely acknowledging the feud and appearing to dismiss it as par for the course—which it pretty much was, given that he would later have a spectacular falling-out with another of his stars, Laurent Fignon. But it's also fair to say that a lot of water has flowed under the bridge since then, and that Guimard and the Badger are back on reasonable terms.

Guimard even suggests that, in becoming the villain in Hinault's eyes, he performed a vital role or function—he became an opponent, of sorts, at a time when Hinault had precious few—or precious few worthy of the name—on the bike. "The Badger could be very relaxed at times," notes Guimard, "but as soon as he came to races where he had certain aims, that aggression would come back.

"You see . . . Hinault's a boxer. He needs to be permanently squared up to someone, in opposition with someone. It can be the peloton, it can be picketers blocking the road [as at Paris-Nice in 1984], it can be the directeur sportif, the teammates. . . . Slanging matches between him and me? Well, yeah, of course there were, but he needed that. He needed some kind of combat to surpass himself, to bury himself, so he had to go looking for that aggression somewhere.

"And yet he's maybe a 10 times nicer guy than someone who's really calm," Guimard adds, laughing. "But he needed combat. He would say, for example, 'Paris-Roubaix is a *course de cons*,' but then he'd get it into his head that he wanted to win it, would go and do precisely that; then the same evening, he would tell you, 'It's still a *course de cons*.' Why was it a *course de cons*? Because he realized it was very difficult for him to dominate there like he was used to doing. Him not going to Paris-Roubaix was a problem for the team vis-à-vis the media, but the day he arrived and saw the weather conditions suited him [in 1981], he fell 15 kilometers from the finish, but you knew as soon as he got up that he couldn't be beaten."

With LeMond in the Renault team and being groomed as Hinault's possible successor, there was, says Hinault, no friction between them. But neither, it seems talking to Hinault now, was there much warmth, at least from him. Indeed, Hinault appears decidedly cool toward LeMond, though this may have more to do with events in 1986 than with anything that happened in their first seasons together.

Given that Hinault had traveled to the United States with Guimard to meet LeMond, you might imagine that he would mentor the American when he arrived in Europe. There was also the fact that the LeMonds initially lived in Brittany. So did he see a lot of LeMond, other than at races?

"Greg lived near Cyrille, so I didn't see him," Hinault says with a shrug.

So he and Martine didn't invite Greg and Kathy around for dinner? "It's almost 200 kilometers!" He snorts. "It's still Brittany . . . well, Loire Atlantique. Here, 200 kilometers seems a lot. In the USA, it might be next door."

LeMond has fonder memories of Hinault. So does Kathy, his wife. Looking at her husband across their big, round kitchen table in Minnesota, she says with nostalgic affection, "He was a really great teammate. He was very fair. I felt he inspired loyalty. You wanted to work for him, didn't you?"

"Yeah, absolutely," says LeMond. "I didn't grow up in a team with the old Merckx-style leadership, where it was, like, 'You work for me no matter what.' The way the team rode was instilled by Guimard. His view was 'Whoever's the best will be leader.' Hinault came from an era where he could have insisted on being a Merckx-type leader, but he didn't. He worked for me in quite a few races. In the Dauphiné one year, I was third, he was leading, and I was having horrible allergies on Mont Ventoux. And he waited for me and paced me up the hill. He was a good teammate, a good role model."

Hinault claims that he was motivated by self-preservation ("I race to last, not to finish broken"), but LeMond maintains that Hinault's approach to racing was not Hinault's choice; it was Guimard's.

"It was Guimard," says LeMond, repeating, for emphasis, "it was Guimard. He was really smart. I don't believe any really great cyclists make good coaches because their ego gets in the way. They believe that it's all due to their gifts, and they don't recognize all the inputs. . . . I wouldn't be the best coach. I've been there and done it, wouldn't be happy being in second place. But for Guimard, one of his riders winning was like him winning. He was not super-talented as a rider, but he was really tactical. As a rider, he was a sprinter, and I think the sprinters make the good coaches; they have to survive, to read the race, conserve energy.

"It simply made no sense to risk everything on one rider for the whole year," continues LeMond. "So I think when Hinault was young, Guimard started that tactic of having other riders lead the team in other races."

The 1982 Tour saw Hinault complete the rare feat of a Giro-Tour double, and, having received a barrage of criticism for his conservative riding in the mountains, he responded with a performance full of panache on the Champs-Élysées. For the second time in his career he won the stage that is supposed to belong to the sprinters, on this occasion not by breaking away but by showing his versatility and exceptional all-around strength by claiming the bunch sprint with a long charge.

When Hinault went early—as he had also done at Paris-Roubaix the previous year—his rivals might counter, but Hinault had the unique gift of being able to go again, as though he had a sixth gear. On the Champs-Elysées, he engaged that sixth gear, winning narrowly and crossing the line with one arm in the air and the familiar expression: clenched jaw, snarling, with the rage and exhaustion of a boxer who, in the final round, has just landed a knockout blow.

5

CHANGING OF THE GUARD

*We're trying to break down the traditional structures
which have converted cycling into one of the last bastions of feudalism.*
BERNARD HINAULT

I knew I could nail it.
GREG LEMOND

The 1983 Vuelta a España was supposed to be the hors d'oeuvre, a prelude to Bernard Hinault's coronation as one of the all-time greats with his fifth Tour de France. What happened changed everything.

In one of the greatest Vueltas, Hinault had to fight as he hadn't needed to in the previous two years' Tours de France. In doing so, he showed the kind of aggression, or "spirit of youth," that had been the hallmark of the early part of his career. Some reporters may even have gone so far as to hail his "panache."

But the circumstances that confronted Hinault in Spain were ideal for bringing out the best in the Badger. There were hostile crowds, throwing stones and spitting at him during one time trial in protest at reports that Hinault and Giuseppe Saronni had made a pact to work together, despite being on different teams, and despite reportedly each receiving £30,000 appearance money from the Vuelta organizers (about $50,000 then, and somewhere north of $120,000 today). There was also spirited Spanish opposition, led by the climber Marino Lejaretta.

Alongside him in the Renault-Elf-Gitane team were two young allies: an unheralded young Frenchman, 22-year-old Laurent Fignon, and Greg

LeMond. Two days in, however, and in appalling weather, LeMond fell ill with bronchitis. He recovered sufficiently to perform a valuable team role for Hinault, finally dropping out with a few stages of the three-week race remaining.

Regardless of LeMond's health issues, and for all Guimard's democratic principles and his rotation of leaders, at the Vuelta, Giro, or Tour, if Hinault was riding, there was no debate: The Badger was captain, *patron*, a Merckx-style leader, even if he didn't possess the Cannibal's insatiable hunger to win every race he started. Indeed, an illustration of the extent to which Hinault was boss had come at the Renault team presentation in Bois de Boulogne, Paris, in early February 1983, when his teammates all appeared on stage wearing Bernard Hinault masks. One by one, they were introduced and lifted their masks to reveal their faces until LeMond, his grasp of French still not perfect, missed his cue. Hinault intervened, lifting the mask for him, thereby further underlining the point, as if that were needed: Hinault was in charge; the others were subservient.

Two and a half months later, Hinault rode into Madrid as the winner of the 1983 Vuelta, but that bare fact doesn't tell the full story. The real and lasting significance of the race was in two apparently innocuous incidents, both on the same day. With three stages left and Hinault trailing another Spaniard, Julian Gorospe, in the overall classification, he ordered his team to attack and, in the words of one Spanish report, to "relentlessly destroy the peloton on the climb to Puerto de Serranillos."

On the road to Ávila, however, Hinault felt that something was wrong with his bike. He spoke to Guimard in the team car and was given a spare bike while his was checked. When it was handed back, it still didn't feel quite right—the saddle seemed too high. "But I was assured it was as normal," writes Hinault in his autobiography, "so I kept it.

"I asked my team to attack and to carry on attacking, so that my enemies had no chance to attack themselves," he continues. "Pascal Poisson and Laurent Fignon did a magnificent job for me. Fignon in particular was going so fast that I thought I would blow up, then, suddenly, [my] problems cleared up." Hinault attacked, taking Vicente Belda with him, and won in the velodrome in Ávila, claiming the overall lead with the slim advantage of 1 minute 12 seconds over Lejaretta.

Overnight, though, Hinault's knee swelled up "on the inside of the joint . . . broken blood vessels and the tendon itself twice its normal size, with hard lumps forming." There were two days to go in the Vuelta, and they were far from straightforward, but with the combination of a strong team and some bluffing to disguise how much he was suffering, he held on to win in Madrid. But then his problems really started. "When I got off the bike, I could scarcely walk," Hinault recalls, "but at least I'd won."

He'd won, but it was effectively the end of Hinault's season; he would not be joining Anquetil and Merckx as a five-time Tour de France winner in 1983. The ramifications were even more far-reaching. You could even argue that the injury Hinault suffered on his way to winning the Vuelta divided his career neatly in two, heralding a second phase quite different from the first.

Apart from Hinault's race-winning attack, the other significant incident—not to say revelation—on the road to Ávila was Fignon. Fignon's version of events is subtly different from Hinault's. On that stage, when he set the pace on the climb, Hinault might well have "blown up," though in Hinault's account he kept going and came around before applying the coup de grâce that won him the Vuelta. In Fignon's version, Hinault had to scream at his young teammate to slow down. "That's where I realized that I really had the stuff for stage races," said Fignon in his autobiography. "I recuperated well, I ate well, I slept well. I felt just fine."

At the Tour de France that followed, Fignon eased into the leader's role vacated by the injured Hinault. Who knows whether it might have been Le-Mond had Guimard not stuck rigidly to his policy of holding him back another year? But Guimard had mapped out a plan for LeMond similar to the one he had drawn up for Hinault, preserving him and protecting him from the ravages of the Tour. To this day, LeMond seems slightly puzzled by that. After all, he and Fignon were more or less the same age, Fignon only 10 months older and aged 22 as he started his first Tour.

"I actually asked to do the Tour in 1983," says LeMond, "and I don't know why, but Guimard had this idea I was too young. Fignon was kinda thrown in there, but all you need's a couple of good guys out of the Tour and you can win it."

Good fortune helps, too—not to mention the kind of talent that those such as LeMond, Fignon, and Hinault appear to take for granted. In the 1983 Tour, Fignon found himself in a position to win after following Pascal Simon on a stage through the Pyrenees as the other favorites hesitated, biding their time. On that stage he moved up to second overall, 4 minutes and 22 seconds behind Simon, only for Simon to crash and break his shoulder blade the following day. Though he struggled on for another five days, Simon was eventually forced to retire, and Fignon, according to one report, "was victor by default." It was an extraordinary debut, certainly, but there was that question against the victory, signifying something—less that Simon had been forced out, more that Hinault was missing.

LeMond had also won a major race by default, also at the expense of Simon, when the Frenchman was stripped of his victory at the pre-Tour Dauphiné Libéré after testing positive. "When you win a race that way, it's a victory clear and simple because the guy who beat you probably wouldn't have been able to do it if he hadn't been taking illegal substances," said LeMond at the time. But it says everything about the lenient attitude toward doping at the time that Simon was permitted to return and start the following month's Tour—a Tour he would almost certainly have won had he not crashed.

A significant footnote to the 1983 Tour was the inclusion of a Colombian team, representing the partial realization of the dream of the organizers, Jacques Goddet and Félix Lévitan, to "internationalize" their event. How to do this had been an ongoing debate—and the source of friction between Goddet, who had taken over the running of the Tour in 1936, and Lévitan, who first covered the race as a journalist in 1947 and was appointed Goddet's deputy in 1965. (Goddet had originally been a journalist, too, with the Tour's founding paper, L'Auto, following his first Tour in 1928. After L'Auto was shut down in August 1944—as General de Gaulle decreed that publications that had continued to publish during the German occupation should close—Goddet established its successor, L'Équipe, in 1946.)

By the early 1980s both men were in their 70s—Goddet was born in 1905, Lévitan in 1911—though neither displayed any inclination to loosen his grip on the race. They remained ambitious for it, too. But it was Lévitan who looked across the Atlantic, toward America, as the promised land. He was excited by Jonathan Boyer's participation in 1981 and saw it as an opportunity to raise awareness and increase the profile of the Tour de France in the States.

Similarly, it was Lévitan who wanted Boyer to wear the stars-and-stripes jersey of American national champion at the Tour, as Boyer confirms. "Félix encouraged me to ride in that jersey. It was the year I rode with Renault [1981]. CBS was covering that Tour as well." Wearing the jersey—or, rather, the system of anointing the national champion based on his position in the world road race championship—would, of course, bring Boyer into conflict with LeMond. But by the early 1980s, it was clear that Lévitan's vision was to raise the profile of the Tour in America, and to that end feature writers from the *New York Times* and *Los Angeles Times* attended the 1982 race along with TV crews from America, Australia, and Japan.

In fact, Lévitan's ambitions went beyond raising the profile of the Tour in America and internationally; he wanted a Tour *of* America. In 1983, this dream was realized, but the first, wildly ambitious incarnation—to which Hinault was invited to fire the starting gun at Virginia Beach—was sunk by huge losses. The inaugural Tour of America was to prove the only one. But Lévitan's commercial instincts were more sound and lasting with regard to the Tour de France. He introduced the showpiece final stage on the Champs-Elysées in 1975, and a year later, there was another innovation: the *maillot à pois*, the polka-dot jersey for king of the mountains, one of the Tour's most distinctive icons.

Lévitan, in his usual attire of a neatly tailored business suit, cut quite a contrast with Goddet, whose trademark uniform, at least in the baking south of France, comprised khaki shorts with knee-high socks, khaki shirt, and pith helmet. Goddet was the senior partner, even if Lévitan became the commercial force behind the partnership, and he could be seen most days at the Tour in the car following the leading riders, standing up (the cars were convertibles or, by the 1980s, fitted with sunroofs), his head protruding authoritatively above the windscreen.

Goddet was an Anglophile, having been educated at a private school near Oxford, and his was a powerful voice in the sport, not least through his column in *L'Équipe*. In one, during the 1982 Tour, he announced the imminence of "Le Tour Mondial," the World Tour, with, every four years, national teams instead of trade (professional) teams invited to take part. There would be 18 teams, said Goddet, 9 from traditional cycling countries, and the route would reflect the "*mondial*" theme, with the start in France, then stages in Great Britain and the United States (Washington, D.C., where the Tour of America had finished, was touted as a likely destination), and then a passage throughout Europe before a finish in Paris.

"We must maintain and safeguard the present structure," wrote Goddet, "while at the same time enlarging international participation by the introduction of professional-type teams that already exist in Colombia, and will shortly exist in the USA. . . . The sport of cycling would be given a form of internationalization every four years, similar to the Olympics, by the organization of a Tour de France contested by national teams with a totally free formula, in which there would be a balance between traditional and 'new' cycling countries."

Goddet's vision of a Tour Mondial was never realized. Rather, Lévitan—who wanted to keep the Tour largely in France but invite national teams from "new" cycling countries—held sway, reportedly after an enormous argument between the two during that 1982 Tour.

Indeed, as Matt Rendell notes in the book *Golden Stages*, the two couldn't have been more different in personality. While Goddet was distinctly bourgeois, Lévitan rose from humble beginnings in Paris, where his father was a shopkeeper. "Lévitan was a devoted husband all his life," wrote Rendell in 2003. "Goddet had four wives and observed, 'I always wanted to marry the woman I loved at the moment I loved her.' Lévitan was rigorously prompt; Goddet was frequently late. [And] the rows between them were legendary . . . [but] if global cycling today belongs to Americans, Australians, Balts, Kazakhs, Latin Americans, Russians, Scandinavians and Ukrainians . . . it is due in great part to the results of Jacques Goddet and Félix Lévitan's slanging match [during the 1982 Tour]."

The impression is of a romantic (Goddet) and businessman (Lévitan), with all the clashes that implies. Yet it is saying something for their ability to work together that Goddet and Lévitan remained partners for more than 20 years.

If the Tour suggested that the future belonged to Fignon—and to a lesser extent, thanks to their performances in the high mountains, the riders from Colombia—the world championships, in Altenrhein, Switzerland, hinted that it could instead belong to another rider from the American continent: LeMond.

LeMond, as he says now, could prepare for a one-day race as few people could. He suffers from attention deficit disorder—"That's diagnosed," he says definitively—but when he focused on a target, he "really, really focused."

So it was ahead of Altenrhein. LeMond knew, as surely as it was possible to know, that he could win. His silver medal the previous year, on the relatively easy Goodwood circuit, had shown his ability, and on a tougher course, at the foot of the Alps, he was certainly a favorite. "I was riding so well," he says now, speaking slowly and quietly. "I mean, the week before, I was riding with Phil Anderson and going so, so well."

By now LeMond had become a neighbor of Anderson, the Australian professional who was a good friend and regular training partner. The LeMonds lived in the Belgian town of Kortrijk, in the cycling-mad Flanders region, with their winter home an apartment in Sacramento, one of several properties in which the financially shrewd LeMond—under the guidance of his father, Bob—invested his earnings. After two years in Brittany, it came as a relief, in Belgium, to be able to speak English and to watch television in their own language—they could get the BBC in their home. "It kept me sane," says LeMond. The LeMonds often socialized with Anderson and his American wife, Anne.

Before the championships, LeMond stayed in a hotel on the German side of Lake Constance. Bumping into a reporter, John Wilcockson, a few days before the championship, Anderson said, "Greg's moved into a five-star hotel at Lindau, on an island. His four-star hotel wasn't good enough." That prompted Wilcockson to reflect, "Yes, the Anglos have brought a new dimension to European professional cycling. No French- or Italian-style training camp for the likes of Anderson, LeMond and, in Liechtenstein, Stephen Roche and Robert Millar. They were preparing for the world championships in their own way."

Ireland's Sean Kelly—of the "new world" in cycling but very much of the old school in terms of his approach—was meanwhile staying with the Irish amateur team "at the modest Hotel Anker, across the road from Rorschach harbor and its railway station. Some of the team complained that the level-crossing bells kept them awake all night . . . a sharp contrast to LeMond's Bavarian retreat, with its swimming pool, tennis courts and expansive view of the lake, island and Alps."

With LeMond in his luxury hotel, continued Wilcockson, was Kathy and her "well-to-do parents."

"That advice about the hotel came from Eddie B," says LeMond now, referring to Eddie Borysewicz, the Polish-born former coach of the American team. LeMond mimics Borysewicz's Polish accent: "Before big race you must stay in good hotel and eat well!"

"I was riding with Phil; I could drop him at will," says LeMond, his voice dropping to a whisper. "I was floating. I knew I could nail a world championship. If I had six weeks to prepare for a one-day race, I knew I could nail it. I'd been second the year before, and I knew I could win. I was certain I would win. But then I got so nervous thinking about winning that, the night before the race, I woke up sweating. I couldn't sleep at all."

"You'd ordered all that room service, remember that?" says Kathy. "At 3 a.m. and 6 a.m. . . ."

"I slept maybe three hours. . . ."

"I don't think you even slept that much—you ate the food, then you barfed it up," adds Kathy matter-of-factly.

"Yeah, I threw it up," LeMond admits. "So I had no food, no sleep, and you can easily talk yourself out of it. 'Oh, my God, I'm going to have a horrible day.' But Guimard . . . Guimard was a psychologist. And he said, 'Greg, all the great exploits are done on no sleep.' And I'm like, yeeeaaah!

"Another coach might have said, 'Why didn't you go to bed earlier; why didn't you do this or that?' Trust me, I've had coaches or directeurs like that. And that would have fed into this negative, defeated attitude. But Guimard had a way. . . . He could take an average rider and make him feel like a world-beater. So much of it is psychology. Plus, he trusted you. If you told him you weren't feeling well, he believed you. He didn't . . . accuse you of not training hard enough, like . . ."

And with that, LeMond is off again, like a spinning top on a frozen surface, and it's an effort to rein him back—to Altenrhein in August 1983, an 18-lap race on a tough, hilly circuit; 15 km per lap, 270 km in total, 4,058 meters of climbing; the Italian Azzurri on £10,000 a man—about $40,000 today—to repeat Giuseppe Saronni's win in Goodwood the previous year; LeMond reunited with Boyer in the American team, though with no pretense this time that the two would help each other. There was no £10,000 at stake for them—they were lucky to be given a jersey—though for LeMond there was a huge financial incentive: the promise of a $25,000 salary hike (more than $50,000 in today's dollars) from Renault if he won.

The men's world championship road race is invariably a war of attrition in which, for lap after lap, nothing of any consequence seems to happen. Generally riders without hope of winning feature in breaks, while the favorites, the big hitters, remain in the bunch, all but invisible. Finally one of them will show his hand—in Altenrhein, it was Phil Anderson. It wasn't a surprise, then, that the Australian would fail to finish, having used up his bullets too early. Most riders reckon they have two bullets: one for the initial attack, the other for the finish. But the temptation to use that first one can be overwhelming.

Stephen Roche and Laurent Fignon—whose Tour win had perhaps made him overconfident; he was overactive, overearly—had digs but got nowhere.

Nothing, meanwhile, was seen of LeMond other than a brief appearance in a 13-man move that slid off the front at half distance. Into the decisive final three laps, the Italians took responsibility, forming, according to one evocative description, "a blue wedge" at the head of the peloton. Then Robert Millar jumped clear, attempting to bridge up to a lone leader. It was lap 16. There were 40 km left: the decisive part of the race, into the final hour. And finally there was LeMond, attacking, taking Moreno Argentin of Italy and Faustino Ruperez of Spain with him, going straight past Millar, who was oblivious to the group bridging up to him ("I might have got on the back of LeMond if I'd seen him coming," he reflected later).

The Italians, content that their national champion, Argentin, was in the break, sat back. The others watched; and in the vacuum created by the disappearance of the blue wedge, nobody took the initiative. Nobody chased. "The consequent hiatus was to prove fatal for those behind," as Wilcockson reported.

The Italians' gamble on Argentin backfired when he was dropped on the main climb. Argentin would finish in tears. Meanwhile, LeMond and Ruperez pressed on, as Fignon now led the chase. Crossing the finish line for the penultimate time, with the bell ringing, LeMond and Ruperez had just over a minute's advantage over their pursuers, led by the Belgian team.

On the first hill, before Vogelherd, LeMond, sensing that Ruperez was weakening, accelerated. His instinct was correct—the Spaniard was finished. Ruperez was dropped and swallowed up by those behind, led now by Adri van der Poel and Roche, but LeMond was untouchable. At the finish, he had a comfortable 1 minute 11 seconds over van der Poel, who won the sprint for silver. At 22, the American became the youngest world professional road race champion since 1970.

Afterward LeMond shed some light on Phil Anderson's curious tactics. It had been strange to see one of the favorites so active so early, covering breaks that stood only the smallest chance of succeeding. But LeMond, asked if he had been worried by one early seven-man move in particular, said, "My good friend was there, so I wasn't too worried."

LeMond celebrated that evening at Anderson's four-star hotel in Grub. Anderson said only that he was "pleased for Greg," but most understood that there had been an arrangement between the two friends. America and Australia remained third-world nations as far as cycling was concerned, and both LeMond and Anderson knew that their best chance of winning was to pool their resources. Since LeMond—able to drop Anderson "at will" in training—was clearly in better shape in Altenrhein, it made sense for Anderson to cover the early moves so he would be in a race-winning position if one happened to stay clear, as occasionally happened, while LeMond held back, conserving energy, awaiting the decisive final phase. It wasn't the first time that Anderson and LeMond were able to form an unofficial pact, and it wouldn't be the last.

"People have said that my victory is a victory for American cycling, but that's far from the truth," said LeMond in an interview the following day. "I fashioned this win in my own way, and the title belongs to nobody but me. There are lots of coaches in the United States who have good ideas on training, but they know nothing about the difficulties of actual competition."

On September 6, 1983, within weeks of LeMond's world title success, there was a shock announcement from the Renault Corporation. The Guimard-Hinault three years' war was over. Hinault, who hadn't raced since starting and failing to finish the Tour of Luxembourg in June, was let go.

In the space of four months, since his win in the Vuelta, Hinault had suffered a fall from grace almost as spectacular as his crash into a ravine at the 1977 Dauphiné Libéré. There was even speculation that he could be finished, with John Wilcockson quoting anonymous riders (probably too scared to criticize the Badger publicly) who claimed that "Hinault doesn't have the incentive to race anymore. He sometimes doesn't shave before a race. He's overweight and feels threatened by good riders in his team."

At the end of July, an out-of-sorts Hinault had appeared in Paris for the Renault after-Tour party—a celebration of Laurent Fignon's victory. "The Badger looked as if his suit was too small for him," writes Fignon in his autobiography. "He seemed distracted, his mind elsewhere, as if he was barely involved in the party. He looked distant, from the three-week race that had just taken place without him, and from cycling in a wider sense. He kept looking away. . . . He was following Guimard's every move, as if he was wary of him and wanted to keep out of his reach. . . . When he became aware that Guimard was in the room it was amazing to see how in a fraction of a second the Badger went back to being a tight-lipped, watchful Breton. His square jaw seemed to be chewing on his unhappiness." Fignon deduced that he was "already looking forward to the battles he would have on the road against

Guimard's riders. Not just riders in the Renault jersey, but the men who were trademarked 'Guimard.' It was written all over his face; everything about him now rejected his old mentor."[1]

A second explanation for Hinault's distraction at the post-Tour party in late July 1983 was his impending operation. Eleven days after the Paris party, on August 2, he succumbed to the surgeon's knife. "I was losing synovial fluid, and the operation was the only solution," he said at the time. "The alternative was a six-month rest cure which offered no cast-iron guarantees of success—and that was a risk I simply couldn't run. I had to have a guarantee one way or the other." Hinault had the operation and three weeks later returned to training.

But as Hinault sat nursing his knee at home in Brittany, not shaving (horror!) and gaining weight (allegedly), he found himself under siege from within his own team as first Fignon won the Tour de France and then LeMond claimed the world title. Abruptly Hinault's position as leader of the Renault team was in grave danger. And for Guimard, these parallel developments—Fignon and LeMond emerging as the new "Guimard-trademarked" riders, Hinault's apparent decline—offered the perfect excuse to end a turbulent relationship with his original protégé and erstwhile leader. Hinault himself offers another explanation, saying that he visited Renault headquarters and offered the hierarchy a choice: him or Guimard.

If that was an effort to call the company's bluff, it backfired. Renault stuck with Guimard, who ordered Hinault's dismissal.

---

1. In Fignon's autobiography, there is a priceless anecdote about a very different night out with Hinault 18 months earlier, during the Tour de l'Armor in Brittany, though here, too, the friction between Hinault and Guimard can be detected. After a stage that finished in Saint-Brieuc, Hinault went home for dinner but promised to return to the team hotel "with a few bottles . . . to toast Brittany!" He kept his word, returning with "his arms loaded with cases of wine," only to find that most of the team members had disappeared to bed. Hinault was furious. "For the first time in my life, I saw Hinault lose his temper," writes Fignon. "He was raging mad and yelled whatever came into his head. 'The bastards, you can't rely on them for anything,' he shouted up and down the corridors, 'and that shit Guimard, he's never around when he's supposed to be.' When he was in a state like this, Hinault was terrifying: he exuded primeval anger and power. Then, still beside himself with rage, he added, 'What the hell, we'll just knock them back ourselves.' So we began drinking. A lot. Right away, Hinault calmed down and his anger metamorphosed into affable pleasure. . . . I couldn't say how many bottles we pulled out of the cases: 10, 12, more? . . . Raging drunk, we chucked empty bottles out of the windows, rampaged up and down the corridors singing fit to bust. It was a riot." When the hotel manager intervened, Hinault replied, "This is my turf," and "told him where to go in no uncertain terms." They got to bed at 5 a.m. The other teams—staying in the same hotel and kept awake for much of the night—tried to wreak havoc in the following day's stage to exact their revenge, but Hinault, incredibly, prevailed. He won the Tour de l'Armor.

Today Guimard is unapologetic in explaining his reasons for instructing Renault to fire Hinault. "I mean, ask yourself why I let the hero leave," says Guimard from behind his desk in the Roubaix velodrome. "The problem wasn't Guimard. It was Fignon. Hinault had won the Vuelta because Fignon had blown everyone away. Then Fignon won the Tour. I then found myself with two riders who had won the Tour. Then what? You can't keep them. One had to go. His knee problem didn't come into it. The team doctor knew exactly what was going on with that. It wasn't a problem. No. The problem was keeping two men, one of whom had won four Tours, the other who was already a Tour winner at 22.

"I was lucky to have done my homework and to know how human beings work," the irrepressible Guimard continues. "You have two bucks, one six years older than the other. The people at Renault had worked it out as well. They knew we couldn't keep both. Every other theory about why Hinault left was just talk, just about selling papers. The harsh reality wasn't very interesting and was hard to take for certain people. If you say that one has to go because they can't both be in the same team, no one's interested."

Then, curiously, Guimard veers into abstract, Eric Cantona–esque terrain. "What people are interested in," he avers, "is Thierry Henry's handball"—a mysterious reference to the French soccer player's handball in a 2010 World Cup playoff against Ireland. "They don't give a shit about the morality of it, the fact that Ireland are staying at home. What they want is the drama, the scandal." I think what Guimard means is that sport is not about nuance; it's black-and-white.

Five days after Renault's announcement, Hinault called a press conference at his home in Quessoy. "I have found two men," Hinault told the assembled media, "who possess the same ideas as me, both on cycling and on the structure of a professional team." He outlined his plans to work with Luis Ocaña, Spain's former Tour de France winner, and Philippe Crepel, the former director of the French La Redoute team. Yet this new team, to be sponsored by the French property group Merlin, was stillborn when "issues" emerged concerning the availability of Ocaña and the suitability of Merlin as sponsor. Hinault was back to square one, and without a team for an attempted comeback in 1984.

Rumors emerged that he was seeking a move away from his native country, with Italy the favored destination. In interviews Hinault suggested that he was disgusted by France and with the French, though in an interview with the radio station Europe 1, he outlined tentative plans to build his own team, in which the relationship between the riders and management would be different. At least one listener was impressed by what he heard.

Bernard Tapie, usually described as a successful "industrialist" or entrepreneur, immediately made contact with Hinault. And within weeks, on Sunday, September 25, on the popular sports program *Stade 2*, Hinault announced, "This is the good news: I want to stay in France and work with Bernard Tapie. I'd like to thank him. Despite my knee injury, he believes in me. With him, I have a good feeling."

When the two Bernards appeared at a press conference two days later, at the Hilton Paris Suffren, some 200 journalists turned up to hear confirmation that a new team would compete under the banner of Tapie's chain of health food shops, La Vie Claire (the clean, or healthy, life). It would be a professional cycling team like no other, promised Hinault, though it didn't quite conform to the model that he had outlined in his interview with Europe 1.

A biography of Tapie, *Le Flambeur* (The high roller), claims to shed some light on how the team came into being and the thinking behind it, at least from Tapie's perspective. "Tapie is a businessman; he knows that managers run things, riders ride," write the coauthors, Valérie Lecasble and Airy Routier. "But he loves the idealism behind [Hinault's plans]. He calls Hinault straightaway, tells him everything he'd like to hear, and promises to invest 10 million francs in the new team [double that of most other teams]. But on one detail he is clear: The team will belong to Tapie, not Hinault. It doesn't matter, because here, again, Tapie wins the argument. He offers Hinault a role as an ambassador of La Vie Claire projects and a development role with other products. Tapie has always had the ability to pull from his hat the most amazing job titles that don't actually tie him to anything. But Hinault believes that this is his retirement plan, and an exit strategy in case he can't get back to his previous level. Comforted, Le Blaireau, of whom nobody had ever asked anything other than to ride faster or longer, is especially flattered. The rebel has found his master."

As this passage suggests, Tapie could be something of a schemer as well as charismatic and hugely persuasive, a potentially lethal combination. His involvement with Hinault, and with cycling, promised to be fascinating—and it didn't disappoint.

Not that Hinault seemed prepared to make a complete break with the past and to move on. Even while announcing his plans with Tapie, he couldn't resist a dig at Guimard over an incident that had happened during that year's Vuelta, and that must—for Le Blaireau—have been humiliating. It was a lecture from Guimard for drinking wine.

"It's no good, believe me, when someone reprimands you in front of a hundred people in a restaurant for drinking a glass of wine," Hinault told the press. "I didn't say anything that day, because I know when to keep my mouth shut. But that day, everything finished with him."

Now Hinault notes, "I did eight years at Renault and saw the big boss once. With Tapie, you were a man, whereas with Renault, you were a number."

Despite the digs, Hinault's sense of anticipation as he announced the birth of La Vie Claire in September 1983 almost—almost—outweighed his bitterness toward Guimard and Renault. Hinault spoke with enthusiasm. But he didn't—he couldn't possibly—speak as much, or with the same passion, as the man sitting beside him, who, physically, bore more than a passing resemblance to Hinault. Both men were formidable-looking and dashingly handsome, with dark eyes and thick eyebrows and prominent, strong jaws.

Neither man could be said, in Sam Abt's description, to be lacking in character. Charisma, too, though of a more obvious and showy kind in the case of "*le flambeur*," Tapie. The new team owner, making his debut on the sporting stage after building his fortune buying up failing businesses and turning them into profitable concerns, appeared in his element in this new spotlight.

There is a photograph of this press conference that is worth a thousand words. It shows Tapie, in smart suit, white shirt, and tie, beside a more casually dressed Hinault. In front of them is a bank of TV microphones; Hinault is gazing down, studying his hands, perhaps examining his fingernails, though his mouth is open. But if Hinault is speaking, Tapie seems oblivious. Tapie has his face tilted upward, eyes raised and lips pursed midsentence. A more animated figure than Tapie would be as difficult to imagine as a less engaged one than Hinault.

According to his biographers, Lecasble and Routier, Tapie knew nothing about cycling and was barely interested in the sport. Indeed, in his press conference with Hinault, as he ran through the major races on the cycling calendar, he neglected to mention the Tour de France. They suggest, albeit with the considerable benefit of hindsight, that he might have seen sport as a stepping-stone into politics, or perhaps "he fancied a new challenge to test his resilience and learn what was behind it."

"As so often with Tapie," they explain, "testimonies diverge; some are convinced he improvises as he goes, his principal strengths being the absence of scruples and his ability to make fast decisions." Comparing him to a chess player, they point out that "he's never been afraid to make a big, risky move in order to take the next step." Is he, they speculate, "spontaneous or calculating? Or both?"

They do suggest that behind Tapie's move into sport lay a deeper ambition: "Instinctively Tapie knows in 1983 that he's going to explode into the heart of French life; he just doesn't know how."

The question is, why cycling? "He wants to become popular, to modify his public image"—which until then was modest and was owed entirely to his ability to transform the fortunes of ailing enterprises. "He decided on cycling after a quick but correct analysis," write the authors of *Le Flambeur*. "It's a sport that's popular without any pretension, that relies on sublime individual effort. But it's a sport that's old-fashioned, and in the hands of old-fashioned managers. It is relatively inexpensive to enter. . . . It draws crowds but of simple, and not very wealthy, people. Among the elite of French society, it's seen as good fun to mock those who stand by the road to watch, and accept the free hats given out by the Tour de France. Often [the fans] come from the same background as the riders, and they have nothing to do with the young, dynamic types, so cherished by advertisers who prefer to invest in sports like tennis, sailing, or, soon, golf."

So had Tapie made a misjudgment? Or did he perhaps see in cycling echoes of his own background and his own struggle to climb the ladder of French society? Tapie had a humble upbringing in a tough Paris suburb. And, on the evidence of his press conference alongside Hinault, it mattered little, if at all, that his knowledge of cycling was next to nothing; he could certainly talk a good game, and loved doing so. He had a clear idea of what he wanted, and what was achievable, from his investment. "It doesn't matter if Hinault rides or not, or whether he wins or not," Tapie told the 200 journalists at the Hilton Paris Suffren before outlining, with unnerving frankness, how his new acquisition would work for him. Hinault, he said, "is the main element in our plan to communicate about our products, to develop them, and in effect to sell them. Hinault is credible, and I trust him to earn us a lot of money. My aim is to earn as much money as possible; this is the only criterion of success."

Now, sitting at his kitchen table in Brittany, Hinault confirms that when he met Tapie in early September 1983, "we came to an agreement straight away. But I was employed as a technical expert, not as a rider.

"Tapie had taken over Look, the company that manufactured ski-boot bindings," he explains. "The ski equipment market is very seasonal, three or four months a year, and cycling is a natural partner for skiing. Tapie wanted me to work with his engineers on developing an automatic pedal." The pedal would use ski-binding technology to offer an alternative to toe clips and straps. "My main role was as a technical expert," says Hinault. "The racing came second. Because I was coming back from the knee operation and didn't know how good I'd be, that's why.

"When we started the team, he was well established as a businessman," Hinault continues. "He must have been the owner of about 40 companies: clothes, perfume, food, sports equipment. He was also in the bar-turning business in the Chamonix Valley. His interests were quite diverse.

"When we went to Tapie, the team was in place—I knew the riders, the mechanics, the support staff. We simply went to Tapie and said, 'This will cost you 12 million francs.' [Tapie said it was 10 million; Hinault insists it was 12, or about $2.5 million.] He said, 'OK, but I don't want to know how much it costs because I've already invested in a boat that cost me three times as much. What I'm interested in is your savoir faire, so I can launch this automatic pedal.'"

With the deal done, Tapie began the business of peeling back the skin of the sport of cycling, examining the inner workings of his latest investment. He did this, according to *Le Flambeur*, by "befriending the journalists." First, he asked for a list of the 10 people from whom he could learn most. And in his Paris home, he entertained them over lunch. Noël Couëdel, the head of cycling at *L'Équipe*, was one such guest, says *Le Flambeur*, of whom "he asks advice, he tries to understand the exact role of the directeurs sportifs; he tries to find out who has the real power and to understand the rules, and unwritten rules, of the system." It is, claim the authors, a familiar method of extracting information—essentially by flattering people—and commonly used by "leaders, businessmen and politicians—but no one masters it as Tapie does." It is, they suggest, "the key to his success . . . . His magnetism performs miracles."

La Vie Claire was, as Hinault predicted, the start of something completely different and new. In structure, organization, even in appearance, the sport had never seen a team like it. And rarely had it seen an image like the one that graced the cover of *Vélo* magazine, which marked the launch of the team with a photograph of Tapie in a smart gray suit, with tie and handkerchief, and Hinault alongside him, in blue blazer and striped, open-necked sports shirt, raising a glass of champagne. Both boasted perfect white teeth and sported dazzling smiles; all that was missing was the Colgate flash.

At the team's official launch, at the Crazy Horse—Paris's legendary nude cabaret bar—in February 1984, Hinault yet again harked back to his rift with Guimard, saying, "I'm convinced that it's inadvisable to try to be team director, coach, manager, and everything else at the same time, as he did." Suggesting that behind all the bluster there was a little sadness, Hinault struck a poignant note as he added, "If he'd shown a little more understanding, we might still be working together."

But their split, Hinault insisted, "emphasized the outmoded structure of a sport in which the rider is systematically prohibited from having a say in decisions that directly affect himself and his teammates.

"I opted for Tapie's offer," he continued, "because it was the only one which gave me the freedom to develop and control my own future. We're linked by a personal contract for the next 10 years, but there are get-out clauses on both sides. The life of the La Vie Claire team is guaranteed, though, for at least three years.

"I want to make it clear from the outset that this is not just another team. It's a new concept, set up as a modern commercial outfit in which each team member has the power to make his own decisions and to shape his own destiny. We're introducing new training methods that are sure to raise a few eyebrows in the ultraconservative world of French cycling. In fact, we're trying to break down the traditional structures, which have converted cycling into one of the last bastions of feudalism. Bernard Tapie won't intervene directly in the running of the team unless he feels we're throwing away his money or damaging the image of his companies.

"I make the general policy decisions," Hinault added, "and have overall control of the budget. But I'm determined to delegate responsibilities, which is something that Guimard never did."

Although some of Hinault's claims were questionable—and would perhaps prove naive on his part—the La Vie Claire team saw the entry into public life of one of the most colorful and notorious figures ever to grace French society. Bernard Tapie would go on to leave his mark on cycling, soccer, politics, and show business before a spell in prison . . . but he was arguably not the most significant person in determining whether this new team would succeed.

And neither, suggests Hinault, was Hinault.

Behind the scenes was someone else, someone who would be far more involved than Tapie in the most important aspects of a professional cycling team: training, team selection, strategy, and tactics. When Hinault earlier talked of the delegation that visited Tapie at his office in Paris, he meant Philippe Crepel, who was still involved, and a little-known Swiss coach, Paul Köchli.

And when Hinault talks with some wonder, even now, about the fact that "I relearned how to train at the age of 28," then heaps praise on a scientist whom he describes as "a real character . . . very interesting," he is also talking about Köchli. In fact, when Hinault talks about Köchli there is—for the first and maybe the only time in our meeting—a sense of warmth and affection as well as seemingly endless admiration.

"What you need to know is that Cyrille Guimard was Paul Köchli's pupil," says Hinault, allowing a small smile of quiet satisfaction to play on his lips as his fingers continue to tap his kitchen table. "So, having been coached by the pupil, I switched to being coached by the teacher."

6

THE KOOKY PROFESSOR

*In a champion's career, the cruelest moment comes
when he realizes the extent of his weakness in the face of the attacks
of insolent youth.*

L'ÉQUIPE ON BERNARD HINAULT, 1984

etting up a meeting with the man whom Bernard Hinault still holds in such high regard, and who is revered by many others as a kind of guru, proves to be difficult. I do locate Paul Köchli, in a small village in Switzerland, close to the French border. But he is elusive and enigmatic. An e-mail is promptly returned with a phone number and an instruction to call "once it gets dark!"

This proves a theme. On the phone, Köchli turns down an interview, explaining that he hasn't spoken to the media for years and has no intention of doing so now. Not that he is abrupt or rude; he chuckles and sounds guarded but friendly as he speaks hesitant English in a strong Swiss-German accent.

I reassure him that it's for a book, not "the media" as such—a tenuous argument, I concede—and he softens. So we pencil in a date, with the recommendation that I should contact him 48 hours in advance to confirm. Later there's an e-mail: "I should be available at my home in Sonvilier. I don't know yet my own program and I want to stay flexible." Again it is made clear that, if I am to visit him, it should be "once it gets dark."

Finally, 24 hours before our meeting, another e-mail arrives with Köchli's address and, below, a brief message: "At 17:00. Best regards, Paul."

It's December, and it has snowed heavily overnight in Besançon, where I have stayed before my intended visit to Köchli's house. Setting out in a ridiculously small rental car, and just over an hour out of Besançon, I find that the main road across the Swiss border is blocked, forcing a detour on a mountain road barely wider than the car and packed hard with snow. The road winds up; the snow deepens and falls in thick flurries, reducing visibility to zero. I pray that I don't meet any other traffic. Of course I don't. Nobody would be mad enough to drive in conditions like this. As I inch slowly up the mountain, I think, How will I get back? But there's no time to worry about that.

Sonvilier is small and quiet. Yet Köchli's house is hard to find. The house numbers are all over the place: So much for Swiss order and efficiency. But eventually I locate what I think must be the right building. It looks like a large apartment block, or a barracks, with the glass door leading into what looks like a communal hallway. I knock. There are no lights on and no sign of movement inside. Köchli's most recent e-mail—with its "I want to stay flexible"—comes back to taunt me.

I push the door. It opens. There's a bike on a stationary trainer in the entrance hall, so I think I must be in the right place. But still it seems eerily quiet. I climb the stairs in front of me and come to a closed door. I knock again, and the silence is broken by shuffling inside. The door opens, and Edith Köchli greets me: smiling, gray-haired but golden-skinned and youthful in cargo pants. "I'm here to see Paul," I say. She smiles, nods, shakes my hand, and gestures for me to enter the dimly lit hallway.

I follow her through a door to the right, which opens up—and looks down—on a surprising scene. It's Köchli's command center: an expansive, brightly lit office a level below us, illuminated by spotlights and seven or eight computer monitors on several desks. The room faces out, thanks to huge bay windows, toward the village. On the wall opposite the windows are floor-to-ceiling shelves of books and files. And directly below me, at the foot of a spiral staircase, is a diminutive figure, straggly gray hair pulled back into a tiny ponytail. He is standing with his back to us, talking in German on the phone. We descend the stairs, but he continues his conversation, apparently oblivious to our presence. I'm thinking, Is that Paul Köchli? The last pictures I have seen of him are at least 15 years old, and in those he was dark-haired. I didn't envisage him being so small, either.

After a minute or so, he concludes the call and turns around. Like his wife, he is wearing loose-fitting cargo pants and a white linen short-sleeved shirt, and he's barefoot, though it's cold. He has large, round glasses, and he squints and blinks awkwardly behind the lenses, one eye in particular seeming to cause him discomfort. He has just had an operation, he explains. It is why the office is so brightly lit, he adds. He seems distracted and unsure how to proceed. "I . . . I haven't really prepared for this," he says. "Are you early?"

"Er, no," I say, neglecting to add, "It's 5 o'clock. It's dark!"

"I . . . haven't finished," says Köchli, gesturing toward his computer.

"Please," I say, "finish what you were doing. I can wait. No rush."

"Ha, oh, no, I can't finish it now," he says in a reprimanding tone.

There follows a curious standoff. Köchli stands in front of me, appearing to wrestle with a dilemma. As he does so, he alternately lifts each foot, rubbing the sole against his leg. Actually, with his outfit and his hippieish appearance, he resembles a yoga teacher.

Edith dispels the awkwardness, asking, "Would you like a drink?"

"Tea would be lovely," I say.

"Fruit tea?" she asks.

"Of course."

Then, finally, Köchli leads me to a corner of the vast office, to two chairs next to the radiator. He pulls his away. "I don't like the heat," he says.

He clears his throat before speaking very precisely: "You must understand . . . I am sure I am different from the ones who were my *conquérants*. My career was very different. I stopped my cycling career very quickly, which gave me the opportunity to not go too far . . . to not get into something from which there is no return . . . no return. Mentally, I mean."

Contrary to what some thought when he was announced as the surprise appointment as directeur sportif for La Vie Claire, Köchli had been a professional cyclist himself—briefly. But he wants to begin his story before then. "It is important," he stresses. "The traditional career of a cyclist—what's the process? They get into it when they are kids. When you are an adolescent, a teenager, it is a very specific, special part of your life. You are not yourself. You try to be what you are not. You have no personality at all; it is something you are unconsciously searching for, looking for. It's a long, hard process to become an adult, with a stable, developed personality."

I am not sure where this is going. Köchli clears his throat again and continues, "The problem with a cyclist is that at this age they get into a context where they have no relation to reality anymore. They are in a system that has nothing to do with real life. In fact, most of them never really become adult.

They don't develop a real personality, a concept of real life. And lots of problems are directly or indirectly related to this—I'm talking about drugs as well.

"Today I understand that I was very lucky not to go too far."

As an amateur cyclist, Köchli represented Switzerland at the 1966 world road race championships at the Nürburgring in Germany. He was 10th; Cyrille Guimard was 11th. A year later, he rode the Tour de l'Avenir for his national team, which was coached by the country's former world sprint champion, Oscar Plattner. At that time, the "Tour of the Future" ran concurrently with the Tour de France. It was the year that Britain's Tom Simpson collapsed and died during the Tour, close to the summit of Mont Ventoux, due to a combination of heat exhaustion, alcohol, and drugs. A day later—the two events are unconnected—Köchli had a fight with Plattner. "I told him, 'You shut your mouth, you asshole!'" recalls Köchli.

Plattner was livid at the precocity of the 19-year-old—not least because he had a VIP in the car on that particular day. "He asked the Swiss federation to suspend me because I told him he was an asshole." Köchli shrugs. "They took away my license for three months, yet Plattner still selected me for the 1967 world championship. I refused to go. Graham Webb [of Great Britain] won; he went 500 meters from the line, but I was a good sprinter, and I'm pretty sure I could have won there."

The day Köchli was handed his license back, he had his revenge on his national federation by turning professional. "But I was too young to turn professional," he admits now. "I immediately got into a context—I'm talking about doping. Because I was a clean rider before. And I was convinced I would never touch it, but everyone is telling you, you have to. You are a kid, you are a child, not an adult, and you don't have the knowledge to take decisions. So you adapt, because otherwise you get . . . marked."

Köchli's professional career lasted only two full seasons. He started the 1968 Tour de France—"I am the youngest Swiss rider that has ever been in the Tour," he says with some pride—but didn't finish. The following year, he began to suffer pain due to an unusual condition, a problem with his femoral artery. "When the pain started, it was terrible," he says. "It was so frustrating."

During the Tour de Romandie in May 1970, the pain became excruciating, and he abandoned the race—and the sport—on the climb of the Col des Mosses. "I stopped. And I called my wife: 'Please just pick me up at the hotel.' I stopped, and it was over. But I know today that if I hadn't had that injury, I would have had a very bad end."

At the time, though, Köchli considered this "a very bad end." At 23, he was finished as a cyclist. He had no idea what to do next, and it is here that his story takes a surprising twist. Oscar Plattner—"who I called an asshole," Köchli takes great delight in repeating—contacted him. "He said, 'Hey, you should become a coach!'" Köchli says, laughing. "That's what Oscar said: 'I want you to become a coach.' Initially I didn't want anything to do with cycling because I was so frustrated. But he convinced me and motivated me, and I started studying at the Swiss National Sports School at Macolin.

"Here starts the difference," Köchli continues, clearing his throat again— which I now understand is a sign that he is about to say something of significance. "Here starts the real difference. Because usually the directeurs sportifs, they are in the car at the Tour de France the year after they have been riding . . . they go from bike to car, like that!" Köchli slaps his hands. "College made me very different from someone who gets off his bike, opens the door of a car, gets in, and starts shouting. Because there is more to being a team directeur than driving the car with your arm hanging out the window.

"At college, I discovered lots of new things, because previously I had been focused on cycling, cycling, cycling. This was a revelation to me. But I also had, in Oscar Plattner—the guy I called an asshole—a very important mentor, because I found that he respected me very much.

"I think I have a deep, broad, and intense knowledge of cycling," continues Köchli. "I had my ass on the bike in the Tour de France. I didn't just learn cycling at university." This point seems important to him—as though the skepticism that surrounded his appointment with La Vie Claire left a scar that can still irritate.

Köchli thrived at his university in Macolin—"I achieved the highest possible coaching diploma," he says—and he didn't have to wait long for his first coaching appointment: Lagos, Nigeria. "They found oil and had lots of money," he explains. "They bought a bunch of Falcon bikes and thought they could buy a good coach. They wanted me to develop cycling, so I went to Lagos, but after 10 days, I realized it was not possible.

"To develop cycling," adds Köchli, "you need roads."

Köchli returned to Switzerland and became Plattner's assistant with the national team. At the same time, he developed a cycling program at the Macolin sports school. "I developed a concept for cycling, how to teach it and how to teach coaches," he says, gesturing enthusiastically. "I was very interested in physiology. But my program included everything! You cannot separate the elements—training, tactics, endurance, power, psychology, motivation. It is wrong to separate these! But everyone does it! No, you need to see the whole thing."

He calms down, settles back in his chair. Clears his throat. "My concept involved revolutionary ideas. I had a conviction that it is very important to have knowledge of physiology and aerobic and anaerobic functions—words I didn't even know while I was a pro cyclist. I wrote my physiology study, which coaches had to read before they came [to Macolin] to work with me."

Köchli gets up, disappears into another room, then reemerges, beckoning me to follow him. In the small adjacent room, filled with more bulging shelves, he produces a thick folder, full of transparent plastic covers containing typewritten pages, with pictures and diagrams of the human body and close-ups of muscles. "This is my paper," he says, handing it over. "People in hospitals started using this—physiotherapists. That gave me confidence in my work. They told me they had never seen something that looked so good, so methodical.

"My program at the university was meant for Swiss coaches," he continues. "But people from other countries heard about it and were asking if they could come. Guimard, for example—he came. He was already the directeur sportif at Renault, and yet he did it. I understood it was difficult for him to do this study and also do his job, but he sent the sheets filled in with the answers to my questions. Most directeurs sportifs think the job is just driving the car and talking at the hotel, but Guimard worked on this paper after stages of the Tour de France. He was a hard worker, a very hard worker. It's why he was pretty successful."

Köchli also shows me shelves, floor to ceiling, of ring binders, each one with a rider's name on the spine; it reads like a who's who of the sport over the past 25 years. The spine of one slim folder reads, "Bernard Hinault," and he pulls it out, then opens it to show sheets of A4 paper, all filled with columns, with codes to indicate the intensity and duration of the training as well as the rider's weight and resting heart rate. "All my riders filled in these sheets every day," he says, "and then they posted them to me—Hinault, too." Köchli smiles as he adds, "Yes, Hinault did his homework."

As part of the course, Köchli rode his bike with his pupils. "There are things you can't understand by reading books. You need to understand cycling, and some don't. I sent some guys home. I told them, 'You are not a coach.' Maybe they were very good at studying, but they had no idea what cycling was."

Köchli was promoted to coach of the Swiss road team, where he enjoyed success. Though he was working with amateurs, his approach was professional—that is, it was team-oriented. "It was absolutely not oriented around protecting one single guy or a leader," he says.

When Plattner retired, Köchli was offered his job as national coach, but he wanted to bring in other coaches "to implement my methodology, under my supervision." The Swiss federation resisted Köchli's proposals and instead appointed another coach to oversee the national squads. "In effect, he would become my boss," says Köchli. "I would not accept that, and it led to a strong conflict." He left.

It was at around the same time that Köchli attended the 1983 world championships in Altenrhein, won by Greg LeMond. "I had met Greg," says Köchli. "I saw him win the Circuit de la Sarthe as an amateur. He had a different way. Nothing to do with the traditional mentality in Europe, which I wanted to cut. I wanted nothing to do with that, and I had different ideas about how my teams should work. And I was very attracted by the American way." So attracted, in fact, that Köchli was in negotiations with the U.S. cycling federation to establish a U.S.-backed professional team.

Those negotiations continued for the next year, with the American cyclists keen to turn professional after the 1984 Olympics in Los Angeles. But in August, Köchli received a phone call from a lawyer representing Bernard Tapie. "I had coached a Swiss rider, Daniel Gisiger, who, in 1981 and 1983, won the Grand Prix des Nations"—the world's most prestigious time trial— "which Hinault usually won. That impressed Hinault, I think.

"I knew Hinault was talking about building a team," continues Köchli. "Hinault also knew that Guimard had gone to school with me in Macolin. And he was fighting with Guimard at this time, so he said, 'We want you— the teacher of Guimard!'"

Hinault says he actually became aware of Köchli through the French national team coach, who told him about an unknown coach in Switzerland whose methods were so innovative as to be years ahead of everyone else's. "That's why he interested me," says Hinault today. "He was a scientist; he had a very scientific approach. Is the sport equally scientific even today? I'm not sure. . . . Köchli was self-taught. A real character. Very interesting."

At one point in my meeting with Hinault, he brings the conversation back to Köchli and proceeds to talk in impassioned tones for several minutes about him, completely unprompted—an unusual thing for Hinault to do. It follows the question of whether he was aware, in the mid-1980s, of the ways in which cycling was changing, becoming more international and adopting more scientific methods of training. "Of course," says Hinault. "And, going back to Paul Köchli, he had a computer with all of the results of all of the riders, from all over the world.

"He wanted to put together the best possible team by cherry-picking from all over the world. He knew who was the best Australian, the best Canadian, and so on and so on. When he came into the sport, the other directeurs sportifs were mocking him, saying, 'The computer can't sit on the bike and turn the pedals,' but that was ridiculous on their part. He was at least 10 years ahead of everyone else. This was before the Internet, don't forget. He used to get every cycling magazine in the world, and he could tell you about every rider in the world, from the junior ranks up. He knew whether they were a sprinter, a climber. . . . That's how he put the team together. There was also the financial aspect of it; he and Tapie took whichever rider could boost the brand in the country where the sponsor wanted to sell its product, just like teams do now."

When contact with Köchli was made, the Swiss traveled to Paris for his first meeting with Tapie and Hinault. "They explained the La Vie Claire project to me," says Köchli, who admits that among the riders they had assembled for their debut season were several he would rather not have had—but his hands, in this regard, were tied. What most concerned him was the relationship he would have with Hinault. "I said, 'For me, the important person is Bernard, because the focus is on him. We have to understand each other.' I wanted to make sure it was right. So I said, 'I want Bernard here for a week.'

"Here," he elaborates, "in this house in Sonvilier, because, I told them, we must be sure. So I had him here. I explained to him my concepts. We were also talking drugs and stuff like this. We talked about everything. I told him, 'I will not adapt to you. I will bring my concept, my ideas, and you must agree to that. You must adapt to me.' This was important: Hinault had to support me."

This is indeed important. Hinault, the four-time Tour de France winner, *le patron*, was being asked to fall in behind a virtually unknown Swiss coach. And he accepted this? "Of course!" Köchli says with a laugh.

"I said to Hinault, 'Listen, your first career was shit.' Because they killed him. They killed him. They killed him until he broke. And then they thought they could put him in the trash, because now they had Fignon. I told him how we'd function; that we would function differently."

Hinault, accompanied by his soigneur Joël Marteil, visited Köchli in the winter, with his recovery from his knee operation complete, to spend a week in the Köchlis' house. How was that? I wonder. "I would say it was easy for me," says Köchli with a nonchalant shrug. "I had a pedagogic approach. I tried to create an environment where we could discuss and make important decisions together; where we could reflect and think and make good decisions. I started to know him better. Of course I knew lots of things about him. Because I knew Guimard, and we talked about Hinault. And I watched the TV, and I read, and I thought, and I listened to other people—all these opinions and ideas about Hinault. But the important thing for me was to get to know him personally.

"Personally, I was surprised," he continues. "I started to understand the person much better."

What most surprised and encouraged Köchli, it seems, was Hinault's willingness to listen and his open-mindedness. This is a recurring—and, yes, surprising—theme with the Badger. (Interestingly, and in contrast to Guimard and most others, Köchli doesn't refer to Hinault by his nickname; this may be because of his seriousness but may also indicate his enduring respect.)

"What made Hinault so successful," continues Köchli, "was that he would act very emotionally in a race—he is challenged by everything." Köchli then brings us right into the present day, to a recent incident, when the podium of the 2009 Tour de France was invaded by a protester in Verbier. Hinault, in his ambassadorial role with the Tour, and with responsibility for the daily podium presentations, turned the clock back 25 years, reacting with the snarling rage of the Badger of old, rushing forward to confront the protester and pushing the man—about 30 years his junior—off the stage with aggressive force. "The guy was challenging him," points out Köchli. "The podium is Hinault's space—he is responsible for it—and this guy was challenging him. Even if the guy was 2 meters 20 tall and built like this"—he imitates a muscle-bound freak—"Hinault would have taken him on and taken him down. You are very lucky, very lucky if you have a guy with this mentality on the team."

Unwittingly, he echoes Guimard's characterization of Hinault as a boxer in need of an opponent.

Early in Köchli's partnership with Hinault, there was an example of what he has just described—very similar, in fact, to the podium protest in 2009 (and indeed to an earlier podium protest, in 2007). In another incident that would help to define Hinault, striking dock workers sought to use the 1984 Paris-Nice as a means to win publicity for their cause, as striking workers frequently did at bike races.

On this occasion, the strikers blocked the road, stopping a lead group that had just gone clear and that contained Hinault, who appeared to be on his way to claiming the leader's white jersey from Robert Millar. Confronted with the mass of striking workers, the riders squeezed their brakes and stretched down to loosen their toe straps as they approached the roadblock. But Hinault didn't. With that familiar snarl—and to the astonishment of his peers—he simply kept going, riding fast toward the line of picketers. When he reached them, he immediately began throwing punches. Fighting isn't easy to do in metal-cleated cycling shoes, and footage shows an off-balance Hinault swinging wildly at one striker in particular while having his hair pulled by another one.

"They wanted to stop us, so we defended ourselves, our right to do our job," Hinault said, shrugging, in a later TV interview. As he recalled the fight—in which he sustained a broken rib but finished the race—his eyes still blazed with indignation. No, he said, he hadn't tried to talk to the strikers, "but neither did they try to talk to me!

"It doesn't make sense," Hinault continued. "It's the only free spectacle we can bring to the public, and it's the only one that gets any bother, because it's easy. They took us hostage on the road. At that stage, the race was on, we'd just broken Millar, he was 45 seconds behind, and I was trying to win Paris-Nice. So I didn't want people coming and bothering me; the race was on. And maybe I lost because of that. When they're at work, I don't go and bother them. I let them work, so they should let me work.

"That's why I went straight in there—*woom!*" added Hinault, the sound effect alluding to a flying fist. "I had a broken rib, all the same. My lower rib, it hurt. But [the striker Hinault took on] must remember it—he got a fat lip."

"That was his right to work," asserts Köchli, echoing the earlier point about Hinault's pragmatism; his unromantic, unsentimental attitude toward his sport, or, rather, his job. (So much, again, for Hinault's claim that cycling is "not a job.") "They were invading his space," adds Köchli, "just like on the podium at the Tour—and challenging him."

Köchli presented Hinault with a completely different kind of challenge. He wanted to test the four-time Tour winner's willingness to put his faith in him. And so he set him a series of small tests. The first was simple: to "train more regularly!" As Köchli says, "He was a guy who did not do so much in the winter. That was one reason for his injuries. He would take it easy, then, *bam!*"—Köchli pumps his arm to indicate a big effort. "That way, you kill yourself."

"I brought in a complete change in the way Hinault worked. And we started with cyclocross." The winter discipline, held on a cross-country course, which demands that its participants jump off their bikes to negotiate obstacles, was a semiregular part of Hinault's routine—perhaps the only intensive training he did between the months of October and January. "I wanted him to learn something he'd never done in his life," says Köchli. "I wanted him to get off his bike on the"—he clears his throat—"on the right side.

"The first time I asked him to do this, he said, 'Paul, that doesn't work. It's not possible.' I told him, 'If you tell me that's not possible, then you are an old man. Are you telling me you cannot learn anything new? If so, then we can just stop now—we can forget it.' So he tried, and after a couple of days, he could dismount on the right, on the left—it only took him a couple of days. And I could show you videos, now, that show Hinault in cyclocross races, coming to an obstacle and going left or right—intuitively doing what is best.

"Very good," adds Köchli with satisfaction. "Surprising. Surprising. It showed me he can go in a new direction."

It isn't altogether surprising to discover that Cyrille Guimard's interpretation of what Köchli repeatedly refers to as Hinault's "second career" is somewhat at odds with Köchli's. Köchli claims Hinault "learned a new way, and used new methods." But Guimard scoffs at the suggestion. "New methods? I wasn't aware of any new methods." He smiles as he adds, "Oh no, no, no. The Badger certainly doesn't change his training methods in his 30s. I know him like the back of my hand. . . ."

Guimard actually had—and retains—a lot of time and respect for Köchli. "I know him well," he says. "He's someone for whom I have the utmost respect, even admiration. I went to Macolin and did the complete course. I did his courses on training, management, everything—which is what led Hinault to say that he'd had the pupil, and now he was learning from the master." As he says this, Guimard hoots with laughter. It takes him some time to regain his composure. So perhaps his respect for Köchli has its limits.

And he confirms this with what he says next, which is fascinating. "The problem with Paul is that he wasn't a commander in chief," says Guimard. "Paul is someone who'll say, 'You have to do this and this,' and he'll explain why, but afterward he's not going to check to make sure you've done what he's said. He'll figure it out eventually because he's clever. But, although you think he has the authority of a Swiss German—a bit *'ein, zwei, drei'*—he doesn't really have a charismatic authority.

"He has a discourse, but when it comes to giving commander-style orders, he's not quite as good. And with the Badger, face-to-face, you had to be very strong, in terms of personality, to make sure he'd obey an order.

"The problem with that team was the chain of command," Guimard continues. "Orders had no legitimacy. Why? Because it was Hinault who wanted Köchli. The chain of command is all wrong. And then, in the background, you have Bernard Tapie. What's he doing?"

Principally what Tapie was doing was setting up a venture that would transform his public image and promote his name as well as his businesses. On all counts, he succeeded. When the team was launched, only 18 percent of the French population had heard of his La Vie Claire chain of health food shops. Within 18 months, the figure had risen to 73 percent. In the meantime, Tapie himself enjoyed—and "enjoyed" does seem to be the appropriate word—a high media profile.

As well as being different in structure, with a scientific expert at the helm rather than the traditional grizzled retired pro, the team also looked different. The design of their shirts was radical, and—25 years on—it remains attractive and, surely alone among 1980s garments, hardly appears dated.

But, as Köchli tells me, the familiar grid-patterned, multicolored La Vie Claire jersey might never have seen the light of day. "Tapie arranged a stylist in Paris to come up with the design," he says later, over dinner. "We went to their office for the unveiling of the jersey—it was behind a curtain. But when the curtain drew back, we were shocked. It was like a Superman outfit, but in black! I can't really describe it, but it was wrong, wrong!"

Hinault has said that the original design was inspired by the trademark outfit of the All Blacks, New Zealand's national rugby team—and perhaps intended to create a similar aura of invincibility. But Köchli was unconvinced.

"I said, 'No, no—cyclists don't wear black jerseys.' It was very embarrassing, very awkward. But a student, a young girl who was there, said, 'What about a Mondrian?' And she sketched this design, with the panels." It was inspired by the Dutch artist Piet Mondrian's 1928 *Composition en rouge, jaune et bleu*, with black lines separating rectangular colored panels. Apart from being attractive, it was functional, with each panel able to accommodate a different (Tapie-owned) sponsor, with Radar on the red panel, Wonder on yellow, and La Vie Claire on white.

"It was genius," says Köchli. "The design is genius. The stylist was not pleased—she was looking daggers at the student. But I still wear my La Vie Claire jersey when I cycle in the valley today."

The 1984 Tour de France promised to be the battleground for multiple wars, the most bloody of which would surely be the returning Badger against his old mentor, Guimard. But Hinault against Fignon also promised to be messy. "France was cut in two," as Fignon notes in his autobiography, "split between him and me."

Then there was Guimard against Köchli and Tapie. And there was the possibility of an internal power struggle at Renault, between LeMond—finally making his Tour debut—and Fignon.

LeMond betrayed his inexperience early, forgetting to "sign on"—as all riders are obliged to do—before the start of the prologue (why does this revelation not come as much of a surprise?). The American resembled, writes the Irish journalist David Walsh, "a boy who was on his first day in secondary school. The incredulous tone of his observations gave one the feeling of a star-struck kid—the young protégé in awe of his Svengali." His Svengali was apparently still Hinault, despite the two being on different teams, with LeMond telling Walsh, after the Badger won the prologue, "I am amazed that Bernard can do such a time, absolutely amazed. It makes you wonder whether it will be possible to beat him."

But it was a Tour that would be decided two weeks later and that was defined by one mountain: Alpe d'Huez. Stage 17, from Grenoble to the Alpe, was set, as so often, to be critical in the battle for yellow. Fignon, second in the overall classification, had been inching toward the yellow jersey, with Hinault 2 minutes 46 seconds behind him and LeMond, who'd been ill early in the race, farther back, over 6 minutes behind Fignon.

In building that lead, by winning the time trial in Le Mans and stealing scraps of time in the Pyrenees, did Fignon manage to plant seeds of uncertainty in the usually doubt-free mind of Hinault? Perhaps, because six days before the decisive stage to Alpe d'Huez, the Badger attempted a move that hinted at his desperation. He attacked alone on a flat stage, 60 km into the 221 km to Blagnac, a move, said Fignon later, "that was unexpected—almost pathetic."

It could also be interpreted as a sign that if the Badger was going to go down, he would go down fighting. But it raised another question: What had happened to the Hinault of the early 1980s, who, though physically so strong, had been on the end of some stinging criticism for his apparent conservatism? It was paradoxical—here he was with his physical powers apparently diminished but his commitment to attacking restored. Often—as on stage 12—there appeared to be neither rhyme nor reason to Hinault's aggression. His moves were born of pride, as more than one commentator noted. Some suspected that Köchli might be partly responsible for his new aggressiveness—a theory implicitly backed up by Laurent Fignon, who would later note that "when he needed to calculate, hold back and race with his head, Hinault had dire need of Guimard."

But there was an unintended consequence of his style of riding—Hinault's popularity soared among the French public.

Public popularity, however, was not—it hardly needs pointing out—Hinault's raison d'être. He didn't launch attacks—particularly hopelessly doomed attacks—to court approval. He did so in order to try to win. His problem—one that Hinault hadn't encountered before—was an opponent, Fignon, who appeared able to match the boxer punch for punch, and then apply the coup de grâce.

While previous challengers might have been worn down, or intimidated, by the merest flexing of Hinault's muscles, that wasn't the case with Fignon, who, though from Paris, possessed the stubbornness of a Breton. Hinault's brinksmanship—"I attack when I'm tired, so the others don't know I'm tired"—simply didn't wash with Fignon, as he notes in his autobiography: "It might have worked on a rider who was mentally weaker than me. But I had an answer for everything, and above all, contrary to how he saw it, I never lost my head, even if the guerrilla warfare [Hinault's repeated attacking] occasionally got a bit tiring, because you had to keep your eyes open all the time."

Fignon's response to Hinault's aggression and his mind games was of the worst, most humiliating kind—he found it tiresome; it bored him; occasionally it even amused him.

Hinault correctly identified the key stage as the 151-km leg from Grenoble to Alpe d'Huez, via the Col du Coq and Côte de Laffrey. His first jab came on the steep Côte de Laffrey, quickly followed by another, and another—he launched no fewer than five attacks on the Laffrey's steep slopes, but each time Fignon and his yellow-and-black-clad Renault team were equal to him.

The brutal sparring between the two riders on that stage was vividly described by one of those caught in the crossfire, Robert Millar, in a 2009 edition of *Rouleur* magazine. Millar writes that his suspicions were aroused, at the foot of the Côte de Laffrey, on spotting "an unhealthy gathering of Bernard Hinault's troops on the front of the group that signals trouble is imminent. . . ."

Millar continues, "The road ramps up and it seems like all hell has let loose. I can see five La Vie Claire jerseys on the front as yellow jersey Vincent Barteau comes sprinting past with [his Renault teammate] Laurent Fignon on his wheel. I make a swift decision not to try to follow them, hoping that the arrival of Fignon [at the front] will calm down the attackers. Ha! Fat chance of that happening—someone has a plan and it's not going to be deviated from, come what may."

After 2 km, with 6 km remaining of a climb "that goes straight up—no corners, no bends, just unrelenting suffering," there are 15 riders left in the group, writes Millar. The speed is high, so high that Hinault has shed all but one of his teammates. Fignon, too, now has only one man left: Greg LeMond.

"The 5 km board and Hinault attacks," Millar writes. "Fignon is onto him directly but the rest of us haul ourselves back to them as if in slow motion. . . . Whack! Another acceleration from Hinault and Fignon responds again. Are they enjoying this sparring, because I'm not. A quick glimpse up from chewing the bars and I make it seven of us remaining . . . another punch thrown—this time Fignon decides he would see what Hinault has to offer. Each acceleration feels like a kick in the stomach—brutal, sickening and designed to hurt as much as possible. Ouch, ouch, ouch.

"A team car pulls alongside and it's for Hinault. I can't hear what's said but immediately there's another injection of pace from him. The Renault car appears next and Cyrille Guimard gives out advice and encouragement to his remaining soldiers. He takes a look at the rest of the group and understands in that glance that this part of the battle won't be troubled by any of us. . . .

"Phew, is that a temporary lull I feel in my legs?" continues Millar. "It is." Most of the group, including Millar, use this opportunity to drink from a bidon, a drinking bottle. But the respite is fleeting. "Whack! There's another attack. LeMond this time, so the Renault boys are going to gang up on poor Hinault. He smiles and sets off after him, Fignon in tow and the rest of us choking on the drinks we dared have."

And so it goes on. "Whack! Another assault from Hinault. Whack! Straight back from Fignon. . . . Alpe d'Huez is still to come and these two are laying into each other like it's the finish. I haven't witnessed savagery at this level before and it seems more like hatred than just plain competition."

And on. "Whack! Hinault tries again and, sure enough, he gets a right hook straight back. . . . Whack! Hinault puts it up two gears and blasts away toward the top." In fact, Fignon eventually rides away from Hinault toward the summit in the company of the Colombian climber Luis Herrera, but Hinault counterattacks on a descent made more treacherous by the "strobe lighting effect" created by tree branches overhead. With Hinault forcing the pace, the photographers' motorbikes that usually travel just in front of the riders struggle to keep ahead; they back up at the corners, increasing the danger. "Could adding this mental stress be the last straw?" wonders Millar. "I guess that's the question Hinault is now asking."

On the valley road to Alpe d'Huez, through the Alpine villages of Séchilienne, Gavet, Les Clavaux, Riouperoux, Livet, and finally Bourg-d'Oisans, there is a general regrouping and "a truce in hostilities," as there often is before the monster climb and its 21 hairpins, winding like a spiral staircase into the sky.

In the valley, Guimard drives alongside Fignon and LeMond, handing them fresh bidons. "Everyone in the car looks serious," writes Millar, "which worries me." Hinault's team car then comes alongside, and "almost reluctantly Hinault exchanges words with them. I'm sure he smiled as he took his bidons. Hmm, I'd guess he's not as tired I am, then."

Then, abruptly, on the approach to the Alpe, "Whack! That man Hinault again. He obviously doesn't feel the headwind or notice that it's a long, drawn-out drag up the valley to the final climb. LeMond and Fignon drag him back as the rest of us scrabble in the gutter for a hint of shelter. Then Guimard comes alongside and shouts out more instructions, but that just seems to encourage more hostility from Hinault. Whack! Now I'm cursing—this isn't remotely funny. Fignon has to do all the work this time as Greg comes tumbling back and joins us weaklings in dodging drain covers."

When the Renault team car draws alongside Fignon again—as Hinault, "hugging the left-hand gutter," persists with his lone attack, building a lead of a minute by the foot of the climb—there are "smiles all round from Guimard, and is that Fignon smirking at his rival's audacity?"

Indeed it is, because this attack of Hinault's in the 1984 Tour, on the approach to Alpe d'Huez, was arguably one of the most reckless of his career. It was another move that Fignon might have described as "unexpected—almost pathetic," which seemed to owe nothing to reason or any coherent race plan and everything to emotion and wounded pride.

Fignon was asked on French TV, immediately after the stage, how he had reacted to Hinault's attack, and his reaction confirmed Millar's impression. "I laughed," he said.

You could argue that what happens as the road begins its relentlessly cruel, 1,100-meter vertical ascent to the summit of Alpe d'Huez vindicates Fignon's derision. First Hinault's shoulders begin to rock. He labors; his pace slows; his usual angry snarl seems to turn into a silent scream of agony. The rage dissolves from his eyes, replaced by a look of increasing desperation. Hinault is caught first by the tiny, birdlike Herrera, the Colombian riding a bike that looks too big for him. In stark contrast to Hinault, Herrera flies gracefully up the gradient.

Then Fignon approaches Hinault's shoulder and eases past. The French TV cameras miss the moment, almost as if they want to spare Hinault the humiliation. But with Fignon opening a gap, Guimard drives up to his leader, telling him not to press on but to maintain his small advantage over Hinault, teasing him into thinking he is holding him, even pulling him back.

"I stayed about 30 meters ahead of the Badger," Fignon later writes in his autobiography. "Guimard wanted to crack him completely."

Or, as Sam Abt puts it, "Fignon seemed to believe that if you couldn't kick a man when he was down, when could you kick him?"

It was cruel, but it worked. Once Fignon finally left Hinault to disappear in pursuit of Herrera—whom he would never catch, allowing the Colombian to win the stage and send 20 million of his countrymen into raptures—Angel Arroyo was the next to catch and drop the Badger; then Millar, Martinez Acevedo, and finally LeMond.

Millar, climbing the mountain alone, absorbed in his own battle with fatigue, describes the moment he catches the Badger: "I'm astonished to see it's Hinault I've caught up with. What a surprise this is. He doesn't look any different to the last time I saw him, still snarling, still fighting, but when he reaches into his pockets and takes out some food I know he's in trouble.

"I could go past him and give him some shelter, some temporary relief from the misery but then I remember Laffrey and the valley and how much it hurt. . . . I let him take a bit more wind . . . I'll have a little rest, thanks." When Millar spots a thickening of the roadside crowd 200 meters ahead, with the promise of shelter, he passes Hinault and gently accelerates. The moment is captured on TV: Hinault grapples in his pocket for food, but it is a distraction from what is happening. His body language is easy to read; he is wasted, lolling like a drunk on a blazing-hot day. When he gets out of the saddle, it isn't to accelerate, it's merely to ensure that the pedals keep turning. It's agony to watch.

Millar's final observation on the moment he caught and left Hinault for dead on the Alpe is almost poignant: "He wanted to be on his own anyway."

Another poignant description is Jean-Paul Vespini's in his book, *The Tour Is Won on the Alpe*. "Hinault was bearing his cross," Vespini writes. "His face was without emotion, his eyes fixed, his muscles tense, and his shoulders heavy from the weight of years of domination . . . the Alpe crucified him"— as, notes Vespini, it crucified Merckx in his final Tour in 1977. The parallels were obvious, and many were moved to wonder whether they were witnessing Hinault's final bow, as they had with Merckx, seven years earlier.

By the roadside, the fans clench their fists and scream encouragement at the struggling Hinault, "as if offering prayers to the glory of a fallen champion."

At the summit, behind Herrera, Fignon took over the yellow jersey. But as Fignon was telling French TV that he had laughed at Hinault's attack, Hinault himself insisted, with his usual stubborn pride, that "I won't stop attacking before Paris." Unusually, though, he admitted, "Today, I have been thrashed."

Fignon was less magnanimous, telling reporters, "I don't know if I'm becoming one of the great riders, but I do know that it all ends one day. Look at Bernard. Two years ago they called him unbeatable."

L'Équipe the next day gave over the front page to a large picture—taken from behind—of the moment when daylight began to appear between

Hinault and Fignon on the slopes of the Alpe. The paper's reporter Pierre Chany wrote that Fignon's "horizons expand every day as he imposes his iron rule." The glory belonged to him and to Herrera, while "the cruelty was reserved for Bernard Hinault, a real scrapper, a proud rider and a man always looking for a challenge, who offered himself up with admirable generosity. . . . During a champion's career, the cruelest moment comes when he realizes the extent of his weakness in the face of the attacks of insolent youth."

Or, as David Walsh, quoting King Lear, put it, "The young doth rise when the old doth fall."

L'Équipe also carried the assessment of Tour director Jacques Goddet, which echoes Millar's assertion and reads almost like a death notice: "Hinault carried himself like a combatant born of cycling legend. He took off down the road the way a boxer enters the ring, to strike, to destroy, to try and finish alone—yes, alone, in whatever condition, as long as he is still standing."

By the time they reached Paris, Hinault was in second place overall but well beaten by the now two-time winner, Fignon. He finished 10 minutes 32 seconds down on a rider who was still just 23 and who seemed set to dominate for years. Yet there was another, unintended consequence of Hinault's defeat—or, rather, his spirited refusal to accept it and to keep fighting the younger, stronger man. "Fignon is the winner, but Hinault is the hero," as one writer put it.

With what might be regarded as breathtaking audacity, Bernard Tapie claimed credit after the Tour for Hinault's restored public image and increased popularity. "I would have been sorry if he had finished second behind Fignon at 2 minutes," said the La Vie Claire boss. "He appeared far more human to the public.

"We succeeded in changing his image, and that's good," added Tapie, who was in the team car that followed Hinault as he struggled up Alpe d'Huez, apparently—according to Tapie's biographers—"with tears flowing down his cheeks, looking like a kid with a broken dream."

Popular or not, Hinault was "uncomfortable in the role of [Raymond] Poulidor," the eternal second. And so was Tapie, for all his claims that he was happy for Hinault to be a popular loser. Tapie was stung by the defeat, and by Cyrille Guimard having the upper hand. Again according to his biographers, "he decided then that Guimard would not win anymore. . . . In the next few months, Tapie is going to pulverize the little world of cycling." (If this was really Tapie's intention, he succeeded. Up to 1984, Guimard's riders had won seven of the previous eight Tours. But, astonishingly, 1984, with Fignon, was to be Guimard's last Tour win. He was still only 37.)

On the third step of the podium in Paris, meanwhile, was another young pretender who confirmed that he would be a presence in the Grand Tours of the future. Third overall, and a close 1 minute 14 seconds behind Hinault by the time they reached Paris, was LeMond, becoming the first American ever to finish on the podium.

The 1984 Tour, and in particular the stage to Alpe d'Huez, was indeed bloody. But the blood spilled was Hinault's.

Speaking now about Fignon's emergence, and his comparatively "lost years" of 1983 and 1984, Hinault states that he didn't feel that he was finished. "I knew that to get back to my best after my operation, I'd need some time," he says with a shrug and a curl of the lip. "I'd need some time, and I'd need to work hard. In 1984, I was going well—I was surprised just how well, so soon. The team was good."

But Fignon and Renault—which won an incredible 10 stages and held the yellow jersey for 19 of the Tour's 23 days—were better, much better. "Yes," says Hinault, "that was too bad. But when, in autumn, I won the Tour of Lombardy and the Grand Prix des Nations, I knew that we were up and running again."

As for his attack on the road to Alpe d'Huez, Hinault says it was a symptom of his attitude; that, in the Tour at least, he couldn't race other than to win. "If you start the race thinking that you'll finish second, you've lost already. You always have to say to yourself, 'I'm the best, and I'm the one who's going to win.'"

For LeMond, meanwhile, finishing on the podium of his first Tour was a triumph of sorts after he'd fallen sick four days into the race. "I was always getting sick," he says, and recalls, also, his first Grand Tour, the 1983 Vuelta. "I got the worst chills, coughing that turned to bronchitis, and I was on antibiotics for two weeks of that Tour. I felt like I was riding with the brakes on. The stage to Guzet-Neige that Millar won, I was losing two minutes every time we went uphill. Guimard kept sending teammates back to help me. He said, 'Take your time, take your time.'

"I stayed in that race because of Guimard. Any other coach would have said, 'What the hell are you doing? Come on, you're not giving your all!' But Guimard could see I was giving my all."

Another problem for LeMond—as it had been for Hinault the previous year—was Fignon. Now with two wins, this one more comprehensive (you could almost say Badgerlike), he was the undisputed leader of the Renault team. There could be no argument with that. But where did that leave the rider who had originally been earmarked, and groomed by Guimard, as Hinault's successor?

"I liked Fignon," says LeMond. "We had a fine relationship. I found him . . . Fignon has an intellectual capacity and an emotional capacity that maybe . . ." That Hinault doesn't? "Put it this way," LeMond continues. "Hinault will probably live until he's 120. He doesn't think; that's the way he is. I mean, I wish I was more like that; that I didn't think so much."

Back to Fignon, and to the quandary in which LeMond found himself in 1984. "I wanted to stay with Guimard," he says. "But I also analyzed my situation. First off, in my mind, I thought I was more talented than Fignon." LeMond laughs. "Hmmm. Actually now I think Fignon was a lot more talented than I gave him credit for back then. He turned pro in 1982, and maybe he's making this up, I don't know, but he told me he trained twice a week and did stuff that was crazy."

Indeed, Fignon cultivated a reputation as a bit of a playboy—certainly compared to LeMond or Hinault—though the description of someone as a "playboy" in a cycling context should be explained. It means drinking to excess some of the time, driving too fast all of the time, and—as Fignon admits in his autobiography—dabbling in drugs, even cocaine, which appeared to be the accepted currency at the 1984 Tour of Colombia. He claims to have won the final stage with his head still spinning from an all-night session.

Let's return to Alpe d'Huez, the scene of Fignon's coronation and Hinault's humiliation, on the evening of July 17. The ski resort at the summit of the mountain was the scene, just hours after the 17th stage had ended, of another significant episode—significant and intriguing, with elements of subterfuge and with profound ramifications for the following year's Tour, and beyond.

It is an incident that suggests that Tapie and Hinault were not licking their fresh and still painful wounds but instead plotting and scheming about how to "pulverize" the little world of cycling, in the process bringing an end to Guimard's period of domination.

What played out that night at the top of Alpe d'Huez resembled a scene from a James Bond movie. Having had dinner, one rider—he had placed sixth on the stage—stepped outside to stretch his legs, as riders often do in the evening. On this occasion, the rider was approached by an attractive female dressed in motorcycle leathers. She addressed the rider by his name, then said, "Monsieur Tapie would like to see you. Please, come with me."

Since the start of the season, Tapie had been in the market for a rider who could provide backup to his leader—and replace him when Hinault retired, as promised, in 1986. Köchli, too, was looking forward to taking a large broom to the squad he had inherited. Most pressingly of all, he wanted to get rid of several of the French riders, particularly the old guard. "Look in the archives," says Köchli. "*Woooosh*. A lot were cleared out after 1984. Riders who were strategically unusable—not useful. But also, I wanted to make a break with the French mentality."

Tapie and Köchli agreed that they needed new riders—in particular a new deputy leader: someone strong enough to support Hinault in his quest for a fifth Tour but also good enough to win in his absence.

Köchli says that Tapie was "very involved in this process, of course, because it was his money," but that Köchli had the final say on signing riders. Otherwise, he admits, La Vie Claire would have signed the Irishman Stephen Roche. "But Roche was more a French rider than anyone!" says Köchli. "Tapie was often talking to Stephen during the Tour; I think they understood each other well, but I told Tapie that I needed a rider who could really play out my concept, which is all about the team, not the leader.

"Tapie said, '*Prends Roche, Prends Roche!* I want Roche!' And I said, 'No, I don't want Roche!'"

Why was he against signing Roche? Köchli sucks through his teeth, coughs, clears his throat. "I didn't want him for several reasons, without explaining all the details. You act on information, on feeling, intuition. . . ."

When I spoke to Roche, I asked how close he had been to signing for La Vie Claire—if, indeed, he had been aware of Tapie's interest. "Oh, yeah," he says. "In 1983, I first met him, and the second time I met him, he said, 'Come and have a drink,' and he took me down off the hill after a stage of the Tour in his car, and he said, 'You should be riding for us.'

"I met him at his house a few months later in Paris," continues Roche. But the move to La Vie Claire "didn't come off. I don't know why. I thought Tapie was a great guy. One day he invited me to Lille to see a football match, and so I drove to Lille, met him at the airport, and we drove to the game. I had a beautiful big Opel Omega, brand new but with no air conditioning. It was too hot, so I opened the windows, and he said, 'What are you doing?' I said, 'That's the air conditioning.'

"After the match, he said, 'Give your car keys to this guy here,' and pointed to this fellow. 'I'll fly you back down.' So Tapie takes me to his private jet and jumps in the cockpit. I said, 'You drive this thing?' He said, 'Yeah.' I said, 'You got a license?' And he said, 'I haven't—but this guy has' as he pointed to the pilot. But Tapie was in the pilot's seat. We made it to Paris, anyway, and I got my car back.

"He was very charismatic," continues the fast-talking Roche. "I enjoyed spending time with him. He could drive cars fast, he could sing, he could dance, he eventually had a talk show—he could do anything. An incredible man, right enough."

Tapie's interest in Roche was clear, the respect and admiration mutual. But it wasn't the Irishman who was approached by the mysterious woman in leather on the evening after the stage to Alpe d'Huez.

7

THE MILLION-DOLLAR MAN

In traditional teams, you have three topics of conversation:
You have cars, women, and drugs.

PAUL KÖCHLI

On the morning of July 18, 1984, the day after the Alpe d'Huez stage of the Tour de France, an interview with Bernard Tapie was published in *L'Équipe*. It was the exact opposite of the modern soccer player's "Come and get me!" plea, communicated via the press when the player in question is angling for a move to another club. It was, instead, a "Come to us!" plea from Tapie that was as unambiguous as it was audacious. It was also typical Tapie.

"I want Fignon!" Tapie told *L'Équipe*.

Which was strange, because it wasn't Fignon who had been summoned to Tapie's hotel room by the leather-clad female motorcyclist only the previous evening. So if it wasn't Roche, and it wasn't Fignon, who was it?

It was LeMond. "I'd got this message earlier that Tapie wanted to meet me, but I kinda didn't take it seriously," says LeMond, "until this woman showed up. She was wearing this black leather suit, a motorcycle suit, and she was holding this black helmet, and she came up—it was like a James Bond movie—and she was . . ." LeMond glances furtively at Kathy and drops his voice to a whisper, "she was really good-looking, and she said"—he adopts a French accent—"'Monsieur LeMond, Monsieur Tapie would like to see you.'

"And I said, 'Yeah?'"

"'You must come with me.' I looked at this motorcycle and got on it, holding on to her black leathers"—he glances again toward his wife, who rolls her eyes—"and we ride off and pull up at a hotel. And we go in, into this hotel room, and there's Tapie—and there's Hinault. And Tapie's first words are 'How would you like to make more money than you ever dreamed of?'

"I said, 'What do you mean?' And he held up a pedal—a Look pedal." It was an early model of the automatic, clipless pedal that Tapie, through one of his companies, Look, was attempting to develop and market. "Tapie told me," continues LeMond, "that I'd get royalties on every pedal sold, and this and that.

"Tapie," LeMond adds, "was the master of manipulation. He was all show, and he was the master of the PR stunt. But, having said that, he did actually deliver on a lot of what he said."[1]

In August 1984, when Tapie announced that LeMond had signed with La Vie Claire and declared him "the world's first million-dollar cyclist," LeMond had not actually signed. Tapie's aim was to put pressure on LeMond, and the tactic apparently worked; he signed in September. As Tapie also knew, news of the "first million-dollar cyclist" was guaranteed to make headlines. In fact, LeMond urged Tapie to keep the amount secret, though he also acknowledged that there was "fat chance of that when he saw an opportunity to zing the cycling establishment and to get lots of publicity." But Tapie's audacity extended even beyond that—his million-dollar cyclist (who hadn't yet signed) wasn't a million-dollar cyclist.

"Tapie wanted to announce that I was the first million-dollar cyclist," says LeMond. "In reality, it wasn't quite what I was paid." It wasn't too far off, though; it was considerably more than the $100,000 a year he had been paid at Renault, and it was stratospheric compared to most cyclists' salaries, with LeMond acknowledging that it was "a stepping-stone for cycling in terms of what riders were paid in the future." (Nor was it the last time LeMond would singlehandedly raise the market value of cyclists; in 1989, he signed a three-year contract with Z worth $5.5 million—a huge jump.)

---

1. Tapie didn't deliver on everything he said, though. An addendum to Tapie's promise of royalties on every clipless pedal sold comes from August 1986, when LeMond's father and manager, Bob, revealed, "Greg has a contract with an equipment manufacturer that Tapie owns. He gets a percentage of every unit that the company sells in America. We signed that contract last summer, and here we are, almost 14 months later, and I haven't seen one cent of what's owed." LeMond confirms that, to this day, he has not received any royalties on sales of clipless pedals.

At La Vie Claire, LeMond signed a contract that saw him receive a salary of $225,000 in year one, $260,000 in year two, and $300,000 in year three (somewhere between $420,000 and $550,000 in today's money), plus various perks—or various promised perks—such as eight first-class flights back to the United States each year, a Renault car on both sides of the Atlantic, free fuel, and "all the Madame Grès clothes your wife wants."

Some of Tapie's pledges proved as reliable as the Guimard-supplied car with the warped windshield that the LeMonds had taken delivery of when they first arrived in Europe. "We found out he had nothing to do with Madame Grès!" says Kathy LeMond.

The access to the elusive and so far untapped "American market" that LeMond's capture could open up was not a consideration, insisted Tapie. He told Sam Abt in early 1986 that his interest in LeMond owed purely to his ability. "We wanted to build the best team in the world," said Tapie. "If the best had been French, we'd have had an all-French team. If I'd needed to recruit a Martian to win, I'd have done so. Greg cost a lot, but he was the best available."

How did the Tapie-generated hype around LeMond's capture—not to mention his reported salary—sit with his new teammate and leader, Hinault? Hinault shrugs. But he visibly bristles at—and strongly refutes—the suggestion that LeMond's capture made Hinault the second-best-paid rider on his own team, even though Hinault's La Vie Claire salary has been widely, and consistently, reported as a relatively modest $150,000 a year from 1984 to his retirement in 1986. There was parity with LeMond, Hinault insists. "At the time, the exchange rate was 1 dollar to 10 francs," says Hinault.

"If they'd given him the same salary as me in francs, then when he went home, he'd have lost 10 percent . . ." Hinault pauses, looks up. "No, a lot more. If you'd converted his salary back into francs, he was earning the same as me. C'est tout!"

Given Tapie's larger-than-life personality and his tendency to feed the media with a stream of juicy quotes, there was a certain amount of interest, curiosity, and intrigue around the team owner's exact role. Confusion over who was in charge was also stoked by Paul Köchli's natural reticence.

Köchli's great strength—as Cyrille Guimard has suggested—was behind the scenes. As well as not being, in Guimard's assessment, an effective "commander in chief," he wasn't, and never would be, a media personality, even to the extent that Guimard, by virtue of his hauteur, was. Tapie, however, fulfilled that role with aplomb. He loved it. Other than as the owner of a professional cycling team, how could he engineer a prominent appearance in *L'Équipe* in the middle of July, as the Tour reached its climax and sales of the daily sports newspaper soared?

Hinault says that Tapie wasn't always around. "He came when there were big races, or big mountain stages, or a crucial time trial. He'd be in the team car." But did he get involved in deciding tactics? "No—not tactics," replies Hinault. "The only thing he did was try to fire us up for, say, a mountain stage in the Tour. He'd be telling us, 'You're going to win! We're going to win!'

"And that's great." Hinault shrugs, almost embarrassed to reveal the lack of detail or sophistication in Tapie's rousing speeches. You imagine that Köchli's instructions contained a little more in the way of instructions, if less panache, although there is a possibility that Hinault is playing down the passion inherent in Tapie's motivational style. According to the autobiography of the soccer star Tony Cascarino, who played for Tapie's Olympique Marseille football team, "Tapie did all the talking before the game and toured the dressing room slapping us on the back and lunging at us with grunts and hoisted testicles," urging them to "*monter les couilles* (show we had balls)."

Explaining the decision to target LeMond for the team, Hinault says there were two considerations. "The goal for Tapie was to invest in the American market, to sell the automatic pedal there." Then he echoes what Tapie told Sam Abt: "We were obviously looking for a good rider as well. And we knew that by signing LeMond, we were destabilizing Renault slightly by taking one of their leaders and lining him up against them, against Fignon.

"If I couldn't beat Fignon with strength alone," Hinault continues, "we thought that we could perhaps beat him by alternating attacks. I go, Greg goes . . . then, finally, *voilà*! Fignon would buckle."

Yet for all that Tapie came to be, in some respects, the public face of the team management—and for all that commercial considerations came into play—it is clear that Köchli's input mattered; otherwise it might have been Roche rather than LeMond who signed with La Vie Claire for 1985. Köchli, as he has said, was keen to dilute the team with non-French influences, adding Swiss and North American riders, including Canada's Steve Bauer as well as LeMond. "I was very impressed by Steve," Köchli says. "Strategically, he was exactly what I was looking for. Adding LeMond, Bauer, and some others—these were important points for a new takeoff with what I could now call 'my' team."

As well as the clandestine meeting with Tapie and Hinault—at which Köchli was curiously absent—the Swiss reveals that he and LeMond also discussed the American's possible move during the 1984 Tour. But the circumstances of their meeting were in stark contrast to the hotel-room rendezvous facilitated by the woman in motorcycle leathers. Köchli and LeMond met a few days after that meeting in Villefranche-en-Beau, following the penultimate stage.

"I was waiting with Hinault in the caravan for dope control," recalls Köchli. "In fact, Hinault was inside, pissing," he clarifies in his matter-of-fact way. "I was waiting outside when Greg arrived. So we were together, only Greg and me, and he spoke to me first, in fact. He said, 'The other guys tell me you are very against doping in your team.' I told him that was true, that it was my goal, my objective, and I'd do everything I could to make sure that we function like this."

LeMond was reluctant to leave Guimard. But Fignon's emergence left him with little choice. Even Guimard, who had taken such care in slowly nurturing LeMond, recognized that Fignon's new status as the hottest property in the sport made LeMond's position almost untenable. But there was also the fact, which Guimard doesn't mention, that Fignon was French and that Renault remained a resolutely French team.

"I realized very early on with Fignon and LeMond that I was going to have two bucks who would want to kill each other," says Guimard. "You can't have two 10-point stags in the same herd of deer. You can't trust it. It can only end in one thing: mortal combat."

For the second year in a row, then, Guimard had to release one of his "10-point stags." He refuses to be drawn on which of the two—Hinault or LeMond—he preferred. "That's like asking which one of your children you prefer." But with the benefit of hindsight—and given that Fignon lost arguably the best years of his career to injury and was never able to add to his two Tour victories of 1983 and 1984—the question is, does Guimard now wish he had kept LeMond?

Guimard turns the question around, seeing the move as LeMond's error rather than his (though, in any case, he couldn't have matched Tapie's financial offer). "Greg's mistake was leaving for La Vie Claire," says Guimard confidently. "If he'd stayed with us, what with Fignon's injuries, he would perhaps have won more Tours."

LeMond confirms that Guimard told him the same thing when the American told him he was thinking of leaving. "He said, 'I think you can win five Tours with us,'" LeMond says.

LeMond also confirms Köchli's account of their encounter outside the dope-testing caravan, though his recollection of the conversation isn't quite so clear. In retirement, LeMond has become outspoken on the subject of doping, but was he aware, as a young professional, of a doping culture, however insidious it might have been, either in his team or in the sport in general?

Unusually for LeMond, he offers a response to this question that isn't expansive but cryptic. "I remember Guimard telling me, when I had the offer from La Vie Claire, that he thought I was the most talented rider he had on the team and that I could win five Tours with him. He said, 'Greg, compared to Fignon, you raced the Tour on one leg.' In a way, I did, because I was sick. But . . . I took it to mean something else.

"I don't know . . . I don't know if I was being groomed before being given the magic potion, I really don't, but Guimard knew my opinion and my attitude toward doping. I never entertained it. I didn't talk about it. Didn't joke about it.

"When I spoke to Guimard about leaving, he said, 'You'll never win the Tour without me.' I don't know what he meant by that, either. But hey, you want to get me going? Tell me I can't do something. Right there the decision was made. I was gone."

It is worth recording that LeMond and Guimard parted on relatively amicable terms and didn't fall out over his departure, which makes their divorce very unusual. Fignon, whose relationship with his mentor eventually went the same way as Guimard's with Hinault, went so far as to claim in his autobiography that "with Guimard, the end is never pretty." LeMond's parting with Guimard seems to have been prettier than most, and as pretty as it could have been.

As for Köchli's determination to run a drug-free team, the question, of course, was how? "The post-Tour criteriums—that's where drug-taking was rife," Köchli claims. These were exhibition races in which the stars of the day, especially of the most recent Tour—stage and jersey winners, even the *lanterne rouge* (the red lantern, or last man)—could command big appearance fees. The irony is that the races weren't overly demanding in a purely athletic sense—they would be fast, to provide the crowds with an exciting show, but the order across the line at the finish was invariably fixed by a mafia of big names and the prize money pooled (as at Châteaulin in 1976, when the upstart Hinault rebelled against Merckx and the others).

Although the races themselves might not have been demanding, the relentless schedule between races was, with riders sometimes competing in two a day. For most of them, there was a very simple equation to consider: More races, more money. But in order to keep the riders going, stimulants, especially amphetamines, were allegedly plentiful and free-flowing—something that also owed to the absence of any doping controls except on very rare occasions (such as at Callac in 1982, when Hinault protested against, and refused to take, a dope test).

Köchli came up with a radical solution to the problem: He banned his riders from taking part in the criteriums. "After the Tour, I said, 'No criteriums!' A lot of French riders complained—the criteriums gave them their income. But I spoke to Tapie and said, 'Give me some space on the jersey.' What I did with that space was get a sponsor—an American sponsor, Red Zinger—and took the team to the Coors Classic [in America] instead. The sponsor gave us enough money to give the guys what they would have earned in the criteriums."

It was a smart and innovative solution, though how effective Köchli's efforts to run a drug-free team were is difficult to say. Apart from the rumors that had swirled around Hinault, there was also Tapie. Tapie maintained that his team was clean, claiming that to be anything other than clean would have been perverse for a team sponsored by a chain of health food stores. Yet some La Vie Claire riders did test positive—including the Dane Kim Andersen, on no fewer than four occasions—and the picture painted by the soccer player Tony Cascarino is hardly encouraging. Cascarino recounts one occasion when "Tapie had summoned his personal physician from Paris, and after dinner we lined up in one of the rooms and rolled up our sleeves for a 'booster' injection. I hadn't a clue what exactly the boost was, [but they] weren't the only injections at the club. Before games we were offered shots—20 tiny pinpricks, injected into the lower back by what looked like a stapling gun. I asked one of the physios what it was and if it was legal. 'Of course it's legal,' he replied. And then he smiled. 'And anyway, our doctor does all of the tests at the club.'"

Köchli maintains, however, that "in traditional teams, you have three top-ics of conversation: You have cars, women, and drugs. That's 99.9 percent of the conversation. Believe me, in our team, it was not like this."

To the supplementary question of whether it was, in that case, "just cars and women," Köchli pauses for a moment, then realizes it's a joke, sits back, and laughs. "Just cars and women, yes!"

While LeMond and Steve Bauer also back up Köchli's claims to have run a clean team—"He was a good influence," says LeMond; "He made it clear that was the philosophy," says Bauer—I was given an even more vivid and con-vincing example of the strength of his opposition to drugs by Shelley Verses, an American soigneur who joined Köchli's team in 1987. "Paul would inven-tory our truck, our van; he would open up our kit to see what was in there—he was paranoid," says Verses.

"In my first month with the team," she continues, "I had period cramps. I had some acetaminophen tablets, and I brought them in my pocket to the dinner table. I remember I was sitting to the right of Köchli. I took the tab-lets out of my pocket and put them on the dinner table, next to my glass of water, so that, after a couple of bites of bread, I could put them in my mouth.

"But Köchli sees them and gets up, and in that funny voice of his, he goes, 'What is this?' And he picks up the tablets, and I say, 'Paul, those are mine,' but he's not listening. He's shouting, 'What is this? What is this? Are you drugging in front of my riders?' And in front of the riders and everybody, he picks them up, says, 'No doping on this team!' and throws them from one end of the room to the other. One of the riders had to duck to avoid them hitting his head.

"I was saying, 'Paul—I have my period . . . menstruation!' But he didn't hear until another woman, the team's PR woman, says, '*Arrête, Paul! Elle a ses règles!*'"

It is an indication of Köchli's progressiveness—the above incident not-withstanding—that he would go on to employ Verses, given that this was an era in which you would be as likely to encounter a leprechaun as a woman in the world of professional cycling, except on the podium. Even now, the glamorous "podium girls" remain, looking beautiful and smiling beatifically alongside a salty, sweat-encrusted cyclist, thus ensuring that some elements of cycling culture remain stranded in the 1970s.

In the mid-1980s, however, apart from the podium girls and until Shelley Verses entered the fray, the only female you might run into at a bike race was

Kathy LeMond, who, from the day she and her husband arrived in Europe, seemed to be welcomed at races and around the Renault team. Both Kathy and Greg confess to not fully comprehending why Guimard accepted and even indulged them as a couple other than to interpret it as further evidence of his people management skills. Regardless of tradition, he realized how important it was for the homesickness-prone LeMond to have his wife around.

Köchli was also sympathetic—to a point. The Swiss experienced at first hand the antifemale attitude in cycling during his brief professional career when he had a spell with an Italian team managed by the retired great Gino Bartali. "My wife was not allowed to even meet me at the hotel," he says. "It was banned. But for me, it was important: I wanted to see my wife. So, at one race in Italy, I put her in a hotel around the block. In the morning, I picked up my bike from the mechanic and said I was going to test the gears. But as I was talking to my wife around the corner from my team hotel, Bartali went out to buy *Gazzetta dello Sport*, and he saw me. You cannot imagine; you cannot imagine." Köchli shakes his head at the memory. "It was terrible, terrible."

It was also, in Köchli's view, ridiculously outmoded and another manifestation of the "traditional European mentality" that he sought to challenge. Yet he did fear that Kathy's presence—or, more accurately, LeMond's ability to pay to have his wife and family with him—could prove divisive. "I said to Greg, 'Listen, you can afford to have your wife with you every day. But think about your teammates who cannot afford that. Be intelligent; don't exaggerate the difference; it'll create resentment, which is not good for you.'"

Notwithstanding the progressive attitudes of Guimard and Köchli, there was a long way to go. And to see how far, we turn again to Shelley Verses, another American who, at the same time as LeMond, challenged—and perhaps helped change—certain prevailing attitudes and conventions.

As a 24-year-old from Connecticut via California, Shelley arrived at the 1985 Giro d'Italia as soigneur to a new American team, 7-Eleven. This was a team that Köchli might, had he not become involved with Bernards Hinault and Tapie, have been leading. The Giro was the 7-Eleven riders' first major European appointment, pitching them in at the deep end against the elite of world cycling—including Hinault, LeMond, and the might of La Vie Claire.

To get a flavor of that Giro—and of the sport at the time—there is perhaps no better witness than Verses. "When they applied for my accreditation, they just put 'S. Verses' on the form," she says, "and they made sure not to send my picture. Then they kept me in the hotel in Verona; they wouldn't let me near the other riders. When Mike Neel, our director, went to collect the team's credentials, he took my passport picture, and they said, 'But this is a girl!' He had to argue for my accreditation.

"I was interviewed all day, every day, by the journalists, and the question was 'How many riders are you sleeping with?' That was the question I was asked all . . . the . . . time. At first I was wearing a T-shirt and little shorts, but at the end of the first week, they gave me a lab coat and told me no more cute tops; from now on, I had to wear that."

Many riders, says Verses, were shocked to see a female working (and not as a podium girl!) and circled her cagily, eyeing her as though she were on show. "Most riders were like *'Ciao, bella!'* I remember [Italian legend Francesco] Moser, surrounded by about five henchmen—these guys in boiler suits running after him—coming and asking me to rub his legs. I'm saying, 'Get him out of here! This is for my riders!' But Davis Phinney [one of the 7-Eleven riders] whispers, 'Shelley, it's Francesco Moser!' So Moser sits down on one of the little stools while these guys are polishing his *chariot* [bike], and I'm thinking, This is a big guy, he's kind of a . . . specimen." Verses laughs bashfully. "Oh, boy, he's a little different from my guys!"

Hinault wasn't as brazen as some of the Italian riders, says Verses—he announced his presence more subtly. "Hinault comes past," Verses recalls, "and he looks like he's going to kill someone; he's just in his Badger zone. But, bizarrely, I did get to know him a little during that Giro. He came over to the team truck one day—I think he was kind of fascinated by me. It was in the Dolomites, and he started speaking—in French. I said, 'Italian?' And he spoke a bit of Italian. He asked, 'What have you got there?' I said, *'Ciliegie'*— cherries—because one of my riders, Ron Kiefel, loved cherries, and when we passed the fruit stalls by the side of the road, I bought him cherries.

"And Hinault says, *'Il mio frutto preferito.'* So I go, 'Here, have some,' and gave him a handful. *'Domani,* I give you more,' I said, and, from then on, I bought him cherries. It was like our secret. It was adorable!"

It was a Giro in which the cherry-fueled Hinault destroyed the opposition, including the Italian favorite Moser, and declared, "I am feeling 100 percent for the first time since 1982"—the year of his last Tour de France win. While Moser finished second to Hinault, the signs for LeMond were encouraging. He was third.

But 7-Eleven left a significant and lasting mark on the race beyond the fact that it had a female staff member, especially in the shape of another slight, slender-framed blond. He was Andy Hampsten. The unassuming Hampsten—whom you hear regularly described as "the nicest man in cycling"—was born in Ohio but grew up in North Dakota. His parents taught English at the University of North Dakota and spent the summers hiking and camping in the mountains, with the exception of one, which they spent in Cambridgeshire, England. It was there that 15-year-old Andy had his introduction to bike racing—riding club time trials—and learned about the Tour de France, "which I had no idea existed."

Back in the United States, he graduated to the national junior team, riding with LeMond at the 1979 world championships. But in the early 1980s, Hampsten's career seemed to stall as he sought to combine cycling with studying. He lasted two years at college and raced domestically in the United States with the small Levis team, despite the fact that "my ambitions were in Europe" and also that his talent—as a climber—was far more suited to the high mountains of Europe. Finally the 1985 Giro—which Hampsten rode at the 11th hour, having signed a short-term contract with 7-Eleven—offered him an opportunity, and he seized it gratefully.

Initially, Hampsten says, the team's rookie status caused problems. "There were a lot of crashes, and there were attempts to blame those crashes on the Americans." There had been a similar attempt to stigmatize the other new boys, the Colombians, when they appeared in Europe to ride the Tour de France in 1983, though with perhaps a little more justification given that their ability to ride in a tightly packed and chaotic peloton tended not to be equal to their astonishing skill in the mountains.

"There was a bit of tension," Hampsten says, "but . . . I don't know if it's an ugly-American trait, but . . . we gave it back. I mean, we didn't fly all the way across the Atlantic so that we could have some Italian swear at us. We knew how to swear back. And then Ron Kiefel won the 15th stage into Perugia [becoming the first American ever to win a stage in a Grand Tour], and he won in very dominating fashion. We got a lot of respect after that.

"I was riding quite well in the second half of the race," continues Hampsten. "I was making it into the first group on the mountain stages. There weren't many mountains, because the course was really designed for Moser. But at the end, there were two days in the Alps, the second very short. Mike

Neel held me back in the long first stage, told me not to attack, to hold it back.

"We warmed up on the course the morning of that second mountain stage," continues Hampsten. It was short—just 58 km, finishing with a climb to the 1,666-meter summit of Gran Paradiso. "I was disappointed, because the second half of the climb wasn't really hard. It was fairly hard at the beginning, and it wasn't my style to attack at the beginning, but I needed an element of surprise, so the plan was to attack on a corner about a kilometer up the climb.

"I was wearing a one-piece suit—the kind you wear for a time trial—which got me teased. You know, it just wasn't done! The other riders were laughing, snickering. Then the team led me out to the base of the climb—and that got us teased a bit as well. But the team killed it; it was the best lead-out. There was a break out front, but we caught the last rider, and there was a bit of a pause—and that was my corner. So I attacked, and I got away very cleanly. I looked back and saw that Hinault and Marino Lejaretta were chasing me. There were about 15 kilometers to go, and I had some doubts, but I kept it drilled, and I won by 57 seconds.

"It's still my favorite win ever," adds Hampsten, making quite a claim considering that he would go on to wear the *maglia rosa* of overall Giro winner in 1988—the first, and still the only, American ever to do so—and win the showpiece stage of the Tour, at Alpe d'Huez, in 1992.

Back in 1985, Hampsten says that his countryman LeMond was "happy on that Giro to have Americans to speak to, but he also told me, right at the beginning, 'Hey, I'm really glad you're here—but as well as just being here, you can kick some ass and do really well.'" LeMond also mentioned, even back then, the possibility of Hampsten joining him and Steve Bauer at La Vie Claire and increasing the quota of North Americans. "He kept saying he was going to tell Hinault about us, that we were neopros and hadn't raced any pro races before. Then he'd come back and say, 'I've told Hinault you'll do something spectacular—now go do something!'"

By the time he did do something spectacular, discussions were already well advanced for Hampsten to join La Vie Claire for 1986.

8

THE CASE OF THE BROKEN RAY-BANS

If I sound sure of myself, it's because I am.
BERNARD HINAULT

The 1985 Tour de France, following a clockwise circuit around France, got under way without the champion of the previous two years. Laurent Fignon succumbed to a serious injury caused by the seemingly innocuous incident of a pedal bashing against his Achilles tendon. An operation followed, but Fignon would arguably never be the same athlete again.

Fignon's absence returned Hinault, especially after his Giro victory, to the status of favorite for a Tour that began in his native and beloved Brittany, with a prologue time trial in Plumelec, which he won at a canter. "If I sound sure of myself," Hinault said afterward, "it's because I am."

LeMond, meanwhile, wasn't. He suffered a mechanical mishap, his chain jamming in the final few hundred meters, forcing him to a virtual standstill, though he still managed to place fifth, 21 seconds down.

Despite Köchli's democratic principles and his refusal to organize his team around a single leader, it was understood by LeMond that he was there to assist Hinault. "I got hired to help win a fifth Tour, which was a major mistake on my part," LeMond says now. And it wasn't long before the limitations of taking on such a role—especially in a Tour lacking an opponent like

Fignon, and especially in a team as strong as La Vie Claire—became blindingly clear to him.

Underlining the strength of La Vie Claire, the squad won the stage 3 team time trial by a full minute, though the Hinault who crossed the line was angry. Mobbed by reporters and photographers, he lashed out, landing a particularly powerful blow on one photographer's chin.

Yet the other, contradictory side to Hinault's personality was highlighted by the role he played in the following days for another La Vie Claire rider, Kim Andersen. The Dane, one of the team's domestiques, claimed the yellow jersey after the fourth stage, keeping it for three days, during which time he was staggered to see Hinault swap roles with him and willingly act as his domestique. This despite the fact, according to Andersen, that Hinault, "unlike other team leaders, who are always calling for assistance from their domestiques even for minor problems, only calls on the help of his team when he has a major problem."

When Andersen punctured while still in yellow, Hinault paced him back to the peloton. And when the Dane took a turn at the front, assisting the chase of a breakaway, he felt Hinault's hand on his arm. "You rest," Hinault told him. "You've worked too hard." Hinault then moved in front, gesturing for Andersen to shelter behind him while he lent his considerable strength to the chase.

"I would die for that man," said Andersen after relinquishing the jersey to Hinault in Strasbourg, at the end of a 75-km time trial that Hinault won by a staggering 2 minutes 20 seconds from Stephen Roche. LeMond was fourth, a further 14 seconds down.

"A devastating result," said the British magazine *Cycling Weekly* of Hinault's performance in the time trial before offering a popular—but, as it turned out, ridiculously premature—verdict: "Press opinion was that the Tour was over and everyone might as well go home."

It was an understandable verdict, though. Going into the Tour's rest day—after the Alps had seen Hinault stamp his authority on the race, then consolidate his lead in another time trial—the Badger held a commanding advantage of 5 minutes 23 seconds over his teammate LeMond.

It confirmed that Hinault was back to his best—his contemptuous best, as the press discovered on the rest day following the time trial. At the Hotel des Alpes, in the village of Saint Nizier du Moucherotte, a press conference with Hinault was scheduled for 11 a.m. But at 11 o'clock, there was no sign. And at

11:30, with the patience of the assembled reporters and TV crews beginning to wear thin, the Badger still hadn't showed up. Where was he? "Out training," said a member of La Vie Claire's support staff.

At 11:40, Hinault deigned to appear. Casually sitting down on the steps rather than behind the table that had been set up as a stage, while photographers buzzed around like wasps, Hinault slipped on a nylon windproof jacket and held court. He was asked if he was afraid of the mountains still to come, with several daunting stages in the Pyrenees. "I'm never afraid of anything," he replied.

It was a case of pride coming before a fall. Because in Saint-Étienne, 24 hours later, the story of the 1985 Tour de France—and Hinault's procession to his fifth win—took the most dramatic and unexpected of twists.

LeMond finished in a small group behind the stage winner, Luis Herrera, almost 2 minutes ahead of a group containing the yellow-jerseyed Hinault. This suited them both, and it suited La Vie Claire; it moved LeMond up the overall classification, consolidating his second overall placing, while Hinault remained impervious in the *maillot jaune* of overall leader. In fact, it was a tactical masterstroke, significantly strengthening Paul Köchli's hand. But as LeMond spoke to reporters after the stage, awaiting the arrival at any moment of Hinault's group, there was drama. A radio reporter burst through the throng surrounding LeMond, yelling, "Hinault's crashed!"

"What?" replied LeMond. "Jeez! Where? He's not here?"

"No," said the radio reporter, "it's five minutes now; he's still not here."

Hinault had been one of six riders to crash in the final 300 meters, and he was the most seriously injured. Dazed, with his yellow jersey scuffed and dirty and with blood gushing from his nose, he sat on the road before slowly and uncertainly getting to his feet. The time lost didn't matter, owing to the Tour's rule that riders who crash in the final kilometer are given the same time as the leading rider in the group. But another rule was important: Hinault still had to cross the line.

And as Hinault lay bleeding on the road, within sight of the finish, that didn't look certain. It was several minutes before he remounted his bike and, with his head bowed and blood dripping to the road, was able to pedal gingerly to the line before being taken by ambulance to the hospital. A broken nose was diagnosed.

Phil Anderson was also involved in the crash. In fact, according to Hinault, the Australian was to blame. "People still talk about that crash," says

Anderson now. "Hinault knew I was a good friend of Greg, and I think he thought I was trying to knock him off on purpose, or something crazy like that.

"Steve Bauer was in front of me coming to the finish, and I was following him. Just as he kicks to sprint, his back wheel hits one of the little reflectors in the road. His back wheel slips out, and his bike goes sideways. He stays upright, but I trip over his wheel, and Hinault goes over the top of me."

In his first autobiography, Hinault recalls the crash and lays the blame squarely at Anderson's door but also—rather comically—rues the fact not that his nose was fractured but that an expensive pair of Ray-Ban sunglasses was broken.[1]

Shelley Verses, who would go on to have a relationship with Anderson, recalls the Saint-Étienne crash as "the Ray-Bans crash," laughing hysterically.

"Yeah, well, he broke his Ray-Bans; I lost my shoes," Anderson says. "Somehow, in the crash, my shoes came off. I remember sitting on the road, trying to get myself up off my arse, but looking around and seeing my bike in one spot and my shoes sitting over there on the road, not too far from the side.

"I started composing myself and got up, and I'm walking over to the side of the road, and both shoes are gone! Both shoes! The crowd took them as a souvenir. Luckily I had a spare pair in the car, but I finished the stage without shoes.

"I got back to the hotel afterward," Anderson continues, "and by the time I got there, the French media were already there, explaining that Hinault had accused me of knocking him off purposefully. It was the last thing on my mind. But yeah, it seems that he still holds a grudge. He came to Australia after I retired, in the mid-1990s, and somebody asked him about me. He explained he was still pissed off with me. That was 10 years after it happened. Now we're talking 20, 25 years, and I think he's still got a chip on his shoulder about it. I never got on that well with Hinault. So be it. But I'm disappointed; firstly that he read that crash wrong. And secondly that he hasn't got over it."

---

1. Before Oakley shades became ubiquitous after LeMond began wearing them, Hinault, in the 1985 Tour, became one of the few riders in the peloton to ride with sunglasses, which is ironic given that the previous year he had issued a reprimand to the British rider Sean Yates, riding his first Tour and wearing a pair of Ray-Bans. "I accidentally hit Hinault in the bunch, just brushed against him," recalls Yates, "and he turned to me and said, 'Take those glasses off, boy, so you can see where you're going!'"

Hinault still remembers the broken Ray-Bans, too. "They weren't broken when I fell," he clarifies when I meet him in Brittany. "It was a fan who stood on them and squashed them."

There were more serious consequences, of course. Not least was the fact—given Hinault's now compromised state—that LeMond had clawed back 2 minutes on general classification, putting him 3:30 down. It wouldn't have mattered had Hinault maintained the impervious form he'd demonstrated before his injuries. But now the question was whether he would, or could, be the same rider as the one who'd dominated the first half of the Tour.

Next day, the beaten-up Hinault soldiered on, for once accepting the full support of his team and spending the entire stage riding in a protective cocoon of La Vie Claire teammates, emerging only to tell Anderson what he thought of him. His swollen nose was now complemented by two black eyes, giving him the appearance of a street fighter. It was—most agreed—a look that suited him.

But Hinault was human, after all. Over the next days, he began to suffer terribly, not least because to his broken nose—as if that were not a sufficient handicap—was added the ailment of bronchitis. LeMond, on the other hand, was a revelation. Without the health issues and injuries that had dogged his previous Grand Tours, he appeared to be getting stronger as the race entered its third, decisive week.

For LeMond, this shift in the balance of power—the momentum he was building, the impetus Hinault was losing—presented exciting possibilities. Although he understood that he was there to support Hinault, he had reached a point in his career when he needed a major win. His biggest victory was still the world road race title, but that was almost two years ago—a lifetime in sport.

Although he consistently placed high in the big races, he was lacking the result that would catapult him from potential star to bona fide star. Part of being a star was seizing opportunity.

LeMond needed to prove that he could assume the responsibility of leadership. He had to show that, in addition to his vast physical capacity, he possessed the ability that Hinault had to get others to rally around him, to bend races to his will. Yet in order to prove that he could handle the responsibility, LeMond needed opportunity. Seizing such an opportunity would inevitably mean usurping Hinault's place, for which he would probably need something of Hinault's Badgerlike instinct—his *méchant* quality, identified by Sam Abt as "a nasty, spiteful, malicious streak" (*"chien méchant"* as the sign says on French homes, warning of a vicious dog). Hinault had it in spades; everybody knew that. But did LeMond?

As the black-eyed, broken-nosed Hinault struggled on in the yellow jersey, a shadow of the rider he had been in the first half of the Tour, LeMond appeared to be presented with his chance in the Pyrenees, on stage 17 to Luz Ardiden. Early in this monster stage, which included the Col d'Aspin, the queen of the Pyrenean climbs, the Col du Tourmalet, and finally the summit finish at Luz Ardiden, the Badger acted the *patron* on the approach to the Col d'Aspin as the Renault team—possibly suspecting that Hinault was vulnerable—set a blistering pace. Hinault rode up to the front of the bunch and began remonstrating with Guimard's men—but in so doing, did he merely alert his rivals to the extent of his suffering? This was certainly a very different Hinault from the rider who, a year earlier, had traded blows with Laurent Fignon on the Côte de Laffrey.

Guimard was right, though; Hinault was vulnerable. On the Tourmalet, he was unable to stay with the leaders and began to slip back. This was LeMond's moment—or was it? He remained vigilant at the front, and when Stephen Roche attacked, he followed. He had to follow the dangerous Roche, a contender for yellow in Paris. But what he did next—whether he cooperated with Roche or sat behind him, riding defensively—was up to his team. It was up to Köchli.

"We kept getting away on the Tourmalet, me and Greg," recalls Roche. "I was in third place overall, and there was a good chance that if the two of us could get away and stay away, then LeMond would take the jersey and I'd go up to second. The main thing was that Hinault was behind us, and he was suffering."

Köchli now found himself in a difficult position. He was in the team car following his *chien méchant* while the eager young puppy was ahead, pulling at the leash, eager to be set free. LeMond admits that he was keen to be given the green light to attack. He knew it was his moment; he was also confident that he was stronger than Roche. Roche agrees: "That's what I felt, yeah."

With Köchli behind, following Hinault, the other La Vie Claire team car accelerated forward to the LeMond-Roche group. It was driven by Maurice Le Guilloux, who'd ridden with the team the previous year. He was now a directeur sportif and Köchli's second-in-command. As Le Guilloux drove up the Tourmalet, following Roche and LeMond, LeMond dropped back to speak to him. "Where's Hinault?" he asked Le Guilloux. "And can I ride with Roche?"

Le Guilloux radioed Köchli while LeMond pedaled alongside the team car, Roche just in front of him. "But after Maurice radioed Köchli, I could hear his instructions coming through Maurice's radio," recalls LeMond.

"I'm riding by the door of the car, and Roche is about five feet away, and I can hear Köchli saying, 'Greg can only ride if he *attacks* Stephen Roche!' But Roche can hear all this as well! We're riding a 5 percent gradient, Lucho Herrera's coming up to us, and I'm asking, 'Where's Hinault?' And they're telling me he's just behind, so I cannot ride." As LeMond notes, a successful attack usually needs an element of surprise—but the element of surprise was lacking given that Roche had overheard Köchli's instruction.

As for LeMond's other question—"Where's Hinault?"—he was told by Le Guilloux, whose information came from Köchli, that Hinault was about 45 seconds behind him. Now LeMond believes—as does Roche—that it was minutes rather than seconds.

"Greg was getting orders to attack me and not to ride," Roche recalls. "The main order was not to ride. That was frustrating. I think he felt he was stronger than me, and if he knew he had a better chance of beating me at the finish and in the final time trial, then why not ride? If we'd ridden at that point, I think we'd have finished first and second in that Tour. Of course the team car was playing it down for Hinault; he was further back than they were letting on. They knew if we worked together, Hinault wouldn't get back on, and LeMond would have won. They were looking after French interests."

LeMond did as instructed, but reluctantly. He didn't cooperate with Roche—and he didn't attack. "I wait and I wait and I wait," he says. "Then a group of about 16 or 18 riders comes up, and Hinault's not there. He's still another minute and a half behind that group. By the time I finished the stage, he was still a minute and 15 seconds down and I'd waited minutes for him."

Hinault was also still in yellow. LeMond's chance had gone.

Köchli defends his instruction to LeMond not to cooperate with Roche. "For me," he says, "it was always clear. Never a doubt. We must win. And when I say 'we,' I don't mean Hinault, and I don't mean LeMond. My basic concept is based on this idea. It's why most of our riders won at least one race per year. We won so many races, with so many different riders, because we acted differently.

"It is a strategic game," Köchli continues. "You cannot jump into the break if you are LeMond, with Roche, and say, 'Hey, Roche, ride!' No! LeMond cannot ride because Hinault is behind. You have to collaborate with your rivals, yes, but you have to collaborate intelligently.

"OK, so Hinault is in trouble on the Tourmalet. Roche attacked, and Greg did what he had to do; he went with him. I was behind Hinault's group, but I had a hard time talking to Hinault [who was being helped by another La Vie Claire rider, the Swiss Niki Rüttimann] there.

"Ahead of us was Maurice Le Guilloux, my assistant. He was one of the riders I wanted to get rid of the previous year, but he was old, he had lots of experience, and he was respected, so I had offered him a job."

It sounds like the traditional career path—straight from bike to team car—that Köchli so disparaged. "Yes, it was the traditional way," he says with a smile, "but, but," he adds, wagging a finger, "he had to, while he finished the 1984 season as a rider, do my course. During the winter he came to Macolin to work with my successor at the sports school. . . ."

Köchli sits back, looking satisfied. So I prompt him back to the Col du Tourmalet. "Maurice was with Greg. I was not there. But there was really no need for us even to talk. Logically, Greg has not to ride with Roche. Just follow him and win the stage—very easy. But then, on the radio, Maurice calls me. 'Greg is telling me he wants to ride; he's asking to ride.'"

Köchli laughs nervously. "I said, 'Is he becoming crazy?' Maurice said, 'He says he can win the Tour now if he rides, and he wants to win the Tour.' I told Maurice, 'That's not a problem—but you tell Greg, he attacks once, full gas, and drops Roche. And then he can go and win the Tour, no problem.'

"Maurice explained this to him, and Greg never attacked. He did never attack. Which means he was not capable, or he didn't feel strong enough to drop Roche and go and win the Tour.

"Because it's not part of the game—not part of the strategic game—to ride with Roche. If Greg rides with Roche, what then? LeMond takes the jersey and we have Roche behind in second place.

"If Greg had done what he wanted to do—ride with Roche—then we go from having the top two riders, Hinault and LeMond, to first and third. What then? The next day, on the Col d'Aubisque, Roche attacked very hard—very, very hard—and we had a hard time because Hinault was suffering still. On that occasion, Greg went with Roche, he didn't ride, and Hinault came back.

But let's imagine Greg punctures at that point. We lose the Tour. Roche wins. It doesn't need a big explanation. It's very easy."

On the Tourmalet, with the Roche-LeMond escape effectively neutered by the instruction to LeMond not to ride with Roche, Hinault was able to recover some ground, though the race splintered again on the climb to Luz Ardiden, where LeMond placed fifth, almost 3 minutes behind the winner, Pedro Delgado. Hinault trailed in 18th, a further minute behind LeMond.

"Greg was a long time before me at the finish line," says Köchli, "and this was the first year that the American TV channels, NBC and ABC, were there, 5 meters beyond the line, grabbing Greg, asking him all the stupid questions. And Greg, with his heart pumping at 200, when he is faced with TV, he has a few things to say, points of view—but we may have others. But he's talking and talking. . . .

"I always told my riders, 'After the race, immediately after it, we don't talk about the race. We talk about it later, when everybody is there. And when everybody is calm.'

"That," he adds, "was part of my strategic concept."

To the reporters at the finish, LeMond did—in characteristically emotional fashion—talk, making absolutely clear his unhappiness and anger. "I had my chance to win today," he told them. "My team stopped me. Köchli said to me, 'How dare you attack Hinault when he's in difficulty?' They lost me the Tour because they told me to stop working, when I was strong enough to attack."

I was gonna quit the 1985 Tour after Luz Ardiden. I was gonna quit that night," LeMond says now, his resentment clearly still simmering 25 years later. "Köchli said he didn't mislead me, but someone in the team definitely said Hinault was just behind. Well, he was way behind.

"It was only at the top I realized, holy shit, I could've won the Tour! I don't know how Stephen Roche was feeling that day, but there's a moment in a race when you can attack . . . and then the moment's gone. We came to a crawl on the Tourmalet after I was told not to ride. I couldn't attack because all the momentum had gone. It was crazy.

"If you watch the stage the next day, on the Col d'Aubisque, Hinault was dropped four or five times," LeMond continues. "I basically pushed him up the climb to keep his lead. That's why it's not just that stage to Luz Ardiden that made the difference; it was the next day. And it was the stuff I didn't do in the Alps.

"I mean, I was a very dedicated teammate that year. And so it wasn't a case of, Hinault had the crash, and he would have been better had he not fallen. The fact is, he had his peak at the first time trial, and then he was slowly going downhill. Everyone can pinpoint Luz Ardiden and say, 'Well, LeMond could've, should've . . .' but there were other things." With a resigned shrug, LeMond adds, "I felt I sacrificed a lot."

Unsurprisingly, Hinault's take on these events differs from LeMond's. Of LeMond's "attack" with Roche, he says, "We said, 'OK, the only condition is that you drop Roche.' He couldn't, so we asked him to come back. When you have the yellow jersey, you defend it by putting Greg at the front. But there's no point in him being up there with other dangerous riders unless I'm in trouble behind. It's a race strategy." Hinault insists he was not in serious trouble; he was always going to come back on the descent, he says.

Asked if LeMond was unhappy afterward, Hinault breezily replies, "No, no." But that wasn't what LeMond told the media after the stage, I point out. "I know he said that," Hinault says with a laugh. "But in general, you don't attack someone [in your own team] who has the yellow jersey. You settle for following the others. If the yellow jersey is in difficulty and is 3 or 4 minutes behind, that's when you say, 'Go, attack,' but in that instance he didn't even have any reason to move because he was second overall. All he needed to do was let Stephen Roche do the work for him."

Hinault insists that the atmosphere in the La Vie Claire team throughout that 1985 Tour was good. "It wasn't tense," he contends. And there was, he adds, no division between the French contingent and the others; no "Hinault camp" or "LeMond camp."

"No. The thing is, if you speak a different language from someone, even if you get by in their language, you're going to form affinities more easily with the riders who speak your language," he observes.

With LeMond, according to his own account, pushing Hinault up the Col d'Aubisque on the final day in the Pyrenees, where Roche won the morning's stage 18a (and later that night, curiously, toasted his success with champagne in the company of Tapie and Hinault), it seemed that Hinault was set to win his fifth Tour. His lead, with the mountain stages now behind them and with only four days to go to Paris, stood at 2 minutes 13 seconds over LeMond, with the final test a time trial on the penultimate day.

Over 45.7 kilometers and around Lake Vassivière near Limousin, the time trial was the kind of stage that appeared made for Hinault. In the first half of the 1985 Tour, his winning margin might have been minutes. But now, post-crash, post-Pyrenees, still sporting the fading remnants of the black eyes, the Hinault who rolled up for this test was a different, wounded beast.

In the morning, Hinault also gave an interview to Jean-Paul Brouchon of *Miroir du Cyclisme*. And he made a surprising pronouncement. The following year, he told Brouchon, "I'll stir things up to help Greg win, and I'll have fun doing it. That's a promise." The timing was in some ways as interesting as the pledge; Hinault hadn't wrapped up the 1985 Tour yet.

But it was also revealing in another way. It seemed to be an implicit acknowledgment that he wouldn't be on the brink of claiming his fifth Tour without LeMond's help. For Hinault, that was quite an admission, while his apparent pledge to sacrifice his own ambitions—and forgo a tilt at a record-breaking sixth Tour—was even more significant.

On the penultimate day of the 1985 Tour, LeMond won the time trial by just 5 seconds over his dogged team leader—an astonishing performance in the circumstances. The gap between the leading pair on general classification was now minuscule compared to some of Hinault's previous winning margins, at just 1 minute 42 seconds—with Roche almost 3 minutes further back in third—but it was enough, with only the ceremonial final stage to go, to see Hinault safely to Paris in yellow.

It was easy to forget, meanwhile—given that LeMond was riding his second Tour and was set to follow third overall in his debut with another podium appearance—that the time trial represented his first stage win. It also represented another small piece of history: the first ever Tour de France stage win by an American.

That could offer one explanation for the fact that LeMond struggled to believe his achievement. As he waited at the finish for Hinault—who started 3 minutes behind him—he kept repeating to reporters, "Bernard's won; he's won. Bernard's won; he's won." Was this a lack of confidence in his own ability or the conviction—hardwired into his psyche after so long in the shadow of Hinault, not to mention the three weeks of a Tour that threatened in the later stages to alter the balance of power in their relationship—that the

Badger, through crashes, a broken nose, and bronchitis (not to mention the heartache of a smashed pair of Ray-Bans), would always prevail in the end?

When Hinault crossed the line, in a time slower than his, LeMond's fist shot up, punching the roof of the caravan in which he was now sitting. Hinault was the first to congratulate him. And then LeMond spoke to reporters. It seemed that an enormous weight had been lifted from his shoulders.

"Now I know I can beat Hinault," he said. "I know I can win a Tour de France."

WE MUST WIN. AND WHEN I SAY "WE," I DON'T MEAN HINAULT AND I DON'T MEAN LEMOND. —PAUL KÖCHLI

PART TWO: ARRIVÉE

THE DAY COMES WHEN THE TWO OF THEM STAND FACE TO FACE OVER THE BOUNTY. AND THEN IT'S ALL ABOUT WHOEVER CAN DRAW FIRST. —ERIC LAHMY

9

THE BULLDOG AND THE BIRD

Next year it's you who will win the Tour, and I'll be there to give you a hand.

BERNARD HINAULT TO GREG LEMOND

BOULOGNE-BILLANCOURT, FRIDAY, JULY 4, 1986

A record 210 riders appear in Boulogne-Billancourt on the afternoon of July 4, the 73rd Tour de France opening with a 4.6-km prologue time trial through the streets of the Paris suburb. Ten riders wear the distinctive multicolors of La Vie Claire, the world's best team, comprising a formidable lineup of big-name stars and lesser-known domestiques.

Wearing number 1 as defending champion is Bernard Hinault, and his teammates' names are listed beneath his on the official start sheet:

2. Steve Bauer (Canada)
3. Charly Bérard (France)
4. Jean-François Bernard (France)
5. Andy Hampsten (USA)
6. Philippe Leleu (France)
7. Greg LeMond (USA)
8. Niki Rüttimann (Switzerland)
9. Alain Vigneron (France)
10. Guido Winterberg (Switzerland)

Of the 21 teams in the race, it's the most international in the peloton: five Frenchmen; three North Americans; two Swiss, with a Swiss directeur sportif in Paul Köchli and two French assistant directeurs sportifs, Maurice Le Guilloux and Michel Laurent.

Short prologue time trials are always tense, fraught affairs, the explosiveness of the effort serving as a metaphor for the nerves of the riders. This year there is an air of unpredictability; yet at the same time there is a sense that history beckons. Some favorites appear confident and assured; others seem edgy and uncertain. Greg LeMond falls squarely into the second category. Any symbolism attached to the fact that this year's Tour starts on American Independence Day is lost on him.

Other symbols seem more real and more ominous, including the number 1 on the back of LeMond's teammate, Bernard Hinault, and his yellow jersey. Both honors are bestowed on the defending champion, but the sight of Hinault preparing to start his favorite discipline, a time trial, with a single, decisive "1" pinned to his yellow jersey, hardly eases LeMond's anxiety. Neither do the headlines in the newspapers, all backing Hinault to win a record sixth Tour rather than LeMond to create his own piece of history, a first win for the "new world," for English-speaking cyclists.

As he has done virtually every day since the final day of the 1985 Tour, LeMond casts his mind back to the promise Hinault made the previous year. Then, as they stood together on the podium on the Champs-Elysées, having finished first and second, Hinault told LeMond a version of what he had told Jean-Paul Brouchon of *Miroir du Cyclisme* the previous day: "Next year, it's your turn."

It seemed unambiguous and should be reassuring. Yet LeMond cannot stop the doubts entering his mind and fluttering like butterflies in his stomach.

"Greg was as fragile as a racehorse," says François Thomazeau, a journalist covering his first Tour in 1986. "This was my impression. He had skinny legs, his upper body was very thin, and you always had the sense that he was on the verge of . . . of breaking. He was the same mentally. He was very talkative, very nice . . . I wouldn't say he was mad or crazy, but he was intense, nervous. Greg was this very special but very strange character, and very nervous. But it kept him going; his drug was adrenaline.

"It was so very different with Hinault, who was more like a bulldog," Thomazeau continues. "So on the one hand, you had this bulldog, and on the other, this birdlike character, very fragile, who you felt could break, even in the race itself, at any moment. He was always on the brink, on the cusp of something. Hinault is a solid guy who knows exactly what he's doing and why, a man with one idea at a time. Whereas with Greg you had the impression . . ." Thomazeau stops and thinks for a moment. "This is another reason why he was like a bird; he was always moving, always in motion, always looking for the next thing. He gives the impression he's being attacked from all sides. Even his face, it's very expressive. He has these lines, wrinkles, around his mouth, which are always moving and creasing."

But in Boulogne-Billancourt on the afternoon of July 4, it isn't just the menacing presence of Hinault that unsettles LeMond, and anyone else with designs on trying to win the Tour. There's a ghost from the past, too. After a year in the wilderness, the blond, bespectacled Laurent Fignon appears to have returned to his best, with a win in the Flèche Wallonne classic in the spring followed by a stage win at the Dauphiné Libéré, just a month before the Tour. Fignon's run of Tour wins had been halted at two with the Achilles injury he'd suffered in early 1985. Halted, or merely paused? In Boulogne-Billancourt, Fignon poses a genuine threat at the head of a new team, Système U, managed by the wily directeur sportif who has cannily guided him, as he also led Hinault and LeMond: Cyrille Guimard.

Yet the prologue seems to confirm that Hinault is indeed the man to beat. He doesn't win the opening test, as he did the previous year, but he is close. Hinault thunders around the tight course and finishes third, behind Fignon's teammate Thierry Marie, using a soon-to-be-banned aerodynamic fin behind his saddle, and the Belgian sprinter Eric Vanderaerden. Fignon is seventh, 4 seconds slower than Hinault. LeMond is a few fractions of a second behind Fignon.

In terms of time won and lost, these seconds and fractions of seconds are insignificant in the context of the next three weeks. But the prologue is revealing of form. It also establishes an early pecking order: Hinault, Fignon, LeMond.

If only, as they dined in the Granita restaurant in Islington, London, one evening in 1994, Tony Blair and Gordon Brown had picked up the telephone to reach a certain legendary directeur sportif of French cycling. Cyrille Guimard's wisdom might have altered the course of British politics. Instead the two men who both wanted to lead their party and become prime minister decided on a pact, shaking hands on a deal intended to give both what they wanted. And it did, to a point. But it also provided British politics with a compelling 16-year subplot of simmering tensions and poisonous feuding.

Guimard could have predicted as much. As the Frenchman animatedly put it in another context, "There is always incompatibility when you put two riders who can win the same race, the biggest race, in the same team! You cannot turn them into friends who'll go dancing together of a Saturday night! It's not possible. You cannot put two 10-point stags in the same herd of deer! One will kill the other!"

But Hinault did make a deal. As he told Jean-Paul Brouchon of *Miroir du Cyclisme* on the penultimate day of the 1985 Tour, "I'll stir things up to help Greg win, and I'll have fun doing it. That's a promise."

Let us look at this pledge afresh. Whether Hinault intended it or not, there is sublime ambiguity at play. Was he saying he would put himself at the service of LeMond or that, by "stirring things up," the likely—or possible—outcome would be a LeMond win? Was his priority victory for LeMond or fun for Hinault? What, in fact, was he saying?

As LeMond understood it, there was no ambiguity. He also remains absolutely clear about when the "deal" was first agreed. In fact, Hinault merely confirmed it on the podium on the Champs-Elysées because, according to LeMond, it had been settled five nights earlier, with Bernard Tapie and Hinault in attendance. The agreement, made in the team's hotel following stage 17 to Luz Ardiden, represented a "peace deal." It was intended to appease LeMond, furious at having been told to wait for Hinault earlier in the day after going clear with Stephen Roche on the Col du Tourmalet. As LeMond has said, "I was going to quit after that stage." But that night, in the hotel, "Tapie and Hinault both agreed that night that he'd work for me the next year." And so LeMond remained in the race.

Hinault's account is different. At his home in Brittany, Hinault tells me that the deal was struck not in Luz Ardiden or on the podium but when they went out in Paris, as a team, in the evening. "It was on the last night of the Tour," says Hinault, his gaze steady and firm. "I told him, 'Next year, it's you who'll win the Tour, and I'll be there to give you a hand.' I said it to Greg, and the press then found out."

But Maurice Le Guilloux, the La Vie Claire directeur sportif, who'd known Hinault during his entire career, has yet another version. "It was on the

Champs-Elysées," says Le Guilloux. "Bernard, in 1985, owed his victory to LeMond. Everybody agreed on that. And he told LeMond after the finish—they hugged, kissed—and he said, 'Next year, my last year, I'll help you to win your first Tour de France.' And LeMond said, 'Oh, thank you, thank you, Bernard.' Then we went out—LeMond, me, Bernard, and Mrs. Hinault."

Yet Hinault—as we know—had also told Brouchon 24 hours earlier of his intention to help LeMond. And he said as much—though, again, in slightly ambiguous terms—at his Tour winner's press conference in Paris, chaired by the distinguished author, journalist, and former war correspondent Jacques Chancel. Chancel's line of questioning was jocular and teasing, while Hinault appeared to be in (for him) a playful mood.

"Next year will be your sixth victory?" suggested Chancel.

"No, no, that's it," said Hinault.

"What do you mean?" asked Chancel. "As a six-time winner, you'd better Anquetil and Merckx. . . ."

"You need to share the experience you've gained," Hinault replied, smiling thinly. "Greg will need me next year."

"That's too easy," said Chancel, turning to face the audience of reporters. "That way, if he loses, he will have called it ahead of time."

Bernard Tapie, who'd been laughing at Chancel's teasing questions, now intervened. "That's not Hinault's style," said the team owner. "If he says at the start that it's Greg who will win, then that means Greg will be leader next year."

Chancel's reporter's antennae must have been twitching furiously. As an experienced war correspondent, he could surely sense the potential for conflict.

The route of the 1986 Tour had been unveiled in Paris in October 1985. On paper, it looked the toughest in years. It was certainly mountainous, with summit finishes at Superbagnères in the Pyrenees, the Col du Granon and Alpe d'Huez in the Alps, and finally the Puy de Dôme in the Massif Central. Hinault was unfazed. "It's a Tour like any other," he said with a shrug. "Of course it's hard, but which ones aren't?"

It would also mark the end of more than one era. It would be the final Tour for Félix Lévitan and his codirector, Jacques Goddet, as it would also be, of course, for the retiring Hinault. The most powerful triumvirate in French

cycling was therefore preparing for its final bow—even if only Hinault actually knew that, with Goddet and Lévitan discovering their fate in March 1987
when they arrived at their Paris office to find the locks changed.

A sixth sense—or the change in ownership of the Amaury group that
owned the Tour—perhaps alerted Lévitan to the imminence of his exit, for
he seemed determined that the 1986 race go with a bang. For him, it had to
serve up more drama and excitement than 1985, when, in his analysis, La
Vie Claire had proved too strong and the others too weak, in body, mind,
and spirit. At the announcement of the 1986 route, Lévitan didn't criticize
Hinault or La Vie Claire but instead blasted the other teams, their managers
and riders, for not taking risks and for their lack of aggression. "I refuse to
believe that one team, even if that of a star, can block a peloton for 20 days,"
said Lévitan.

"If I understand correctly," said Hinault, responding with irritation to
Lévitan's remarks, "he is saying that the rest are a lot of Charlies, and so I won
a race of Charlies. . . ."

In late November, in the Alpine town of Briançon, the 21-man La Vie Claire
squad, bolstered by the arrival of Andy Hampsten—now one of five North
Americans along with LeMond, Roy Knickman, Thurlow Rogers, and the Canadian Steve Bauer—convened for their first training camp ahead of the 1986
season. It was a strange kind of training camp, with not enough snow for skiing (as had been planned) but too much for cycling, leaving them to impro-
vise with Köchli-supervised running sessions, interspersed with discussion
of the season ahead.

As ever, one race loomed larger than any other in those discussions: the
Tour de France. Briançon was an appropriate place to discuss the 1986 race,
with the town set to host a key stage, stage 18, which would climb the nearby
Col du Galibier before eventually finishing at the summit of Alpe d'Huez.
There was every chance it would be a stage—perhaps *the* stage—that would
help decide the Tour.

Hampsten recalls Hinault being in a relaxed mood on the eve of his final season before his long-planned retirement, 11 months hence, on his 32nd
birthday. Hinault also seemed preoccupied by the Tour, and, as he looked
ahead, he sought to "gee up" his teammates, to inspire them with enthusiasm

about what they might achieve as the undisputed—as in fact they had recently been voted by cycling journalists—"best team in the world."

One big question, of course, was whether, for the first time, an American could win. Hinault seemed to think so. "Greg will have the yellow jersey here," Hampsten recalls Hinault telling them in Briançon. "I remember Hinault saying, 'This'll be great—Greg will have the yellow jersey, and Andy, you'll really help in the mountains,'" says Hampsten, who, on account of his slender frame and prominent front teeth, was nicknamed *"le petit lapin"* (the little rabbit) by Hinault.

"He was just being really encouraging," Hampsten continues. "Maybe I paid too much attention to some interviews he gave at the time, but I also remember him saying, 'Andy, the little rabbit, he'll fly up the climbs in July and help Greg win the Tour.'

"So, yeah, I thought that was the plan all along, to help Greg win. But then, I was hanging out with Greg most of the time. . . ."

For Hampsten, joining La Vie Claire was the fulfillment of a dream, and in Briançon, at that first get-together, he was almost pinching himself as he looked forward to riding alongside Hinault and LeMond. "I had given myself 1985 to make it as a pro or go do something else," he says. "But La Vie Claire was certainly the team, above all others, that I wanted to join.

"All my negotiations were with Köchli," continues Hampsten. "I think he's the most brilliant coach I've ever met, period. And he was very much the kind of coach I wanted to work with. Instead of being some kind of dictatorship, with some guy who raced 20 years ago telling everyone what to do and having a one-way discussion, Köchli really engaged all his riders in conversations."

Hampsten initially based himself in Switzerland, where Köchli was a neighbor. "That was on purpose," Hampsten says, "so I could travel with him and learn from him. I would also watch a lot of races on TV with him. We'd be watching Flèche Wallonne or something, and Köchli would tell me more in two minutes than I'd learn in months. I did think he was the kooky professor, but I really liked him."

In many respects, Köchli lived up to the caricature of the eccentric scientist or mad professor, though he objected strongly to this nickname. "They called me . . . the professor," Köchli says, spitting it out. "I didn't like that, of course. It was not meant in a complimentary way. I said to one journalist, after winning the Tour in 1985, 'That was practice rather than theory.' Because he treated me as a theorist."

Hampsten looked ahead to the 1986 season with the Tour de France as his main goal but was aware that he "had a lot to prove, especially on the number-one team in the world." Yet Köchli wasn't the only one who offered support and encouragement and with whom he quickly forged a good relationship. Hinault took Hampsten under his wing and showed the 23-year-old (who would turn 24 in April 1986) a side of his personality that he generally kept hidden from the media and opponents. "Hinault was supernice," Hampsten says warmly. "I don't think he could have been nicer as a teammate."

The only occasions when Hinault wasn't supernice, says Hampsten, was when the weather was bad and—a familiar gripe—he had to train. "Hinault was grouchy about training and racing in the rain," says Hampsten. "He really didn't like that.

"The team had me share a room with him at the winter training camp in Briançon," Hampsten continues, "and it was a little strange because I felt I should call him 'Mr. Hinault.' My French wasn't good. I'd studied it at school, but when I went to France, I couldn't really speak it in the group. But one-on-one was OK, so we could communicate."

I had heard stories about Hinault's nocturnal habits, which I was eager to check with Hampsten. One that Köchli mentioned was his apparent fondness for popular science magazines—one that surprised me, I must confess—which he would pore over late into the night. "Nobody wanted to share a room with Hinault because he stayed up reading so late, well past midnight," Köchli recalls.

"And after he finished an article, he would have to explain the theory to his roommate, sometimes even waking him up to tell him. If a rider had to share a room with him for a few days, he would come to me with black rings around his eyes and say, 'Please, Paul, can you move me?'" As Köchli explains, most riders wouldn't feel very comfortable asking the great Hinault to turn the light off, far less telling him to put a sock in it as, in the small hours, he began to regale them with tales of obscure scientific discoveries.

Guimard, asked about Hinault's sleeping habits, smiles knowingly. "When he wasn't sleeping, let's say he was . . . keeping watch," he says. "There are riders who go to bed early and get up early. With the Badger, it's not that he went to bed late. He went to bed at the same time as the others, but he'd read or watch TV. He was almost never asleep before midnight."

Hampsten can't recall being kept up late, though, as he says, "We rotated, so we never shared for too long. But also, I liked to read, too."

A more vivid memory of Hampsten's is Hinault's main obsession. "He was infatuated with farming," Hampsten remembers. "We had Niki Rüttimann, this wonderful kid from Switzerland, who was my age, and he was a farm kid. Niki grew up on a farm and still lived on a farm, and he'd always bailed Hinault out in the mountains, so Hinault adored him. But he would just ask Niki farm questions all night long. It was full-on. 'OK, what am I gonna do when such-and-such happens? What about when the calf doesn't come out of the womb?' All this kind of thing.

"Hinault was really passionate about things. He liked food, he liked wine, but he loved farming," continues Hampsten. "I was a professional for 12 years, and the other guys talk about bikes, cars, girls . . . I realized that early, and thought, Why even bother learning this language? I talked about this stuff when I was 14! But Hinault would really like a good conversation. It was often about his interests, but the important thing is that it wasn't just bikes, cars, and girls. He was an interesting guy."

Aside from conversations that revolved around farming, Hampsten was most struck, as he found his feet in Europe, by his leader's qualities as a teammate. They were, he says, considerable, and not what he expected. "Early in the year, we were riding the same program, doing weeklong stage races in Spain, and in one [the Vuelta Ciclista a la Comunidad Valenciana], Hinault took the lead. I thought, This is great; he's my captain, he's leading, I'll do what I can to help him. There was this crosswind section in the race, he was at the back, and I went to find him and started pulling him up. The wind was coming from the left, and as I pulled him up, I was staying very close to the guys who were riding in the right-hand gutter.

"He put his hand on my hip and gently but very firmly pushed me to the center of the road. He said something I didn't understand, but I obviously knew he didn't want to monkey around near the other riders. I got him pretty near the front, and then he jumped the rest of the way to the front.

"Later I humbly apologized, and he said, 'No, no, it was great, thank you so much.' I said, 'Well, really, whatever you can tell me, I just love racing on the team, you're the captain, please just tell me, show me what I can do.'

"And I think he could tell I was serious. He said, 'OK, in a situation like that, if I'm at the back picking my nose and you're going to take me to the front, the last thing I want to do is hang out with these other nose-pickers. I don't care if it's only for 20 meters—just get me away from those guys. If you can get me all the way to the front, that's brilliant. But I don't want to deal with those guys.'

"Later on, he had a flat tire on a mountain stage," Hampsten continues. "I was the only teammate around to help him, so I waited. And afterward we were bombing down this really sketchy descent, and I was waving him ahead of me because, despite going as fast as I possibly could, I wasn't catching the group, which I could see ahead.

"But, although I'm waving him through, Hinault doesn't come around me. Then we get to the bottom of the descent, and finally he draws level and just shakes his head and says, 'We'll get them now.' Later he said, 'Look, if you don't want to crash on some little road in Spain, I don't want to crash on some little road in Spain.'" Hampsten laughs. "He was Mr. Hinault; he was our captain, and we were all trying to help him. But he knew I was trying to do it right." With feeling, Hampsten adds, "And at the Tour of Switzerland, he repaid me in spades for the help I tried to give him in those early-season races."

The Tour of Switzerland, in early June, is one of the main pre–Tour de France stage races, where the favorites fine-tune their form and the teams finalize their rosters. Hampsten approached the weeklong Swiss race with trepidation. In the spring, he had been hampered by bronchitis and had "no big results, though I finished the tough races." Crucially, he didn't feel he had done enough yet to make the 10-man La Vie Claire team for the Tour de France.

Before the Tour of Switzerland, he rode another important pre-Tour stage race, the Dauphiné Libéré. There he suffered *la fringale*, or "the bonk"—the expressions used for running out of fuel and hitting the metaphorical wall—while in a break during a mountain stage before performing decently on another mountain stage. It was, Hampsten concluded, "OK, not brilliant." And, in his mind, it still wasn't enough to ensure him a place in the Tour.

Which meant that for Hampsten, it was Switzerland or bust. Yet, on the eve of the race, having been "very discouraged about my training, and the pressure of chasing selection for the Tour de France," the American felt himself relax. "I realized, I don't have to make the Tour de France. It's just something I want to do." The pressure vanished. And in this newly liberated frame of mind, Hampsten went out and won the prologue time trial, ahead of

Hinault, in second, and LeMond, seventh. "I kind of apologized to them for beating them," says the ever-humble Hampsten.

"But Hinault loves the fact I've won!" Hampsten continues, laughing. "It's his time to get fit for the Tour, and he becomes very determined to make sure I won the Tour of Switzerland.

"Next day, it's bucketing rain. There are four loops of a circuit—it's hard, not brutal. It's going to be a bunch sprint. I, of course, don't put on a rain jacket because I have the leader's jersey, and I don't want to cover it up because, you know, I'm trying to look cool.

"On the last lap, Hinault comes up to me, says, 'How's it going, Andy?' And I say, 'Well, to be honest, I feel really bad. I'm really cold.' It was hard at that point, with the big teams leading out their sprinters on these rollers [steady rises and falls]. Hinault says, 'No problem.' And he sat on the tops of his bars and took me into the center of the road while everyone else is fighting in the right-hand gutter in the rain and the spray coming off the road from the wheels in front. And I followed him, and on the flats and downhills he took me to the front, and on the little uphills he slid back with me, found me, took me out of trouble and straight back up to the front. It was the greatest armchair ride I ever had in my career, by the greatest rider I've ever ridden with."

With Hinault's help, Hampsten became the first American to win the Tour of Switzerland. The following week, Köchli gave him the news. He would be riding the 1986 Tour de France.

10

WHO IS BERNARD TAPIE?

He must take the initiative. As long as he doesn't,
he will not be a leader.

BERNARD TAPIE ON GREG LEMOND

reg LeMond finished third in the Tour of Switzerland, though he, too, encountered difficulties in the first half of a season in which there was suddenly a lot of pressure on him. Indeed, this was another aspect of the "deal"
with Hinault: It left LeMond no room to maneuver. This year, 1986, was the
year in which he had to deliver, to step up from contender to champion, from
pretender to king. No excuses.

LeMond's year got off to a very bad start, however, when, in February,
while he was training with Steve Bauer in California, a motorist drove past
blasting his horn angrily. LeMond and Bauer responded in kind, "waving
their fists," according to reports at the time—a description that is presumably accurate only in the sense that they used their hands to make their feelings known to the driver.

The driver was incensed; he hit his brakes hard, then reversed until Le-
Mond and Bauer were almost on his bumper before accelerating away.
LeMond and Bauer took a deep breath, cursed the driver afresh, and carried
on. But five miles farther down the road, they encountered the same vehicle,
its driver standing beside it. And as they got closer, they realized that he was

wielding a pistol. LeMond stopped. The driver fired the gun into the air just feet away from him.

What might have happened next is anyone's guess—LeMond is not one to back away from a confrontation, though the driver's gun should have ensured that he made an exception here—but the two were saved by a mystery truck, which appeared from nowhere and stopped, allowing LeMond and Bauer to jump in the back. The gun-wielding driver was later arrested but released on parole after being charged with firearm offenses.

The incident came in the midst of a bad winter in California, which disrupted LeMond's training. But when he returned to Europe, he rode strongly. Indeed, a casual glance at his résumé up to the Tour of Switzerland reveals that there was nothing wrong in terms of his fitness or form. He finished second in the Milan–San Remo classic, third in Paris-Nice, third in the Critérium International, and fourth overall in the three-week Giro d'Italia. In all the major races, he was there or thereabouts. But that was just the point: LeMond's record was peppered with high placings. Wins, other than a stage of the Giro, proved more elusive.

The Giro in particular was a disappointment. "Last year, all my efforts were aimed at helping Hinault," he told the Italian journalist Giuseppe Matarrese on the eve of the race. "This time I will be team leader, and I'm sure I can do better than third overall." LeMond added that in his previous attempt the year before, "In the first week of the race, I ate too much Italian food. I was overweight. I like Italian food, but I must control myself."

In the event, LeMond's fourth overall, behind an Italian clean sweep of the podium, was due in part to a heavy crash early on, but his performance fell below expectations. There was some redemption in his stage win, which came when he attacked in the final kilometer. "I wanted to win to reassure myself," he said. At the finish, he looked ahead to the Tour. "My team wasn't as strong as I'd have liked, but I'm looking forward to the Tour, when Bernard Hinault will be at my side again."

But a more sinister episode during that Giro upset LeMond. As he would later tell *Rolling Stone* magazine, an Italian rider on a rival team had requested La Vie Claire's assistance to help him win the Giro d'Italia. Such deals are made, but often on a quid pro quo basis—a stage win, for example, in exchange for help in the mountains. Here, however, LeMond claimed to have been offered $50,000 to put his team at the service of the Italian rider. When LeMond refused, he was alarmed by his teammates' reaction. "I was naïve about this side of the sport, but my teammates got pissed off that I'd rejected it," LeMond told *Rolling Stone*. "They sold themselves out. It was pretty poor of them. They're paid by my team, and they were there to work for me. But they'd given up. Their only responsibility [they felt] was to Hinault." And Hinault, of course, was absent from the Giro.

Another unsettling issue was LeMond's relationship with Köchli. It wasn't bad. But it wasn't perfect. It certainly wasn't as good as Köchli's with Hinault. In some respects, it's surprising that they didn't get on like a house afire since LeMond and Köchli appear to be, in many respects, well suited, both being preoccupied by training theory and early devotees of sports science. Indeed, so much a fan of Köchli's theories was LeMond that, later, he published a training book based on them.

Theory was one thing, however. Day-to-day relations were quite another, and their very different personalities and temperaments meant that LeMond and Köchli rubbed against each other. LeMond, often spontaneous and frequently giving the appearance of being chaotic and disorganized—because he frequently was chaotic and disorganized—naturally resisted Köchli's desire for organization, order, and discipline. The inevitable result was friction. Or, as Kathy LeMond puts it, a little more strongly, "We drove him crazy!"

"You can see from the way our house looks," she explains, "and the way we are; we're so casual. He couldn't cope with that. And Greg always cuts it to the last minute. Köchli would be at the airport, looking for Greg . . . thank God we didn't have cell phones then."

"Köchli was a good influence," LeMond chips in. "I actually like him. But we're opposites. He's Swiss, very programmed. But it affected his tactics."

And here LeMond, as he so often does, segues quickly into an anecdote that at first seems to veer off at a tangent to the discussion we've just been having, only to home back in on the point and to reveal something fundamental. In this case, LeMond's story sheds light on Köchli's intransigence, which, with someone as dizzily hyperactive as LeMond, must surely have been the most significant barrier to a flourishing professional relationship forming between the two.

"I remember one stage of the Giro in 1985," says LeMond, "and it's an example of his weakness and inflexibility. Racing's all about adapting to the moment. You can plan it in your mind, you can visualize it, but everything can change in the course of the race. Well, we had these Michelin maps with *flèches* [arrows] to indicate the steepness of a climb. And we're in Italy, looking at these Michelin maps, and according to the *flèches*, the climbs had 10 percent gradients. So we decide on this tactic, to blow the race apart on these steep climbs, and Hinault and Köchli are saying, 'This is what we're gonna do,' while I'm thinking, Guimard would never plan out a race like this.

"But we get to the first climb, and everyone from the team is there at the front, going as hard as we can, and I'm trying to be up there with Hinault. He's first, I'm third. But I'm thinking, The map doesn't match the course. It's supposed to be a 10 percent climb, but this is only 4 or 5 percent—it's not as steep as we thought. Moser and Saronni are sitting there behind us, just getting sucked along. You can't drop guys on a 4 percent climb. But Hinault's up there, giving it everything, sticking to the plan.

"So I go back and speak to Köchli, and I say, 'This isn't gonna work, Paul. I think we should wait until we have a harder hill.' And he says, 'No.'

"The maps in Italy were different to the ones we used in France," LeMond continues. "The number of *flèches* to indicate gradients was different. Our tactics weren't working—but they would never work. It was the wrong tactic. But there was no flexibility, and so we carried on, attacking these small climbs while Moser and Saronni just sat there.

"That was tough . . . it was arrogance, stupidity, in a way. It was this idea that we were so strong that all we needed was a fighting plan. But that's like having a military plan that assumes that you're not going to have any enemy when you invade a country. And then you get there and find 20 million people. . . ."

On the question of Köchli's tactics, Hinault contradicts LeMond. He notes his attention to detail but casts it in a more favorable light, and also suggests that Köchli was flexible (leading you to speculate that he might have been more flexible with Hinault than with LeMond. If, for instance, it had been Hinault who had dropped back to speak to Köchli during the 1985 Giro, might Köchli have been more inclined to change tactics?).

"Köchli gave you a lot of freedom," says Hinault. "He formulated a tactic in the morning, but in the race, you could try something different. You have to adapt according to what your opponents do. If they attack earlier than you expected, maybe you have to counter."

A big factor at the time was the absence of race radios. In the modern era, riders are in constant contact with their directeurs, who can issue instructions on the move—a development that unites Köchli, Hinault, and LeMond in their opposition, each feeling that it kills much of the spontaneity and unpredictability of racing. "We didn't have radios, so you had to study the map, think about wind directions and so on," says Hinault. "You work out a tactic, but then, in the race, it's you that has to react to the circumstances. You can't wait for someone to tell you, 'You have to go now because the others are two minutes down the road.' That's what I don't like about racing now. The riders wait for the directeur sportif to tell them when the race is going to light up. No! You have to watch your opponents, see if there's one of them at the back of the peloton and surprise him. If you can break it up, start an echelon . . . you can surprise your opponent: 'Shit, he got me!' The race is over."

Köchli says that, during his career as a directeur, he was offered early prototypes of two-way radios on numerous occasions. "I thought about it once, and I decided we will *never* use a radio," he says. "I wanted my riders to take responsibility. You must [as a rider] be an excellent tactician. Tactics is what happens *now*." He snaps his fingers to emphasize the point. "Immediately. It's nothing to do with strategy. A directeur should never, during the race, interfere with the riders on tactics. Anyway, by definition it's not possible. Tactics are what happen in the race." He snaps his fingers again. "Intuitively a rider must decide, which means taking responsibility."

It is the difference between the big picture and the detail. The strategy—such as the plan to attack Moser and Saronni on the (less steep than expected) climbs of the 1985 Giro—represents the big picture, while tactics—whether to follow an attack, for example—are the minutiae, the microdecisions that need to be made quickly in the heat of battle.

"The strategy," says Köchli, "is me, in the morning, saying, 'OK, guys'"—he claps his hands several times—"'today we defend,' or 'today we attack.'

"Because the Tour is a strategic war," he adds. "You cannot attack everywhere, and what it means to defend or to attack must be translated into the context. You must have a strategic plan."

Hinault, in his final season, appeared initially to be his usual self—as a 150-km lone break to win February's Luis Puig Trophy suggests—though in the spring, some doubts emerged as his old knee injury flared up. He was erratic, inconsistent, with hints of being slightly happy as the prospect loomed of retirement and fulfilling his dream of working on his farm. Paul Kimmage, the Irish ex-professional, recalls riding a four-day stage race with Hinault in Brittany on the eve of the Tour. Hinault "sat at the back of the bunch from the start and frowned whenever anyone came near him." Then he abandoned—on the first stage. In his book, *Rough Ride*, Kimmage writes, "Le Blaireau was a weird fellow; he frightened me. I was always afraid of crashing in front of him and bringing him down. Sometimes he would attack and the bunch would string out in a long line behind him. Then he would sit up and start laughing, mocking us."

If Hinault's knee problems suggested vulnerability in the Badger, then, coupled with LeMond's faltering efforts to step into Hinault's shoes, it might have been a mildly anxious period for Bernard Tapie, who gave an interview at the time to Sam Abt. "I'm not unhappy with Greg," Tapie told Abt before immediately going on to confirm otherwise by revealing exactly how disgruntled he was with his (almost) million-dollar man.

"He's among the five best in the world, but he is missing that little bit extra to make him number one," explained Tapie. "He has class, he has the will, the physical tools, the team, but he must take the initiative. As long as he doesn't, he will not be a leader. He has never been the boss, and he still doesn't realize that the boss is the one who says to his team in the morning, 'This evening, when the race is over, I'll be the winner.' That's what he's missing.

"Second, third, second, third—his record is full of those finishes," added Tapie. "Second place is the same as 25th place. There are 10 cyclists on a team, but only one can win. So for the others to accept him as a leader and be willing to fight for him, Greg must win."

And yet, just as there were questions about LeMond's ability to lead and about Hinault's knee and perhaps even his motivation in his final year, there might equally have been questions about Tapie's commitment to his La Vie Claire cycling team. On April 12, 1986, the entrepreneur deepened his involvement in sport, but in the process diluted his interest in cycling, by becoming president of the Olympique de Marseille soccer team.

It brought the 43-year-old to a bigger audience—which could explain his motivation, at least in part (again, Hinault says he has no recollection of Tapie being particularly interested in soccer, just as he hadn't been especially interested in cycling before establishing his own team). Tapie's move into soccer saw him take over the running of a sleeping, deeply troubled giant of the French game, whose most recent League 1 title had been claimed way back in 1972.

In many respects, Tapie's approach to sport mirrored his approach to business. His modus operandi was to take over failing enterprises, often for the token sum of one franc, and turn them around. They were businesses that had been given up on and written off, and you could say the same for his cycling and soccer interests. Hinault, around whom the La Vie Claire team was constructed, had been written off after his knee injury; he had been discarded by Cyrille Guimard and the Renault team and given a 50-50 chance, at best, of returning to his previous level. He was, in other words, the sporting equivalent of a failing enterprise.

But perhaps to an even greater extent than a failing business, an injured, aging athlete represents a huge risk. Backing Hinault in late 1983 was, therefore, a gamble. But Tapie, in the style of the new breed of 1980s entrepreneurs/moguls, enjoyed risk, and he loved to gamble. In a sense, he was in the mold of "charismatic CEO and businessman superstars" who possessed, as Michael Wolff's biography of Rupert Murdoch (to whom Tapie otherwise bears scant resemblance) puts it, "a particular eighties kind of temperament." Wolff defined this as "a high tolerance for uncertainty, the ability to keep numerous balls in the air, and a lack of any evident ambivalence." This sums up Tapie: tycoon, sports impresario, man of the people, politician, entertainer, and prisoner.

Olympique de Marseille, ensconced in the vast Stade Vélodrome, was viewed by many as a similar proposition to Hinault—damaged, even cursed goods. Tapie relished the challenge of trying to transform the team's fortunes. As with La Vie Claire, he threw money at it. A succession of star players arrived, and between 1989 and 1992, Marseille won four league titles in succession before, a year later, it became the first French team to win the European Champions League. Yet it was an achievement that led ultimately, in a parable of hubris, to Tapie's spectacular fall from grace, culminating in a two-year prison sentence for match-fixing in the run-up to Marseille's European triumph.

In 2001, a low-budget documentary film was made about Tapie: *Who Is Bernard Tapie?* It was American director Marina Zenovich's attempt to meet the man and come to grips with the legend who, by then, had earned notoriety for his spell in prison, which followed (and effectively ended) his time as a politician and cabinet minister and came in the midst of his reinvention as an actor. It was his role in Claude Lelouch's 1996 film *Hommes, Femmes, Mode d'Emploi* (Men, women: a user's manual) that brought Tapie to Zenovich's attention, and she subsequently spent two years trying to track him down to arrange an interview, staking out his Paris home and the theater in which he was performing (in *One Flew over the Cuckoo's Nest*) and pestering his personal assistant but ultimately failing to interview a man she describes as having "the charming good looks of Warren Beatty, the bravado of Donald Trump, the charisma of Bill Clinton," who "fell from grace like O. J. Simpson."

Among the choice quotes from those Zenovich interviews about Tapie are comments from Lelouch—"If he were American, he'd be president by now . . . or he'd be in the electric chair"—and Franz-Olivier Giesbert, editor-in-chief of *Le Figaro*, who contends, "He's very charismatic, very, very charismatic—it's incredible . . . men or women, people fall in love with Bernard Tapie. And he works it. He's developed a technique for this."

"Essentially," says Alan Riding of the *New York Times*, "he has been a performance artist all his life" (he did start out as a singer, in fact), while Lelouch also describes him as "a human being who has a heart of gold, who is very generous, but who can be lethal as well."

The stories that Tapie is shady, that his methods are underhand (if not illegal), and that he is a bit of a shark all emanate, claimed Tapie in a TV interview in the early 1990s, from "mundane dinners and business lunches" involving "mediocre people." "Mediocre people always feel the need to justify their mediocrity by putting other people down."

It was no wonder that Tapie was attracted to sport, and to decidedly unmundane and nonmediocre people like Hinault and LeMond. He seemed to like Hinault's very different, less showy brand of charisma and to be in awe—wasn't everybody?—of the sheer force of his will, his strength of character, his complete lack of ambivalence. If he admired LeMond, it was for his American attitude, even, albeit grudgingly, his and his father's hardball negotiating skills, which Tapie later claimed "added an extra zero to LeMond's contract."

But beyond their personalities, the raw test of strength and endurance presented by the Tour de France must also have appealed to Tapie, who is credited by one friend with having "colossal energy." And he may actually have fancied himself as being in possession of similar powers of endurance if a 1980s TV advertisement for one of his companies is anything to go by.

The ad was for Wonder batteries, and it ran regularly on French TV during the 1986 Tour. Not many owners of battery companies star in their own advertisements. But then, Tapie was no ordinary battery-company owner. The Wonder name was featured prominently down the side panel of the La

Vie Claire jerseys, and the commercial opens with the dashing Tapie, his glossy mane of dark hair bouncing gently (his resemblance here to James Brown is striking) as he strides through an office while pursued by a gaggle of flailing acolytes and assistants, all waving bits of paper in his direction, trying desperately to get his attention. "What keeps Bernard Tapie going?" is the question posed as Tapie continues his whirlwind progress through the office.

He then marches straight through a solid wall. "What keeps you going?" asks yet another fawning female assistant on the other side of the collapsed wall as Tapie marches on. "Me?" he says, "I run on Wonder," before opening a flap in his back to reveal two Wonder-brand batteries. When the assistant removes one, he topples over.

It is a production that displays Tapie's main strengths—showmanship, confidence, audacity, and irresistible charisma. Even more revealing, though, is another interview, which is also featured in *Who Is Bernard Tapie?*, in which Tapie is asked, "Have you ever cheated, lied, or broken the law in order to succeed in business?"

"In business, no," replies Tapie. "Everywhere else, yes. But not in business."

By early 1986, Tapie had a new favorite. Although Hinault and LeMond were the stars in his stable, a young Frenchman by the name of Jean-François Bernard became the apple of his eye as the Tour approached. The pale-skinned, dark-haired, rangy 24-year-old from Burgundy had been French amateur champion in 1983 before turning professional with La Vie Claire in late 1984. Now, though, Tapie saw him as the rider to succeed Hinault as the great French hero and future Tour de France winner.

Tapie's instinct certainly seemed sound. As the Tour loomed, the rider who would come to be known to the English-speaking world as "Jeff Bernard" was in the midst of a season that confirmed his promise and perhaps hinted at his destiny as a future Tour winner. Bernard began by claiming an early-season stage race, the Tour of the Mediterranean. He then won the prologue time trial and a stage of the Tour de Romandie and followed that with a stage at the Dauphiné Libéré, which sealed his place in the La Vie Claire team for the Tour. Tapie was so impressed that he made a promise: If Bernard won a stage of the Tour, Tapie would give him a Porsche.

Bernard wasn't the only talented young rider on the team, of course, and the parallels between Bernard and *le petit lapin*, Andy Hampsten, are glaringly obvious. Their interteam rivalry even mirrored, in many respects, LeMond's with Hinault, albeit with not so much at stake—at least not yet.

Both 24, Bernard and Hampsten were rising stage race stars. The boyish Hampsten was a rider in the mold of some of the great climbers, with his slender frame and his ability to suffer up the legendary passes of the Pyrenees and Alps in a rhythmic, fluid, almost balletic style that belied such suffering. Bernard, taller but also with a thin, fragile-looking frame, was more of a *rouleur* and all-rounder, though he could certainly climb. In fact, Hampsten and Bernard were almost uncannily similar—except only Bernard had been promised the Porsche.

Going into the Tour, then, La Vie Claire was an international blend, if "blend" is the right word. One of LeMond's greatest fears was of the team being divided along international lines.

Bernard, Hampsten, Niki Rüttimann, and Steve Bauer, who'd made such a strong Tour debut in 1985, finishing 10th overall, were the riders who were expected to be La Vie Claire's key men in the all-important mountain stages of the 1986 Tour. Of the other four riders—three French, one Swiss—Charly Bérard was a 26-year-old, seventh-year professional, a longtime teammate of Hinault, having ridden alongside him in the Renault team before switching, with Hinault, to La Vie Claire in 1984. Philippe Leleu, 28, was another Breton, from Lamballe, and another trusted lieutenant, having joined La Vie Claire from the Wolber team in 1984. He was also a useful rider, a Tour de France stage winner, into Dijon three years earlier. Alain Vigneron was similar to Bérard: The 31-year-old had joined Renault in 1981 and followed Hinault to La Vie Claire at the squad's inception.

While Jean-François Bernard would be a force in the high mountains, these riders were domestiques primarily for the flatter stages, where they'd be at the disposal of the team leader. Their job was to offer unquestioned and unstinting support and protection in the big peloton, fetching water bottles, food, and rain capes from the team car when needed; giving up a wheel in the event of a puncture; offering their own bike in the case of a crash. Bérard also had a decent record of high overall finishes in the Tour, and he could offer some support in the mountains.

As for the Swiss, Winterberg was 23 and a second-year professional with La Vie Claire who would remain in Köchli-managed teams for the duration of his eight-year career. Rüttimann was more talented, also 23, in his third year with La Vie Claire, and the winner, already in 1986, of Étoile de Bessèges, an important early-season stage race in southern France. He too would remain with Köchli throughout his career. It seems fair to assume that their loyalty going into the 1986 Tour was not to Hinault or to LeMond but to their Swiss mentor, Köchli.

Yet the big question for them, and indeed for the other riders of La Vie Claire, remained: Who would be leader? Hinault or LeMond? The question had even greater implications for the two potential leaders, of course. LeMond, having sacrificed his personal ambitions in 1985, now expected Hinault to do the same. That meant not attacking; it meant marking moves, not contributing to them unless it tactically made sense to do so. If Hinault found himself in a break with a favorite like Stephen Roche—as LeMond had on the Col du Tourmalet the previous year—he would not work with him.

In theory, the ultimate decision over who would lead the team would be made not by Hinault or by LeMond but by the directeur sportif, Paul Köchli. What, then, did Köchli make of Hinault's agreement to ride in support of Le-Mond? In fact, Köchli is vague on the very existence, and certainly the validity, of this deal. It is telling that he was not present in the hotel room in Luz Ardiden when, according to LeMond, it was brokered by Bernard Tapie.

"If Hinault said there was an agreement to help LeMond . . ." Köchli says, then pauses. "I don't know in what context he said that. For one year, all the papers repeated the story [that Hinault would help LeMond win the 1986 Tour]. But that doesn't mean we change our strategy. It goes against our strategy. It's exactly what we don't do." Indeed, as he made clear when he talked about the 1985 Tour, "we must win. And when I say 'we,' I don't mean Hinault, and I don't mean LeMond."

In other words, Köchli wanted to start the Tour with two potential leaders rather than one designated leader. He might even have fancied that his hand was stronger still; that Jean-François Bernard or Andy Hampsten could do what Fignon had done in 1983 and take the yellow jersey to Paris.

Still, Köchli must have been aware of the agreement by Hinault to assist LeMond and of the speculation over whether or not Hinault would honor his bargain. So how did he feel about it? When the question is put to him, Köchli pauses at length, then leans forward and clears his throat. "So," he says, clasping his hands, "tension? That is, in a race like the Tour, something that you cannot exclude. My speech at the beginning of every Tour was always and exclusively focused on that. And in 1986, it was very short and focused on that.

"For the guys who also come to the Tour for the first time, it was important to tell them that this is a different race and that we must be very, very careful that we do not build up aggression and tension within the team environment. For example, the Tour of Switzerland is an important race, but it's like a holiday by comparison with the Tour de France. You don't have ABC, NBC, hundreds of reporters. My speech at the beginning of the Tour was this: Let's face this intelligently. Problems will appear—of course they will appear. But we must be able to talk to each other in an intelligent way, to solve problems. Otherwise you create more.

"But I believe Greg was nervous," Köchli adds. "He was anxious before the Tour. Hinault was not. And in my opinion, of course Hinault wanted to win the Tour. It was not his goal to give the Tour to Greg. And there were the French people, who preferred things to be old-fashioned, who tried to persuade Hinault, 'You must win; you mustn't let an American win.'"

A nd so, on the eve of the 1986 Tour, as 210 riders gathered in Boulogne-Billancourt, the French media salivated at what lay in store: the most mountainous race in years; the return of Laurent Fignon; Le Blaireau going for his sixth Tour win on the eve of his retirement; and, in much smaller print, the possibility of a historic first victory for an English-speaking and non-European cyclist.

For most, it was a two-horse race, and a rerun of 1984. "Hinault-Fignon: Legend and Glory," read the front page of *Miroir du Cyclisme*, with the cover split in two: Hinault on one side, Fignon on the other. Jacques Anquetil, the five-time winner, agreed. Now 52 and looking to be in rude health, his full head of hair as immaculately coiffed as it had always been throughout his career (he was said to carry a comb in the pocket of his racing jersey), Anquetil was only 15 months from his death from stomach cancer. Anquetil told Channel 4, "The favorites are Fignon and Hinault. It's natural, because Fignon has won twice and Hinault five times, but there's also Millar, Zimmermann . . . Delgado. Five or six riders could win if Fignon and Hinault cancel each other out or falter in the mountain stages." Not a mention of LeMond.

"On his way to a sixth victory?" That was the question posed by *Cyclisme Internationale* on a front page devoted to Hinault. Such confidence in the five-time winner extended to the very top of French society. President

François Mitterrand, who on January 21, 1986, had awarded Hinault the Legion of Honor, telephoned Le Blaireau on the eve of the Tour to tell him, "Ride your own race."

L'Équipe also backed Hinault unequivocally. On the morning of Friday, July 4, the day the Tour started in Boulogne-Billancourt (yes, on a Friday, not a Saturday, as is the custom today), the front page declared, "Hinault for the Tour record."

The *L'Équipe* headline, in commanding block capitals, squeezed tennis stars Boris Becker and Henri Leconte into a section at the top and French Formula 1 champion Alain Prost into a small corner at the bottom alongside the other Tour story on the front page, about Fignon. The main picture, meanwhile, showed Hinault, stripped to the waist, receiving the traditional pre-Tour medical examination. For some reason, and despite his compromised pose, it is a picture that conveys a clear message: ready for business.

L'Équipe's front page made passing mention of Hinault's "deal" with LeMond, but the paper seemed in little doubt that the Badger would be trying to win. "Hinault attacks the record of victories held by Jacques Anquetil and Eddy Merckx in this Tour (his last), despite affirming that he will ride for LeMond," it read. "On a hilly course, the Breton will be exposed to many dangers, as well as the ambitions of Fignon, Herrera and others. . . ."

Buried inside, on page five, another story appeared beneath the headline "Hinault: 'All for Greg.'" As so often with such headlines, it is a little misleading since "all for Greg" doesn't appear to be exactly what Hinault says, nor what he actually means. He says he is prepared to "play the LeMond card" but goes on to observe that, as a team, La Vie Claire has "many strings to our bow." Ultimately, Hinault stresses, it is not Bernard Hinault but the race that will decide. "The strongest rider will win," he says.

Hinault, ordinarily so certain, so lacking in ambivalence, was now guilty of serial ambiguity.

There are several ways to read his comments. Had he decided to start the race with an open mind and genuinely let the race decide? Or did he intend to keep his promise to LeMond but ease the pressure on his American teammate by playing down his chances? Did he feel pressure himself—was he influenced by the weight of expectation, especially in France, and did that prompt him to think, "The hell with the deal with LeMond—I'm going for number six"?

Now, Hinault says merely that his mood ahead of the Tour was one of confidence. "I think the whole team felt supergood. In our minds, we couldn't lose the Tour. Everyone was motivated and confident." He shrugs off the suggestion that he might have been beginning to feel some pangs of nostalgia, even sadness that his career was almost at an end. Indeed, he acts as though the idea didn't even occur to him. "Not at all. I knew that the day I stopped, I'd still be with Look, as part of a five-year contract I'd signed, and with the Société du Tour de France, and I'd be busy on the farm I'd bought. For me, one page in my life was turning, and I was starting something new. A new page in my life. The feeling wasn't one of regret. Not at all.

"It was never in my head, to beat records," continues Hinault with the penetrating, defiant gaze that dares you to challenge him and at the same time ensures that you don't. "I didn't race to break records; I raced to have fun. Whether it's five, six, or seven [Tour victories], it doesn't make any difference. If you're not having fun, there's no point."

But according to François Thomazeau, working for Reuters at the 1986 Tour, everything with Hinault stemmed from his natural aggression and innate desire to win. Thomazeau is among many—LeMond included—who laugh at Hinault's assertion that he "just wanted to have fun" in his final Tour.

"To those who knew Hinault, who'd seen him win his five Tours, it was inconceivable that a guy like that would be satisfied being a domestique," says Thomazeau, shaking his head. "It was not in his nature."

Yet that was the sporting pact he had made with LeMond. In fact, Köchli rejects the suggestion that any of his riders were mere domestiques—"We did not recognize the word 'domestique,'" he says. But LeMond thought differently. He expected Hinault to sacrifice his personal ambitions, as LeMond felt he had done in 1985.

Maurice Le Guilloux, the La Vie Claire assistant directeur, thinks that other pressures began to tell on Hinault, especially in the weeks leading up to his final Tour. It is perhaps difficult to imagine Hinault being swayed by the media, but Le Guilloux believes that all the headlines anticipating a sixth victory had an insidious, cumulative effect. "The French press couldn't imagine, and didn't want to believe, that Bernard Hinault would be the loyal teammate of an American," says Le Guilloux. "They didn't want to see a French team, led by a French legend, supporting an American rider. Bernard was pushed by France; he was pushed by the press; he was pushed by everyone. And there was strong anti-American feeling." Le Guilloux shakes his head; he seems anguished. "It was incredible."

Then there was the French president phoning Hinault, urging him to "ride his own race." "For Bernard, it was about pride as well," Le Guilloux continues. "But he wasn't insensitive to [the media pressure]. And so, even before the Tour, I think he is starting to feel really strong pressure to win his sixth Tour. Everyone is talking about it, even the Tour organizers, saying, 'You'll be the first rider ever to win six Tours.'

"Everyone," adds Le Guilloux, "was talking him into it."

⬆ Bernard Hinault in his La Vie Claire jersey in 1985, showing off his four Tour de France yellow jerseys and eyeing a fifth with his new team.

⬇ A young Greg LeMond speaks to his directeur sportif, Cyrille Guimard, during the 1982 Tour de l'Avenir, which LeMond dominated for his first major victory in Europe. It was LeMond's second professional season.

⬆ Innocents abroad: LeMond, in the yellow jersey, talks to fellow Americans Andy Hampsten (center) and Alexi Grewal (left) at the 1982 Tour de l'Avenir. Grewal would go on to win the 1984 Olympic road race and would later tell Hinault during the 1986 Tour, "You blew it, Bernie."

⬅ The kooky professor: Paul Köchli, directeur sportif for La Vie Claire, issues his instructions from the team car during the 1984 Tour de France.

LeMond fulfills his domestique duties, shepherding his team leader, Hinault, on stage 20 to Limoges, just 48 hours before Hinault claimed his fifth Tour victory in 1985.

"Next year, it's you who'll be in yellow," Hinault reassures LeMond at the 1985 Tour.

LeMond, Hinault, and Sean Kelly sit on the podium in Paris, awaiting the final presentation of the 1985 Tour. Hinault's black eyes, the legacy of his crash in Saint-Étienne, are still visible.

Hinault leads Pedro Delgado of Spain during his surprise attack on the first Pyrenean stage of the 1986 Tour.

⬆ The big guns of the 1986 Tour, from left to right: Robert Millar, Greg LeMond, Thierry Claveyrolat, Andy Hampsten (behind, in La Vie Claire jersey), Bernard Hinault, Urs Zimmermann (in red), and Luis Herrera.

⬇ LeMond shadowing Urs Zimmermann on stage 17 to Bourg-lès-Valence. While Hinault struggled with injury, LeMond rode into yellow on this stage, becoming the first American rider to lead the Tour de France.

LeMond with his family—mother Bertha, father Bob, and wife Kathy—on the Tour's rest day at Alpe d'Huez.

LeMond and his wife, Kathy, celebrating LeMond's capture of the yellow jersey, which he'd claimed from Hinault earlier that day at the summit of Bourg-lès-Valence.

Andy Hampsten, one of the revelations of the 1986 Tour, on his way to fourth overall in Paris. He left La Vie Claire the following season to join the American team 7-Eleven, reasoning that he "didn't want to hang around for round two, the Jean-François Bernard show."

↑ Le Flambeur (the high roller): Bernard Tapie with his two stars, Hinault and LeMond, at Alpe d'Huez on the rest day of the 1986 Tour. Twenty-four hours earlier, Tapie had claimed, "They were at each other's throats until 4 a.m."

↑ The champagne's on Tapie: a bottle each for LeMond and Hinault as they put the bitterness behind them and toast Tour success.

↑ LeMond gives Hinault a helping hand as the two teammates destroy the opposition on the road to Alpe d'Huez and their showdown on the mountain. Hinault had struggled with a leg injury on the previous stage and asked LeMond to slow down on one climb earlier in the stage, though he maintains he was as strong as LeMond on the Alpe.

↑ You can't teach an old Badger new tricks: Hinault deals with a podium protester at the 2009 Tour.

↓ Old "friends" reunited: Hinault and LeMond meet in Brittany at the 2008 Tour de France, during one of LeMond's rare appearances at the race in recent years.

11

THE AMERICAN INVASION

We love our Bernard Hinault, a pure champion: a rascal, rabble-rousing,
proud cyclist, capable of upsetting, of taking the initiative in the most
unusual way, and of producing a miracle.

JACQUES GODDET

NANTERRE, SATURDAY, JULY 5

Twenty-four hours after the prologue time trial, the riders of the Tour de France face two stages. They remain within an easy pedal of Paris. As if French national fervor hasn't been whipped up enough by the expected battle between Bernard Hinault and Laurent Fignon, the opening days of the Tour also serve to promote Paris's bid for the 1992 Olympic Games.

The first of the two stages should be routine; it's an 85-km road stage from Nanterre to Sceaux. But it is followed in the afternoon by the first significant test: a team time trial, over 56 km, from Meudon to Saint Quentin.

As expected, in the morning, the Hinault-Fignon-LeMond showdown takes a backseat. And yet the story is compelling. A debutant team, 7-Eleven of America, claim the lead through its Canadian, Alex Stieda. Stieda thus provides the 1986 Tour with its first major deviation from the anticipated script: the first North American ever to wear the yellow jersey—and it isn't LeMond.

Only an American team, and one determined to be different—from Andy Hampsten's claim that 7-Eleven, with whom he had ridden at the 1985 Giro, "had more fun" than other teams to its groundbreaking employment of a female soigneur, Shelley Verses, to the presence of an embedded journalist, Don Alexander, who would later write a book titled, with characteristic understatement, *The American Invasion*—only that kind of team could have had the immediate impact of 7-Eleven.

There was, admittedly, nothing understated about its debut. Yet it seemed symbolic that it was listed in the official Tour literature as the 21st and final team and allocated the lowliest of numbers, 201–210. The 7-Eleven riders were seen as arrivistes, upstarts. Jim Ochowicz, the directeur sportif, claims that when they arrived in Boulogne-Billancourt with their eight American riders, as well as one Canadian and one Mexican, they had no idea what to expect. Nevertheless, they set their goals as a stage win and a rider in the top 20 overall. "We were guessing," says Ochowicz. "We were pioneering; we had no counsel; we were exploring and testing and trying to find our way."

Ochowicz had begun the process of gaining entry to the Tour—so much more complicated than merely paying the $35,000 entry fee, which provided each team with hotel rooms for the three weeks as well as two Peugeot team cars and one station wagon—12 months earlier, after the 1985 Giro.

"I went to speak to one of our sponsors, [Italian company] Hoonved, and asked them, through their connections, for an introduction to Félix Lévitan," says Ochowicz. "I went to the 1985 Tour and met with Lévitan for about 15 minutes. I told him what we wanted to do, and he said, 'Uh, OK. We'll see. Maybe.' It wasn't encouraging, but I stayed on top of it for the next 9, 10 months."

Ochowicz, known universally as "Och" (rhymes with "coach") and someone who would go on to be arguably as significant a figure in the growth of the sport in America as anyone, refutes the suggestion that the Tour was desperate to have an American team—a natural assumption given LeMond's emergence as an overall contender and also Lévitan's doomed efforts to establish a Tour of America. To the question of whether the Tour de France appeared keen for an American team, Ochowicz shrugs. "Well, yes and no. American TV was covering it, and I think they thought it might be an advantage to have an American team, but they had never been approached by anyone other than me before. There wasn't great enthusiasm, in fact. It took a lot of work, and constant contact."

As to whether he found Lévitan "approachable," Ochowicz laughs. "He was . . . not approachable, no. But my persistence, the support of our sponsor, and, I think, the performance the team was starting to demonstrate all made the case for us pretty compelling. We eventually got the invitation in June, just before the start. But hell, we were right out of the blocks at that '86 Tour."

Stieda had been the very first of the 210 riders down the start ramp in the prologue, but he set a fast time, one that stood as the fastest for over an hour. He eventually placed 21st, just 12 seconds behind Thierry Marie. It was a good result, and one that was to prove significant within 24 hours.

Saturday's first stage got off to a bizarre start when, in the early kilometers, through the Paris suburbs, a skydiver narrowly avoided landing in the peloton. He landed instead on a motorcycle-mounted gendarme, forcing the race to stop. When it restarted, Stieda was one of the first attackers, the blond Canadian jumping away on his own and gobbling up the bonus seconds available in Levallois-Perret. After that he pressed on, stretching his lead to more than a minute and picking up more bonuses, accumulating 36 seconds in total before being joined by five other riders after 68 km, 17 km from the finish.

As Belgian rider Pol Verschuere won the sprint to decide the stage, Stieda's fifth place was enough for him to claim the overall lead from Marie, and the yellow jersey. With just 89.6 km of the 4,094 km raced, Stieda's leap into the jersey single-handedly subverted his team's outsider status. On only the Tour's second day, it made 7-Eleven's debut Tour—almost regardless of what lay in store over the next three weeks—a remarkable success. Even stranger, or more wonderful, depending on how you looked at it, Stieda—laid-back, good-humored, face-paint-wearing, harmonica-playing, bleached blond; the antithesis of the stereotypical European professional cyclist, in other words—was supposed to be there as a domestique.

Saturday afternoon's stage is a 56-km team time trial, an event La Vie Claire dominated in 1985, winning by over a minute. But now, in 1986 on the road from Meudon to Saint Quentin, something very, very odd happens.

It's the La Vie Claire nightmare, the reemergence of the ghost. In fact, it's the triumphant return to center stage of Laurent Fignon. Fignon's—and, of course, Guimard's—Système U squad doesn't just win the team time trial, and doesn't just beat Hinault, LeMond, and La Vie Claire. It hammers them by 2 minutes. Two minutes! In doing so it sends out a message as resounding as any, while La Vie Claire—the team who "in our minds couldn't be beaten"—well, what on earth happens?

One oddity is the difference in approach and appearance of the two teams—the Système U cyclists are all riding the in-vogue low-profile bikes, with upturned "cowhorn" handlebars, and using disc wheels. They look slick, compact, efficient. The La Vie Claire riders look like throwbacks, riding standard road machines, their only concession to aerodynamics their teardrop-shaped helmets. Système U looks fast. La Vie Claire—which had been the first team to use the low-profile bikes in individual time trials and the first to use Tapie's beloved clipless Look pedals—doesn't.

Such impressions aside, there are two versions of what happens to La Vie Claire. One—Hinault's—is that Hinault does a masterful job of keeping the team together, looking after Niki Rüttimann, who was still recovering from a crash at the Tour of Switzerland, and Guido Winterberg, who had crashed in the morning stage and ensuring they finish as a complete team. The other version—LeMond's—is that it is Hinault, not the Swiss pair, who struggles.

In this event a year earlier, Hinault's role as captain had been instrumental, says Steve Bauer. On that occasion, he'd held back the stronger members of the squad—principally Bauer and LeMond—encouraging them to keep the team together as one efficient unit, especially in the early stages, and to pace their effort. On that occasion he got it spot-on, reckons Bauer. And he is at it again, calling the shots, upbraiding those—Bauer and LeMond again—who want to go harder, faster. But there is a significant difference. In 1985, they were on their way to winning by over a minute; here, they are conceding 2 to Fignon's team.

Tapie was devastated. "He thought the team time trial would bring glory for us," says Köchli. "I told him, 'Calm down. The Tour is not over on the second day.'"

"I reflect back on 1985, thinking how well Hinault gauged the team's efforts on the uphills," says Bauer. "I almost felt like we were holding back too much, but it really helped the team stick together for the final 25, 30 kilometers, when we were really ripping . . . his tactic really paid off there, that's for sure. But in 1986 . . ." Bauer leaves the sentence unfinished, but the implication is clear: Hinault got it wrong.

In his second autobiography, *Hinault by Hinault*, published in 2005, Hinault admits of the stage that "I am not at my best" but adds, "We want to finish as a complete team, so I decide to slow the team when the Swiss riders Rüttimann and Winterberg are weaker. LeMond is unhappy, but we need to react quickly while riding, and I'm the boss."

"Hinault was holding back?" asks LeMond, incredulous, when I read this passage to him. "He was holding back?" he adds, his eyes almost popping out.

Well, I explain, he doesn't exactly say that he was holding back—but he does imply that he could have gone harder; that it was the two Swiss who were struggling and at risk of elimination if they were dropped (as 12 riders from other teams were).

"He was getting dropped," LeMond explains. "He was gasping; he was screaming at me because he couldn't keep up. Oh, no, no. Who'd he blame? Steve Bauer and I did about 60 percent of the work. I mean, it's OK," adds LeMond more calmly. "It was one day—you can have an off day. But that was the first time I ever saw Hinault in trouble in a team time trial. . . ."

It was, in contrast, a very good day for Fignon and Système U, whose riders now filled the top seven places. And a bad one for 7-Eleven, which, suffering four punctures and a crash, finished 20th, more than 6 minutes down—meaning Stieda's spell in yellow lasted only a few hours. But at least 7-Eleven was still ahead of Café de Colombia, which saw four riders eliminated. It was nothing short of a disaster for the team and for its leader, Luis Herrera, whose chances of winning the Tour were now virtually nil.

Stephen Roche's Carrera team rode strongly into second, elevating not only Roche but the Italian squad's dark horse, Urs Zimmermann. The tall, gangly Swiss—who seemed to have managed in the previous 12 months to shed even more weight from his lean frame—was poised for a challenge in his favored mountains.

Phil Anderson, of the third-placed Panasonic team, meanwhile, had an interesting and intriguing take on what the result of the team time trial meant for his friend LeMond and for La Vie Claire. "Hinault could still win this race, and he could win it without LeMond," said Anderson. "But LeMond cannot win without Hinault."

After an opening weekend in and around Paris, the Tour proceeded north through the Somme, then west into Normandy before it was due to head south and circle France in a counterclockwise direction, traversing the Pyrenees, then the Alps. The stages in the opening week were notable mainly for their unnoteworthiness. And yet it is interesting, from today's vantage point, to record how many of that opening week's stages were won by plucky break-aways and how few—none, in fact—were decided by bunch sprints.

Indeed, it is yet another reason why the 1986 Tour might be considered pivotal, in this case marking the end of an era. The following year, 1987, saw the emergence of the Dutch sprinter Jean-Paul van Poppel, who won two stages (and four in 1988) thanks, increasingly, to the highly disciplined and organized lead-out work of his Superconfex team, which began to perfect the art of reeling in breakaways and setting up sprint finishes. In doing so, Super-confex prefigured some of the modern teams—Mario Cipollini's well-drilled squads of the late 1990s and early 2000s; Mark Cavendish's HTC-Columbia team from 2008 onward—which commit so fully to their sprinter and seem able to time their pursuit of the day's escapees to perfection, invariably catch-ing them in, or close to, the final kilometer. But whereas for Superconfex and others this was an art form, nowadays it is more of a science, with race ra-dios, which allow directeurs sportifs to keep their riders constantly updated on time gaps, removing the need for guesswork and instinct. As far as many observers are concerned—including Hinault, LeMond, and Köchli—the sport is poorer for that.

Twenty-four hours after the calamitous team time trial, Davis Phinney, for whom the Tour was his first professional race in Europe, added another glorious chapter to what was rapidly becoming an extraordinary 7-Eleven story, winning a rainy stage 3 into Lievin, close to Lille, from a break of six that had clipped off the front of the peloton. Phinney's win went down well in this part of France, according to the team's embedded chronicler, Don Alexander. "The inhabitants of the North Country have not forgotten the 'Liberators' of World War II," Alexander would later write in *The American Invasion*. "While they would probably prefer to see a French victory [prob-ably?] in the Tour de France, to have an American win a stage in their re-gion was a special treat. As Phinney accepted his trophy, the crowd chanted 'American! American!'"

These early stages, after the skirmishes of the prologue and team time trial, resemble the early laps of a world championship road race. They al-low the leaders to find their legs, to ease themselves in, and the lesser lights to shine—after Phinney, Spain's Pello Ruiz Cabestany takes stage 4, and the Panasonic rider Johan Van Der Velde wins stage 5, taking over the yellow jersey.

CHERBOURG, WEDNESDAY, JULY 9

Next day, stage 6, to Cherbourg, witnesses a surprise attack by a favorite. The only nonsurprise, perhaps, is the identity of the perpetrator, especially given the region to which the Tour is heading: Brittany. Bernard Hinault goes for the intermediate sprint at Saint-Manvieu-en-Morray after 50 km, placing second. And then, rather than sitting up and drifting back to the peloton, he continues his effort. Stephen Roche jumps after Hinault along with 10 others, including 4 from Roche's Carrera team, and by 58 km the leading dozen have 1 minute 30 seconds on the peloton.

The cat has been put among the pigeons—or the badger set loose in the henhouse. Still, given the relatively easy terrain and the lack of crosswinds, the mood in the peloton is one of slight unrest rather than out-and-out alarm. Fignon's Système U team chases; then Fignon himself joins a counterattack. He is joined by nine riders, including his teammate Charly Mottet; Hinault's right-hand man, Jean-François Bernard; and LeMond. As Fignon's group begin to chase, closing the gap to 22 seconds, Hinault's group responds, the Badger driving it on, keeping up the pressure, maintaining the gap. It's thrilling stuff, but the peloton gets its act together, a coalition of Spanish teams hunting down Fignon's group, catching it after 117 km of the 200-km stage and hauling in Hinault and company 3 km later. Eventually the Italian sprinter Guido Bontempi wins the stage. But the significant act of the day is Hinault's aggression.

In his second autobiography, Hinault explains the motivation behind his attack on the road to Cherbourg. "The Tour had fallen into a lethargy, [so] I restored its color" is the self-effacing Badger's take. Jacques Goddet, the Tour director, was similarly impressed, writing the next day in his column in *L'Équipe*, "We love our Bernard Hinault, a pure champion: a rascal, rabble-rousing, proud cyclist, capable of upsetting, of taking the initiative in the most unusual way, and of producing a miracle."

NANTES, SATURDAY, JULY 12

Hinault's attack on the road to Cherbourg only serves to make Greg LeMond even more uncertain and edgy. They have barely left the blocks, but already the pledge that Hinault made to help the American seems as believable as Santa Claus. A new reality is dawning on LeMond: He is on his own in this Tour. He also begins to suspect that Hinault has reached a fresh agreement, made a new deal—with himself.

But it hinges, thinks LeMond, on the outcome of stage 9, the first individual time trial, a week into the race, on Saturday, July 12. The time trial is in Nantes, where Guimard lived, and where the LeMonds lived when they first arrived in Europe. At 61.5 km, it is long, the kind of test Hinault excels at and in which he is so confident that he can apparently enter a state of extreme relaxation in the hours before, sleeping, waking, and then pulverizing the opposition.

"I detected a change in Hinault as the Tour got nearer," says LeMond now, "and then, about two weeks before it started, he didn't actually say it, but his attitude seemed to be 'We'll see after the first time trial. We'll let that decide who's leading the team.' The way he was talking, it all seemed to be about that time trial.

"Which was not," LeMond laughs nervously, "the deal we cut."

On the day of the time trial, Hinault, in his dark glasses, white aero helmet ("Hinault B" in small black letters directly above his brow), and distinctive blue Patrick shoes (which were uniquely Hinault; nobody else wore them) rides the entire time trial with his jaw clenched aggressively and his legs churning a huge gear. He exudes power. No *souplesse*, just brute strength. Even when the road rises, rather than searching for the lever to find an easier gear, he seems simply to clench his jaw even tighter and push harder. Like a bull preparing to charge, he drops his shoulders as he rises from the saddle, heaving his way up the small inclines.

As the wind rises for the later starters, Hinault, resembling a vision of the future on his low-profile time trial bike with double disc wheels, cuts through it like a blade—or a cleaver being wielded by a butcher with arms like Popeye's. LeMond, whose style is more punchy, more—mirroring his personality—erratic as he stands up on the pedals, sits back down, stands up again, sits down again, starts the time trial two places and 4 minutes in front of Hinault. And at the first check, he sets the fastest time at 24 minutes, 2 seconds.

But here, ominously soon after LeMond has passed, comes Hinault—he is 20 seconds up on LeMond already. LeMond endures bad luck; in the course of the 61 km, he punctures and needs a bike change after breaking a wheel. It costs him "at least 30 seconds but probably closer to a minute," LeMond recalls now. At the finish, LeMond is nevertheless the fastest so far, with 1:19:30. Behind him is the charging bull, Hinault, and behind Hinault, owing to his higher overall position, is Laurent Fignon.

When Hinault flashes across the line, the clock above the finish stops at 1:18:46—44 seconds faster than LeMond.

Hinault wheels across the line, taking deep gulps of air, then turns his attention to the performance of the man still on the course and considered his main rival: Fignon. Hinault is wiped down by his soigneur and given a tracksuit top, and within a couple of minutes of finishing his ride, he takes his seat in the stand, a TV monitor in front of him. He dons a chunky set of headphones and, leaning forward, rests his chin on his crossed arms. Then he stares at the screen. He wears Ray-Ban aviator sunglasses, which help disguise his expression. In fact, Hinault remains expressionless, impassive, even as Fignon appears, weaving in ungainly fashion toward the finish, a pale imitation of the rider of two years ago, whose superiority over Hinault was so absolute that he could play with him, torment him, and laugh at him. Today Fignon's time, when the clock stops, is good enough only for 32nd, 3 minutes 42 seconds slower than Hinault. But, as he registers his rival's disastrous performance, Hinault's expression doesn't change; he calmly sits up, removes his headphones, and makes his way to the podium. There he is acclaimed as the stage winner, but not the overall leader. The Dane Jørgen Pedersen, who has held the yellow jersey since Cherbourg, hangs on to it—just.

The time trial reshuffles the pecking order. It now reads Hinault, LeMond, Fignon. But with the time he has lost, Fignon is a distant third; he could be out of it altogether.

Given that LeMond has become aware of the significance Hinault attached to the time trial, he is disheartened. "I had a puncture and I broke a wheel," says LeMond now of the time trial, "so I lost the time trial by 44 seconds, which I would not have lost had those two things not happened. But in Hinault's mind . . . I mean, I would have said to his face, 'You wouldn't have beaten me if I hadn't had the flat and broken the wheel; I would have won the time trial.' But it didn't matter to him. To him all that mattered was 'I won the time trial.'"

And it confirmed LeMond's suspicion that, in Hinault's mind, the time trial had decided who should be the team's designated leader. "But he made that rule himself!" protests LeMond. "I didn't agree to anything. I didn't race like that. He, in his mind, was the leader. But in my mind . . . I was clear that—"

Kathy LeMond finishes her husband's sentence. "The whole winter, the whole spring, Hinault had been clear. He said he'd support Greg." Kathy witnessed the first time trial, arriving in Nantes with baby son Geoffrey and a special treat for her husband—his favorite Mexican food. And so after the time trial, in their hotel in Nantes, LeMond and Andy Hampsten evict the chef and take over the kitchen, LeMond laying out the tortillas while Hampsten crushes avocados for guacamole. The chef is curious and asks them what they're making. "Burritos, tortilla, refritos!" LeMond tells him.

Hampsten is a more than willing accomplice. On his first Tour, he's already disillusioned with the way the riders are treated. "The beds are cots in a school classroom," he complains to one reporter. And the food is no better. "We do 125 miles balls out, I come back and can hardly see straight, and they give me terrible, overcooked pasta."

The chef isn't the only one who's curious—their French teammates are fascinated, too. "Greg had a different mentality," Jean-François Bernard remembers with a smile. "A different way of doing things. A bon vivant! He could go and eat Mexican food in the evening, even if the next day he had diarrhea, just because he felt like he wanted to eat Mexican.

"I liked that!" adds Bernard, who is himself something of a bon vivant these days.

As for the other Americans, who had done so much to animate the first week of the Tour, providing the race with another compelling subplot, the riders of 7-Eleven also seek out home comforts in Nantes. In their case, it's beneath the familiar golden arches; for the first time since Paris, they discover a McDonald's, though it's unclear whether there is any link with their inability to sustain their early form. Week one was as good as it got for 7-Eleven. But with a stage win for Davis Phinney and half a day in the yellow jersey for Alex Stieda, Jim Ochowicz is not complaining.

FUTUROSCOPE, SUNDAY, JULY 13

Paul Kimmage, the Irish professional with the French RMO team, was riding his first Tour, and riding high. Two days before the time trial, he made it into the day's main break, with his breakaway companions including a promising young Spaniard, Miguel Indurain. Kimmage even managed a late attack before eventually finishing ninth on the stage. But it meant, at the end of "the most exciting week of my life," that the Irishman was his team's highest-placed rider on general classification going into the time trial. "It lulled me into a false sense of . . . extending myself more than I should have in the time trial in Nantes," he says.

"I went into that time trial thinking, Fuck, I'm going for it. I had [Bernard] Thévenet [the RMO directeur sportif and a double Tour winner in the 1970s] telling me to go easy. But this was my chance. I went out and fucking buried myself. And I still lost about 8 minutes to Hinault!" Kimmage laughs, then instantly turns serious. "It was crushing. I remember going back to my hotel room. I was aching, lying on my bed, so sore. No relief. The TV was on, I was watching guys coming in and thinking, Holy fuck, how the fuck can they do that? It was astonishing. Really crushing. Really crushing. I was toast after that. I never recovered from it. From then on, it was survival for me."

Yet the day after the time trial, on the 184-km 10th stage from Nantes to Futuroscope, offered Kimmage another, in some ways even starker and more shocking perspective on the Tour de France and on those strange, almost freakish creatures trying not merely to survive but to win. He remembers seeing LeMond, in apparent distress, drop back to the convoy of team cars that followed the peloton. Some 10 or 15 minutes later, he reappeared. "His team was moving him back up; I remember the La Vie Claire train, four or five riders, coming up the outside.

"LeMond was third or fourth in line, and the fucking smell was horrendous," Kimmage adds, screwing up his face. Now, however, it's not so much the smell—or the remembered sight of brown liquid running down his legs—that horrifies him as the indignity of LeMond's sudden, violent bout of diarrhea. "I remember looking at LeMond," continues Kimmage, "and thinking, Christ, how the fuck can he do that?

"When you look at other sports it's just ludicrous, really. A soccer player's touched; he collapses like he's been shot. Tennis: A player cramps, there's a break, he gets a massage. But the embarrassment, the humiliation LeMond had to endure. But I tell you one thing: He went up in my estimation for that. There was always a sense that LeMond was . . . classy but soft. Yeah, classy but soft. He was looked on as being a curiosity, as not being serious. Being in a French team, I tried to fit in by pretending I was French, following the French rules—no ice cream but a ton of cheese. He refused that, refused to compromise. But what a bike rider. What a fucking bike rider."

If LeMond feels embarrassed now to be reminded of his bout of diarrhea, he doesn't show it. On the contrary, the deep lines around his mouth crease into a wide smile; he laughs loudly and long. He appears to remember the incident as though it were a cherished memory. "I think it was a bad peach," he says. Interestingly, he doesn't mention the Mexican food he and Hampsten had indulged in the previous evening.

"It's crazy," he adds. "It was the same in the Tour de l'Avenir in '82 [which LeMond won]. Guimard was shocked by my strong ride in the team time trial there because two or three days before that, I'd had serious diarrhea. I had to stop all the time. I was all over the place.

"But earlier that year, in '86, in May, I remember flying into Geneva with . . . who was it? Eric Salomon! It was before the Tour of Italy. Köchli picks us up, and we're riding to the top of the Col du Grand Saint Bernard. Köchli gave us a map, but I was kinda delirious with tiredness, I was so jet-lagged. But we rode this mountain and we were . . . overdressed. It was warm; I was sweating, I was so hot. And we were going so hard.

"That mountain is in the middle of nowhere, but we get to a bar, and I'm so thirsty, but there's a tap, with fresh springwater, and we fill our bottles. And I just pounded six bottles. And I put another bottle in my back pocket, and I'm walking out . . ." LeMond's eyes widen, and he begins laughing again. "I'm like, 'Eric, oh, *putain!*' I tried taking my shirt over my head [the bib shorts cyclists wear cannot be removed without first removing the shirt], and then I had just a . . . complete loss of bowel control."

Across the LeMonds' kitchen table, Kathy LeMond's expression is one of horror and revulsion. LeMond, oblivious, carries on: "I filled my shorts, it was down my legs, but there was a trough across the street. I was totally naked there on the road, with my shoes off, all my clothes. I tried to wash my clothes in the water and then put them back on, but they stank. Then we rode to the top and met Köchli."

"He gets terrible food poisoning," offers Kathy. "To this day, if he has a shrimp which isn't right, he'll be throwing up before he's outa the room."

"Did you feel good after that?" she asks, bringing the conversation back to stage 10 of the Tour, when LeMond battled the agony and the inconvenience of his attack of diarrhea on the road to Futuroscope.

"It was 60, 70 kilometers to go, and I took a peach," LeMond says. "About 10 km later, I went to a teammate, 'Pass me your hat.' He was like, 'What?' I said, 'Pass me your hat, please.' 'What do you want my hat for?' 'Pass me the goddamn hat!'

"I shoved it down my shorts; it didn't feel like it was going to be diarrhea, but oh, my God, it was so severe. I just felt the shorts go *woooooop!* And it fills my shorts, then slowly dribbles down my legs into my shoes. I mean literally, it was dripping into my wheels, it was flying off the spokes. And then everyone separated off from me. We were single file, we were going hard, and I was cramping, my stomach.

"When you get that kind of deal, it's a really personal thing, and you need isolation. You're dying. I needed to be alone. Sitting in the peloton, like, ooooh, I wanna be alone. I got to the finish line with severe stomach cramps. I get off and there are all those people, they want to talk to you, but I'm like 'Get out of my way!' and I go over to the team's motor home, and I'm so grateful we have one, and I'm rushing, I go in, and I go to open up the toilet, and they've removed it. It's full of boxes of postcards. The one sitting where the toilet was . . . God, the irony! Imagine a box this high," LeMond gestures with his hand to a height about four feet off the ground, "with all these Hinault postcards. There had to be 30, 40 thousand of these cards . . . I took them all out of the center so I could sit, like it was a toilet seat . . . and I sat there for an hour and a half."

"That was disgusting," says Kathy. "Everyone said he should have quit." Turning to her husband, she adds, "They couldn't believe you wanted to win that badly."

"But I was fine the next day." LeMond shrugs. "Maybe it's selective memory, but that Tour, 1986, I can barely remember having . . . a bad day. I didn't feel my legs.

"That," he adds quickly, "wasn't the problem."

12

YOU BLEW IT, BERNIE

It's a very confusing situation for me.
I'd rather quit the Tour than get second again.

GREG LEMOND

nticipating the possibility of a first ever American win, *Rolling Stone* magazine sent a writer, Trip Gabriel, to the 1986 Tour de France. It was hardly typical *Rolling Stone* territory, yet the event supplied Gabriel and the magazine with the kind of material—and intrigue—that could perhaps have featured in some of the stories for which America's bible of music and popular culture was renowned, and on which its reputation was founded.

After all, Hunter S. Thompson might have written the following about the "myths and legends," and also the heroes, of the Tour de France: "We love them for the extra dimension they provide, the illusion of near-infinite possibility to erase the narrow confines of most men's reality. Weird heroes and mould-breaking champions exist as living proof to those who need it that the tyranny of 'the rat race' is not yet final."

By the same token, after speaking to Greg LeMond, Thompson might have written this not of Richard Nixon but of Bernard Hinault: "He could shake your hand and stab you in the back at the same time."

Gabriel's—and *Rolling Stone*'s—take on the Tour makes for fascinating reading. It is clear that what began as a quirky assignment, and an attempt to come to grips with this alien event that captivated mainland Europe but barely registered in the United States, turned into a different kind of story, one not of cultural curiosity but of pure (and impure) sport and the extraordinary and epic battle that began to be played out between two men on the roads and in the mountains of France.

At first, though, as the race snaked across the north of France before heading down the western flank toward the Pyrenees, Gabriel appears struck most powerfully by the culture surrounding the Tour, in particular the fans. When they reach the mountains, he finds "the Gallic depths of their passion unfathomable to the foreign mind." Claiming that one in three Frenchmen watch the Tour, he continues, "At folding tables all along the route, they set out goose terrine, artichokes, Camembert, cold chicken and bottles of wine to hold down the four corners of the tablecloths. Post-office windows are abandoned. Drivers hop down from their Mercedes trucks. Cows go un-milked, mooing in their fields while the entire country halts to watch the race."

The culture surrounding the sport in Europe is at odds with what passes for "cycling culture" in the United States. "In America bicycling may be the sport of the fitness-conscious yuppies. But in Europe it's the equivalent of boxing or basketball in the U.S.—a way up from the lower classes, practiced by tough rural kids like Bernard Hinault, whose family did not own a car while he was growing up."

Entering the Pyrenees, Gabriel's attention switches away from the Tour's quirks and curiosities. Instead he finds himself sucked into the drama of the sporting battle, a battle that, on July 15, is detonated in abrupt fashion, thus ending any notions of a "phony war"—and apparently also ending the suggestions of an accord, a deal, between Hinault and LeMond. "In the midst of competition," writes Gabriel, "Hinault attempted to snatch victory like a furious, clawing rodent . . . he acted not only for himself but for a nation horrified that its great race might be hijacked by an American outlaw."

On day one in the Pyrenees, on the stage to Pau, "Hinault dynamited the race," launching "what is instantly recognized as one of the most daring breakaways in years."

PAU, TUESDAY, JULY 15

The first of two stages in the Pyrenees, over 217 km from Bayonne to Pau, follow a morning train transfer from Bordeaux to Bayonne. In the carriages of the train, as it speeds south, the riders sit dressed in their Lycra racing kits,

ready for action but with a collective sense of foreboding. Ahead of them lies
the main battleground of any Tour: the mountains. It is enough to induce a
sense of anxiety and fear in each and every rider, from the team leaders and
climbers, who can no longer hide in the peloton, to the sprinters and domestiques, for whom the mountain stages are all about painful survival; a daily
battle to finish within the time limit.

The day that looms ahead of them—day one in the Pyrenees—is not as
tough as the monster stage that will follow 24 hours later. But still, the climbing is relentless, starting after 70 km with the Col d'Haltza, which turns into
the first-category Col de Burdincurutcheta before the road drops down and
begins ascending the Col Bagargui. Then it's into the valley before the second-
category Col d'Ichère at 150 km and then the day's big one, the first-category
Col de Marie-Blanque, followed by a long, mainly downhill, run to Pau.

As mountain stages go, this one is testing rather than brutal. LeMond argues that it hardly even merits the description "mountain stage." "It was like
a flat stage with the Marie-Blanque," he says dismissively.

There is a sense that the riders are being eased in. The next day, over four
major climbs and with a summit finish, is different—it is brutal. And yet this
first stage, held in the searing heat of southern France, close to the Spanish
border, starts off aggressively, with attack after attack. La Vie Claire is particularly active, seemingly determined to cover every move. Philippe Leleu
is in the early break; Niki Rüttimann features in the next. Steve Bauer and
Jean-François Bernard are also prominent, marking groups that sprint off the
front of the pack. The leaders are still hiding, keeping their powder dry for
the big climbs, in particular the Marie-Blanque; the expectation is that today's stage will be decided there. But as early as the Col de Burdincurutcheta,
90 km into the stage, Bernard Hinault makes a surprising appearance at the
head of the race, forcing some of the other leaders, notably the Colombian
climber Luis "Lucho" Herrera, to chase him.

"It was superhot," recalls Andy Hampsten. "And early on, on one of the
first climbs, Hinault was really working to drive a group clear. Over the top
of the [Burdincurutcheta] climb he was really driving, and I thought, That's
a little weird. There was a long way to go. He wasn't attacking, he was just
riding a really hard tempo on the front. I asked Greg, 'Why's Hinault doing
this? Did he talk to you?' And Greg said, 'No.' He had no idea why Hinault
was riding so hard; it was like he was on a mission. So I went to the front and
hesitantly said to Hinault, 'Eh, I'll do that if you want . . . but, um, why are

you riding so hard?' And Hinault was supergruff. I don't even know what he said."

After this skirmish, the race calms down in the valley roads linking the Col Bagargui and Col de Marie-Blanque. Or that is the impression. For in fact it is here, not on a climb but on an apparently inconsequential section of road, when few are paying attention, that Hinault lights the fuse. He slips clear in the company of two other riders, with a fourth making contact as daylight opens up back to the peloton.

The move catches LeMond off guard. Hinault's attack came close to the feed zone, and LeMond was more concerned with collecting his musette,[1] containing food and drinking bottles. For several miles, LeMond rides along in the peloton, unaware and blissfully ignorant of the fact that Hinault has attacked.

"I was thinking, Nothing's happening," LeMond says. "We don't have radios, and my teammates aren't telling me anything. But Hinault just . . . slipped away."

LeMond's first inkling of what has happened comes when the timer's motorbike—which, on a blackboard, relays time gaps from peloton to break, identifying the riders in the break by their numbers—drops back to the bunch. "When the motorbike appears with the blackboard showing the numbers of the breakaway . . . I had to do a double take. There was number 1. I saw that and just thought, that's Hinault. *Hinault?*"

It seems inconceivable now, in the era of race radios, that LeMond could be oblivious to the fact that Hinault had escaped, along with another fancied rider, Spain's Pedro Delgado, and a second La Vie Claire rider, Jean-François Bernard. Yet such things did happen; it was a time when inattention could cost a rider dear, as it had cost Robert Millar a year earlier.

Millar was riding to overall victory on the penultimate day of the 1985 Vuelta a España when, unbeknownst to him and in highly suspicious circumstances, two riders broke away. Millar realized too late and lost the leader's jersey—and the Vuelta—to one of the escapees. Coincidentally, the beneficiary on that occasion—the man who mastered the Houdini act amid a welter of conspiracy theories and rumors of skulduggery—was Pedro Delgado.

---

1. A bag containing food and water that is designed to be grabbed easily by a cyclist, handed up by the roadside soigneurs in the feed zone.

Now, a year later, the same rider teams up with Hinault as they escape on the valley roads leading eventually to the Marie-Blanque. Initially there are another two riders with Hinault and Delgado: Eduardo Chozas of Spain, who doesn't last very long in their company, and, of course, Jean-François Bernard.

Bernard rides hard, taking long turns on the front of the break, forcing the pace, helping establish the lead. "Hinault taking Jean-François with him put Greg in a pretty good bind," says Steve Bauer. "He really had Greg on the ropes there."

Bernard's presence in the break with Hinault fuels LeMond's suspicion. He wonders if the escape was planned—if, within his own team, a French conspiracy is at play.

As Hinault's stealth break stretches its advantage to 2 minutes, very little happens behind. Laurent Fignon, it becomes clear whenever the road begins to rise, is finished. The double Tour winner, as his performance in the time trial in Nantes foretold, loses 11 minutes and abandons the Tour. More surprisingly, the challenge of Stephen Roche—third the previous year—also crumbles on this first, relatively easy day in the mountains. The Irishman loses 21 minutes. For Phil Anderson, the Australian, the day is even more catastrophic; he loses 33.

This leaves . . . whom? In the absence of Fignon, in particular, there is arguably only one favorite whose Tour ambitions are being torpedoed by Hinault's attack: Greg LeMond. But LeMond, growing ever more anxious, is in an impossible situation. He cannot chase his own teammate. He can only sit behind his other rivals and watch and wait for them to take the initiative, growing more and more frustrated as they appear reluctant to do so.

Of those other riders who can chase Hinault and Delgado, who is there? There is Urs Zimmermann, the Swiss rider on Roche's Carrera team. Robert Millar also looks strong. And there's the Colombian Luis Herrera, who tries to force the pace on each of the climbs before looking around and waving someone else through. Each of these riders is a strong climber, but each—as Herrera's actions suggest—appears to lack the belief that he has the all-around ability to win the Tour. They chase Hinault and Delgado, but in chasing they don't fully commit. It's too early in the Tour for that. And so they hedge their bets. They play a classic game of poker. They ride at the front and contribute to the pace-setting, mainly in order to encourage the others to commit more fully and chase harder.

"When Hinault attacked with Delgado, Greg was broken, exhausted," recalls Maurice Le Guilloux, who was following in the second La Vie Claire team car. The first, driven by Paul Köchli, was behind the break—behind Hinault, Bernard, and Delgado. Le Guilloux admits he was as "surprised" by Hinault's attack as LeMond was. "Greg came back to the team car and said, 'Look, I don't understand what's going on. Why is Hinault attacking?' He was very upset."

Steve Bauer remembers that "on day one in the Pyrenees, we were all at the front, we were in control of the race, total control, and [Hinault] used that to his advantage by attacking. After he'd gone, we were looking at Greg, thinking, Oh, shit, what do we do? Greg was pretty frickin' upset when he realized what was happening; he figured he might have lost the Tour right there."

After speaking to Le Guilloux, LeMond accelerates back to the peloton, which by now is a select group of team leaders and specialist climbers. In what could be interpreted as an act of disloyalty toward Hinault—but is equally an act of desperation—he begins to urge the others to start chasing.

"Why don't you work?" he asks Millar. Millar shrugs. Millar won't chase at the front if Zimmermann won't; Zimmermann won't chase if Herrera won't; and so it goes on. One of the main problems, in fact, is the presence of LeMond: Knowing that he is under team orders not to assist the chase of Hinault, they don't want to give him a free ride. If they do, he will arrive fresh at the base of the Marie-Blanque and then—perhaps—take off.

As Bauer says, LeMond is in a bind. And it is his own teammate, Hinault, who has put him there.

"I'm sitting there," recalls LeMond, "with the TV cameras and the photographers on me, and Hinault's riding away. No one's chasing him, and I can't. It's crazy."

On the lower slopes of the final climb, the Col de Marie-Blanque, Hinault and Delgado drop Bernard, who has given his all, and press on, their lead now having grown to 3 minutes. Herrera has another go on the climb, with LeMond marking him. Zimmermann and Millar chase them down, but Herrera keeps trying, and LeMond keeps following him. Eventually it is LeMond who initiates a counterattack, and this time Herrera follows him. But the chase has been so erratic, so stop-start, that Hinault and Delgado— riding steadily—continue to pull away, their lead approaching 6 minutes, 30 seconds.

At the finish in Pau, Delgado outsprints Hinault for the stage win. Hinault admits that he made a deal with the Spaniard—"I asked him to help increase the gap, and I'd give him the stage"—and Hinault takes over the yellow jersey from the Dane Pedersen. LeMond is best of the rest, placing third, just ahead of Herrera, but 4:30 behind Hinault, a huge margin.

"The field was decimated after the Marie-Blanque," says LeMond. "Sitting in that bunch, we were going nowhere. If you've got two guys doing 40 kph, and a group doing 30 kph and riding erratically, it doesn't mean those two guys are stronger. . . . They were just riding steady, but we were down 6, 6½ minutes at one point, and I'm dying with frustration. I can't chase him. I'm going nuts.

"I should've just chased him," LeMond continues. "As soon as I realized he was away, I should've chased him. Eventually I thought, Screw it, I'm going, and I went and took Lucho Herrera with me, and we pulled back a minute and a half by Pau."

In Pau, LeMond finished in a state of frustration and confusion. And yet it was Hinault, who had taken the yellow jersey and now had a commanding lead of 5 minutes 25 seconds over LeMond, who seemed angry. "Hinault found out I had been chasing him down with Lucho Herrera, and on the finish line he was almost punching me," says LeMond. "He was asking, 'How dare you chase me down?' We almost had a fistfight right there. They had to hold him back.

"I mean, I waited till everyone else had been dropped, and I took Lucho Herrera, who's not going to win the Tour [the Colombian had lost too much time in the team time trial]. And Hinault was pissed at me! And that's when I started realizing, holy shit . . . and I started piecing everything together.

"The thing is," continues LeMond, "I was riding incredibly well. But Hinault and I . . . we're tiptoeing around each other. He seems to have this idea that whoever won the time trial [in Nantes] would win the Tour almost by default because the team was so strong. Psychologically I think he's convinced himself of this. But he hasn't said it to me. And, after the time trial, I don't really make a big deal of the flat tire or broken wheel, but I think Hinault felt he'd beaten me fair and square."

It takes Hinault's attack on the road to Pau, 14 days into the Tour, for the issues between them to come to a head. Or to begin to come to a head. Whereas the time trial was a simple, straightforward test of strength—no tactics, no interference from others, no possibility of collusion—the road stages are different, multidimensional, largely uncontrollable puzzles, with the possibility of combines between rival riders (witness Hinault's deal with Delgado). As it began to dawn on LeMond what he could be up against—given the respect Hinault commanded and the number of friends he had in the peloton—his imagination began to run riot.

"The way the peloton just shut down after Hinault went away," says Le-Mond. "I mean, Maurice Le Guilloux told me that the French riders and a couple of teams, maybe some of the Spanish riders . . ." He trails off, but the implication is that he was beginning to wonder if he might be up against not just Hinault but others in the peloton, including rival riders and teams. His mind flashed back to the Giro, when an Italian rider had tried to "buy" La Vie Claire. Could a similar deal be struck by Hinault at the Tour? "Put it this way," says LeMond, "Hinault didn't get away on that stage through physical ability."

At the stage finish in Pau, LeMond—apparently still overlooking Paul Köchli's rule about not speaking to journalists about the race immediately after the stage—admitted to reporters, "It's a very confusing situation to me. I'd rather quit the Tour than get second again."

Later that evening, he spoke to Sam Abt of the *International Herald Tribune*. "Greg was in the dumps," recalls Abt. "I talked to him that night, and he was real down. He just said, 'It's over. I'm gonna have to settle for second again.'"

Kathy LeMond, who had returned to the family home in Kortrijk, also spoke to her husband on the phone in the evening. "He called me and said, 'I lost the Tour today.'"

"Well, I was 5 minutes down on Hinault," says LeMond. "I thought, That's it. I'm not going to make up this time."

"Darling, you couldn't," says Kathy. "Five minutes? On Hinault?"

"But I remember that night, I was able to sleep," adds LeMond, looking relieved and then determined. "I was just like . . . he's gonna pay. I'm gonna make it back. Right away I thought I'd lost the Tour. But then I was saying to myself, I have to make it back. The objective tomorrow is, I've got to make the time back. Because if I go into the Alps with that deficit . . ."

LeMond pauses as his eyebrows shoot into the air, and he shakes his head. *"Ooooof!"*

Despite Hinault's blast at LeMond after the stage, the atmosphere in the La Vie Claire hotel in the evening after the Pau stage wasn't as fraught as it could have been—or as fraught as it would become—but there was tension, unspoken, between LeMond and Hinault. Incredible as it might seem, LeMond says that at this point, he and Hinault had still not had a conversation about who was leading the team, at least not with each other; it was the elephant in the room, unacknowledged but obvious to everyone. When he appeared at dinner, Hinault sought to lighten the mood in bombastic style.

"That's how it is in the first day in the mountains," he told his teammates. "You need to stir the pot." (It recalled his comment the previous year. "I'll stir things up," he had said, though the second part of the comment seemed less certain: "To help Greg win.")

While LeMond was skeptical, to say the least, others seemed prepared to give Hinault the benefit of the doubt in Pau. "I really didn't think that Hinault had attacked to try and win the Tour," says Andy Hampsten. "I was going along with what he said, that it was for the team. But Greg, I think, was more astute than I was. Now I recognize Greg was worried; he was terrified.

"The atmosphere wasn't bad that night, after the first stage in the Pyrenees," continues Hampsten. "It was just confusing, for everyone. It hadn't been the plan [for Hinault to attack]. But that was the thing; nothing was really planned. We were La Vie Claire—these guys, Greg and Hinault, would clobber everyone in the time trial; then in the mountains we were going to tear people apart. That was the only plan I got. Köchli was brilliant because he didn't try to choreograph everything we did."

For others in the team, such as Hinault's accomplice in the break, Jean-François Bernard, the escape amounted not to treachery but to genius. As far as Bernard was concerned, the Tour was now Hinault's to lose. "In Pau," he says, "the game is done." He claps his hands decisively. "When Hinault took the yellow jersey in Pau, that's it—it's over. He will win the Tour."

Most agreed. The following day's *L'Équipe* was gushing in its praise, hailing "one of the most spectacular breaks of his career." Jacques Goddet, meanwhile, wrote, "This Hinault, I didn't think he still existed. He seemed motivated by profound happiness at the certainty that he has regained all his powers and reestablished himself as the absolute boss."

The goal," says Hinault now, placing his coffee mug on the table as he begins to explain the rationale behind his attack on day one in the Pyrenees, "was to force our rivals—Phil Anderson, Delgado [Has he forgotten Delgado was with him, in the break?], Stephen Roche, Millar—to chase. As soon as I went off the front, in theory, the others should have followed me, or at least tried. But on the stage to Pau, when I went, they didn't really move."

Hinault looks confused, as LeMond was on the day. There was still a long way to go in the Tour, he points out. And his intention—he continues to insist—remained to help LeMond win. And also, he adds, to have fun. "I never enjoyed myself in a Tour as much I did that year," he says.

Surely Hinault realized, though, that with his attack on the road to Pau and the huge advantage he established, LeMond began to perceive him not as a friend or ally but as a threat or enemy? "He thought so," Hinault says with a shrug. "I didn't. Never. I'd given my word, and I wasn't going back on it. I didn't pay any attention to what was being said. I gave my word from the first day. I don't have to justify everything that I do.

"He had nothing to worry about." Hinault shrugs again. "He had nothing to worry about. First of all, the aim was to force the others to ride. Zimmermann, Roche . . . who else? Millar, Anderson. A lot of good riders, left behind. All he had to do was sit there. The next day he could attack."

The next day, a La Vie Claire rider did attack. But it was Hinault.

SUPERBAGNÈRES, WEDNESDAY, JULY 16

"Bernard Hinault won the Tour de France on the first day in the Pyrenees," says Gilles Le Roc'h, the Breton journalist. "And he was so proud, so proud of his career. For LeMond, it was treason. But Hinault wanted to be the first to win six Tours de France. He had a great hand. But he made a big mistake the day after, when he tried to kill Greg LeMond."

That is certainly one interpretation. Stage 14, from Pau to Superbagnères, is one of the toughest of the race, featuring four climbs, all stacked toward the end. The climbing begins with the Queen of the Pyrenees, the Col du Tourmalet, starting 75 km into the 186-km stage, followed by the Col d'Aspin and the Col de Peyresourde. It will end with the first summit finish, at Superbagnères.

The Tour leaves Pau without Laurent Fignon. Photos show him dressed in civvies—shirt and strange, baggy pinstriped trousers—stepping into a Système U camper van. Exits from the Tour—especially by a favorite—are rarely dignified affairs, though this beat Fignon's withdrawal from the 1988 race, when he'd taken his leave shortly after throwing his water bottle at one of the motorcycle-mounted photographers attempting to capture the moment of his retirement. Later it emerged that the cause of Fignon's poor form in that Tour was a 60-cm tapeworm.

With the Tourmalet coming relatively early on stage 14, the race doesn't fully ignite on the slopes of the most famous of Pyrenean climbs. A Frenchman, Dominique Arnaud, had attacked from the start, and he begins the 20-km, 2,115-meter climb with an enormous 13-minute lead over the peloton. Behind him, Roche, Delgado—on the attack again—Charly Mottet, and 39-year-old Joop Zoetemelk—the winner in 1980 and three times second to Hinault—break clear as the Tourmalet winds up through banks of spectators.

Behind Arnaud, the favorites crest the summit together and ready themselves for the long descent, slipping bits of newspaper down jerseys to protect chests from windchill. Hinault doesn't bother with the paper; he seems to have other ideas.

He attacks as they begin to plunge down the other side. And on the twisting, dangerous descent, he quickly opens a gap. Hinault speeds through the gray concrete ski resort of La Mongie, 4 km down the mountain, at 80 kph and continues to plummet like a stone. By the valley, he leads by 1 minute 43 seconds.

Behind Hinault, LeMond experiences an uncomfortable sense of déjà vu. Once again he is powerless to chase. Once again he finds himself—to use Steve Bauer's description—"in a bind." And once again he's been put there by his teammate, the rider who was supposed to be helping him win: Hinault.

LeMond is confused, and he's not alone. For the second time in 24 hours, Maurice Le Guilloux, driving a La Vie Claire team car, is scratching his head. "I'm asking, 'Why are you attacking? You are 5 minutes ahead!'" recalls Le Guilloux. "But Hinault, when we went up to him in the car, said, 'I'm not going back, I'm not waiting.'"

Le Guilloux says that, by attacking, Hinault was going against instructions. Even Jean-François Bernard, his loyal teammate who'd helped Hinault capitalize on his escape the previous day, echoes this. "There was a meeting before the stage," says Bernard, "and the word was, 'We don't need to attack. Hinault has the yellow jersey; there's no requirement to attack; we stay as we are. It's up to our adversaries to attack us.' Hinault agreed to that. And then, out of the blue, Hinault attacked!"

Why? is the question. Why attack so early on the stage? Why persist on his own? One theory is that the Badger might have been inspired by a stage that did as much as any to create the Eddy Merckx legend. During the 1969

Tour, Merckx attacked on the Tourmalet, near the top, and carried on alone, for 140 km, to win in Mourenx by 8 minutes. In *L'Équipe*, Jacques Goddet coined a new expression in response to that astonishing performance: "Merckxissimo!"

Yet Merckx's move had gone down in history as one of the greatest ever rides in the Tour precisely because it was so unusual. Another description for a solo break in the mountains, early in the stage and with multiple mountain ranges to come, is "suicide attack." The question now, as Hinault flexes his muscles and fixes the road with an expression that combines aggression and defiance, is whether his move will come to be described as Merckxissimo or kamikaze.

The next climb that Hinault faces is the Col d'Aspin, and he grinds up it, face fixed in that angry snarl, legs churning his customary huge gear. By the summit of the Aspin, he has stretched his lead on LeMond and the others to more than 2 minutes. He catches Arnaud on the descent, but, behind, the chase is beginning to pick up momentum. Unlike the previous day, Millar, Herrera, and Zimmermann are committing to it, especially Zimmermann, who realizes, "The race has gone, it's over, if I don't chase Hinault." And on the slopes of the Col de Peyresourde, the day's penultimate climb, the Zimmermann-led chasing group begins to eat into Hinault's lead.

But for the TV audience—and even for the chasing group—it isn't clear how quickly they are catching Hinault, still snarling, still grinding his way up the climb. It's only on the descent of the Peyresourde, as a swarm of press and TV motorcycles surround the man in the yellow jersey, that a small group of riders suddenly appears in the corner of the picture, catching everyone by surprise. As for the apparently sudden disintegration of Hinault's lead on the upper slopes of the Peyresourde, this raises the question: Is he cracking?[2]

The group that catches Hinault on the descent of the Peyresourde contains all the strong men: LeMond, Zimmermann, Millar, Herrera, and one of the revelations on this brutal day in the mountains, the young American, Hampsten. But now there's virtually no respite before the day's final climb up to the finish at the top of Superbagnères. There's just a dash through the spa

2. Even the TV commentators were caught by surprise when Hinault was captured on the descent of the Col de Peyresourde, expressing their shock when they saw LeMond et al. catch him. When Channel 4 later put together a highlights montage of the 1986 Tour, it showed Hinault flying down the Tourmalet to a very 1980s soundtrack of Billy Ocean's "When the Going Gets Tough, the Tough Get Going." Then, as Hinault climbs the Aspin and the picture cuts to a haunted-looking LeMond, the music changes to the Eurythmics' "Would I Lie to You?"

town of Luchon, a regular on the Tour route and a place with another link to Merckx's epic ride in 1969—Luchon is where stage 17 began.

Today, as they ride through the pretty, café-lined central boulevard of Luchon, it becomes clear that Hinault is paying for his effort and suffering. Really suffering. "Hinault suddenly began drifting aimlessly across the road," as one report would later put it—a classic sign of the dreaded bonk, or *fringale*, when the body's blood-sugar levels become so depleted that the rider runs out of energy. It means Hinault's in trouble because there's still the 15.3-km climb to the 1,569-meter summit of Superbagnères.

Before they start climbing Superbagnères, and in the lull after the capture of Hinault, there's a small regrouping. Three riders bridge up to the lead group, and among this trio is Alexi Grewal of 7-Eleven. As they ride through Luchon, Grewal, who stood out as a maverick even in such a maverick team as 7-Eleven, does something that few would dare do.

He rides alongside Hinault, turns to him, and says, "You blew it, Bernie. You fucked up."[3]

Later Grewal, the winner of the 1984 Olympic road race, will describe Hinault's solo attack on this second day in the Pyrenees as "undoubtedly the most stupid move of the race so far. Here Hinault is leading by 5 and a half minutes, he's got Greg at an extreme disadvantage, then he breaks away with three big mountains left. What does he expect? That everybody's going to give up? He did it because he thought he was too good. He said to himself, 'I'm Bernard Hinault, a superstud. I'll show 'em.' If it had worked, he'd have been a legend."

But as Grewal rides past the drifting Hinault and takes in the Badger's glazed expression, he realizes Hinault is done. "He was dead in the water, standing still. I thought, God, he's finished," Grewal told Trip Gabriel, the *Rolling Stone* writer. "From the time we caught him to the time we passed him, his speed never changed. He was in a huge gear—he's always in a huge gear—but he didn't even try to pedal. He didn't even see us go by. To him, the rest of us weren't even in the race."

---

3. After the original publication of this book, Alexi Grewal got in touch to say that he never said, "You blew it, Bernie," to Hinault, though the quotation was published in *Rolling Stone* at the time and is fondly remembered by all who have read it. Indeed, Grewal claims never to have spoken a single word to Hinault, though he concedes that it is possible he thought, "You blew it, Bernie," as he passed Hinault in Luchon, or that he may have said it at the dinner table. Instead, he vividly remembers that Hinault somehow recovered on the climb to Superbagnères and, with 300 meters to go, came "roaring" past him, "flying and gritting his teeth."

LeMond also spoke to Hinault in Luchon, just before the climb. "Do you want anything?" he asked.

"I'm dead," replied Hinault. "Follow the others."

At least, this is how their exchange was reported. Today, LeMond can't recall if Hinault spoke at all. "I asked him how he was feeling," says LeMond, "and he just grunted. I don't know what he said. I didn't care. I was just seething."

And *Hinault is cracking. Hinault is cracking. . . .*" It's the voice of Phil Liggett, the TV commentator, as the riders tackle the lower slopes of Superbagnères, rising out of Luchon.

Hinault, it is clear, is enduring a thousand agonies. He persists with the huge gear, his legs turning ever more slowly, as though he is pedaling through treacle, and he loses contact with LeMond's group. Now the shackles are off; this is LeMond's moment, his time. As the road steepens, Luis Herrera sets the pace. LeMond follows him. Zimmermann sits third. Millar, who had been trailed off, has just regained contact and comes up to Zimmermann's back wheel. LeMond has to attack. He has to go. But, as Hinault struggles behind, the story of this Tour is about to take another unexpected twist.

An American in a La Vie Claire jersey attacks. But it isn't LeMond.

Andy Hampsten—who has just returned to the group in the company of Millar and has been sitting behind the Scot, in fifth—accelerates up the left side of the road on the approach to a right-sweeping hairpin bend. No one reacts. A few seconds later, he looks around his shoulder and sees daylight as he takes the hairpin so fast he almost overshoots it. Behind, in the group, it's as-you-were: Herrera, LeMond, Zimmermann, Millar. Now LeMond is looking around, too. Waiting for the reaction. It doesn't come. And then Herrera, who'd been providing all the impetus, swings across to the side, looks down at his bike, and sticks his hand in the air—he's punctured. There's an impasse. The three riders fan across the road and look at each other as Hampsten—*le petit lapin*—bounds up the climb. As Hinault always said he would.

Let me tell you something you won't know," says Hampsten. "Before that last climb, Hinault's bonked, he's blown, and the favorites are racing neck and neck to the base of Superbagnères. I got dropped because I was kinda bonking there, too. But I could see Greg with the leaders—all the really dangerous guys—just up the road. There was a bit of a false flat in the valley. And Robert Millar was going well; I could get on his wheel and get back up to the group. I could tell Greg was full of energy, but everyone was looking at him to attack. He really needed someone else to attack, to stir the pot, so he could counter.

"I came back to the group with Millar at exactly the point where the road turned and got steeper, so I attacked just to . . . because no one had any idea we were coming up, and I could see Greg needed someone to do that. I gave him a look as I went by to say, Hey, I'm not trying to win.

"On TV, it looks fantastic!" Hampsten laughs. "It looks like Andy Hampsten's going to win the Tour de France, you know? After about four seconds I think this myself, then remember, Oh, yeah, I'm bonking! I can't sustain this.

"There are 10 kilometers to go or something, and Köchli came up to me, because I really did get a good gap, though I could see behind that Zimmermann was chasing. I was going to tell Köchli, 'Don't worry, I saw that Greg needed an attack; I'm going to work with Greg as long as I can, then I'll be finished.' But Köchli comes up and encourages me. I said, 'That's great, but I'm not trying to win.'

"And Köchli says, 'No, no, but there's all this fighting within the team, and there's no reason that you can't win the Tour de France. All I care about is that La Vie Claire wins, and your two bigheaded teammates are bickering over it like it's their privilege. The best thing for this team would be for you to take the yellow jersey tonight.'

"I'm blown away." Hampsten laughs. "I said, 'Well, that'd be great, but . . .'"[4]

As the group begins to fragment behind Hampsten, LeMond makes his move. He jumps around the hardworking Zimmermann—Millar is behind the pair, head bobbing, struggling to remain in contact—and quickly bridges the gap to his teammate. LeMond in full flight can be an ungainly sight. He is in and out of the saddle, and when he's making an effort, his head drops until his forehead is almost making contact with the handlebars. But it is certainly effective.

---

4. This information is news to LeMond. When I tell him that Köchli told Hampsten this was his moment to win the Tour, he looks surprised, then laughs. "I never even heard that!" And in a quiet, serious voice, LeMond adds, "Wow. Think what that would have meant to Andy."

When he catches Hampsten, Hampsten offers him a bottle, asks if he's OK, tries to pace him for a bit, but, as he suspected, he can't sustain the effort; he can't stay with LeMond. Now alone, LeMond rides up the mountain to victory—his second stage win after the final time trial in 1985—sprinting to eke out every last second's advantage. Then, almost as he crosses the line, he throws his arms in the air and clasps his hands above his head.

For LeMond, it's a glorious moment—his greatest since his 1983 world championship. And yet, incredibly, it isn't decisive.

Behind him, Hinault, it transpires, is merely wounded, not—as he had seemed in Luchon—dead. On the climb to Superbagnères, he stages a recovery that is little short of remarkable but that is perhaps typical of the Badger. Given his state in the valley, in Luchon, total collapse was in the cards. Instead, like a boxer staggering through round after round and somehow making it to the final count, Hinault fights his way up the climb. Looking punch-drunk, he limits his loss to 4 minutes 39 seconds, though the sight of him approaching the finish is painful to behold. His gears jump not once but twice when he is out of the saddle, causing him to lurch forward, putting his manhood at risk. It is undignified, but he makes it across the line, to a huge cheer. And he has kept the yellow jersey by 40 seconds.

The margin between the stage winner, LeMond, and the 11th-placed Hinault is scarcely credible. The previous day, to Pau, Hinault had gained 4 minutes 37 seconds. Today he has conceded almost exactly the same margin—plus 2 seconds. Result: yellow for Hinault. Status quo maintained.

Hinault is interviewed at the finish. Had he given LeMond permission to attack? "I'm not his father," replies Hinault. "He can do what he likes. What's important is to keep the jersey in the team." Explaining his attack, Hinault adds, "If I had succeeded in reaching Superbagnères, I would have won the Tour, and everyone would have lavished praise on me. If I failed, I knew that Greg was behind me ready to counterattack and that I was tiring his adversaries. It was a sound strategy."

Once again Hinault proves a master of ambiguity. His motives, his motivation, remain a mystery, though his remark—"I would have won the Tour"—represents his first admission of self-interest. Yet the admission is barely necessary. LeMond, though relieved to have won the stage and regained the time lost to Hinault the previous day, appears even more wary of his teammate than he was 24 hours earlier. "He's trying to bury me," he tells one reporter.

That night, after the stage to Superbagnères, we were coming in destroyed," recalls Jean-François Bernard. "We realized that we'd come close to catastrophe. We all said to Hinault, 'Why did you attack?'

"He said, 'Because I felt like it.' He was like that. He was instinctive; he didn't plan or prepare things; he rode on instinct. Panache. It's what people expect of cycling—a bit of spectacle—but that kind of rider doesn't exist in the peloton anymore. . . .

"I like panache," continues Bernard. Then he shakes his head and throws up his arms as he adds, "But we were lucky we didn't lose the Tour that day, uh?"

"Hinault was crazy," says LeMond now. "Tactically, his attack on the second day in the Pyrenees was suicide. It couldn't have worked better for me. Everything happens in the last hour of the race. Hinault went out there, but, had he been thinking about it, he should have stayed in the group. He wouldn't have lost close to 5 minutes; he'd have lost maybe 2."

For Steve Bauer, too, it was a "fatal error" for Hinault to launch his attack so early on the stage. He, too, interpreted it not as a strategic move on behalf of the team but as an effort by Hinault to attain immortality, an act of machismo or Merckxissimo. "He tried to do the superhuman, godly Hinault move, which could have won him the Tour de France," says the Canadian. "I guess he was too cocky, maybe. I mean, he still had the Aspin, Peyresourde, and a mountaintop finish at Superbagnères. I mean . . ." Bauer chuckles. "Can you imagine one of the favorites trying a move like that in this era? It would be pretty suicidal, I think. You wouldn't see Lance [Armstrong] doing that. Or anyone, for that matter."

LeMond's conviction that Hinault—still in yellow, of course—was trying to "bury him" led to an intervention by Bernard Tapie the evening of the stage finish at Superbagnères. After the stage, Hampsten made an effort to convince LeMond that the stage had, in the end, "worked out for the best," to which LeMond replied, "You don't know Hinault. This is going to be bad."

"It was supertense by now," says Hampsten. "I was thinking, This is not what I'd signed up for."

Unlike the previous day, when Hinault had angrily confronted LeMond, it was LeMond who was furious with his teammate. Finally he spoke his mind and vented his frustration. "Paul Köchli had a problem trying to calm Greg down," Hinault writes in his second autobiography. "I said that on this Tour, I attack when I want. My role is to make the race hard, and I succeeded. After two days in the high mountains, 27 riders have either dropped out or been disqualified; our main adversaries have all lost members of their team. I always said that, in this Tour, Greg only needs to worry about himself. I will take care of the other 208 riders."

In a TV interview in 2005, Hinault sought to backtrack on his admission, at the summit of Superbagnères, that his attack had amounted to an effort to win the Tour. "If I'd really wanted to win the Tour, I wouldn't have attacked," he said. "I would have eased off at the bottom of the [descent of the] Tourmalet and waited for them. I tried to force them to work so Greg could counterattack, which is what he did on Superbagnères."

It's true that in the end Hinault paid for his effort, even if he did manage to hold on to the yellow jersey. "I wasn't that tired," Hinault claims. "I pulled back 1 minute in 5 kilometers at the end." He smiles, looking satisfied. "But I was pretty hungry. Having worked so hard and not really thought about refueling, I did have a bit of a bad patch. I wasn't dying of hunger. I wasn't completely gone, you know? I refueled, but it was too late. The bad patch was between Luchon and the bottom of Superbagnères. At the bottom I still wasn't great; then I pulled back a minute. . . ."

Thus, two decades on, does Hinault manage to spin his virtual collapse into a virtual triumph. It's certainly true that his retention of the yellow jersey represented something of a triumph. Yet it was written by some at the time that his attack had been motivated by pride; that he was attempting an epic, heroic feat that would bury LeMond and effectively win him the Tour.

"They can write what they like," replies Hinault testily. "They can write what they like. They're not in my shoes, so they don't know. It's easier to write about it than to do it."

13

THE ENEMY OF MY ENEMY
IS MY FRIEND

He was Mussolini, he was Stalin, he was Hitler,
he was all of them, rolled into one.

SHELLEY VERSES

He was like my big brother. You wouldn't want to go against
your big brother; he's your family.

GREG LEMOND

"Come, I show you something," Paul Köchli says, getting up from his chair and walking toward one of his computers.

In the vast office of his house in Sonvilier, Köchli has been explaining the "strategic game" he tried to play at the 1986 Tour. Now, hunched over his computer, he drags the mouse, clicks, clicks again, and locates the file he's looking for. He opens it. It's a picture of a surfer in the barrel of an enormous wave. The surfer looks poised, perfectly balanced and in control, though the wave looms ominously overheard.

"OK," says Köchli, straightening up, "this is the race." He points at the wave. "We are here." He points at the surfer. "You must race with the race, with your *conquérants.*

"Anticipate," he emphasizes. "A surfer must not compete with the wave, and a cyclist must not race against the race."

Köchli is explaining Bernard Hinault's tactics. He doesn't agree with his assistant, Maurice Le Guilloux—or most others, for that matter—that Hinault's tactics made no sense. But using the surfing analogy, does he not agree that Hinault got it wrong on the second day in the Pyrenees? After all, he was perhaps fortunate not to be completely swamped and overwhelmed by the race/wave when, on the climb to Superbagnères, he was dropped as the race exploded in front of him.

No, says Köchli. The important point is that on both Pyrenean stages it was Hinault who seized the initiative, who anticipated the race and dictated it, or anticipated the race by dictating it. LeMond, in contrast, found himself at its—and Hinault's—mercy. Hinault suffered through forgetting to eat, and that was a mistake, but it owed nothing to anything LeMond did.

"If you want to win, you have to attack," says Köchli. "The problem Greg had in the Pyrenees is that Hinault is the better rider. I make a big, big distinction between a good rider and a strong rider. Here, Greg was probably stronger than Hinault. But Hinault was clearly the better rider.

"The difference, most often, is better tactics. And Hinault was tactically better. His personality was very different from Greg's. Greg was a guy who waited and waited and counterattacked. That was how he won the world championship in 1983. Hinault, in his first career [when he rode for Cyrille Guimard], was a guy who just decided when he wanted to"—Köchli twists his wrist, as though opening the throttle on a motorbike—"*vroom!* He was so strong he could drop everybody.

"But later, with me, Hinault liked the game, and he started playing the game. Greg was always there, observing . . . but Hinault had already taken the opportunity. I could not be against that. He was a good example for other riders in the team, who started acting like Hinault and winning lots of other races. Greg was not familiar with that, and he could not adapt. Within the team, he was at a disadvantage.

"It is a strategic game that must be applied by everyone in the team with a certain . . . feeling," adds Köchli with feeling. "Because you have to play. And you have to collaborate, but intelligently."

Hence, says Köchli, Hinault's "deal" with Pedro Delgado when the two escaped on the stage to Pau and Hinault agreed to give the Spaniard the stage in exchange for his help in building the lead, was intelligent—it worked in both their interests and, more importantly, the team's. Whereas LeMond's escape with Stephen Roche in the previous year's Tour was different; collaborating with Roche, reckons Köchli, was not intelligent because Roche represented too serious a threat to the team's ambition of winning the Tour. "The enemy of my enemy is my friend," Köchli says with a smile.

"In a football game, it's very simple. There are two enemies against each other. A bicycle race is much more complicated. So many dimensions.

Twenty-one teams, 200 riders. It's hot; it's cold. Uphill, downhill. Headwind, crosswind. The wind changes. Very interesting strategically. Very, very interesting. You can be friends in a certain situation, but maybe in 10 minutes not friends anymore. It always changes. It's dynamic."

Expanding on his "strategic game," Köchli continues, "I never wanted a sprinter on my team. Mark Cavendish on my team? No. Nothing against Cavendish, and nothing against using a different concept, but my concept was to win the Tour. You cannot win the Tour with Cavendish on your team. Instead of a sprinter, I want one more rider to attack, to play my strategic game.

"I think this was hard for Greg, this strategic game. It was not an easy game we were playing; it was a complicated one. If you play an easy game, you will not win because all the others see what you are doing, and they will profit from you.

"In 1986, we are the focus because we are strong. We must take responsibility. And yet we never rode on the front." What Köchli means is that his team never sat en masse at the front of the peloton, controlling the race. "Never," he adds for emphasis. "Instead we had riders in the break, to force the others to chase. The important thing is that you run your team in a way that your riders are not afraid to make decisions. Because if an opportunity appears, the rider must react intuitively and make the decision in a second."

This might explain Köchli's encouragement of Andy Hampsten when he launched his attack on Superbagnères. Hampsten had only just caught the group, and before the others even realized he was there, he was gone. No wonder Köchli was delighted; no wonder he urged Hampsten on, telling him he could win the Tour. Hampsten was playing his game, dictating the race, forcing the others to chase—just as, earlier on the same stage as well as the previous day, Hinault had done. "It's a game," says Köchli. (It is surely no coincidence that Hinault echoes his old directeur, saying, "It's ultimately a game. If you know how to play, you can do fantastic things.")

Köchli chuckles. "Ha ha ha! I'm laughing because I hear people talk about 'play sports' and cycling as an 'endurance sport.' Ridiculous! Cycling is a play sport; it's a game. I tell my riders in the morning"—he claps his hands loudly several times—"'OK, today we play cycling! Let's play cycling!'"

BLAGNAC, THURSDAY, JULY 17

Following the stage to Superbagnères and over the next few days—classic transitional stages across the south of France from the Pyrenees and into the foothills of the next battleground, the Alps—La Vie Claire delivers a master class in how to "play cycling." The riders infiltrate breaks, win stages, and generally do not behave as many would expect the team with the yellow jersey to behave.

Stage 14, from Luchon to Blagnac, provides a perfect illustration of Köchli's "strategic game" in action. Here is a stage that, on paper, presents little danger. La Vie Claire has the yellow jersey as well as the rider placed second overall. So what should it do?

What most teams would do in such a situation, on such a stage, is to ride defensively, putting the team on the front of the peloton and controlling the race, the single priority to protect the yellow jersey. Lance Armstrong's team, during his seven-year winning run, mastered the execution of such a strategy, reducing the three-week Tour to two or three decisive moments in the mountains and stifling the rest of the race by putting the entire team on the front. It's a strategy, says Köchli, that is "opposite in outlook to ours. We created the race every day. Armstrong's team hopes there is no race every day, except the one day when Armstrong makes the difference."

For Köchli, the race is fluid, malleable. Even with a rider in yellow, his riders raced with aggression and imagination. Köchli has already claimed that his team "never" rode en masse at the front of the peloton. Now he says, "It's impossible—impossible!—for you to show me any TV recording that shows my team riding at the front of a peloton. It was strictly forbidden." Really? "Yes! I don't want my riders on the front. Why? Why?" He clears his throat. "We just make sure we have a rider in the next break, to force the others to chase. That's all. It's simple."

On the road to Blagnac, there are several early attempts to form a break. Guido Winterberg features in the first, Jean-François Bernard in the second. It seems inevitable that, when a break does become established, it will include a La Vie Claire rider. And it does. After 100 km, Niki Rüttimann, 14th overall at the beginning of the day, is one of four riders who escape.

With his three companions, after they build a lead of 8 minutes, Rüttimann plays a starring role in a brilliant finale of attack and counterattack. Into the final 5 km, Twan Poels attacks. Rüttimann is the first to react, but the four regroup. A momentary lull, then Paul Haghedooren goes; a second later, Christophe Lavainne pounces after him. Then Poels hunts down Lavainne, taking Rüttimann with him. They regroup. Now Rüttimann is fourth man, the ideal position. And he knows, intuitively—as Hampsten did 24 hours earlier—that this is the time to go. He jumps hard, switching to the other side of the road to make it more difficult for one of his erstwhile companions to latch on to his back wheel.

The timing is perfect. The other three look at each other. Each has just made a big effort; they are unwilling, possibly unable, to make another. And while they hesitate, Rüttimann solos to a stage victory, La Vie Claire's second in consecutive days. In addition—and the real masterstroke—Rüttimann moves up to eighth overall. With Hinault, LeMond, and sixth-placed Hampsten, La Vie Claire riders now occupy half of the top eight places on general classification.

Two days later, from Nîmes to Gap, on a stage that sees the race enter the foothills of the Alps, they pull a similar trick with Jean-François Bernard. And yet it is a stage during which LeMond has cause, once again, to question whether his team's strategy is unfolding according to Köchli's attacking principles and "strategic game" or being dictated by—and for—Bernard Hinault.

On the road from Nîmes to Gap, as the mistral wind wreaks havoc, the Badger goes on the rampage.

GAP, SATURDAY, JULY 19

"We had incredibly strong crosswinds that day," says LeMond. "We rode through a canyon, a valley, and there were attacks all day long. Typically, if you're trying to win the Tour, you have protection from your team on a stage like that—these are very, very dangerous conditions. Guys are assigned to help you, to keep you up front, help close the gaps."

"But, uh . . ." LeMond pauses, "that didn't happen for me."

"There was a lot of attacking in the valley," he continues. "Guys jumping away, being caught; gaps opening, being closed. You follow the breaks, they come back, but all of a sudden a group goes away—and this one's got Hinault in it. I'd followed him in, I don't know, about seven attacks. And this is the one I don't follow. It wasn't an attack; it was a split, but it goes, and boom! Everyone stops.

"It's so windy," LeMond explains. "You couldn't get across on your own; you needed to be in a group." It's the most basic principle of road racing: A group is much faster than an individual, and an individual will use far more energy to ride at the same speed. The principle applies especially in crosswinds; an individual rider faces a Herculean task in trying to bridge any gap alone in such conditions. As LeMond says, breaks in a crosswind are very dangerous. (Köchli disagrees with LeMond's description of such conditions as "dangerous": "Greg saw danger, but our team saw opportunities that only appeared in such crosswinds.")

"But the group goes," says LeMond, "and I'm stuck behind in a group that's going nowhere, and I'm thinking, Oh, my God, it's happening again. . . ."

Hinault's group of four, which escaped after 120 km, quickly latched on to another group of four, making eight as they raced east toward the Hautes-Alpes along valley roads in which the mistral was swirling. It wasn't just the presence of Hinault that worried LeMond, though. In the initial group of four—which Hinault's group caught—were two other La Vie Claire riders, Niki Rüttimann and Guido Winterberg. With Hinault, meanwhile, was Urs Zimmermann, the rider placed third overall. That surely spelled danger. Yet despite the presence of Zimmermann, the eight, including the three La Vie Claire riders, put the hammer down and rode hard. After only a few kilometers, they had gained 52 seconds.

"This time, I thought pretty quickly," says LeMond. Knowing that he couldn't ask his team to chase down three teammates, he approached a rider on a rival team. "I spoke to Robert Millar. I said, 'Robert, I'm getting screwed here. Can you get your team to ride—and, if you're close to me on a mountain stage, I'll let you have it.'" Millar, a man of few words, nodded his agreement. "He got his team to ride," says LeMond. "They chased, and got them back."

But it was a chase that lasted 28 km, which tells you how hard the front group was riding given that Millar's Panasonic team was arguably, after La Vie Claire, the strongest in the race. When the groups merged, LeMond made his displeasure known, gesturing angrily at Hinault. Hinault reacted equally angrily. "I'm the boss of this race," he told LeMond. "I know what I'm doing."

A sheepish Rüttimann meanwhile rode alongside LeMond in the peloton. "He came up to me and apologized," says LeMond. "He told me he had to ride; that he and Winterberg had been told by Hinault to ride." Köchli reveals that Rüttimann also spoke to him. "When it calmed down, Niki came back and he was pretty tense, nervous, and he was shouting at me, asking, 'Why would Bernard tell us to ride full gas with Zimmermann?' I shouted back! I told him it was bullshit [to complain]; that it was a rule in our team to make breaks happen. I always said, 'We ride hard in every break to make it happen.

And once it is established, we can start thinking about it strategically.' On this stage to Gap, we were hours from the finish. It was a great opportunity. And when the break came back, we had to start again."

"There was all this tension," LeMond says. "Very little was really said or spoken. Hinault and I were barely communicating. We were just pissed at each other. Steve and Andy were thinking, Shit, what do we do now? It was hard for them. And the Swiss . . . well, the Swiss were neutral."

On the road to Gap, with Hinault and company having been brought to heel, La Vie Claire played another card, putting "Jeff" Bernard in the next break. There was no thrilling finale today, with Bernard fortunate that both his breakaway companions punctured on the descent of the Col d'Espreaux. But it was far from a lucky win for the young Frenchman; he arrived in Gap with a lead of more than 3 minutes on his pursuers and moved up to 13th overall, thus giving the team yet another man in the higher echelons of the general classification. Now they had 5 in the top 13. La Vie Claire's grip on the Tour was tightening.

Bernard Tapie proved as good as his word. For his stage win, Jean-François Bernard was given the Porsche he'd been promised. "I kept that Porsche for a long time," says Bernard, speaking in the Village Départ of the Tour de France on the morning of stage 10 of the 2010 race, a stage that, coincidentally, would later finish in Gap, where Bernard had enjoyed his victory in 1986. "I only got rid of the Porsche recently," he adds with a smile.

In retirement, Bernard, who now works at the Tour for French TV, seems to have become something of a bon vivant—a description Bernard himself used to describe LeMond. The evidence, in Bernard's case, is written in his pallor, in the wine, in the long, sociable dinners that he can be seen enjoying in the evenings, and in the cigarettes that are invariably held between his fingers. He reaches for his box of Marlboros now as he recalls life on the La Vie Claire team during that tempestuous Tour. "The problem was that the team was half French, half foreign," he explains.

Bernard is affable; open; animated; and, at 48, dressed youthfully in T-shirt, faded jeans, and sneakers, with the same combed-back dark hair—graying at the edges—and the trademark sideburns—just narrow strips to the bottoms of his ears—that distinguished him as a rider. He was 24 when he won his first stage of the Tour, thus confirming in many people's eyes that he would be the Frenchman to succeed Hinault when the Badger retired. It was, he admits now, too much to ask. "If Hinault had done another year, I could have become the new Hinault," he says. "It's like a bird in a nest—if you try to fly too early, you fall. . . ."

But if the weight of expectation eventually got to Jean-François, the background turbulence in his debut Tour might not have helped. "The team was divided in half, with the French supporting Hinault and the others supporting LeMond," Bernard explains matter-of-factly. "The atmosphere wasn't great; we had two teams within one team.

"This division was real," he continues with a shrug. "Even if it wasn't evident day-to-day, or on the surface, it was there the whole Tour. You could feel it.

"I was close to Hinault," he adds, sounding a little circumspect—as though he means that he was as close as it was possible to be to Hinault. "As a young French rider, being taken on by this team, for me it was brilliant . . . but it was great to be with Greg LeMond as well. I never had any problem with him. I liked him. If I see him now, we're friends, I hope. But within the race, you always take sides. And the French were supporting Hinault; we were thinking about the sixth victory and him overtaking Merckx and Anquetil. It was a big thing. For the French, for Hinault to win six, would have been amazing."

Bernard dismisses Hinault's agreement to help LeMond. "*Pah!* It's the strongest who wins the Tour." Yet he does agree that the confusion over who was the team's leader, and the subsequent divisions, created an increasingly difficult atmosphere. It needed, he thinks, a stronger directeur sportif than Köchli. This is where Bernard's opinion is different from Hinault's; he does not rate Köchli highly. "Köchli had his head at 3,000 meters! His head was in the clouds," says Bernard, waving his cigarette in the sky as if to indicate on which cloud Köchli resided. "He wasn't directing anything. Hinault was leading, then Tapie. . . . Köchli was just there to drive the car. Anyway, Hinault, LeMond were both very strong personalities. What do you do with two strong personalities? It's very complicated to manage, and Köchli couldn't manage personalities like that.

"With Guimard," adds Bernard, "I think it would have been clear from the start. But it was never clear. It was a mess. And there was a lot of ambiguity because of that."

Others have suggested that it was Tapie who was really calling the shots. Bernard laughs and rolls his eyes. "Tapie was everywhere," he says. "He was close to everyone, because of his personality. It's true he could intervene anywhere, very easily; his personality allowed him to enter any conversation. So he could get involved in talking about the tactics of the race. He was the same in business, in politics, in soccer. And yes, he was better suited than Köchli to manage this type of situation."

Tapie appeared in Gap that evening. With Köchli absent from the team hotel in Gap—he was away (successfully) appealing the disqualification of Alain Vigneron, allegedly for holding on to the team car during the stage—Tapie talked to every member of the team, visiting their hotel rooms and having one-to-one chats. He also appeared on French TV's prime-time news program. "The mountains will decide the winner," he said. "Everything is good between Greg LeMond and Hinault. Perfect harmony! They both know what they have to do."

"I remember sitting with Tapie in the car on the way to the hotel after the stage," says LeMond, "and him trying to calm me down, saying, 'I'll work it out with Hinault.'

"I said to Tapie, 'Fuck it, I'm done, I'm going home.' I said, 'I'm not going to race against Hinault, against my teammate. I can't do it anymore.'

"OK, I wasn't really going to quit," LeMond concedes, "but I was trying to draw a line in this bullshit. I was a puppet. They played me. I took [Hinault's] word; that was the problem. And Tapie's saying, 'I'll work it out with Hinault.' But I believe Tapie went back into the hotel, spoke to Hinault, and said, 'Fuck LeMond—he's just an American—go for it.'" LeMond adds that he has no evidence to support this belief. But he and others suspected afterward that, after telling LeMond what he wanted to hear, Tapie did the same with Hinault. In other words, nothing had been resolved. Status quo.

By this stage—after Hinault's double ambush in the Pyrenees, after his attempted coup on the road to Gap—how bad had the atmosphere become? Rumors have abounded since 1986 of the team being split in two—with the Swiss in the middle, as befitting their neutral status—and dining separately, or at least at different ends of the table. Köchli is guarded when asked about the divisions in the team. "I think we were prepared for tension," he says. "In this case, you are right, the tension was extremely high. But because we were prepared, it was controlled."

And did the two contingents dine separately? Köchli sighs, then cryptically says, "I would say that is not incorrect. But it is not true, either . . . it is not true, either."

Andy Hampsten remembers that the tension between Hinault and LeMond spawned meetings galore, starting in Gap. "Tapie was going to meet with Hinault; Tapie was going to meet with Greg; Tapie was going to meet with Köchli, Greg, and Hinault. Tapie is going to meet with everyone!" Hampsten laughs. "At the dinner table, you have the French guys at one end, the Swiss guys in the middle, and the three North Americans at the other end. In Gap, after Greg spoke to Tapie, Steve and I asked, 'So, how'd it go?' Greg says, 'Oh, they're not going to do shit.' We can see Greg's totally pissed off. Then Tapie walks into the room, and he's, you know, 'Hi, everyone!'—he's larger than life. You know, he hung around the team, and it was great," continues Hampsten with heavy sarcasm. "When Tapie laughed, we'd all laugh. That kinda thing. I never got a good vibe off him.

"Here he'd come to sort things out—but we've all found out," and here Hampsten drops his voice to a whisper, "that he hasn't done anything. The French guys have found out the same thing, that nothing's been resolved. So nobody's talking. And there are two minutes when you could have heard a pin drop. But, you know, Greg's pissed off, but he's someone who can't sit around and not have fun. And so, when Tapie comes in, Greg shouts out, 'Hey, Tapie—Andy's got the white jersey [for best young rider]; are you going to give him a Porsche?'

"There were three North Americans laughing," Hampsten says, "and everyone else sitting in silence."

W hat happened in that Tour, what happened every day in that Tour, what Bernard Hinault put Greg through, makes me want to cry."

Shelley Verses, the soigneur for the 7-Eleven team who experienced her own baptism at her—and the team's—first Tour in 1986, does sound on the verge of tears as she speaks from her home in Santa Barbara, California. We had already spoken on the phone, at some length, about this Tour, and about the 1985 Giro and her bonding with Bernard Hinault over her daily gift to him of cherries, and about her post-1986 experiences with La Vie Claire and Köchli. But a few weeks after our first conversation, she e-mails: "I have a confession; I lied by omission during our interview. I left out things regarding the 1986 Tour. I felt like I should protect Paul Köchli somehow because I went on to La Vie Claire. It was torture to see what Greg was going through, and I would like to tell you. It has been bothering me terribly."

I reply, and we arrange another time to speak. "Oh, my God," she says, "I didn't say what I really felt, and I just kept thinking, Shelley, you can't do that. But you have to understand the power Bernard Hinault had. Hinault was this commander, this commander in chief. You couldn't take a piss in the peloton unless you asked Bernard Hinault. If you wanted to ride ahead to your village and see your family, you had to ask Bernard Hinault. That was the respect he commanded. He was a man in the peloton. A man, not a boy. And he ruled in every fucking country.

"He was Mussolini, he was Stalin, he was Hitler, he was all of them rolled into one. Off the bike, there was a sweetness to him. But at the same time, here was Greg LeMond, this kid, this gifted child, this prodigy, this incredible athlete, who had the VO_2max nobody had ever seen before. And Hinault just decided, after promising he'd help him, 'I'm not giving it to you.' And he would chase down his own teammate."

Verses sounds close to tears. "During that Tour, at night," she says, "we've got Greg coming to our hotel, we've got Hampsten coming, Bauer coming, saying, 'This is our nightmare. We gotta get out of this.' We were their friends. You had to pretend everything was OK—my directeur sportif always told me that the most important thing for me was to stay calm, to not tell the riders anything, to not upset the stallions in the stable. But I was frickin' petrified every day. We just wanted our friend to win and go and have a Mexican dinner with him at the end in Paris. But we didn't know how it was going to happen. He was our hero. Hinault was our hero, too, but to watch him do such a vile thing was just so awful, so unsportsmanlike.

"Some people can't drop the bone," adds Verses. "Like an angry dog, they've got this bone in their mouth, and you're saying, 'Drop it, drop it!' And he's growling! It's like . . . he'd eat his young. Look at Hinault with Phil [Anderson], when he growled at him and swiped that Coke can out of his hands when he was offering it to him . . . Phil was a 20-year-old kid!" As she talks, Verses's emotions seem to bubble to the surface. Her recall is extraordinarily vivid, not merely in the minutiae of the details but in the feelings she attaches to them, as though she is living the moment all over again, and no less powerfully than the first time around.

Even if they don't express their disappointment with the same emotional force as Verses, others too were upset not only by Hinault's apparent determination to ride roughshod over the agreement he'd made with LeMond but with what they deemed underhanded tactics and psychological warfare. Maurice Le Guilloux, for instance, who comes across as a gentle bear of a man, with his large, deep-set eyes giving him a hangdog, melancholic appearance, seems to have been upset by Hinault's antics. "Greg," says Le Guilloux, "lost confidence in Bernard day after day, bit by bit. He was asking, 'What's happening? What's happening? I'm about to lose the Tour.'

"I like that when you give your word, you keep it," says Le Guilloux. "A champion of the stature of Bernard Hinault needs to recognize that it was thanks to Greg LeMond that he won his fifth Tour de France in 1985. It's true that in 1986, Hinault was under pressure; people couldn't accept he'd help an American and not try and win his sixth Tour. Bernard even told them, 'I gave LeMond my word.' But they told him, 'In cycling, we say the word of a rider means nothing.'

"But that's not the way I see things," adds Le Guilloux. "I don't like it."

Fear comes from uncertainty," said the American writer Eric Hoffer. As Le Guilloux suggests, it was uncertainty that was threatening to destroy LeMond. He became suspicious of every move Hinault made. But Hinault, by his devil-may-care approach to the race, his repeated attacks, his panache, his apparent fearlessness, was in effect holding up a mirror to LeMond's weaknesses, revealing his anxiety and hesitation. And his paranoia? That may be too strong. "Insecurity" is the description favored by the journalist François Thomazeau.

Then again, LeMond could perhaps be excused for feeling paranoid. A poll, published in L'Équipe on the eve of the decisive Alpine stages, claimed that 80 percent of the riders left in the race wanted Hinault to win. If true, the question was, how far would they be prepared to go to help him? LeMond knew that the threat to his hopes of winning the Tour could be more sinister than Hinault's aggression or any amount of psychological warfare, if that is what Hinault was consciously waging.

LeMond had learned about how the sport could work at the Giro, when the $50,000 offer was made to "buy" his and his team's help. Rumors of races, riders, and even entire teams being bought are as abundant and juicy as those about riders' methods for avoiding dope control, though less frequently verified. Trip Gabriel in *Rolling Stone* quoted the journalist John Wilcockson: "'There are excellent riders whose records don't show it because they've sold most of the races they could have won.'" LeMond admits he was "naive about this side of the sport." The Giro, just a month before the Tour, opened his eyes a little.

But now he began to wonder who, other than Hinault and possibly the French riders on his team, might be riding against him. Le Guilloux shared his own fears with LeMond that other French teams, and perhaps even some Spanish teams, would align themselves with Hinault and combine against him. Then there was Anderson's comment early in the Tour. "Hinault can win the Tour without Greg," Anderson had said. "But Greg can't win without Hinault." What did he mean? Possibly, as Verses has noted, that Hinault's power and influence stretched way beyond his own team.

In fact, few attempts were made by most of the other French teams to disguise the fact that they supported Hinault. Yet that didn't mean they necessarily offered practical help. One of them, RMO, was led by Bernard Vallet, an old Hinault cohort. Paul Kimmage, the Irish rider, was also on that team. Kimmage laughs at the suggestion that he might have been "bought" by Hinault. "The view within RMO was certainly pro-Hinault," says Kimmage. "But it was basically coming from Vallet. We weren't good enough to help him. We didn't have riders who'd be there [at the front of the race on the key stages] to be capable of influencing things.

"I'm sure, had we had guys who were good enough, we'd have weighed in," Kimmage says. "But I feel I was almost like a golfer's caddy, holding the flag." This, indeed, is the lot of perhaps a majority of the riders in the Tour, particularly in the third and final week, when many are on their knees. Kimmage continues, "It's amazing to think how little I engaged with the actual race, but that's true of all the pro riders who aren't at the coal face. You get on with your business; you live in this cocoon of your own race, your own world. Meanwhile, this great race is going on—probably the best fucking race of all time—and you're part of it, but you're pretty much a passive observer."

Kimmage knew who was the boss, though. "Oh, yeah, Hinault. I heard about one of my teammates attacking during the 1984 Tour and Hinault chasing him down himself and saying, 'I'll tell you when you can attack.' He was the last of the greats to impose his will on the race in that way. Things changed a lot after he retired. It could work in your favor, too. There was a stage toward the end in '86 when I was on my hands and knees, almost dead, and Hinault said, 'Right, it's controlled today; no mucking around.' I was grateful for that."

Certain teams were said to be "up for sale," meaning they could be "bought" to help another team to work at the front and reel in a breakaway, for example. Not that all such transactions would see money change hands. When LeMond asked Millar for help to catch Hinault on the road to Gap, the deal he struck was that he'd allow Millar to win a mountain stage, if in a position to do so. Which proved that LeMond could play this game, too.

But friendships also mattered. LeMond's friend Anderson was another who was riding for Panasonic, though he had suffered from illness earlier in 1986 and was, in the Grand Tours at least, never quite the same rider again. "I never rode against Greg," says Anderson. "I certainly never chased him down. If a job has to be done for your team, you've got to do it. But even so, I certainly wouldn't have done anything to jeopardize Greg.

"Anyway, at Panasonic we were involved in our own race; we had to beat Jan Raas's team." Raas had ridden for Peter Post, the Panasonic directeur sportif, before the two fell out. "Jan Raas's goal in life was to make sure Peter Post was unsuccessful," says Anderson. "And Peter Post's goal in life was to make sure Jan Raas was unsuccessful." The Dutchmen's rivalry reached its illogical conclusion in 1990 when a rider from each team featured in a two-man break. Each rider was promptly instructed by his directeur not to cooperate with the other. Ludicrously, they came to a virtual standstill and were caught.

That incident highlights the disparate, sometimes random motivations and loyalties of teams and riders, though Anderson has no doubt that Hinault was calling in favors from friends in 1986. But how many of those friends would be capable of helping him in the high mountains, where the race was likely to be decided, was another question altogether. Anderson and others also point to LeMond's temperament as putting him at a disadvantage in the face of any perceived or imagined threat from Hinault and making him susceptible to the mind games the Badger might have indulged in.

"Greg was always very emotional, and not afraid to show his emotions," says Anderson. "It's what I like about him. But yeah, it could make him more vulnerable; it makes him different from most cyclists, that's for sure."

But paranoid? Jean-François Bernard suggests so. "He would sometimes go and eat on his own, and he would have his bike in his room," says Bernard. "He was afraid someone would sabotage it. But I think a lot was exaggerated. At this level of competition, things can happen, but Greg was a bit paranoid, I think."

I really liked Hinault," says LeMond now. "But I was also intimidated by him because he was my hero. I think that's what got to me in '86. It would have been easier for me to get through that race from a psychological and competitive point of view if I'd said, 'Let's just split the team down the middle. You have your guys; I'll have mine.'

"That was the thing that was so confusing: saying one thing, doing the opposite. But for some reason, I got intimidated by Hinault as a figure. I mean, I looked up to him. He was like my big brother. You wouldn't want to go against your big brother; he's your family. And at first, he treated me like his brother, or his son. For me, that was the biggest disappointment.

"But I think he was manipulated. You wouldn't think Hinault's a guy who could be easily manipulated. But I think he was, in a way." Manipulated by whom? I ask. "By Tapie," says LeMond.

"Anyway," he adds, his face softening, the lines disappearing from around his mouth, "although nothing was sorted after Gap, I was lucky. The next day, he had a real bad day. What was it . . . knee pain?"

COL DU GRANON, SUNDAY, JULY 20

Stage 17, from Gap to the summit of the Col du Granon, saw the race enter the Alps, and—after the climbs of the Col de Vars, the Col d'Izoard, and the Tour's highest-ever finish, atop the 2,413-meter Granon—it saw history made. On the Izoard, as the Spaniard Eduardo Chozas rode alone to the stage win, Hinault began to struggle. Earlier in the stage, he dropped back to the doctor's car for medical attention—apparently for his knee—and he would later, while negotiating a twisting descent, be seen fiddling with a hex key, adjusting his saddle height, searching for a more comfortable position.

As they climbed the Col d'Izoard, LeMond shadowed Urs Zimmermann, the rider placed third overall. But with Hinault flagging, there was an opportunity for Zimmermann—and LeMond. According to Zimmermann, several riders attacked as the descent began; a group became detached at the front, including, among others, Charly Mottet. LeMond attacked this group, says Zimmermann, and he followed. Ahead of them was the Col du Granon, a little-known mountain making its first (and still only) appearance on the route of the Tour de France. LeMond worked with Zimmermann to establish the gap, but it was Zimmermann who led them up the Granon, piling on the pressure on what was, he says, "maybe the best day of my whole career."

Behind them, there was carnage. As Zimmermann took second on the stage, 6 minutes 25 seconds behind Chozas—who had managed a Merckx-esque 150-km lone break—LeMond remained glued to his back wheel to place third on the stage. The others were scattered behind them, but the big loser was Hinault. He was 13th, 3 minutes 21 seconds behind LeMond, losing the yellow jersey to his teammate and dropping to third overall, behind Zimmermann. LeMond now led the Swiss by 2 minutes 24 seconds and Hinault by a further 23 seconds.

It was what LeMond had dreamed of: He was in yellow. Yet as he talked to reporters at the finish, as the first rider from the United States ever to wear the yellow jersey, LeMond seemed less than ecstatic. He appeared guarded and cautious. "The race is not over yet," he said. In fact, he had just endured his toughest physical test of the Tour. "I suffered on the Col du Granon," says LeMond. "I ran out of fuel." He managed to avert the dreaded *fringale*, but having run his reserves so low, he was concerned about the following day's stage, the most talked-about of the Tour, beginning in Briançon and tackling the Col du Lautaret, the Col du Galibier, and Col de la Croix de Fer before finishing with the fabled ascent of Alpe d'Huez.

This was the Alpine showdown that would be decisive in settling the final destination of the yellow jersey—of this everybody was sure, as Hinault had been sure at the La Vie Claire training camp in Briançon the previous winter, when he predicted that LeMond would be in yellow with Hampsten, the "little rabbit," setting the pace on the climbs. Turns out Hinault had been right. But LeMond—through his distrust of Hinault, his fear that Hinault's many "friends" in the peloton could become his enemies, and now his concern over his ability to refuel and fully recover from digging so deep to stay with Zimmermann—looked ahead to the stage with some trepidation. It was not the frame of mind he had imagined being in on his first day wearing the yellow jersey.

There was another source of uncertainty: the threat, virtually ignored thus far, posed by Zimmermann. The Swiss rider was now sandwiched between the two La Vie Claire men, only a shade over 2 minutes behind LeMond. In the mountains, as Hinault had proved with his yo-yo performance, 2 minutes was nothing. On a good day, a rider could gain 4 minutes; on a bad day, he could lose many more. Clearly the 26-year-old Zimmermann could no longer be overlooked.

In fact, Köchli knew his fellow Swiss well. "He was our hardest opponent," says Köchli. "I knew him by heart; I was his coach on the national team. And I knew where he was not good. So we had a strategy for that. The strategy was that at least once per day, he must believe that we are attacking him; he must feel under threat. Whether it is true or not, he must believe it."

After tracking down Zimmermann in Switzerland and talking to him now, I didn't find it difficult to imagine why Köchli believed such a strategy could work. Zimmerman comes across as highly sensitive—and he admits that, although the 1986 Tour represented the pinnacle of his career, it was also, for him, fraught with stress and tension. As well as having to fight LeMond and Hinault on the road, he spent most of the three weeks engaged in another battle within his own team, the Italian Carrera squad, with his directeur sportif, Davide Boifava.

Zimmermann—who, with his long, skinny limbs, sunken cheeks, and lank blond hair, had a ghoulish appearance—had emerged as an overall contender after having shed weight, though he dismisses claims made at the time that it was the consequence of an extreme diet. "I had left home and the farm I lived on with my parents," says Zimmermann. "Living on my own, I started cooking for myself. That's all. It was more like a decision to be serious; cycling was my profession. I trained much harder, and by the end of 1985, I was really strong on the hills."

Going into the 1986 Tour, Zimmermann was cautiously optimistic. "I wasn't the kind of guy to say, 'I'm going to win this thing.' But I remember that I talked to the media before the Tour and said there was a good chance for me to be in the top six. But I actually thought I could do better."

Zimmermann emerged as one of the strong men in the Pyrenees. When Hinault attacked on the stage to Pau, Zimmermann says he "got kind of furious. I thought, That's not possible. But I had a bad day and I couldn't react and nobody reacted, I think because everybody was a little scared of Hinault. The next day, when he attacked again, I reacted quite strongly. Otherwise the race had already gone. When Hinault slid away on the descent [of the Tourmalet], all the guys looked at each other. Then I took responsibility, and

I started working, especially with Millar. I paid for my work that day, and I couldn't stay with LeMond on Superbagnères, but at least the race was open again."

Yet Zimmermann's tactics on this stage caused a rift with his directeur. "He told the media, 'Zimmermann was so wrong' to do so much work because I was then dropped [to Superbagnères]. But if I hadn't worked, no one else would have, and the race would have been over. It caused a problem for me with my directeur for the rest of the race. And it got worse. It was very stressful. That was a really bad situation, and really sad."

But going into the Alps, Zimmermann had a chance, and on the stage to the Col du Granon, with LeMond shadowing him, he made his move. The wounded Hinault was falling behind, losing minutes. And, as he climbed with LeMond, Zimmermann believed he had the measure of the American.

And did he believe he could win the Tour? "There was a spirit inside of me," Zimmermann says, though hesitantly. "I said to myself, If there's a chance, I am going to take it. That spirit I had made me proud. It still makes me proud, if I think about it. But I was kind of young, even a little bit naive, and I didn't have the support from the team that I should have. But I was making my own decisions now. I was great that day. Greg attacked at the top of the Izoard, and I went on his wheel, and we took some minutes from the others."

Zimmermann reflects a moment, then says, "I didn't know Greg really well, but I always felt good around him. I could tell he was a good guy. I feel that he always played inside the rules of the game. You know, I feel that there's an official history of this Tour, that tells the story of these two guys [LeMond and Hinault], but I think the real story is rather different, and for me, I felt the race completely differently. Anyway, that's part of cycling. So many stories, and then stories behind the stories.[1]

"What happened between Hinault and Greg," continues Zimmermann, "with Hinault saying he'd help Greg win when deep inside him he didn't want to—for Greg, that was terrible, but for me, it was great." He laughs. "And 1986 was my best Tour; it was a year where everything was right. When I felt I was someone else."

---

1. It's not a complete surprise to discover that, after retiring from cycling, Zimmermann wrote a semiautobiographical novel. In his lugubrious tones, he explains, "I had some problems in my life, and I started writing. My writing is cooking on a low fire now, but when there's inspiration, it goes ahead. I write small stories, looking at life in a different way."

Which, on the eve of the Alpe d'Huez stage, was exactly what Köchli feared. The Zimmermann who matched LeMond on the first hard day in the Alps had become a serious threat precisely because he resembled "someone else," or someone other than the talented but reserved, fragile, and insecure rider, so prone to self-doubt and so well known to Köchli from his days coaching the Swiss team. Especially after the Col du Granon stage, Zimmermann seemed possessed by a performance-enhancing cocktail more potent and more effective than any drug: the fitness and form of his life allied with self-belief and confidence.

This added another, unexpected dimension to the final week of the Tour. Would it see a shift in the battle from LeMond versus Hinault to LeMond versus Zimmermann? Jacques Anquetil, writing in *L'Équipe* on the morning of the Alpe d'Huez stage, wasn't so sure that Hinault should be discounted just yet. *"Le Blaireau n'est pas mort"* (The Badger is not dead), wrote Anquetil on Monday, July 21. Either Anquetil was putting on a show of confidence for the benefit of the French public, which had started to believe that the sixth title was within the Badger's grasp, or he had the inside track on the state of Hinault's mysterious injury.

One man who did have the inside track was Maurice Le Guilloux. But Le Guilloux first makes an important point about the stage to the Col du Granon—the stage that saw history made as LeMond wrested the yellow jersey from his teammate. "Greg never attacked Hinault," says Le Guilloux, repeating, "he never attacked Hinault. He only followed Zimmermann, as he only followed Roche on the Tourmalet the previous year. He didn't attack Hinault.

"Bernard had a big problem with his leg," continues Le Guilloux. "Not his knee, as most people thought. It was in his calf. It was incredible; it was touch and go, borderline, whether Bernard would quit the next day. He was given anti-inflammatories and lots of medicine [including mesotherapy, the insertion of needles to allow medicine to be more quickly absorbed]. But we were thinking that maybe he wouldn't start the next stage because it's a big stage, to Alpe d'Huez.

"But the next morning, a miracle!" adds Le Guilloux, throwing his hands into the air. "His leg is fine."

14

A TWO-HEADED EAGLE

The true secret of the Alpe's success is that it is a climb that delivers a verdict—absolute, impartial, and final.

JEAN-PAUL VESPINI

ALPE D'HUEZ, MONDAY, JULY 21

The night he lost the yellow jersey to Greg LeMond and slipped to third overall, Bernard Hinault called a team meeting at the La Vie Claire hotel in Briançon. The Badger was unhappy. Not about his injury. Not even about the fact that his teammate LeMond had taken over the jersey that he had been wearing for the last six days. No; Hinault was unhappy about Zimmermann.

It was unacceptable, Hinault told his teammates, that Zimmermann now split the two La Vie Claire riders. He harked back to the previous year's Tour, when having riders placed first and second on general classification had put them in such a strong position. And so tomorrow, said Hinault, they, as a team, would have to take Zimmermann out. They would do so by attacking him. And they would keep attacking him until he was broken.

When, and by whom, Hinault didn't say. But LeMond knew that his first day in yellow would be fraught. It was never going to be easy, not on such a tough stage. But riding defensively, with Hinault as his lieutenant, following moves and marking other riders rather than trying to set the race alight, might have made sense. There were, after all, only two more mountain stages, neither as tough as this one, and the time trial in two days would suit Hinault and LeMond—not Zimmermann. But no. Not a chance. Hinault was, recalls LeMond, talking "insane tactics . . . about how he's got to keep attacking Zimmermann." There would be fireworks.

In fact, there were—according to Bernard Tapie—fireworks later that same evening, on the eve of the Alpe d'Huez stage, as the dispute between Hinault and LeMond flared up. According to Tapie, they were "at each other's throats" all day. "I took my plane that evening," said Tapie, "and, after arriving, spent from 2 to 4 o'clock in the morning with them."

As the 143 surviving riders—some 67 having now pulled out, a testimony to how brutal this Tour had been—gathered in Briançon on the morning of Monday July 21, LeMond, wearing the yellow jersey for the first time in his career, felt a knot of anxiety form in his stomach. The Badger, meanwhile, resembled a boxer striding toward the ring in his satin gown, puffed up with purpose, brimful of confidence, buoyed and cheered by the throngs of supporters in Briançon chanting, "Hi-nault! Hi-nault!" as they glimpsed their hero. Hinault had said he wanted to have fun at this Tour, and he did appear—despite his partial collapse in the Pyrenees, despite his injury in the Alps the previous day, now apparently overcome and forgotten—to be having fun. LeMond was only concerned that it was at his expense.

Today Hinault's arena, his boxing ring, would be one of the greatest in the Tour: Alpe d'Huez. This was the stage everyone had been looking forward to. It would be packed with fans from bottom to top, many of them French, most rooting for Hinault. It could be an intimidating place at the best of times. "People didn't clear a path until the last second," as Andy Hampsten, who, six years later, would win at the summit of the Alpe, said. "I felt like I was going at 60 kilometers an hour. The sensation of passing through such a narrow opening in the crowd was the most beautiful and emotional thing I've ever experienced in my life."

But the sheer number of spectators, their proximity to the riders, their overwhelming support for one rider over all others could make Alpe d'Huez seem like a hostile place, too. It was the greatest feature of this particular climb—its suitability as an arena for sporting battles, the 21 hairpin bends, snaking up the mountain, forming a natural amphitheater, a gladiator's ring, on an epic scale. Then there was its place in Tour folklore, established since Fausto Coppi's win there in 1952, the first time the Alpe had been used— indeed, the Tour's first-ever summit finish. Coppi's performance was full of panache, it was conclusive in winning him the Tour, and it meant the Tour "had discovered its Fenway Park, its Wimbledon, its stadium of reference . . . [its] modern temple," according to the French writer Jean-Paul Vespini in his book *The Tour Is Won on the Alpe*. "The true secret of the Alpe's success," he added, "is that it is a climb that delivers a verdict—absolute, impartial, and final."

There is no easing in, no opportunity to gradually loosen the muscles, as the riders roll out of Briançon on the N91 and almost immediately begin to climb the Col du Lautaret. The attacks begin at the gun. Julian Gorospe, Dag-Otto Lauritzen, and Maarten Ducrot all have a go. And then, as the road curls up, there are more jabs—this time Jean-François Bernard going clear in a small group. More try their luck, among them another La Vie Claire rider, Guido Winterberg, followed by the Colombian Luis Herrera, whose hopes of winning overall were compromised as early as the team time trial and have by now collapsed.

The Lautaret turns into the majestic Col du Galibier, winding up over one of the highest passes in Europe, where Herrera and Winterberg ride away from their companions, who are mercilessly gobbled up by the peloton. Herrera and Winterberg form an alliance and carve out a lead of 1½ minutes. Near the summit, Winterberg struggles to stay with the small Colombian climber, and by the summit, at 2,645 meters, he trails by 10 seconds.

Behind this pair, the large group contains all the favorites. Hinault is prominent all the way up the Galibier, trying a few tentative jabs with brief accelerations, testing the others' legs. LeMond pays close attention to him, never allowing Hinault, wearing the multicolored patchwork jersey awarded to the leader of the combined competition, to stray too far, while Zimmermann, in the red Swiss champion's jersey, spends much of the climb following LeMond, in yellow. Zimmermann, it appears, is glued to LeMond's wheel. He seems uninterested in Hinault. "The great danger now is Zimmermann," as the TV commentator Phil Liggett intones. "He's the biggest threat, but not far behind lurks the Badger; is he thinking he could profit from the attention the top two will be paying each other? If they watch each other, perhaps Hinault could slip away unnoticed.

"Hinault," says Liggett, "is like a time bomb."

As they begin the descent of the Galibier, there is a flash of color. The patchwork jersey—yellow, green, red, and white—shoots out of the yellow-jersey group. It's Hinault. The "insane tactics" have started. On the descent of the Galibier, barely 40 km into the stage, he has attacked.

It's the Tourmalet all over again, but with a crucial difference. This time, two other riders chase after Hinault and catch him: the Spaniard Pello Ruiz Cabestany and Hinault's La Vie Claire teammate Steve Bauer. Bauer will later confess to being confused as to what Hinault is doing and why he is attacking. Hinault will argue that he is not attacking LeMond; he is attacking Zimmermann, as he said he would do.

"Hinault started attacking on the Galibier," says LeMond. "He was saying, 'We've got to secure second place.' At one point on the climb, he got away, but I went after him myself. Then he attacks on the descent, and people counterattack, and he keeps going, while Zimmermann's just staying on my wheel. All of a sudden there are three guys together [Hinault, Bauer, and Cabestany]. I stopped pedaling to see what Zimmermann would do, if he would jump after them. But he stayed behind me. I thought, Holy shit. I was given strict instructions not to work with Zimmermann, so I was stuck."

Again Hinault has seized the initiative. And LeMond is in a bind. If he can't catch Hinault, Hinault could win the Tour.

"The Galibier is not a steep descent," LeMond says. "It's a descent you have to ride on, actually pedal and ride hard. But I'm stuck with Zimmermann. I can't ride because I'll just take him up to Hinault."

After the 17-km descent of the Galibier, the road briefly rises up again as it tackles the easy side of the Col du Télégraphe—a 5-km rise before another long descent. It gives LeMond an opportunity to drop back to speak to Köchli in the team car. He rides alongside the open window, speaking for about a minute to the directeur sportif. "Greg asked me, 'What shall I do?'" recalls Köchli. "I said, 'You don't know what to do? You want to win the Tour?'

"'Yes,' he said, 'I want to win the Tour.' So I told him, 'Just drop Zimmermann and go with them before it's too late.' Simple!

"Before that," continues Köchli, "Winterberg had been first over the summit of the Galibier [in fact, he was second to Herrera]. We played all over the place. They created the race, with this strategy giving us the possibility to be everywhere."

"On the Télégraphe," says LeMond, "I'm with Zimmermann, and Bauer, Hinault, and Cabestany are a minute and a half up on me. Köchli's telling me, 'You must not work with Zimmermann, you must attack him—is that clear?'

But there's only a couple of hundred meters of the climb left. What the hell, I think. I just put it in a pretty good-sized gear and sprinted as hard as I could past Zimmermann. I got about 10 meters in front, and all I could hear was his bike creaking as he sprinted to try and catch me."

As he begins the descent, LeMond looks around and sees Zimmermann struggling to negotiate one of the early bends, almost overshooting it. Beyond the road lies vast scree, boulder-strewn slopes; the closer Zimmermann gets to the edge, the more scared and more cautious he becomes. His self-doubt has returned. And as he tenses up, he slows down. LeMond knows this. He also recognizes Zimmermann's limitations on the descent: He is tall, gangly, with a high center of gravity. When LeMond goes flat out, Zimmermann can't keep up. So LeMond twists the knife, taking the bends even faster. The gap between them is like an accordion; it stretches on every corner and contracts on every straight as Zimmermann sprints for LeMond's rear wheel. But finally it stretches until it breaks, even though Zimmermann adjusts his body to get as aerodynamic as possible, moving his backside over his rear wheel, lowering his chest onto his saddle. With the Swiss left behind, LeMond nails it, riding as hard and as fast as he has ever ridden in his life and eventually making contact with Hinault's group.

When he does, there is no acknowledgment, no eye contact, indeed no communication at all between him and Hinault. Even nonteammates would often exchange a word or a glance of recognition. But LeMond's gaze is focused squarely on the road ahead. Hinault only briefly glances up to see who, if anyone, is with him. Perhaps he silently congratulates himself that Zimmermann is not there. Perhaps he seethes inwardly that LeMond is.

Bauer, meanwhile, is relieved; he has been extricated from an awkward situation. In a lead group with Hinault, with his friend and teammate LeMond chasing behind, he was unsure what to do. But now he goes to the front and, in the teeth of a headwind, acts the perfect teammate, driving the four-man group through the valley, further distancing Zimmermann. "I just rode the whole valley like a time trial," he says. "We got to the Croix de Fer [at 85 km], and we had about 3 minutes on the chase group by then. I sat up and said to Greg and Hinault, 'OK, my job's done. The race is yours.'"

Cabestany, a passenger in the lead group, remains with Hinault and LeMond on the Croix de Fer, where, as they begin the climb, Hinault asks LeMond to slow down. "He said his knee was hurting," says LeMond. "He said, 'Let me ride in front.'" And so Hinault leads most of the way up the climb, then drops like a stone down the other side, finally getting rid of Cabestany in the process. LeMond sticks like a limpet to Hinault; he doesn't want to suffer the fate suffered by Zimmermann on the earlier descent. But he is astonished at the risks Hinault seems prepared to take on the way down.

Félix Lévitan, the Tour's director, in the car behind the leading pair, cannot believe what he is seeing, either. "In all my years on the Tour de France, I have never seen such a descent," Lévitan says on race radio. "No word describes this. . . . Hinault is doing 90 kilometers per hour, and LeMond is with him." And there's another shock in store for Lévitan: Midway down, Hinault slows marginally, sits up, yanks at his shorts, and leans over to the side of the road—he is relieving himself.

Hinault's kamikaze descent, even allowing for his natural break, succeeds in increasing his and LeMond's advantage over Zimmermann. At the summit of the Croix de Fer, the Swiss was 2 minutes 50 seconds behind the La Vie Claire pair. After the descent, as they begin the 15-km ride through the valley to the base of Alpe d'Huez, the gap has increased to 4½ minutes. Through the valley, Hinault and LeMond ease off a little; the urgency goes. They appear to be steadying themselves, preparing for what's about to come, what will surely be the defining moment of the 1986 Tour.

Midway through the valley, the La Vie Claire team car pulls alongside, though this time it isn't Köchli but Bernard Tapie who addresses his riders. He speaks to them both. They nod and carry on.

And now, as LeMond and Hinault ride together through the village of Bourg d'Oisans, at the foot of Alpe d'Huez, they can glance up and see the road zigzagging up the mountain, easily picked out by the sun glinting off the parked cars that line the route all the way to the summit along with a heaving mass of humanity estimated later to number half a million people. Ahead of Hinault and LeMond now is the climb that "delivers a verdict—absolute, impartial, and final."

You have to ride with your head," says Hinault. He is explaining why he told LeMond to slow down on the Croix de Fer and to ride steadily—not too hard—in the valley before they reached Alpe d'Huez. "There's no point riding really hard in the valley if on the climb you're going to collapse. You can always make up more time on the climb than in the valley. You have to give Zimmermann a bit of hope—leave him thinking, 'I'm coming back to them.

I'm coming back. . . .' And then, when you get to the end of the valley, he's worn himself out trying to recoup the time, thinking you're weak.

"Then you get to the climb, and you turn the screw," Hinault continues, adding with a whistle, "*Au revoir*. And he's out the back. That's what we did on the Croix de Fer before that. We got to the bottom with a gap of a minute, a minute and a half, and Greg wanted to go hard. I said, 'Let him come to us. Give him some hope.' We let him come back a bit, then we turned the screw. *Vrooom! Au revoir!*

"That's what tactics are. You don't just have to ride like a beast all the time. We were also lucky to have Steve Bauer and Cabestany, so there were four of us riding and only one behind [Zimmermann]. So just to get close to us in the valley, he'd more or less exhausted himself. You let them come back, let them think you're tired, then at the very moment when they think they're back in it, you twist the knife. Mentally, that's when you kill them."

With Zimmermann done for, what now for LeMond and Hinault as they begin to climb the Alpe? Entering the human corridor, Hinault leads, LeMond follows. "The crowd is massive," Hinault will later write in his autobiography, "and they are chanting my name. Greg looks worried; I tell him to stay behind me, that it will be OK, that I know how to deal with the crowd."

For hairpin after hairpin, the order remains the same: Hinault leads, LeMond follows as they proceed through banks of braying fans who have waited all day, perhaps several days, for their fleeting glimpse of the race. No wonder their excitement is at fever pitch; they're seeing the national hero and the yellow jersey tearing the race—if not each other—to pieces. The fleeting nature of their exposure to the action only makes the experience more intense: the three weeks, the battle that has raged on the roads of France, distilled into a single moment. In the circumstances, LeMond seems content to follow Hinault rather than to set the pace himself or, as payback for Hinault's repeated attacks over the previous two weeks, to give the Badger a taste of his own medicine by attacking him.

But in fact LeMond is following the instructions issued by Tapie. When the team car drove alongside the pair on the approach to the Alpe, Tapie told LeMond, "You've won the Tour, Greg. But this is really important: Let Hinault lead—it's his last Tour—and let him win the stage." LeMond had nodded his agreement; it was a deal that appeared to suit him and also Hinault.

But fear also weighed on LeMond's mind and influenced his thinking. "I was worried," he says. "I was thinking of Eddy Merckx, who was punched in his side. I was thinking there could be someone out there . . . there was such strong feeling out there. It was so frenzied. And I'm racing against France's best-known athlete."

Such fears were not far-fetched. As LeMond says, there was a precedent. Merckx, as he chased Bernard Thévenet on the Puy de Dôme, was punched hard in the kidneys by a spectator during the 1975 Tour. The blow knocked the stuffing out of Merckx and arguably cost him the Tour. Much was also made of the fact that it happened on Bastille Day and that Merckx was up against a Frenchman.

"I kept telling him to stay behind," says Hinault. "There was absolutely no need for him to go and wear himself out on the climb. We were 6 minutes ahead. I told him, 'You stay calm, don't panic, and we go to the finish together.'"

And so Hinault leads, LeMond follows as they proceed up the mountain at a steady pace, taking 48 minutes from bottom to top, which, incredibly, is almost 3 minutes slower than Fausto Coppi's ascent in 1952 (and more than 10 minutes slower than the almost certainly drug-fueled record time Marco Pantani would establish in 1997). Not that the processional nature of their progress really matters to those watching, who believe they are witnessing the most extraordinary reconciliation and a mountaintop finish destined to be recognized as one of the greatest of all time.

It is perfect, in fact. A scriptwriter couldn't have come up with a more fitting, or more moving, denouement. Hinault is fulfilling the promise he made to LeMond, performing the role he said he'd perform as though he has finally come to terms with it. His shepherding of LeMond up the mountain is almost paternal. It seems to signify that the old warrior, in his final Tour, having given his all, is conceding defeat. But in doing so, he is also ensuring that he goes out with his pride and dignity not merely intact but enhanced. He is handing over to his successor, but on his terms. The climb stands in stark contrast to Hinault's last ascent of this mountain, two years earlier, when he managed a desperate attack on the approach to the Alpe, then wove and wobbled to the summit as Laurent Fignon toyed with him and laughed at him. There is a nobility, even heroism, to what Hinault appears to be doing here, particularly given the implied threat to LeMond from the roadside fans, virtually all Hinault supporters.

The fans spill in unruly fashion onto the road, and Hinault cleaves through them, clearing the way for LeMond, who is able to follow in the protective cocoon between his teammate's rear wheel and the TV motorbike that follows just behind him. They climb in silence. Hinault's snarl has vanished, replaced by an expression not—for once—of anger but of pure, concentrated effort. His jaw is still clenched, but the rage seems to have disappeared from his eyes. Even LeMond looks relaxed. "They look as though they're out on a club run," says Liggett as they begin to enter the ski resort at the summit.

At the plateau, as the road levels, LeMond puts in the smallest of accelerations to emerge, for the first time since the valley, from Hinault's shadow. He pulls alongside his teammate while Hinault turns and looks at him almost indulgently. LeMond reaches out to touch his shoulder blade and then puts his arm around Hinault's shoulder. LeMond smiles. Hinault smiles. They exchange a few words, chatting as though they are indeed out for a leisurely ride. As one speaks, the other nods; they smile, nod again, and carry on riding side by side.

Kathy LeMond is watching in the commentary booth at the finish line in the company of Phil Liggett, who invites her to share her thoughts with the Channel 4 audience. "It's fabulous," she says, her voice crackling with emotion. "I'm glad to see they're just good friends now."

What did Greg say to Hinault? Liggett asks Kathy. "You win," she says.

As they near the line and LeMond eases up slightly as they join hands in the air, Kathy offers a running commentary. "All right, they're going to cross the line like this. . . . Watch, I knew it, I knew it. All right. All right!"

Hinault crosses the line first, for his 26th stage win, a haul that puts him behind only Merckx in the all-time list.

"This Tour has been the hardest one I've ever raced; everybody's on the verge of just cracking," says the drawn, tired-looking LeMond after crossing the line. "I was worried today myself, you know. Zimmermann rode a really good race yesterday, and I kind of got the bonk with only a kilometer. . . . I was great until the last kilometer, and I was afraid that when you get the *fringale*, the bonk, and lose all that energy and sugar, it's hard to replace, and I was worried about today. But I felt really, really good on the last two climbs."

When he pulled level with Hinault, what did LeMond say? "Thank you and, uh . . ." As he pauses, the crevasses around LeMond's mouth deepen, his eyes start to sparkle, and his drawn face breaks into a smile. "I told him, 'This has been a great stage for you and me, and I hope we're both winners.'" To reporters, LeMond also admits, "It would have looked scandalous if I'd put a few minutes on Bernard today. They [the French supporters] are looking to fry me out there."

At the summit of Alpe d'Huez, around the podium, the support for Hinault appears even more enthusiastic than it had been on the narrow passage up the mountain. "Hi-nault! Hi-nault!" the spectators chant as their hero appears on the podium to receive his garland for the stage win. He embraces LeMond, who has just been presented with the yellow jersey for a second day. Then he accepts his own array of bouquets: for most aggressive rider, for best *rouleur*, and . . . for best teammate.

From the podium, Hinault negotiates the crowds, holding a large bouquet of red-tipped flowers high in the air, heading for the La Vie Claire motor home. He shaves, combs his hair, and changes into a white team tracksuit. Putting on his Ray-Bans as he steps back into the sunlight, he is introduced to the French sports minister, Christian Bergelin, and then heads for a post-stage interview with French TV's daily review show, *A Chacun Son Tour* (To each his Tour).

In a makeshift and crowded studio at the summit of Alpe d'Huez, the yellow-jerseyed LeMond sits beside a relaxed-looking Hinault, who, in his white tracksuit top and with a towel wrapped around his neck, slumps in his chair, sipping from a bottle of beer. While Zimmermann is interviewed by Jacques Chancel and asked if he understood what Hinault and LeMond had done to him, Hinault laughs. And when Chancel turns to the still smiling Hinault, he can hardly be heard above the chants of "Hi-nault! Hi-nault!" It may as well be the Hinault show. "I thought Greg learned a lot again today," Hinault says between glugs of beer. "I only hope the strongest man wins this Tour."

"You are going to fight one another?" asks a surprised Chancel, who, like everyone else, believed the hand-in-hand finish signaled a truce.

"The Tour is not finished," Hinault replies. "There could be a crash; many things can happen. [But] if we have a war, it'll be a fair war, and the stronger one will win."

"So, LeMond," Chancel turns to LeMond, "you'll be forced to attack?"

"But I don't want to attack!" LeMond says, forcing a nervous laugh. "Why would I attack? I could've attacked last year as well."

As the chants of "Hi-nault! Hi-nault!" continue, the Badger holds court in front of an audience that includes Bergelin, the actor André Dussolier, and the ex–soccer star Michel Hidalgo. Chancel goads Hinault: "You're only 2 minutes away from LeMond—you can catch him!"

And Hinault shrugs again. "I don't know. We'll see."

LeMond, meanwhile, shifts uncomfortably in his seat. And, in the description of *Rolling Stone* magazine, "he turns ashen."

A two-headed eagle" read the banner headline on the following day's *L'Équipe* above a picture of LeMond and Hinault at the summit of Alpe d'Huez, with arms raised, beaming, LeMond looking almost gratefully across at Hinault. "Like tragedy or comedy, the epic has its strict rules, with its own particular characters and set of circumstances," writes Jean Amadou, the distinguished French playwright. "In the one written yesterday . . . the performance of the Breton, Hinault, and the American, LeMond, will stay in the memory and appear in the books just like all the Tour legends before them.

"At Alpe d'Huez," Amadou continues, "Hinault jumped even further up the popularity scale as the hunter turned gamekeeper. By acting as the American's mentor, Hinault underlined his perfect understanding of what it takes to trigger the crowd's enthusiasm. And whatever happens, he's won in the public's eyes: If he wins, he's a hero; if he loses, he's an idol."

Finally, Amadou adds, "my natural skepticism means that I should be suspicious of top riders hugging and kissing each other just when the cameras are pointing in their direction. I suspect a touch of affectation. Yet when Hinault and LeMond fell into each other's arms on the podium, it seemed to me that the gesture was spontaneous. Despite everything that I've seen and the cynicism that's built up in me, the Tour has restored a feeling of naïveté that had long since been dulled."

Another *L'Équipe* writer, Eric Lahmy, strikes a slightly different note, perhaps having heard Hinault's ambiguous interview on French TV. He suggests that the script might not yet be finalized, that there could be one more twist in the final act. "Once again Hinault has shown us what he can do. He's taken Fignon, Herrera, Millar, and Zimmermann out of the equation. All of his rivals except for his teammate. What will Hinault do tomorrow? The situation reminds me of the film *Vera Cruz*, an old Gary Cooper and Burt Lancaster Western. The two heroes are out to find the treasure, but, together, they must first beat the bad guys.

"Then the day comes when the two of them stand face-to-face over the bounty," adds Lahmy. "And then it's all about whoever can draw first."

The trouble was that neither had drawn on Alpe d'Huez. Hinault's and LeMond's guns remained in their holsters. Steve Bauer, who had been so prominent before slipping back on the Croix de Fer, was exasperated when he heard that his two team leaders had ridden together all the way to the summit without one attacking the other. "They should've battled it out," says Bauer. "But Hinault played the game where he said, 'I'll lead you up the mountain so nobody [in the crowd] will attack you.' Greg was really furious later, when Hinault came out with that stuff about the Tour not being over, because he said he could have dropped Hinault, and then Hinault's saying he could've dropped Greg.

"Greg was fearful, believe me," Bauer continues. "I think that's why he bought what Hinault said and rode up behind him. And I think it was a legitimate concern. There was such a rivalry between them that I believe there was the possibility of sabotage or some kind of attack. Everybody wanted Hinault to win a sixth Tour, and that was playing pretty strong in the media and with the fans. Greg was worried, for sure. And, on some levels, he had good reason to be.

"But I still think they really should've battled it out right there, man. That should've been the race."

In his autobiography, Hinault makes a bold statement: "I could have had his scalp at Alpe d'Huez if I'd wanted to." Now, asked whether he really feels he was stronger than LeMond on the climb to Alpe d'Huez, he strikes an ambivalent tone: "Maybe. We'll never know. I had him behind me, but I don't know if I could have dropped him. So no one will know which of the two was better."

Does he regret that his main rival, LeMond, wasn't on a rival team? Hinault puffs out his cheeks. "*Non.* I've never regretted what happened."

ALPE D'HUEZ, TUESDAY, JULY 22

At 9 a.m. on Tuesday, July 22, the day after the Alpe d'Huez stage, on the Tour's first and only rest day, Hinault and LeMond appeared together in the Church of Our Mother of the Snows for a press conference. Hinault spoke about the previous day and the upcoming days, then proceeded to tear up and rewrite the script, or at least the version of the story that had been written following the hand-in-hand finish the previous day. "It's not over" was his mantra, expressed more forcibly now than it had been during the previous evening's TV interview. The reforged friendship that Kathy LeMond had so wanted to believe in the previous day was a fallacy.

For the duration of the press conference, Paul Köchli sat between his two riders, all three of them dressed in pristine white team-issue tracksuits, and dwarfed by the enormous pipes of the church organ that rose up behind them. "They looked like angels," one journalist noted wryly. "Daylight from the conical tower above poured light on them. Had they come to confession?"

By now the atmosphere was very obviously strained, and there was no more of Tapie's talk of "perfect harmony" between the two leaders. Köchli tried in vain to dispel rumors of "a rift," but it was written in the demeanor and body language of LeMond. It was also clear that Alpe d'Huez had, according to Hinault, decided nothing.

"I'm very proud of what we did together," Hinault told the journalists. "But the Tour isn't over. Who was stronger on the climb? Go on, ask Greg." LeMond just about managed a weak smile. Hinault then went on to explain that the race would be decided by the 58-km time trial at Saint-Étienne in two days' time. The day after that would see the final summit finish, at Puy de Dôme.

But—once again—Hinault had decided that the outcome would hinge on his specialty, the individual time trial. "In no case will I attack Greg at Puy if I haven't won back the yellow jersey [in the time trial]," said Hinault. For Le-Mond, this was cold comfort, if it was comfort at all.

When Hinault, LeMond, and Köchli stood up to leave, they stepped out of the church and each headed in a different direction. But LeMond stopped to speak to reporters. "This is a very stressful Tour for me, both mentally and physically. It is an unusual situation," he said. *L'Équipe*'s front page the following day performed the journalistic equivalent of a backflip. In contrast to the joyous hand-in-hand image of the "two-headed eagle" of just 24 hours before, the headline now was tantamount to a war cry by the French sports daily on behalf of its hero: "*HINAULT: CE N'EST PAS FINI!*"

I mean, what a moment it was," says Sam Abt. "The two of them coming up Alpe d'Huez, Greg's arm around Hinault, lifting the two hands as they crossed the line. It was a beautiful moment. And they had buried Zimmermann.

"Then," continues Abt, "I go to the press conference on the rest day the next day. And I just noticed, when I looked at my own clips [newspaper clippings], that I buried what Hinault actually said there." In other words, Abt didn't go down the same road as *L'Équipe*, with Hinault's battle cry that it wasn't yet over. Abt preferred to be seduced by the romance of the original story, of hatchets buried and of reconciliation.

"I don't think I could believe it," Abt explains. "Here's this press conference, and Hinault's saying, 'It isn't over yet.' I couldn't quite comprehend this. I mean, here was one of the great moments in sport. And then you get this . . . surly Hinault the next day, with LeMond sitting next to him. And Hinault's saying, 'It isn't over.' Everybody looked at each other, and we're thinking, You gotta be kidding.

"Here's my own opinion," continues Abt, measuring his words carefully. "Hinault just didn't get it. It's sort of understandable. He's a coarse guy, he's not educated, he comes from a very poor background. He's not the kind of guy who would say, 'This was a beautiful moment yesterday; let's not spoil it.' He didn't get it. It wouldn't even occur to him, I think, to consider that this was now part of his heritage. Of course, Anquetil said, 'This is Hinault's greatest Tour. If he wins it, he wins six. And if he helps LeMond win it, he's a hero.' And that was correct. But Hinault almost managed to blow all that.

"I've always thought Hinault was sadistic," adds Abt. "But now, after re-reading my clips, I'm less sure of that. I think it's part of it. It's like with [Lance] Armstrong. There's a part of him that is sadistic—the mind games and all. But in Hinault's case, I don't think he was as calculating as that. I don't think he knew any better."

SAINT-ÉTIENNE, WEDNESDAY, JULY 23

After the rest day, acting as a bridge to the time trial, the 179.5-km 19th stage from Villard de Lans to Saint-Étienne fueled LeMond's suspicions that dark forces could be massing against him. After declaring a go-slow in the first part of the stage—much to the relief of Paul Kimmage, among others, who had scraped inside the time limit at Alpe d'Huez—Hinault tried, close to the finish, to break away on the descent of the Côte de la Croix de Chaubourtet. He escaped with the rider who had unwittingly been at the center of the La Vie Claire controversy the previous year: Stephen Roche. But on this occasion, it was Roche whose team loyalties demanded that he not collaborate with Hinault. With his Carrera teammate Zimmermann third, and theoretically still with a chance of beating Hinault into Paris, Roche refused to work with Hinault and sat up.

Hinault's intentions seemed clear, though. He was still attacking, still seeking to claw back time ahead of what he had declared would be the deciding stage, the following day's 58-km time trial, also in Saint-Étienne. Andy Hampsten recalls Hinault attacking through the feed zone—a breach of etiquette to which, oddly, the rest of the peloton turned a blind eye. "I thought the [Hinault-LeMond] battle would resolve itself after Alpe d'Huez," says Hampsten. "But we saw Hinault go in the feed zone, and Greg thought, Oh, shit. We were shocked."

But there were other incidents in that stage, LeMond recalls, that left him feeling uneasy—a vague sense that he might be in danger; that people were out to get him; that he wasn't being accorded the respect or the protection usually afforded the yellow jersey. For example, if the yellow jersey stops to answer a call of nature, it is another of cycling's unwritten rules that the peloton slows and waits until he is safely back in their number. But on stage 19, to Saint-Étienne, LeMond couldn't be confident that would happen. He might have had the yellow jersey, but Hinault remained the *patron*. He spent the stage, as he would spend the remainder of the Tour, riding in fear of a puncture or more serious mechanical problem.[1]

LeMond had been diplomatic during the press conference at the summit of Alpe d'Huez. He hadn't criticized Hinault and appeared resigned to accepting his diktat that the time trial in Saint-Étienne would decide the race and the final destination of the yellow jersey. In truth, that wasn't difficult for him to accept; with a lead of 2 minutes 45 seconds over Hinault, and with his legs feeling strong, he was confident that he would beat Hinault in the time trial. And he really wanted to. The 40-second defeat in the first time trial, at Nantes, after he'd suffered a broken wheel and puncture, played on LeMond's mind, not least because the result had seemed to vindicate Hinault's aggression in the subsequent stages. LeMond had his one stage win, at Superbagnères, but another would add a golden seal. And it would confirm him as a deserving winner, in contrast with the picture that was being drawn of him in the French press as the "cavalier," riding to Paris on Hinault's back.

---

1. Even more sinister was a rumor that reached LeMond some years later: "I heard this story that one guy, a very senior French rider, was willing to crash me, to bring me down. But Hinault said, 'No.' He didn't want that."

On the road to Saint-Étienne, as Hinault tried to get away, LeMond was
bailed out by his most loyal teammates, Steve Bauer and Andy Hampsten.
"It's the only time I ever chased a teammate in my life," says Hampsten. "It
felt weird; I felt sick doing it. I'm chasing my hero, who also happens to be
my teammate, but you know what? I'm thinking, This isn't cool. Greg had
the jersey.

"I knew it was the right thing to do," adds Hampsten. "I was pissed, sick of
the whole situation. Emotionally, it was really, really hard. We were just confused by Hinault. I mean, I know there was pressure on him, and he has the
president of France saying, 'Why not go for six instead of helping an American?' But it went too far.

"Steve and I needed to support Greg," Hampsten continues. "And so we
said to him, 'Look, we're behind you.' Greg said, 'What if other teams are
helping him?' And we said, 'We don't think that's going to happen. We'll
keep you in the front.' That wasn't hard because Greg was so strong. And he
has good tactical sense. We tried to reassure him; we told him, 'So what if
Hinault has a bunch of buddies? You are strong. With me and Steve helping
you, you'll be OK.'"

And LeMond did have a few other friends. At the finish in Saint-Étienne,
Phil Anderson scolded Hinault for attacking his yellow-jerseyed teammate.
There was a strange synchronicity in this; in the same city a year ago, Hinault
had crashed, breaking his nose and blaming Anderson.

Speaking to reporters in Saint-Étienne, LeMond appeared close to breaking down. The strain was telling; his face was even more drawn. By this point,
as *Rolling Stone* put it, "the Tour de France had taken the youthfulness out
of LeMond's face, glazing his small, blue eyes and stretching his skin tightly
over the contours of his skull. At 25, he was like the survivor of a death camp,
hanging on to first place overall in what the French papers called a 'march
through hell,' the hardest Tour de France in 40 years."

"I don't see any natural threats," LeMond told TV reporters when asked
what might now stop him winning the Tour. His eyes were red and raw, but
they burned with intensity; he looked like he'd been crying. "I keep hearing rumors about stuff, and I sure hope nothing like that happens. People
say that 80 percent of the peloton will race against me, and I just feel that's
kinda absurd. I mean, this is sport. I've been racing with Bernard for years.
But if I don't win because of an accident, and Bernard wins because I've been

knocked out by some rider in the peloton, I just say it will be his worst victory ever, and that's a bad way to go down in history.

"It's the tension from the organizer of the race, the public," continued LeMond. "They want to see Hinault win. But if they want to crash me, I'd rather they told that to me right now, and I'll give the jersey to him. I'll stop the Tour de France rather than continue and have someone punch me and knock me down. I can understand the pressure he's under. But I really can't understand his attitude—that he wants to win so bad that he'd stab me in the back after promising to work for me in this Tour. You can never trust anybody. Life is that way. The only people you can trust are your family."

LeMond was now surrounded by his family. Kathy had rejoined him, and his parents, Bob and Bertha, had arrived from America. In Hinault's view, this was the problem, not the fact that LeMond suspected a conspiracy against him or that he was confused, on a daily basis, by his teammate's tactics. "Greg had his family, his wife and entourage, around him," says Hinault. "What I saw from the outside was that it was more his parents who were afraid, who were making him doubt."

In the background, meanwhile, was Bernard Tapie. He would later describe the spectacle of the two riders—his two riders—arriving hand in hand at the summit of Alpe d'Huez as "the first great moment of my career in sports. . . . It wasn't winning the Tour; it was the stage victory." Tapie then expanded on his role as peacemaker, mentioning that "they'd been at each other's throats." (Incidentally, neither Hinault nor LeMond backs up this claim; LeMond says the closest they came to physical violence was after the stage to Pau, when Hinault accused him of chasing him down. Hinault insists, implausibly, that "there was never any antagonism.") "Hours after separating them," added Tapie, "I watched them arrive at the summit of the Alpe together. It was more wonderful than any other experience."

Observing from the outside, Cyrille Guimard believed then, and believes now, that the furor that surrounded Hinault's battle with LeMond actually suited Tapie down to the ground—indeed, that he encouraged it. "Bernard Tapie was conducting the orchestra," he says. "Bernard Tapie is no choirboy, and the rivalry suited him fine. The more rivalry there was, the more media coverage they got and, most importantly, he got. Because, let's not forget, that was Tapie's life; he was magnificent at using other people. He was an artist at it. Love him or hate him, question his morals, but that's what he was.

"It was a phony war!" protests Guimard. But he appears to contradict himself when he adds that Hinault and LeMond could never be compatible. "One will die or both will die. That clear?" he explains, making it sound anything but phony. He expands on his thesis in philosophical mode: "Man is an animal who can understand this system, but this is the way he works, too. So when you put LeMond and the Badger together, you can say what you like to them, but these are two guys with a pride, a charisma, an ego that will not give an inch. If you put them into the same playground, there'll be a fight."

Guimard doesn't believe what Hinault said then—and continues to say now—about helping LeMond by, as he said at Superbagnères, eliminating the rest of the field with his aggressive riding; he laughs at the very suggestion. "It's not possible," says Guimard. "Plus, the fact is that if Hinault hadn't made a mistake on the second day in the Pyrenees, LeMond would never have had a chance of winning.

"The Badger was 6 minutes ahead! If he hadn't gone on that suicide mission and had a *fringale* on Superbagnères, the race would have been over. There, his pride got the better of him."

15

BORN IN THE USA

I waged a psychological war against him to find out if he had any guts.
BERNARD HINAULT

SAINT-ÉTIENNE, WEDNESDAY, JULY 23

On the evening after the 19th stage, which had witnessed Bernard Hinault's latest attacks on the road to Saint-Étienne, Greg LeMond had dinner with his teammates before joining his parents and Kathy at their table in the hotel restaurant. They were staying at the Sofitel.

"I wasn't really worried about something sinister happening until that night," says LeMond.

"I sat with your mom and dad," remembers Kathy. "And after dinner, you came and sat with us. That's when they came and talked to us."

They?

"It was Goddet," LeMond says. Jacques Goddet, the Tour director. "He said he was so happy to see an American in yellow, and for an American to win the Tour. But then he says, 'You must be very careful, Greg—there are a lot of people who want to see Hinault win.'"

"Goddet," adds Kathy, "says, 'I'm hearing many things that are very worrying, and I promise you, Greg, I'll do everything I can to protect you, but I can only do so much. You have to be so careful, Greg. With your bottles, with your food, with your mechanics...'"

"A lot of the stuff he was suggesting hadn't really entered my mind. . . ." LeMond says.

"We crapped our pants!" says Kathy. "The organizer of the Tour comes to your dinner table! . . . And says, 'I'll do everything I can to protect you, but watch your food, watch your water'? We went out and we bought every single thing that Greg ate from that moment on."

"I think it was pretty novel the way I did the drug test the next day," LeMond says, smiling. "I was so worried about the drug control after what Goddet said. I thought how easy it would be—if someone really wanted to screw me over—to sabotage that. So I watched what I ate, I made my own drinks, I would purposely miss my musette at the feed and take someone else's.

"And I had my wife bring me a Kodak [camera]," he continues. "I went to drug control with the camera and a sealed bottle of fresh springwater. You go in and you strip down naked and pee in a cup. I've always looked at it as the most archaic method. Back then, you go in, and you've got these three old farts sitting there. You pee in the cup, they pour it into two vials—an 'A' sample and a 'B' sample. Then they take—like Thomas Jefferson—the red wax to seal it. They seal the top, and they put a UCI stamp on it—a stamp you could probably have made in any town in France.

"I started thinking about that: how easy it would be to mess with a urine sample. Cycling's a mafia. It's corrupt. So I went in there, and I said to the guys, 'I know this sounds crazy, but I'd like to take a picture.' First I washed the cup out with the springwater. I really made sure it was clean. Then I peed in it. Then I washed out the vials with the water. And then, just as they're sealing the 'B' sample, while the wax is still hot, I say, 'Hold on a minute,' and I shove my finger into it. I leave a fingerprint right there in the wax. And then I take photos of it. That way, if there's anything wrong with the 'A' sample—if they come back and say it's positive—I can check the 'B' sample myself before they test it, and I can be pretty sure it hasn't been tampered with or manipulated.

"Actually," adds LeMond, "that was pretty brilliant!" And he laughs.

SAINT-ÉTIENNE, THURSDAY, JULY 24

At least in the time trial—the stage that would finally settle the Tour, according to Hinault—there would be no danger to LeMond from riding in the peloton in close proximity to the other 133 riders who remained in the race. It was a 58-km solo test starting and finishing in Saint-Étienne.

LeMond, "never a good sleeper," has not slept well since Alpe d'Huez. The time trial is in the afternoon. LeMond, as the yellow jersey, is the last man to go. Hinault starts 2 minutes in front of him.

Maurice Le Guilloux is looking after LeMond and will follow him in the team car; Paul Köchli follows Hinault. While each directeur sportif has somehow remained neutral in the struggle between the two riders—perhaps because, ultimately, neither has any control over Hinault and recognizes as much—Le Guilloux has become more aligned with LeMond than with the rider he has known throughout his career.

In the morning, LeMond heads out on his time trial bike to reconnoiter the course. And during the ride, his pedal breaks. Le Guilloux is following him in the car and can't believe it. "Incredible!" he says. "That never happens." It leaves LeMond unsettled, and Le Guilloux, too. "But I tried to calm him. I told him, 'It happens, pedals break; don't think about it.'"

Before he started his time trial, LeMond was interviewed. He didn't look like a man on the verge of winning the Tour; he sounded defensive and defiant. "Hinault attacked me from the beginning," he said. "He's never helped me once. I don't feel confident at all with him. You know, you never know what can happen. I could crash or flat, but I feel really strong. I don't think there should be any problems."

As LeMond sets off for his ride, with a replacement pedal, he quickly finds his rhythm. He shifts a little on his saddle, as he always does, but his legs are spinning smoothly. Hinault, in contrast, rocks gently as he turns his usual monstrous gear. But LeMond is going well; he feels on top of the effort, and he can't feel his legs: a good sign.

Twenty kilometers into the race, LeMond is up on Hinault by 8 seconds. It is the reverse of the first time trial in Nantes, when he was 20 seconds down at the first checkpoint. But 10 kilometers later, the positions have reversed: Hinault leads; LeMond is 4 seconds slower. And then, after 37 km, as Kathy LeMond and Bob and Bertha are watching the action live on a television in a caravan by the finish in Saint-Étienne, and LeMond is racing through the tight, crowd-lined streets in the town of Saint Chamond, disaster.

The TV images show LeMond flying into a 90-degree right-hand bend. Then the picture wobbles. Crash! He's down!

"A crash? With Greg?" asks Kathy, rising from her seat, clasping her hand to her chest.

LeMond's mother leaps to her feet. "No, no," she screams. "What happened? What happened?"

LeMond, meanwhile, is frantically picking himself up and remounting his bike. Again Le Guilloux is trying to reassure him. "It's OK, Greg; it's OK." But panic is natural in such a situation—on a road stage, all you have to do is rejoin the peloton, which may even wait in the event of a crash. In a time trial, the clock ticks relentlessly.

Tick tock. Tick tock. Every second LeMond loses—as he picks himself off the road, checks for injuries, checks his bike, squeezes the brakes, makes sure the chain is still on, remounts—is time lost to Hinault.

Tick tock. Tick tock. His grip on the yellow jersey is being pried away, finger by finger. To heighten LeMond's anxiety, he doesn't know how much time, if any, he has to lose. Though Le Guilloux is telling LeMond that he and Hinault are virtually neck and neck, LeMond can't hear him; the aerodynamic helmet he's wearing covers his ears.

As quickly as possible, LeMond is back on his bike, shifting around on the saddle, adrenaline pumping. He settles back down, pumps the pedals, but the smoothness has gone. He feels ragged. Something's wrong. The bike isn't running freely. It feels like it's dragging. LeMond realizes what it is: The front brake has been nudged in the crash, and it's rubbing against the rim. He sticks his hand up, indicates to Le Guilloux that he wants to change bikes, and stops.

He's handed the spare from the roof rack—a standard road bike with a rear disc wheel rather than the low-profile machine he had been riding. Within a few seconds, he's away again. But the cumulative cost of the crash and bike change and loss of momentum must be at least 30 seconds, probably closer to a minute, as he begins the only climb on the course: the Côte de Rochetaillée. At 46 km, he is 30 seconds down on Hinault; at 51 km, it is 16 seconds. But it is all downhill to the finish, dangerous in places, and fear lurks in LeMond's mind.

Ahead of him, Hinault, wearing the polka-dot jersey of King of the Mountains, continues his relentless, and in contrast incident-free, march to the line. He negotiated the same tight corner in Saint Chamond without mishap, and as he closes in on the finish, he catches the rider who started in front of him: Zimmermann. As Hinault finishes in 1 hour 15 minutes 35 seconds, all eyes turn to the finishing straight on the Cours Fauriel, and the ticking clock. There's only one rider left to finish: LeMond.

Tick tock. Tick tock.

As he appears on the finishing straight, the time clicks past Hinault's and heads toward 1 hour 16 minutes. And that's when it stops: bang on 1:16. Twenty-five seconds slower than Hinault. LeMond has done enough to hold on to the yellow jersey, with 2:18 to spare. But he's disappointed—disappointed that he hasn't beaten Hinault. Adding injury to insult, he is handed a can of Coke and gashes his finger while trying to open it.

The broken pedal, the crash, the rubbing brake . . . in the immediate aftermath of the time trial, with blood dripping from his finger, LeMond suspected foul play. His family, too, was convinced that dark forces were at work. But as he calmed down, LeMond considered each incident and was able to find a rational explanation. "Kathy thought my bike had been messed with," he says now. "But I just took that corner too fast."

Le Guilloux was downcast. He felt that it wasn't just the crash and the mechanical problem that cost LeMond another stage win in the time trial but the psychological consequences of his accident. "Greg panicked," says Le Guilloux. "He got the scare of his life when he crashed. And on the descent to the finish, he was scared. He had no confidence in his bike. He got stressed because of this, and he rode with a lot of fear—following him in the car, I could see that."

By now Le Guilloux, disappointed by Hinault, was fully behind LeMond. "When you're a directeur, and you follow a rider, you want him to win," Le Guilloux says. "That's natural. So yes, I wanted Greg to beat Hinault. And without the crash, Greg would have won in Saint-Étienne. That's what I wanted. And I wanted Bernard to see it, and for him to shake Greg's hand afterward and say, 'You are the strongest, and you won.' Rather than for Bernard to say, 'I let you win.' I wanted Bernard to recognize the value of Greg because it's wrong for him to say that he let Greg win the Tour. For 25 years now, he has said this, and it's false. Bernard did everything he could to try and win.

"It's true that if Bernard hadn't had the problems with his leg in the Alps, I'm not sure what would have happened," adds Le Guilloux. "Greg would have been forced to attack him. But I am sure of this: Hinault in 1986 might have been as strong as Hinault in 1985. But LeMond in '86 was much stronger than LeMond in '85."

Le Guilloux admits that his friendship with Hinault was damaged by the 1986 Tour. "I was always a friend of Bernard Hinault," he says, "but I like

Greg, I like him a lot. I'm still and always will be his friend. For me, things have changed with Bernard. We were teammates, we were neighbors, and we did our careers together; we were together all the time. But this experience was very difficult for me, and our friendship has been damaged by it. Because . . . I like that when you give your word, you keep it."

Bernard Tapie was one of the first to congratulate LeMond after the time trial. "It's over," he told LeMond. "You've won."

"I'm not so sure," replied LeMond. "It's not done till it's done."

LeMond told Tapie about his fears concerning possible foul play or an act of sabotage, particularly with the drug testing.

"Oh, it's OK," Tapie replied. "I have my own people flying the urine samples to the lab in Paris."

As he recalls the conversation, LeMond rolls his eyes and laughs. "And that's supposed to make me feel better?"

After talking to Tapie, LeMond headed to the drug-testing caravan with his Kodak camera. Hinault, meanwhile, spoke to reporters. "I've really thrown everything at Greg in the last 48 hours," he said. "I've pushed him as hard as I can and spared him nothing—not words, not deeds—and I have put him under maximum pressure. If he doesn't buckle, that means he's a champion and deserves to win the race. I did it for his own good. Next year, maybe he'll have to fight off another opponent who will make life miserable for him. Now he'll know how to fight back."

It was to become Hinault's official line, that he actually "helped" LeMond by not handing him the Tour on a plate, by making it difficult for him, in the process adding luster to his victory. But LeMond, unsurprisingly, didn't buy it, and still doesn't.

The evening of the time trial, Hinault spoke to LeMond. "I went to see him in his bath" is Hinault's rather bizarre recollection. "I said, 'You've won the Tour.'"

Hinault sits back from his kitchen table, leaving the briefest of pauses, then adds, "Even though I'd won the time trial, I said, 'You've won the Tour.'"

PUY DE DÔME, FRIDAY, JULY 25

Four stages remained, but only one of them, to the Puy de Dôme—the spectacular dome-shaped volcanic plug in the Massif Central, 48 hours before

Paris—presented danger. The Puy de Dôme is a climb of rich symbolism and incident, where Hinault had fancied claiming his first yellow jersey in 1978, where Eddy Merckx had been punched in the kidneys three years earlier. In 1986, it was included as the sting in the tail, an attempt by Messrs. Goddet and Lévitan to keep interest alive as late as possible, perhaps even to allow a challenger to make one last, desperate bid for the yellow jersey.

Hinault led up one of the early climbs, the Croix de l'Homme Mort. But there was a different air about him. He rode with authority, as the *patron*, but the large group of riders bunched comfortably behind him indicated that the pace he was setting wasn't ferocious. Hinault was controlling rather than igniting the race. He wasn't trying to drive a group clear as he had done in the Pyrenees. His goal now seemed more modest: to stay at the head and arrive at the summit first to collect points to consolidate his lead in the King of the Mountains competition.

LeMond kept his loyal teammates Bauer and Hampsten in close attendance, acting as watchdogs, following their master as he moved around the peloton, trying to keep him among the first 20 riders, where it was safer and he could remain vigilant. In fact, it was Hampsten, not LeMond, who had a problem. A puncture saw him drop back for a wheel change. Yet as he remounted his bike and began to chase, he was joined by Alain Vigneron and Charly Bérard, who had dropped back when they saw he had a problem. Now they were helping him recapture the peloton. Given the division there'd been in the team, Hampsten was a little surprised, pleasantly surprised. "Hey, thanks," he told them.

"Are you kidding?" Vigneron responded. "Your fourth place is worth about 45,000 francs." (It is the custom in cycling that all the money won by the team is pooled and shared equally, meaning they stood to gain financially from Hampsten's high overall placing, splitting about $10,000. As Hampsten says now, "Those pros sure as hell know where to find buttered bread.")

As they began to climb the Puy de Dôme, past an enormous banner that read, "Hinault—6 Tours," the lead group began to splinter. And Hinault conceded his place at the front. With his job done and his King of the Mountains title secure, he began to slip back. At the summit, LeMond finished among the leaders, in 17th. Hinault came in 34th, 52 seconds farther back. As he approached the line, he eased up, stood on the pedals, and stretched his back. It indicated he wasn't concerned about losing a little more time. It was his way of running up the white flag.

PARIS, SUNDAY, JULY 27

There was one more minor scare still in store for LeMond, on the final, tra-ditionally ceremonial stage into Paris. It usually has the air of the last day of school or an end-of-term party, with champagne poured into glasses and handed around the peloton and lots of posing for photographs. What tends to be overlooked is that they still have to ride and, once on the Champs-Elysées, race. The final stage in 1986 happened also to be a marathon 255 km, on un-dulating roads, from Cosne-sur-Loire into central Paris. After the champagne and the photos and the general cavorting, there was a crash in the middle of the peloton. At the bottom of the heap was LeMond.

Jeez, here we go again, he thought.

But it was a crash caused by inattention, probably induced by extreme fatigue, rather than sabotage. As LeMond picked up himself and his bike, which he inspected and remounted, he was relieved that body and machine were intact. But after 4,300 km, 3 weeks, 23 stages, and 110 hours of racing, LeMond, as he began to chase back to the peloton, looked up and was con-fronted, in the no-man's-land between him and the pack of riders, by a sight that almost knocked him straight back off again. Ahead of him, standing on the pedals and slow-pedaling as he waited to pace his American teammate back to the peloton, was Bernard Hinault.

Le Tour du Nouveau Monde" (The Tour of the New World) declared L'Équipe on Monday, July 28. It was a headline that was prescient to a degree that neither the paper nor anyone else connected with the sport could have pre-dicted. And apart from the imminent rise of cycling in the English-speaking countries, the United States in particular, nobody would have foreseen the decline in the mother country. With the retirement of Hinault would disap-pear any hope of a French victory for several generations. At the time of this writing, in 2011, the wait goes on for a French Tour winner to follow the last one: Bernard Hinault in 1985.

Blissfully ignorant of the drought that was to follow, the tone of the French sports daily's front page managed to be triumphant. "The 1986 tour will go down in legend: first, for being one of the most exciting in history, and also for being the first victory by an American, Greg LeMond. Bernard Hinault is going away, leaving the way clear for a new generation, but the Breton grew in stature in this Tour, even if he could not get a sixth victory."

On the Champs-Elysées, the Italian sprinter Guido Bontempi sprinted to his third stage win—he had also won the previous day's penultimate stage, from Clermont-Ferrand to Nevers—with Hinault in the thick of it in fourth, a competitor to the end. LeMond crossed the line in the middle of the bunch. What did he feel? Joy? Euphoria? Relief? "I just wanted to go home," he says.

On the podium set up in the middle of the Champs-Élysées, LeMond and Hinault embraced. "It felt good to have Hinault congratulate me on the podium after everything that has passed between us," LeMond told reporters. Hinault, meanwhile, stuck to his line that he had kept the promise he'd made a year ago; that his attacks had simply been an effort to shake off the competition and to add prestige to his teammate's victory; that he had, after all, helped LeMond win. But what else could he say? As the singer Bono once said, "Sometimes, my friend, the lie is ugly, but the truth is unbearable."

Hinault could of course point to the final result to back up his claim, however implausible it seemed. But it was Anquetil who summed up what most felt, especially in France. LeMond might have been the winner, said Anquetil, but Hinault was the hero. Not necessarily for "helping" his teammate win but for lighting up his final Tour; for sustaining the drama; for making it the spectacle it was; for making it arguably the greatest, dirtiest, and most intriguing Tour of all time.

I make the argument, with the subtitle of this book, that this was the greatest ever Tour de France. It's an entirely subjective opinion, of course, owing partly to very personal, and objectively irrelevant, factors such as my impressionable age (13) and the fact that it was the first Tour de France broadcast in its entirety on British television. Nevertheless, most longtime observers agree that it was an exceptional Tour. Apart from its historical significance—heralding seismic change in the sport by crowning the first English-speaking winner—the race itself was gripping, exciting, and unpredictable, and in LeMond and Hinault it had two protagonists who were utterly compelling. Theirs was a titanic battle, made all the more intriguing by the fact that they were teammates and polar opposites. Hinault was the evil pantomime villain, LeMond the blue-eyed innocent.

But it would be ridiculous not to acknowledge that the 1986 Tour wouldn't have been great had it not been for Hinault. Anquetil was right; Hinault was the hero (or antihero) of the race. Frankly, it would have been boring without him.

Does that make the Badger the hero of the story? Perhaps; perhaps all is fair in love, war, and (within the rules) sport. I confess I saw Hinault ride only two Tours, but in 1985, with his broken nose and black eyes, and the following year, with his raw aggression and breathtaking arrogance, I developed a deep fascination with him. Sport needs characters like the Badger to make it unpredictable and interesting, to give it character. To me, he seemed like cycling's Muhammad Ali; he had a similar aura. Cycling has lacked a character of similar stature since Hinault retired.

But Sam Abt and other commentators are also right. In 1986, Hinault did blow an opportunity to bow out gracefully and with his honor intact. Had he openly and without qualification admitted that he was trying to win—as he did on a couple of occasions during the Tour, such as at the summit of Super-bagnères and at Alpe d'Huez—then the verdict could be different. But there was something underhand about his tactics, disingenuous about his arguments, even cruel in his treatment of LeMond.

In his defense, Hinault might have made the point that all is fair in love, war, and sport. He could have added that he didn't break any rules, "only" a promise. But it was a promise made—if LeMond is to be believed—to keep LeMond on side during the critical phase of the 1985 Tour, when Hinault's grip on a fifth title appeared to be weakening. Had LeMond attacked Hinault in 1985 as Hinault attacked LeMond in 1986, the American might well have won a year earlier. Hinault might have ended up as "only" a four-time Tour winner.

As to why Hinault broke that promise, I think the answer is quite simple. While he was prepared to help his teammates in lesser races—witness his riding in support of Andy Hampsten at the Tour of Switzerland—at the Tour de France, Hinault couldn't bring himself to ride any way other than to win. It was in his nature, hardwired into his DNA. His every instinct was urging him not to sacrifice his own chances but to attack and fight until Paris, tearing the opposition to pieces. You might as well put a fox in a chicken coop and tell it not to cause any trouble.

But Hinault also, as he argued, had too much "respect" for the Tour, and for what it meant to his country, not to fight. Just as leisure cyclists in replica yellow jerseys offend him ("When I see potbellied cyclists with stomachs like they're pregnant wearing the *maillot jaune*, it appalls me"), to ride the Tour de France and not try to win was anathema to Hinault. The proposition disgusted him.

Perhaps for this reason—that he didn't win; that he feels, despite the evidence to the contrary, that his effort was compromised by having LeMond in his team—Hinault's memories of his final Tour seemed initially to arouse feelings of bitterness. In his first autobiography, published two years after his retirement, he makes several barbed, even caustic, remarks about LeMond. "I could have had his scalp at Alpe d'Huez," he writes. And on LeMond's fears that his bike might have been sabotaged in the final time trial, he says, "I began to wonder whether he was right in the head."

Now Hinault is slightly more measured in his comments about LeMond. But he does stick, doggedly, to the line that he helped him win the 1986 Tour. "From my point of view, there was never any antagonism," Hinault says. "There was no conflict. It was his entourage, his wife, his parents, who said so. In the time trial in Saint-Étienne, when he fell, his wife was saying that the mechanic had tightened his bottom bracket so he couldn't win. But we have our own, different mechanics! So what are they talking about? It's a bit stupid. It wasn't in our interests to [sabotage his bike], anyway."

Hinault says he can't fathom the suspicion of LeMond and others who accused him of treachery. "I kept my word to help him," he protests. "I've always been used to people keeping their word, and keeping mine. I don't know whether, in [American] culture, they always say, 'I'll give my word' and then screw you over if they have the chance. I don't know. But that's not how I roll.

"From the moment I said that he would win," Hinault continues, "I did everything in my power to make him win. I'd given my word, and I wasn't going back on it.

"If I'd really wanted to be nasty," he adds, "I could have fucked him up the ass."

The Badger smiles thinly, but he isn't joking. He means it, if only metaphorically. He can't help himself.

My time with Hinault is almost up. He has glanced at his watch at least twice in the past 10 minutes. It is difficult to get the measure of him; he remains impressively inscrutable while at the same time resolutely black and white. In 25 years, he has not budged an inch in his version of the 1986 Tour. I had been told, by Gilles Le Roc'h, a journalist who knows him well, that "he's not relaxed with the story of the '86 Tour. He doesn't like to talk about it because he guesses that people will think it doesn't reflect well on him. He knows that."

But there have been few signs of discomfort today. In fact, it's difficult to imagine what an uncomfortable Hinault would look like. He is a man supremely confident and comfortable in his own skin, unburdened by doubt, reassured by absolute certainty. Asked if he's ever experienced moments of doubt or prevarication, he answers quickly, decisively, "No. Once I've taken a decision, I move forward. I might think hard about it first, but once I've decided, I say, 'C'est bon. C'est parti. On y va.'"

It's time to go.

"Can I give you a lift to the station?" asks Hinault, getting up from the table.

The Badger leads me out of his kitchen, through the dark hallway, switching on his phone as he walks across the yard toward the Skoda parked beside the tractor. As he drives along the private road, away from his house, the phone beeps twice, and he peers at the screen. As he does so, two wheels leave the narrow lane, veering into the dirt, kicking up clouds of dust, and Hinault looks up quickly, alters course, and returns to his phone without saying a word. On the open road, he drives fast. A Renault Clio appears in front of us. Hinault speeds up to its bumper, then brakes. "Out of the way, Granny," he mutters as he swerves out into the other lane, accelerating hard to overtake.

"I think he is not being 100 percent honest," says Paul Köchli of Hinault's assertion that he "helped" LeMond win the 1986 Tour. Köchli laughs as he adds, "It's probably unconscious, but when Hinault says, today, 'I just had amusement; I just played in the 1986 Tour,' I don't think he is 100 percent honest. He understood that this was the way he could win." By "win" Köchli could mean win the Tour or win the hearts of the French people. Either or both objectives could be achieved by the aggression—the panache—with which Hinault rode his final Tour.

"He was clever," continues Köchli. "He was smart; Greg was not. Hinault could see the opportunity and take it. He was a good tactician. Also, maybe he made some small deals with other riders in the heat of the race—deals that didn't go against our strategy, that helped us." Köchli could be referring here to the "deal" Hinault made with Delgado in the Pyrenees, using the Spaniard to help him build a bigger lead and giving him the stage victory in exchange. But there could have been other deals as well; Köchli won't say.

"But Hinault could not destroy Greg," he adds. "Why? Because he needed him. He was part of the game." Köchli laughs. "He knew that, because he was smart."

For Köchli, the 1986 Tour represented his greatest achievement as a directeur sportif. In fact, there is a strong case for arguing that the La Vie Claire performance that year stands as the greatest team performance the Tour has ever seen. The roll call of honors includes six stage wins; first overall with LeMond, second with Hinault, fourth with Hampsten, seventh with Rüttimann, and twelfth with Jean-François Bernard; the team prize; the combined competition (LeMond); the King of the Mountains (Hinault); and the white jersey for best young rider (Hampsten).

Köchli must look back with immense pride. "Oh, I don't know if it's pride," he says. "'Pride,' I think, is not the right word." He pauses as he searches the English language for a more fitting description. I offer a suggestion: "satisfaction"?

"No," replies Köchli. "'Pride' is better than 'satisfaction.' Is there something stronger than pride?"

A ndy Hampsten did not receive a Porsche from Bernard Tapie. In fact, so sick had he been made by the experience of his first Tour—despite finishing fourth overall and winning the white jersey—that he engineered an escape from the three-year contract he'd signed with La Vie Claire at the beginning of 1986. "Which wasn't very cool of me," he says, "but after that whole scene, I could see it was going to be Jean-François [Bernard]'s team. And I thought, I'm not sticking around for round two of this, for the Jean-François Bernard show."

Hampsten signed with 7-Eleven, which, after its successful debut Tour, in which it won a stage, held the yellow jersey (albeit briefly), and failed only in its aim of having a man finish in the top 20, stepped up a level in 1987. 7-Eleven continued to improve in each consecutive season until, still under Jim Ochowicz's direction, it morphed into the Motorola squad and, in late 1992, introduced a prodigious young American named Lance Armstrong to the world of cycling. But in 1987, when Hampsten joined, it was still markedly different from most other teams, and very different from La Vie Claire. "It was very different," agrees Hampsten. "A lot more fun."

But despite the awkwardness and stress of those three weeks in 1986, Hampsten's verdict on that Tour de France, and on Hinault, has softened a bit over the years. "OK, it was really hard for Greg," says Hampsten, "but Hinault destroyed the rest of the field. Greg only had one guy to compete against.

We're never going to see that again. Zimmermann was at, what—10 minutes? [10 minutes 54 seconds]. He was nowhere. I mean, yeah, Greg had to ride against his teammate, and that was supertough, and it was superstressful. But he didn't have to ride against anyone else. And when I look back on it now, I don't know . . . I think, in some ways, Hinault did what he had to do."

LeMond almost agrees. "Some of Hinault's stupid moves actually did help me," he concedes. "But what bothers me is when people ask, 'Did Hinault give you the Tour?' That's a perception that's out there, which devalues my win. Actually, the fact he rode so aggressively against me did help in a way, because he destroyed himself. But it was clear he was trying to win. He didn't intentionally destroy himself. I would have loved to have been on a different team and been able to go head to head with him instead of having to figure out how to . . . politely win the race.

"But I don't have any hatred toward Hinault at all," LeMond continues. "Realistically, I'm an American. Hinault had everything to gain by trying to win. I do think he'd have kept his promise to ride as my teammate had Guimard been there. Guimard would have said, 'You made a deal.' But instead Hinault has Tapie on one side, saying, 'Who cares about LeMond? He'll be out of your life in a year.' And he's going for six Tours. I mean . . . my God. That must have been mighty tempting. It just annoys me that I'm sometimes not given full credit for my win in '86. I did win, after all."

On the night of his triumph, after the official presentation on the Champs-Elysées, LeMond and Kathy checked into their hotel. And then, with Hampsten, they visited the American Embassy in Paris. Then it was back to the Champs-Elysées, to a Bernard Tapie–organized team party at the Lido. It was a tame affair. "These guys don't know how to party," LeMond told Hampsten.

"Everyone was paralyzed with tiredness," LeMond recalls now. "There was no joy at all. We went to the Lido to follow protocol, but, you know what? If you win the Tour, you want to share it with your wife and family, not these guys I've spent three weeks with.

"After a while at the Lido, Kathy, me, and Steve Bauer sneaked off. We found a small bar in the middle of Paris, and we celebrated ourselves. That was good; it was nice. We were out till 5 a.m., and I had to be up at 8 for media stuff. But what sticks in my mind is the first song they played in that small bar . . . you know what it was?"

LeMond looks up at his wife, Kathy, and they both laugh. "It was Bruce Springsteen. 'Born in the USA.'"

EPILOGUE

All this cycling stuff, that's in the past.

BERNARD HINAULT

reg LeMond and Bernard Hinault competed together in one more stage race, a month after the Tour de France. It was the Coors Classic in Colorado, with Hinault the designated La Vie Claire team leader. On the eve of his retirement, the Badger wanted to go out with a bang.

But with Hinault in the leader's jersey, LeMond, who was sitting third overall, attacked. Hinault reacted furiously. According to LeMond, he "got off his bike, threw it down, said he was going to quit, and accused me of riding against him. I said, 'Bernard, you're paranoid if you think I'm doing to you what you did to me in the Tour.' But he got madder and madder. He yelled for half an hour and wouldn't talk to me."

The next day, LeMond told Hinault he wouldn't attack him again, that he'd stay by his side and work to help him win (which he did). "That's a promise," LeMond told him. "Which is something you can't keep."

Reminded now of what happened in Colorado, Hinault shrugs. "Yes, but I had the jersey," he says. "In a team, you never attack the rider in the jersey. You wait behind the jersey until he's in trouble, then you can go. If your team has the jersey, you stay on the wheel and smoke your pipe."

I put it to Hinault that perhaps, in Colorado, LeMond had been following his example by "stirring the pot" or "having fun." (LeMond also indulged
in another kind of fun: He played 18 holes of golf on the rest day, for which
Hinault accused him of a lack of professionalism.) Or perhaps LeMond re-
sented what had happened at the Tour?

"Maybe, maybe," says Hinault. It is as close as the Badger ever comes to
conceding that he may not have played fair at the 1986 Tour.

The 1986 Tour should have launched LeMond's career into orbit. It didn't.
He didn't even ride the following year's race, having almost died three
months before it started. In April 1987, he was accidentally shot in the back
by his brother-in-law while turkey hunting in California. Only the availability of a helicopter, which transported him to the hospital, saved his life. His
recovery was long and arduous, with no guarantee that he would be able to
return to cycling.

When he did attempt to come back to the sport, the following season, Le-
Mond struggled to recapture his basic fitness, never mind his Tour-winning
form. He missed two Tours before returning, finally, in 1989. As in 1986—
though with more justification this time—he wasn't mentioned among the
favorites. In fact, he had been close to quitting the sport at the Giro d'Italia
in May, but Kathy had persuaded him to carry on. But in July, with 37 shot-
gun pellets still lodged in his body and 2 in his heart lining, he fought an astonishing duel with another rider coming back from several years in the wilderness: Laurent Fignon. It was the closest Tour in history, LeMond winning
the final stage into Paris—a time trial—to claim the yellow jersey by just 8
seconds from a devastated Fignon. In any argument over what is the greatest
ever Tour de France, 1989 will figure.

LeMond returned to win his third Tour in 1990, but his career entered its
decline soon after. He retired in 1994, climbing off during the Tour, when he
was unable to stay with the leaders in the mountains. Some blamed the ef-
fects of lead poisoning from the pellets that remain lodged in his body, a condition he continues to fight. During my visit, in 2010, LeMond spoke in anguished terms about this debilitating affliction and the possibility of visiting
an Israeli surgeon who specializes in removing lead shrapnel from delicate
areas, including the heart lining.

In retirement, LeMond has been outspoken on the subject of doping. He
began to wonder if his own decline as a rider, and his inability to challenge
for a fourth Tour victory, owed something to the alleged rampant abuse of

the blood booster EPO by many of his opponents in the early 1990s. And he had a public falling out with another American rider, Armstrong, after Le-Mond commented, in the midst of the Texan's record run of seven wins in the Tour de France, that, "if Armstrong's clean, it's the greatest comeback in sport. And if he's not, it's the greatest fraud."

LeMond's outspokenness has seen him fall out of favor with many in the sport, where a law of omertà on the topic of doping has long prevailed. But he isn't the only one to have been distanced from professional cycling on this account. Paul Köchli and Urs Zimmermann both told me that the escalation and increasing sophistication of doping methods in the 1990s hastened their departures from professional cycling, though Köchli, "the first guy to use computers in sport," remains at the vanguard in his use of computers to analyze cyclists' training data.

In his semiexile from the sport, LeMond resembles a dissident political leader, loved by the masses, disliked or misunderstood by many of those in positions of power, and banished to the cycling equivalent of Siberia. But he has had to cope with far more serious traumas than his disillusionment with, and distance from, professional cycling. In 2007, it emerged that as a teenager, LeMond had suffered sexual abuse at the hands of a family friend, Ron, on hunting and fishing trips in Montana. Coming to terms with this meant acknowledging it, and LeMond did so publicly, telling Paul Kimmage, the cyclist-turned-journalist who had finished 130 places behind LeMond in the 1986 Tour, about "the secret that nearly destroyed me."

It was this secret—and the shame that he felt as a result of it—that might explain his drive to succeed in cycling, LeMond told Kimmage. As LeMond described it, "Cycling was a way to reinvent myself." He also told Kimmage that as he stood on the podium on the Champs-Elysées, having won the 1986 Tour, he thought of his abuser and wondered if he was watching him from somewhere. It is a chilling revelation. And it puts his problems with Hinault in perspective.

On the possibility of reengaging with the sport, LeMond is characteristically hard to pin down. He flutters like a bird between two apparently opposing positions, leaving doors tantalizingly ajar for a possible return. "I'm done with the sport," he tells me when I visit him. "I can't really see a place for me." And yet, a couple of months later, talking on the phone about a promising young American rider, LeMond's enthusiasm bubbles to the surface. "When I hear about 19-year-old kids smokin' top-level pros, I really love hearing that." His suspicion that doping is still rife is what keeps LeMond away. But with real feeling, he adds, "I want to believe, but the question I always ask is, 'Can I believe?'"

It is a question that continues to torment LeMond, driving him to despair, just as it did—in another context—throughout the 1986 Tour.

While LeMond has distanced himself from cycling, Hinault is a familiar presence and part of the furniture at the many races organized by ASO, the company that owns and organizes the Tour de France. At the Tour, the Badger appears on the podium every day, presenting the jerseys, introducing the day's winners to the VIPs, and acting as an attack dog if—as has happened twice in recent years—any uninvited guests invade the podium, even if they are bigger than he and up to 30 years his junior.

It might seem surprising that Hinault appeared to settle so easily into retirement. Did the fire, the "destructive rage," just disappear? "It's another competition," Hinault told me of his life postcycling. "There's bike racing, and there's the competition of daily life. It's the same. Everything you do, you want to be the best. It's all about finding a way of being the best. If you haven't got that desire to fight and win, you'll never win. You have to have that in your head."

Hinault claims he has no regrets about stopping so soon, when he was still only 32. Others aren't so sure. Gilles Le Roc'h, the Breton journalist, recalls the 1988 Tour of Lombardy, when Hinault told him, "I should have stayed in; I could have raced all over the world and won so much money." Then again, thinks Le Roc'h, "I'm not sure money was his petrol. He wanted to be first; winning was his petrol. Not money." If Hinault regretted his early retirement, it would have been because he thought he could carry on winning, not just accumulate wealth.

In different ways, and for different reasons, LeMond and Hinault both drifted away from, or out of, cycling, LeMond from the professional world of cycling he inhabited for 15 years, Hinault from the simple habit of riding a bike. Yet, coincidentally, both rediscovered their enjoyment of riding a bike at the same time, in 2007.

Hinault had made another pledge in 1986: He wouldn't cycle in retirement, even for fun. It fit with his black-and-white view of the world. He was going to apply himself to his new life, in particular the farm, and there was no place, no space, for cycling (it even harks all the way back to the teenaged Hinault's argument with his father about prioritizing cycling over his apprenticeship "because I don't like doing things by halves").

"I didn't ride my bike for 20 years," Hinault tells me. "I started again in 2007, simply because we stopped working on the farm at the end of 2006. In 2006, we rented it out, and I had some free time. I needed to stay fit.

"Prior to that, I'd been working on the farm, which is intensive enough. When I stopped, I said to myself that I needed to do something, and I started enjoying cycling again after 20 years, even though it was hard at first, because you have to rebuild your muscular mass."

LeMond began riding his bike again at the same time. His eldest son, Geoffrey—a baby during the 1986 Tour—had taken up the sport, and Le-Mond—just as his father had done in 1975 in Montana—began cycling regularly with him. In 2007, father and son traveled to France to ride L'Étape du Tour—a stage of the Tour de France—together.

It was the first time Hinault had seen LeMond in years. "He came with his son to do L'Étape du Tour," recalls Hinault, "and I saw him then, and we spoke. But if we see each other . . . the first thing you do is ask how things are going. That's more important.

"All this cycling stuff, that's in the past." Hinault shrugs. "There's no point dredging it all up."

AFTERWORD

When this book was first published in the UK in 2011, it sparked a bit of a debate about the claim made by the subtitle (changed in the U.S. edition from "Lemond, Hinault and the Greatest Ever Tour de France" to "Greg Lemond, Bernard Hinault, and the Greatest Tour de France"). One or two people, stroking their chins, furrowing their brows, asked, "Do you really think 1986 was the greatest ever Tour de France?"

It hadn't been my intention to be put on the spot about this, or even for it to be much of an issue. Naive, I know. But it seemed beside the point, a needless distraction from the story of the LeMond-Hinault duel. It had only been intended as an eye-catching subtitle!

And yet the discussion proved rather interesting. What was also interesting was that, among those who initially objected most strongly, a certain wavering, or uncertainty, could be detected. Not because they were convinced by anything I said but because, when they considered other Tours, they realized how difficult it is to settle on one as *the* definitive greatest ever.

As other possibilities were pondered, some alighted on 1989, when LeMond claimed his second victory, this time on the final day and by the smallest margin of victory ever in the Tour, those 8 seconds he clawed back to beat

Laurent Fignon. Another popular one was 2003, when Lance Armstrong overcame adversity—and an in-shape Jan Ullrich—to win the hardest-fought of his seven Tours. Those with a sense of mischief—and an appetite for the drama of a drug scandal—nominated 1998, the year of the Festina Affair, as well as of police raids, rider strikes, and the subplot of a gripping duel between Marco Pantani and Ullrich.

Such choices reminded me a little of those "Greatest Albums of All Time" lists published in newspapers and magazines, which are always stacked with recent releases—and therefore anomalies. The cycling equivalent of placing Lady Gaga's "The Fame" ahead of the Beatles' "Revolver" might be to suggest that Carlos Sastre's narrow win in 2008 deserves consideration.

So what about 1969, the first of Eddy Merckx's five victories, when the Cannibal won by over 17 minutes and picked up the points and King of the Mountains competitions? Or even one that features prominently at the start of this story and that saw the maiden win by another of the all-time greats: Bernard Hinault in 1978?

Delving much further back, there is Octave Lapize's victory in 1910 as the Tour tackled its first major mountain range: the Pyrenees. Lapize was a climber who was nonetheless moved to scream, "Assassins!" at the organizers' car parked at the top of the Col d'Aubisque.

Or there is 1947, when the Tour was reborn after World War II. An air of mystery prevailed. After a seven-year absence, there was no benchmark; there were no obvious favorites (a bit like 2007, when Operacion Puerto and other doping scandals removed so many favorites). That 1947 Tour had a thrilling and somehow fitting denouement when, on the final day, a little-known Frenchman, Jean Robic, attacked to claim his first yellow jersey at the point where it mattered most. It was a notable Tour for other reasons. It was the first organized by *L'Équipe*; it contained the longest successful solo breakaway, by Alberto Bourlon, who won stage 14 after being away for 157 miles (253 km); and it also presented the longest individual time trial—86 miles (139 km).

Another barometer for greatest ever Tour could be how often a particular race is evoked in subsequent years. It happens a lot with 1986. It was 1986 that provided the reference point in 2009, when two of the favorites, Alberto Contador and Lance Armstrong, lined up in the same Astana team. There was the familiar sense of an uneasy truce. "Just like 1986!" was the cry of many.

Armstrong played the Hinault role as the grizzled old champion and *patron*, while Contador fulfilled the LeMond role as the fresh-faced young gun (or *pistolero*, to use his nickname), even though the Spaniard had already won the Tour, in 2007. And there were definitely shades of Hinault in Armstrong's "ambush" on stage 3, in the crosswinds of the Camargue, when he made the split and stole some seconds on Contador. There were echoes here of the 16th stage of the 1986 Tour into Gap, when, buffeted by similarly strong winds, Hinault infiltrated the split along with two teammates, Niki Rüttimann and Guido Winterberg.

Back then, you will recall that Hinault instructed his teammates to ride on the front, distancing LeMond. And 23 years later, Armstrong instructed his two teammates, Yaroslav Popovych and Haimar Zubeldia, to drive the break, distancing Contador. At the finish, the American's observations were cutting. "It doesn't take a rocket scientist to figure out that you have to go to the front in those conditions," Armstrong said. "I've won the Tour de France seven times. Why wouldn't you ride at the front? It makes no sense that you wouldn't ride there."

Hinault might have sought to undermine LeMond in a similarly subtle, devastating way. And indeed, it is tempting to compare Armstrong with Hinault—though, personally, I don't think the comparison is valid.

In fact, the relationship between Hinault and Armstrong is interesting. Although there seemed to be much mutual respect, if not quite friendliness, during Armstrong's seven-year winning run (Hinault on one occasion advising Armstrong to give his opponents "no gifts" in the form of stage wins), the Badger and Armstrong appeared to be at odds during Armstrong's comeback Tour. Hinault couldn't understand why on earth the American had returned; had he not found something better to do? He openly criticized him, telling *Le Parisien*, "I hope he will not be at the Tour. Is he afraid of France? Nobody forces him to come; he only has to stay at home! He cannot win the Tour. I hope that Contador gives him a beating."

When he read Hinault's comments, Armstrong, via Twitter, responded, "What a wanker. Five TdF wins doesn't buy you any common sense."

In a funny way, this—or Armstrong's method of retort, shared with his two million–plus Twitter followers—highlighted one key difference between Hinault and Armstrong. It sounds simple but is actually quite telling: Hinault would *never* join Twitter. It seems inconceivable.

During the 2009 Tour, there is no doubt that Contador suffered through being in the same team as such a dominant, overbearing personality—just as LeMond had done in 1986. But each time, the outcome was the same: The younger man won. Another similarity was that afterward, when asked to name his toughest opponent, Contador replied, "The hotel." Like LeMond, Contador had the sense that, by leading the Tour and being the strongest rider in the race, he was rewriting the preferred script.

During the race, Hinault was asked if the Armstrong-Contador situation reminded him of his tussle with LeMond in 1986. "No, no," he replied. "There was no controversy between Greg and me. In 1985, I was designated to win the Tour. In 1986, he was there to win the Tour. And it happened like that.

"What we see [in 2009] is that there are two who want to win. It is the opposite of 1986. Armstrong says he wants to win. Contador says, 'I am also here to win.'"

As Hinault says, completely different from 1986.

Sure.

We can agree on one real difference, though. Whereas 1986 pitted two outstanding riders, both close to the top of their game, against each other, 2009 was, in a sporting sense, no contest. Armstrong in 2009 was not as capable as Hinault in 1986 of "stirring the pot," of igniting the race with the kind of attacks that, 23 years earlier, put LeMond on the ropes. There was also a sense, for all that Contador suggested he struggled to retain his sanity in the team hotel, that the Spaniard is much tougher than his fragile-looking body suggests. He doesn't seem as prone to doubt and anxiety as perhaps LeMond was.

Unexpectedly, the "greatest ever Tour" question received an airing again during the 2011 race. That owed too much, I think, to the closeness of the four riders at the top of general classification in the final week. And maybe to the identity of one of those riders: the man in yellow, with an outside chance of becoming the first home winner since Bernard Hinault in 1985. Plucky, gutsy, tenacious Thomas Voeckler, his tongue lolling, his face fixed in a look of fright, his body apparently permanently on the verge of collapse, defended the yellow jersey as though the pride of an entire nation depended on it. Which it did. Voeckler performed heroically in the final week as the Tour entered the Alps and Cadel Evans and the Schleck brothers, Andy and Frank, nibbled away at his lead.

Finally, just 48 hours before Paris, the Tour came down to a familiar showdown on—of course—Alpe d'Huez. And here, finally, Voeckler's luck—or his legs—expired. But not without a brave, agonizing effort to keep the lead. In the end, Voeckler couldn't even retain a place on the podium, slipping to fourth as Evans became the first Australian winner. The French, meanwhile, continue their wait for a successor to Hinault.

A memorable Tour, then, that captivated fans across the world and proved as historic, in Australia at least, as 1986. But the greatest ever? I don't think so, for the simple reason that for all that it was close and exciting, it lacked an all-time great. It seems unlikely that Evans, the Schlecks, or Voeckler will ever be mentioned alongside Coppi, Anquetil, Merckx, Hinault, and the rest. Also missing was an edge to the various rivalries in 2011. There wasn't the undercurrent of fear, suspicion, and intrigue that made 1986—and other great Tours—so compelling.

And so I return to 1986. It remains a Tour that meets all the criteria, checks all the boxes, pushes all the buttons. It was a close battle. It was deeply symbolic, with the new world–versus–old world confrontation. It featured not one but two of the all-time greats. And there was an edge to their rivalry that was sharpened to a lethal point by the fact that they were teammates.

It was during the final week of the 2011 Tour, in the Italian town of Pinerolo, that I finally laid eyes on a relatively unoccupied Bernard Hinault. It was about 10 minutes before the stage started, and he was standing by his official car, parked just in front of the gathering peloton, talking to one of his ASO colleagues. I approached him, reaching into my bag and pulling out a copy of *Slaying the Badger*.

"*Monsieur Hinault, un cadeau pour vous,*" I said, handing him the book.

"Aaahh," he replied, not making eye contact but taking the book, opening it, flicking through some of the pages, and lingering briefly on the pictures. "*Merci,*" said Hinault, snapping it shut, tossing it into the car, and resuming the conversation I'd interrupted as I shuffled away.

I confess to not being too surprised that I haven't heard what Hinault thinks of my book (and also to relief that his English probably doesn't extend to "slaying"). I'm not sure he would be troubled by his depiction in these pages (which, in any case, I hope is balanced). Hinault, as should now be abundantly clear, isn't swayed—far less dependent on—the opinions of others. (Another reason why I don't think we'll ever see him on Twitter.)

Greg LeMond, of course, is another case. I heard from Kathy LeMond, in a breathless e-mail: "Oh my god Richard. I am sitting in a coffee shop parking lot and just finished your book. I needed coffee because I was up all night reading. We got the book yesterday."

It's a little embarrassing to reprint the e-mail verbatim because it was, to my great relief, complimentary. "I was brought back to 1986 as though I was reliving it," Kathy continued. "I actually feel nervous even now. I learned things that I never knew." Naturally, I received this as the very highest praise. She said she felt the portrait of LeMond and Hinault was "honest and authentic."

But there was no word from LeMond. I sent him a few e-mails but didn't hear back. Eventually Kathy wrote again: "I think it is hard for him to read about himself but he wants me to tell you that he thought you did a fantastic job on it."

The most interesting reaction from one of the main protagonists came from the rider who finished third: Urs Zimmermann.

Zimmermann sent a long, idiosyncratic, quite wonderful e-mail. "When I was reading the book in the last two weeks I was always in something like a hidden world of my mind," he wrote. What he went on to say prompted me to consider an aspect of the story that I hadn't given much thought to. While we in the English-speaking world are preoccupied with the way the English speakers—LeMond, Kelly, Roche, Anderson, et al.—changed the face of the sport in the 1980s, what did those in the traditional cycling nations make of this invasion? Did they recognize the phenomenon, and are they familiar with the story? Zimmermann suggests not. Though he says that reading the book forced him to "consider the past in a new way," he adds, "Despite the fact I was [later] a member of the 7-Eleven and Motorola teams, I never would have known all this detail about the English-speaking cycling world."

Zimmermann also said that there is one episode in the book with which he is "not 100 percent satisfied."

It concerns the 17th stage, to the Col du Granon, during which Zimmermann and LeMond broke away behind the stage winner, Eduardo Chozas. It was the stage on which Hinault, in the yellow jersey, struggled with injury and LeMond took over the race lead. But there is, as Zimmermann puts it, "a black hole." It concerns the question of who attacked first: LeMond or Zimmermann? Maurice Le Guilloux assured me that LeMond "never attacked the yellow jersey." Zimmermann suggests otherwise.

Zimmermann cast his mind back to that stage, and to what exactly happened on the climb before the Granon, the Col d'Izoard—or, more accurately, on the descent. It was here that he and LeMond went clear. It is a "black hole" because reports of what happened, and who initiated their escape, are vague and because the TV cameras missed the crucial action (as they often do on descents).

"It was Greg who did the initial attack," says Zimmermann. "I was on his wheel, in the first sharp turns of the descent. Some other riders crashed at this point, and we were gone. In the second part of the descent I gave Greg some support, but overall, Greg did 90 percent of the work down to Briançon. And—there was no team car."

Zimmermann continues, "Finally, in this famous climb into Briançon, Paul Köchli moves up to Greg and says, 'What the hell are you doing Greg?' This was the moment I knew; now it's exclusively up to me to work." The impression that day—formed by the footage of Zimmermann leading all the way up the Granon—was of Zimmermann leading the charge with LeMond sitting on, riding defensively. But Zimmermann witnessed something else.

Zimmermann continues, "Up to that moment there was nothing that made me sure there was a war between Hinault and LeMond. Everything could have been a game of strategy, or the impact of Fignon's failure. But for me, Greg's attack on the Izoard was evidence there was a war. It looks like this is a black hole of that Tour; nobody wants to have a look at it."

Zimmermann draws a comparison with 1985, when LeMond escaped with Stephen Roche and was instructed not to cooperate. In 1986, the Swiss rider found himself in the Roche role, only this time there was no team car to tell LeMond not to work. "You suggest that Greg never attacked the yellow jersey," Zimmermann writes. "But what about if he does? What a pleasure to have Greg as the bad boy for once!"

Zimmermann raises an interesting point. But given the wider context— what had happened in 1985 and Hinault's agreement to help LeMond; his repeated attacking; LeMond's distrust of Hinault and others; the fraught atmosphere in the team—few would perhaps blame LeMond for breaking with protocol and, away from Köchli's watchful eyes and with Hinault suffering with injury, seizing his chance when it came. Interestingly, Köchli himself did not identify this stage as a key moment in the 1986 Tour.

Köchli had asked to see the manuscript prior to publication, and several weeks later, I received a Skype message from him: "Are you available on the phone? I don't like Skype and I would like to talk to you."

I braced myself for what he had to say; I could picture him going through the manuscript in his Sonvilier office with a red pen. But Köchli, who had seemed so reluctant to speak in the first place and initially so guarded, could not have been more generous. "I can't say that for me, it was enjoyable to read," he said, chuckling awkwardly. Yet for more than an hour, he went through the text from beginning to end, correcting and clarifying. He called another couple of times with additional clarifications; as you'd expect from Köchli, it seemed important to get the details right.

In true Köchli style, he found fault with the most unexpected things: LeMond's claim that the cause of his diarrhea might have been a bad peach, for example. Köchli seemed offended by the idea that LeMond could have been given a piece of rotten fruit while riding for his team.

"A bad peach!" Köchli said indignantly. "This is not possible. In my team? No! If you eat a bad peach, you know it is bad and you throw it away. You don't eat it. No. I'm sorry."

He also took exception to Shelley Verses's description of Hinault as "Mussolini, Stalin, and Hitler rolled into one."

"No!" he said. "This is not true, not true. You cannot say this."

Köchli remains fiercely protective of Hinault—someone who doesn't appear to need much protection.

And others' reactions? Of the current peloton, David Millar, an avid student of the history of the sport, muses, "I have my theory on Hinault. He did keep his promise, is a man of his word, but the only way he could do that was by racing for the win in a totally reckless manner. His Pyrenean adventure, the kamikaze solo while in yellow, he did that because it was the only way he could satisfy everybody, the French people and his inner demons.

"If he pulled it off, which deep down he would have known he couldn't, LeMond would have had no choice but to admit he didn't deserve to win," Millar continues. "But if he lost, he went down in flames satisfying those who wanted to see him win his sixth. His heroism and panache vindicated his pact with LeMond."

If Millar's analysis is correct, you wonder if Hinault had it all thought out or whether such a rationale existed only in his subconscious. It is why Hinault continues to fascinate. Did he merely follow his instinct ("As long as I breathe, I attack"), or was he more calculating? Another reader suggests that Hinault was searching for a "decisive moment" in order "to excuse himself from having to consciously make the decision to compete with or support LeMond," at which point he could say—perhaps to himself, perhaps to the French people—that he was either going to win or lose. His problem was that the decisive moment he so craved never came.

The reaction from one reader prompted me to think about another aspect of the story—an obvious one, but one that I hadn't given much consideration to because it seemed so obvious. The reader, Gabriel Karaffa from New York, notes that the 1986 Tour was "a stark example" of so many different people "pursuing their own agendas." The problem, of course, was that so many of the dominant players—from the charismatic, wealthy team owner to the coaching genius to the two strongest riders—happened to be in the same team. In cycling, perhaps more than any other sport, this is a recipe for conflict. Because, as Karaffa notes, cycling "was not originally a team sport, but it evolved into one. . . . The problem with this, of course, is that only one rider can win the general classification. . . . Were it to completely convert to a team sport, all events would be decided by team classifications."

Those of us who follow cycling closely accept that it is a team sport and rarely reflect on how unnatural this is. Perhaps it's best described as an individual team sport.

But it is an aspect of the sport that cuts to the heart of the 1986 drama. Neither Hinault nor LeMond was drawn to cycling in order to become a member of a successful team. Teenagers do not embark on the road to a career as a professional cyclist harboring dreams of becoming a domestique. The team role is something that is forced on the majority of riders by their own limitations. For those without limitations—Hinault, LeMond—it is a near-impossible compromise.

With his kind permission, I end with Karaffa's conclusion—which also returns to the question posed at the start of this Afterword and represents a decisive vote in favor of that contentious subtitle:

"The combination of Tapie's goals, Köchli's lack of decisive leadership (though his hands may have been tied by Tapie's goals and Hinault's personality), Hinault's inability to plot a moral course, and LeMond's desire to win (coupled with his unparalleled strength) created what you have described as 'The Greatest Ever Tour de France.' Every other race has paled in comparison."

ACKNOWLEDGMENTS

I owe huge thanks to Greg and Kathy LeMond and Bernard Hinault for inviting me into their homes and for so willingly revisiting the events of 1986 as well as the background to their epic battle at that year's Tour de France.

And I am very grateful to many other key players from the 1986 Tour and from this golden era of cycling, in particular Paul and Edith Köchli and Shelley Verses but also, in no particular order, Andy Hampsten, Cyrille Guimard, François Thomazeau, Gilles Le Roc'h, Jean-François Bernard, Jim Ochowicz, Jonathan Boyer, Maurice Le Guilloux, Paul Kimmage, Phil Anderson, Sam Abt, Trip Gabriel, Sean Yates, Stephen Roche, Steve Bauer, and Urs Zimmermann. Thank you, too, to Robert Garbutt and the staff at *Cycling Weekly* for allowing me access to their library and Barbara Rumpus and Thierry Dengerma at *L'Équipe* for access to *L'Équipe*'s back catalog.

Merci bien to Daniel Friebe, my colleague and linguistic maestro, without whose help this book would be greatly diminished. Likewise, to my editor at Yellow Jersey, Rowan Yapp, for her good ideas and helpful suggestions and to Matt Phillips and his predecessor, Tristan Jones, for liking the idea in the first place. For their help with this book, thanks to Victoria McArthur, Brian Palmer of the Washing Machine Post for his eagle eye, my good friend Peter Orr for his enthusiasm and forensic attention to detail, and of course my agent, Mark "Stan" Stanton—but Stan, you were definitely wrong about the title. Special thanks to Jill Douglas. Thanks as ever to my dad, Brian, and Jennifer; my brothers, Robin and Peter; and my "sister," Iciar Gomez. And *merci ma chérie*, Virginie Pierret, for love and support.

I watched Marina Zenovich's film, *Who Is Bernard Tapie?*, with great interest and amusement and recommend it to anyone interested in this fascinating character. The following books and publications also proved interesting and, in some cases, invaluable: *Hinault par Hinault* by Bernard Hinault with Jean-Paul Brouchon (Éditions Jacob-Duvernet); *Greg LeMond: The Incredible Comeback* by Samuel Abt (Stanley Paul); *Memories of the Peloton* by Bernard Hinault (Springfield Books); *We Were Young and Carefree* by Laurent Fignon (Yellow Jersey); *Off to the Races* by Samuel Abt (VeloPress); *Le Flambeur: La Vraie Vie de Bernard Tapie* by Valérie Lecasble and Airy Routier (Grasset); *Viva la Vuelta* by Lucy Fallon and Adrian Bell (Mousehold Press); *Kings of the Road* by Robin Magowan and Graham Watson (Springfield Books); *Librement* by Bernard Tapie (Plon); *The American Invasion* by Don Alexander and Jim Ochowicz (Alexander and Alexander); *Alpe d'Huez: The Legend* by Gérard Ejnès; *Rough Ride* by Paul Kimmage (Yellow Jersey); *The Tour Is Won on the Alpe* by Jean-Paul Vespini (VeloPress); *The Sweat of the Gods* by Benjo Maso (Mousehold Press); *Uphill Battle: Cycling's Great Climbers* by Owen Mulholland (VeloPress); *Golden Stages of the Tour de France*, edited by Richard Alchin and Adrian Bell (Mousehold Press); *Légendes du Tour de France 100 ans de Pyrénées* by Pierre Carrey (Grimal Editions); and "Into the Valley," the brilliantly vivid article by Robert Millar in *Rouleur* magazine, issue 13.

INDEX

Note: n. indicates footnote. When articles or prepositions in foreign languages (*le, la, van,* etc.) occur in people's surnames, the name is alphabetized by the first letter of the article (e.g., Le Guilloux is alphabetized under *L*). When they occur in riders' nicknames or in the names of organizations, places, etc., those names are alphabetized by the first letter of the first nonarticle word (e.g., La Vie Claire team is alphabetized under *V*; Le Blaireau is alphabetized under *B*).

Alpe d'Huez, 238–239
    Fignon's defeat of Hinault (1984), 123–126
    and LeMond-Hinault cooperation, 2–4
    and Merckx (1977), 124
    1984, 119, 123–126
    1986, 237–250
"L'Américain." *See* LeMond, Greg
The American Invasion, 185–186
Amstel Gold, 76
Andersen, Kim, 137
    and Hinault, 144
Anderson, Phil
    and Altenrhein world championships
        (1983), 95–98
    and Hinault, 252
    on Hinault, 22–23
    on Hinault and LeMond, 189, 229
    and LeMond, 94–95, 230
    on LeMond, 57, 64, 230
    and Tour de France (1985), 145–147
    and Tour de France (1986), 189, 203,
        207–208
Anquetil, Jacques, 6, 22, 27, 43, 79, 181, 279
    death of, 180
    on Hinault, 263
    public image, 79
    retirement of, 39
    on Tour de France (1986), 180
Arbes, Hubert, 47
Argentin, Moreno, 97
Armstrong, Lance, 77, 215, 220, 267, 276
    and Hinault, 277
    and LeMond, 71, 271
    and Tour de France (2009), 276–278
    VO₂ level, 58n.

Arnaud, Dominique, 209
Arroyo, Angel, 123
L'Auto, 92

"The Badger." *See* Hinault, Bernard
Bauer, Steve, 6, 268
    encounter with gun-wielding driver,
        169–170
    on Hinault, 44, 188
    on Hinault and LeMond (Tour de France,
        1986), 203, 204, 209, 215, 248
    Köchli on, 134
    on LeMond, 10, 57, 60
    and Tour de France (1985), 146
    and Tour de France (1986), 162, 178, 188,
        201, 223, 226
    and Tour de France (1986, Alpe d'Huez
        stage), 240–243
    and Tour de France (1986, Puy de Dôme
        stage), 261
    and Tour de France (1986, Villard de Lans–
        Saint-Étienne stage), 252
Baylet, Mayor of Valence d'Agen, 15, 17, 19
Belda, Vicente, 90
Bellocq, François, 49
Bérard, Charly, 178, 261
Bergelin, Christian, 246
Bernadeau, Jean-René, 18, 78
Bernard, Jean-François ("Jeff"), 6, 177–178
    author's interview with, 223–225
    description of, 223–224
    and Hampsten, 177–178
    Hampsten on, 267
    on Hinault, 209, 224
    on Köchli, 224

on LeMond, 194, 231
on LeMond and Hinault, 224
and Tapie, 177, 223, 225
and Tour de France (1986), 178, 179, 191,
    267
and Tour de France (1986, Alpe d'Huez
    stage), 239–240
and Tour de France (1986, Bayonne-Pau
    stage), 201–204, 207
and Tour de France (1986, Luchon-Blagnac
    stage), 220
and Tour de France (1986, Nîmes-Gap
    stage), 221–223
and Tour de France (1986, Pau-
    Superbagnères stage), 215
Beth, personal assistant to LeMond, 10, 11–
    12
Bidot, Jean, 23
"Le Blaireau." *See* Hinault, Bernard
Bobet, Louison, 23, 46
Bontempi, Guido, 191, 263
Borysewicz, Eddie, 95
Bourlon, Alberto, 276
Boyer, Jonathan "Jock," 63, 65, 92
and Goodwood race (1982), 66–70
on Hinault, 80–81
on LeMond, 67–68
Brittany, 7–8

Cabestany, Pello Ruiz, 190
and Tour de France (1986, Alpe d'Huez
    stage), 240–243
"The Cannibal." *See* Merckx, Eddy
Cascarino, Tony, 134, 137
Cavendish, Mark, 190
    Köchli on, 219
Chozas, Eduardo, 203, 231, 280
Cipollini, Mario, 190
Circuit de la Sarthe, 113
Club Olympique Briochin, 25
Contador, Alberto, 276–278
Coors Classic, 56, 269–270
Coppi, Fausto, 244, 279
Crepel, Philippe, 100, 106
Crise de foie (liver pain), 83–84
Cycling
    European, LeMond's youthful enthusiasm
        for, 59
    as game, 83
    individualism and teamwork in, 283
    as job or vocation, 78–79, 116–117
Cyclists

in Hinault masks, 90
interrupted maturation of, 109–110
Cyclocross, 117

De Maerteleire, Kenny, 61, 61n.
De Vlaeminck, Roger, 35
Delgado, Pedro, 6, 151
and Tour de France (1986, Bayonne-Pau
    stage), 202–205, 207–208
and Tour de France (1986, Pau-
    Superbagnères stage), 209, 218
Dierickx, André, 35–36
Doping, 276
    accusations against Hinault, 48–49
    Cascarino on Tapie and, 137
    Köchli's opposition to, 110, 131, 135, 136–
        138, 271
    LeMond's opposition to, 270–271,
        272
    Zimmermann's opposition to, 271

L'Équipe, 92
Evans, Cadel, 278–279

Fignon, Laurent, 6, 115
    Achilles tendon injury, 143
    and Altenrhein world championships
        (1983), 96
    and Guimard, 85, 135, 136
    and Hinault, 185
    on Hinault, 98–99, 99n.
    on Hinault, Köchli, and Guimard, 120
    and Tour de France (1984), 119–127, 244
    and Tour de France (1986), 159, 180–181,
        185, 203, 247, 281
    and Tour de France (1986, Meudon-Saint
        Quentin stage), 187, 189
    and Tour de France (1986, Nantes time
        trial), 192–193
    and Tour de France (1986, stage 6), 191
    and Tour de France (1986, withdrawal),
        208–209
    and Tour de France (1989), 270, 275–276
    as Tour de France winner, 99, 100
    and Vuelta a España (1983), 89–92, 100
"Le Flambeur." *See* Tapie, Bernard

Gabriel, Trip, 199–200
Giro d'Italia, 46, 59, 141–142
Gisiger, Daniel, 113
Goddet, Jacques, 40–41, 42, 47
    on Hinault, 185, 191, 207

and inclusion of Puy de Dôme, 261
and internationalization of Tour de France,
  92–94
last Tour de France, 161–162
and Tour Mondial idea, 93
warning of danger to LeMond, 255–256
Gordis, Kent, 59, 63, 79
Gorospe, Julian, 90
Grand Prix des Nations, 113, 126
Grand Tours, 59
and Hinault, 76
Grewal, Alexi, 211, 211n.
Guimard, Cyrille, 6, 27–28, 29, 110
  on conflict between two riders who can
    win, 159
  conflict with Hinault, 80–81, 85, 98–100,
    99n., 101–102, 105
  description of, 31–32
  as directeur sportif, 31, 32
  early training regimen for LeMond, 64
  and English lessons, 54, 63
  falling out with René Hinault, 76–77
  and Fignon, 85, 135, 136
  Hinault, work with, 27, 28, 29, 34, 35, 45
  on Hinault, 31, 32–34, 85–86, 100, 118,
    164–165
  on Hinault's abandonment of Tour de
    France (1980), 47
  and Hinault's crash on Col de Porte, 36–37
  on Kathy LeMond's presence, 139
  and Köchli, 112
  on Köchli, 117–118
  and LeMond, 28, 62–64, 135–136
  on nice men and success in sport, 34, 70
  and Système U, 159
  on Tapie, Hinault, and LeMond, 253–254
  and Tour de France (1984), 119, 122–123,
    125–127
  trip to U.S. to meet LeMond, 50–51, 53–54

Haghedooren, Paul, 220
Hampsten, Andy, 6, 44, 141–142, 268
  and Bernard, 177–178
  on French affection for Hinault, 238
  on Hinault, 162–167, 226, 267–268
  on Hinault's break in Bayonne-Pau stage,
    201–202, 207
  on J.-F. Bernard, 267
  on Köchli, 163, 207, 226
  Köchli on, 219
  on LeMond, 61–62, 71, 226, 267–268
  on 7-Eleven team, 185

on Tapie, 226
and Tour de France (1986), 178, 179, 194,
  221, 223, 232, 267
and Tour de France (1986, Pau-
  Superbagnères stage), 210, 212–214,
  213n., 215
and Tour de France (1986, Puy de Dôme
  stage), 261
and Tour de France (1986, Villard de Lans–
  Saint-Étienne stage), 252
on Tour de France (1986) and move to
  7-Eleven team, 267–268
and Tour of Switzerland (1986), 166–167
Herrera, Luis "Lucho," 6, 122
  and Tour de France (1985), 145, 149
  and Tour de France (1986), 201, 203–205,
    210, 212
  and Tour de France (1986, Alpe d'Huez
    stage), 239, 247
Hinault, Bernard, 279
  and accusations of doping, 48–49
  and "appointments" (winning selected
    races), 44, 77
  and Armstrong, 277
  and "attacks of insolent youth," 107, 124
  author's visit to home of, 7–10, 82–83
  bike as graduation present, 24
  as "Le Blaireau" (the Badger), 5, 19–20
  breakout season (1978), 39–44
  and brother Gilbert's bike, 24–25
  comparison with LeMond, 56–58, 75
  conflict with Guimard, 80–81, 85, 98–100,
    99n., 101–102, 105
  confrontations with protester and striking
    workers, 115–116
  crash and win in Dauphiné Libéré (1977),
    36–39
  and cycling as game, 83
  and cycling as job, not vocation, 78–79,
    116–117
  deal to help LeMond in 1986 Tour de
    France, 157, 158, 160–162, 181–183, 225–
    231 227, 228–231, 264
  "destructive rage" of, 21
  and "La Doyenne" (1977, win in), 35–36
  early career (as amateur), 25–27
  early life, 20–21, 23–25
  on excessive dope testing, 78
  as farmer, 23
  father's brief criticism of, 20–21
  and Fignon, 185
  "first career," 29

first official race, 25
and Ghent-Wevelgem (1977, win at), 35,
    36, 76
Goddet on, 185, 191
and Guimard, 27, 28, 29, 34, 35
Guimard on, 31, 32–34
Hampsten on, 162–167
Hinault by Hinault (autobiography), 18
on his boyhood, 15
on his self-confidence, 13, 143
home in Brittany, 9–10
knee problem, 21, 45, 46, 48, 49, 90–91,
    99, 100
and Köchli, 112, 113–118
on Köchli, 113–114, 172
on Köchli and Guimard, 106
Köchli on tactics of (Tour de France, 1986),
    217–219
as leader, 165
and LeMond, 86, 200, 225–226
on LeMond, 74, 157, 158, 160–162, 255, 260,
    265
and LeMond in Coors Classic (1986),
    269–270
LeMond's defecation on postcards of, 2,
    197
on LeMond's family, 265
on LeMond's salary, 133
and Liège-Bastogne-Liège, 45–46, 76
as "little Napoleon," 16
low initial salary, 28
Memories of the Peloton (autobiography),
    18
and Merckx, 34–35, 36, 38
military service, 26
and 1986 season (pre–Tour de France),
    173–174
nocturnal habits, 164–165
as "old world" cycing representative, 3
open-mindedness of, 115
opposition to race radios, 172–173, 190
and Paris-Roubaix, 45, 76
as *patron* of peloton, 22–23, 73, 80–82, 84,
    90, 99
personality of, 4–5, 7, 9, 17, 34, 199, 264–265
physical description and abilities, 9, 33
and pragmatism vs. panache, 78–79, 81, 89
pre–Alpe d'Huez activities (1986), 237–238
professional career, beginning of, 27–29
as proud, stubborn Breton, 23, 24
public image and media relations, 74–80
reaction to his final Tour, 262–264

reaction to this book, 279
on Renault's style, 102
in retirement, 272–273
retirement, effect of, 262
as rival and teammate of LeMond, 2–3, 6
"second career" (La Vie Claire), 91,
    100–106,
on self-control, 26
as sheet metal worker, 25
stoic response to pain, 21–22, 82, 83–84
as team player, 43–44
and Tour de France (1978, first win), 39–43
and Tour de France (1978, leader of strike
    in), 15–19, 40–42, 78
and Tour de France (1979, winner of), 44
and Tour de France (1980), 46–48
and Tour de France (1982, performance
    on), 87
and Tour de France (1984), 119–126
and Tour de France (1985), 143–154, 146n.
and Tour de France (1986), 1, 157, 158–160,
    179–183, 193–194, 217–228, 262–267, 277,
    280–282
and Tour de France (1986, Alpe d'Huez
    stage), 237–250
and Tour de France (1986, break in
    Bayonne-Pau stage), 200–208
and Tour de France (1986, Clermont-
    Ferrand–Nevers stage), 263
and Tour de France (1986, final stage into
    Paris), 262, 263
and Tour de France (1986, Gap-Col du
    Granon), 231–235
and Tour de France (1986, Meudon-Saint
    Quentin stage), 187–189
and Tour de France (1986, Nantes time
    trial), 191–193
and Tour de France (1986, Nîmes-Gap
    stage), 221–223
and Tour de France (1986, Pau-
    Superbagnères stage), 208–216, 210n.
and Tour de France (1986, Puy de Dôme
    stage), 260–261
and Tour de France (1986, Saint-Étienne
    time trial), 256–260
and Tour de France (1986, stage 6), 191
and Tour de France (1986, Villard de Lans–
    Saint-Étienne stage), 250–253
and training, 29, 40
trip to U.S. to meet LeMond, 50–51, 53–54
and Vuelta a España (1983), 89–91
on why he races, 73, 74, 77, 81

world title at Sallanches, 48–50
and Zimmermann, 237–238
Hinault, Gilbert (brother of Bernard), 18, 24
Hinault, Joseph (father of Bernard), 20–21, 24, 27
Hinault, Josiane (sister of Bernard), 24
Hinault, Lucie (mother of Bernard), 24
Hinault, Martine (wife of Bernard), 10, 28, 47, 60–61, 77
Hinault, Mickael (son of Bernard), 28, 29, 47
Hinault, Pierre (brother of Bernard), 24
Hinault, René (cousin of Bernard), 25, 37
   falling-out with Guimard, 76–77, 80
Hommes, Femmes, Mode d'Emploi, 175–176

Indurain, Miguel, 77, 194

Kelly, Sean, 42, 67, 68, 95
Kiefel, Ron, 140, 141
Kimmage, Paul, 173–174
   on Hinault, 229–230
   as journalist, 271
   on LeMond, 195
   and Tour de France (1986), 194, 229
   and Tour de France (1986, Nantes time trial), 194–195
   and Tour de France (1986, Nantes-Futuroscope stage), 195
   and Tour de France (1986, Villard de Lans–Saint-Étienne stage), 250
Knickman, Roy, 162
Köchli, Edith, 108
Köchli, Paul, 6, 29, 106, 158, 206
   author's visit to home of, 107–110
   on Bauer, 134
   beginning of coaching career, 111–113
   brief career as cyclist, 109–111
   and Guimard, 106, 112
   Hampsten on, 163, 207
   and Hinault, 112, 113–118, 282
   on Hinault and Tour de France (1986), 180, 213, 225–226, 266
   on his "strategic game" (Tour de France, 1986), 217–219, 220, 222–223
   on interrupted maturation of cyclists, 109–110
   on Kathy LeMond's presence, 139
   and LeMond, 113, 135, 136, 138, 171–172, 215
   on LeMond and Tour de France (1986), 180, 213, 218, 222, 225–226, 266
   and LeMond at Alpe d'Huez (1986), 240
   opposition to doping, 110, 131, 135, 136–138,

271
   opposition to race radios, 172–173, 190
   and Plattner, 110, 111
   and post–Alpe d'Huez press conference (1986), 249
   as the "professor," 163–164
   reaction to this book, 282
   on Roche, 128
   role with La Vie Claire team, 133–135
   and Swiss riders, 178–179
   and Tapie, 113, 114
   and Tour de France (1984), 119
   and Tour de France (1985), 143, 145, 148–151
   and Tour de France (1986), 179–180, 188, 204, 267, 281–282
   and Tour de France (1986, Saint-Étienne time trial), 257
   on La Vie Claire jersey design, 118–119
   on Zimmermann, 233

Lama, André, 37
Lapize, Octave, 276
Laurent, Michel, 158
Lavainne, Christophe, 220
Le Clerc, Patrick and Pierre, 78
Le Guilloux, Maurice, 19–20, 27, 45, 158
   on Hinault's deal with LeMond, 160–161, 182–183, 228
   on LeMond and Hinault, 235, 259–260
   and Tour de France (1985), 148–150
   and Tour de France (1986), 204, 206, 209
   and Tour de France (1986, Saint-Étienne time trial), 257–259
Le Roux, Robert, 25–26, 28–29
Leblanc, Jean-Marie, 50, 53
Lejaretta, Marino, 89, 90
Leleu, Philippe, 178, 201
Lelouch, Claude, 175, 176
LeMond, Bertha (mother of Greg), 54, 56, 253
   and Tour de France (1986, Saint-Étienne time trial), 257–258, 259
LeMond, Bob (father of Greg), 54, 56, 95, 253
   as cyclist, 56
   and Tour de France (1986, Saint-Étienne time trial), 257, 259
LeMond, Geoffrey (son of Greg), 193–194
LeMond, Greg
   and ADD, 94
   on aftermath of Tour de France (1986), 268
   and Altenrhein world championships (1983), 94–98, 99

on American racers working as a team,
  68–70
and Anderson, 94–95
and Armstrong, 71
on Armstrong, 271
author's first interview with, 10–11
author's visit to home of, 11–12
bike-throwing incident, 62
on Boyer, 68–70
comparison with Hinault, 56–58, 75
conflict with U.S. national coach, 62–63
diarrhea attacks, 1–2, 195–197
as difficult to contact and pin down, 10
early life, 54–56
early professional career, 63–64, 73–74
encounter with angry, gun-wielding driver,
  169–170
and excessive heat, 65–66
on Fignon, 127
first races, 57–58
first races in Europe, 59
on French food superstitions, 84
and French language and culture, 54, 63,
  64–66
general opinions of other riders on,
  70–71
and Goddet's warning of danger, 255–256
and golf, 5, 71
and Goodwood race (1982), 66–70, 94
and Guimard, 28, 62–63, 135–136
on Guimard, 86–87, 96, 268
and Hampsten, 142
and Hinault, 86, 200, 225–226, 232
on Hinault, 86, 119, 127, 189, 231, 260, 268
and Hinault, easing off to allow him to win
  at Alpe d'Huez, 3–4
and Hinault in Coors Classic (1986),
  269–270
and Hinault's deal to help him in 1986 Tour
  de France, 157, 158, 160–162, 181–183,
  217–231, 264
on his focus on cycling, 71–72
on his individualism in sports, 13, 55
injury in hunting accident, 270
introduction to cycling, 55–56
and Köchli, 113, 135, 136, 138, 171–172
Köchli on, 218, 222
list of goals (1977–1978), 59
meeting of and marriage to Kathy, 60
move to France, 63–64
natural talent, "accumulative advantages"
  of, 57–59

as "new world" cycing representative, 3
and 1986 season (pre–Tour de France),
  169–171
and Olympic road race (1980), 59, 62
opposition to doping, 270–271, 272
opposition to race radios, 172, 190
personality of, 5–6, 7, 10–11, 65, 70–71
reaction to this book, 280
as rival and teammate of Hinault, 2–3, 6
semiexile from cycling, 271–272, 273
on sexual abuse experienced as teenager,
  271
and skiing, 55–56
and Tapie, 132–134, 132n., 176, 225
on Tapie, 260, 268
and Tapie's summons, 127–128, 131–132
and Tour de France (1984), 119–127
and Tour de France (1985), 143–145, 147–
  154, 281
and Tour de France (1986), 158–160, 179,
  193–194, 195–197, 199, 221, 280–282
and Tour de France (1986, Alpe d'Huez
  stage), 237–250
and Tour de France (1986, Clermont-
  Ferrand–Nevers stage), 263
and Tour de France (1986, final stage into
  Paris), 262, 263
and Tour de France (1986, Gap–Col du
  Granon), 231–235
and Tour de France (1986, and Hinault's
  break in Bayonne-Pau stage), 201–208
and Tour de France (1986, Meudon-Saint
  Quentin stage), 187–189
and Tour de France (1986, Nantes time
  trial), 191–194
and Tour de France (1986, Nîmes-Gap
  stage), 221–223, 230
and Tour de France (1986, Pau-
  Superbagnères stage), 208–216, 210n.
and Tour de France (1986, Puy de Dôme
  stage), 260–261
and Tour de France (1986, Saint-Étienne
  time trial), 256–260
and Tour de France (1986, stage 6), 191
and Tour de France (1986, Villard de Lans-
  Saint-Étienne stage), 250–253
and Tour de France (1986, winner of),
  262–263
and Tour de France (1989, 1990, victories
  in), 270, 275–276
training approach, 56–57
victory yell, 53, 64

and visit from Guimard and Hinault, 50–51, 53–54

VO₂ level, 58, 58n.

and Vuelta a España (1983), 89–92

and world junior championship races, 59–60, 61–62

youthful enthusiasm for European cycling, 59

Zimmerman on, 234

LeMond, Karen (sister of Greg), 54, 56

LeMond, Kathy (sister of Greg), 54, 56

LeMond, Kathy Morris (wife of Greg), 10–11, 12, 53–54, 95–96, 268

on Goddet's warning of danger to Greg, 255–256

on Greg and food poisoning, 196

on Greg and Hinault, 245

on Hinault, 86, 193–194

on Köchli, 171

meeting of and marriage to Greg, 60

move to France, 63–64

reaction to this book, 280

as sole woman around Renault team (1980s), 138–139

and Tour de France (1986), 193–194, 245, 253

and Tour de France (1986, Saint-Étienne time trial), 257, 259

Lévitan, Félix, 19, 39, 40–41, 42, 47

and inclusion of Puy de Dôme, 261

and internationalization of Tour de France, 92–94

and Ochowicz, 186–187

and Tour of America, 93, 186

last Tour de France, 161–162

Liege-Bastogne-Liège, 35–36, 45–46, 76

Maglia rosa, 142

Maillot à pois, 93

Maillot jaune, 59

Marie, Thierry, 159

Marteil, Joël, 115

Martin, Raymond, 34

Martinez Acevedo, Serafin, 123

Merckx, Eddy, 6, 22, 27–28, 41, 76, 181, 245, 279

and Alpe d'Huez (1977), 124

and Hinault, 34–35, 36, 38

as patron, 84, 86, 90

punched by spectator (Tour de France, 1975), 243–244, 261

retirement of, 39

and Tour de France (1969), 209–210, 211, 276

Milan–San Remo, 59

Millar, Robert, 65

and Altenrhein world championships (1983), 95, 97

on Hinault, 81, 230, 282–283

on LeMond, 230

and Tour de France (1984), 121–126

and Tour de France (1986), 203, 204, 207–208, 210, 212–213, 218, 222, 230, 247

and Vuelta a España (1985), 202

Moser, Francesco, 140

Motorola team, 267

Mottet, Charly, 191, 209, 231–232

Neel, Mike, 141–142

Noah, Yannick, 80

Ocaña, Luis, 76, 100

Ochowicz, Jim

and Lévitan, 186–187

and Tour de France (1986), 186, 194

Olivier, Jean-Yves, 25

Olympique de Marseille (soccer team), 174, 175

Pantani, Marco, 244, 276

Paris-Roubaix, 45, 59, 76

Patron of the peloton, defined, 22

Pedersen, Jørgen, 193, 205

Peeters, Ludo, 45

Pevenage, Rudy, 45

Phinney, Davis, 190, 194

Plattner, Oscar, 110

Podium girls, 138

Poisson, Pascal, 90

Pollentier, Michel, 43

Popovych, Yaroslav, 277

Post, Peter, 230

Poulidor, Raymond, 27, 43, 74, 79

Powels, Twan, 220

Puig, Luis, 75

Raas, Jan, 17, 230

Race radios, 172–173, 190

"Ray-Bans crash" (Tour de France, 1985), 145–147

Red Zinger Classic, 56

Relocation of athletes, 54n.

Renault teams, 40, 50

cyclists in Hinault masks, 90

and Guimard, 68
and Hinault, 80–81, 85
and LeMond, 53–54, 65, 73, 86
Robic, Jean, 276
Roche, Stephen, 6, 65, 179
   and Altenrhein world championships
      (1983), 95, 96, 97
   on LeMond, 70–71
   and Tapie, 127–129
   and Tour de France (1985), 144, 148–153,
      218, 281
   and Tour de France (1986), 189, 191, 203,
      207–208, 209
   and Tour de France (1986, Villard de Lans–
      Saint-Étienne stage), 250–251
Rogers, Thurlow, 162
Rolling Stone coverage of Tour de France
   (1986), 199–200
Route de France, 33
Ruperez, Faustino, 97
Rüttimann, Niki, 150, 165
   and Tour de France (1986), 178–179, 188,
      201, 220–223, 267, 277

Saronni, Giuseppe "Beppe," 67, 70, 89, 96
Schleck, Andy and Frank, 278, 279
Schuiten, Roy, 27
7-11 team, 6, 141–142, 267
   and Tour de France (1986), 185–187, 189,
      190, 194
Simon, Pascal, 91–92
Simpson, Joanne, 11
Simpson, Tom, 11, 110
Soigneurs, 18, 18n.
Stablinski, Jean, 27, 28–29
Stieda, Alex, 185, 187, 189, 194
Superconfex team, 190
Système U team, 159
   and Tour de France (1986, Meudon-Saint
      Quentin stage), 187–189
   and Tour de France (1986, stage 6), 191

Talbourdet, Georges, 19
Tapie, Bernard, 3, 6, 268
   as actor, 175–176
   attitude toward doping, 137
   and Hinault, 176, 225–226
   and Hinault, alliance with, 101–106
   and Hinault's deal with LeMond, 160, 161,
      225–226
   imprisonment for match-fixing in soccer,
      175

and J.-F. Bernard, 177, 223
J.-F. Bernard on, 225
and Köchli, 113, 114
and LeMond, 132–134, 132n., 176, 225–226
motivation for funding La Vie Claire team,
   118
on LeMond, 159, 174
and LeMond, summons to, 127–128,
   131–132
personality of, 132–134, 175–177
as politician, 175, 176
as publicity hound, 131, 132–133
and Roche, 127–129
as sports turn-around artist, 174–175
and Tour de France (1984), 119, 125–126
and Tour de France (1986), 188
and Tour de France (1986, Alpe d'Huez
   stage), 238, 242–243, 253
and Tour de France (1986, Saint-Étienne
   time trial), 260
Tertre, Paul, 28
Thévenet, Bernard, 36, 38–39, 74, 195
   public image, 79
Thurau, Dietrich, 35
Tour de France, 59
   1947, 276
   1969, 209–210, 211, 276
   1978, 15–19, 39–43, 78, 276
   1981, 73
   1984, 119–127
   1984 (Alpe d'Huez stage), 119, 123–126
   1985, 143–154
   1985 (Alpe d'Huez stage), 2–4
   1986, 157–162, 177–183, 262–263, 277, 278,
      279, 280–284
   1986 (Alpe d'Huez stage), 237–250
   1986 (Bayonne-Pau stage), 200–206
   1986 (final stage into Paris), 262
   1986 (Gap-Col du Granon), 231–235
   1986 (Köchli on Hinault's tactics), 217–219
   1986 (Luchon-Blagnac stage), 219–221
   1986 (Meudon-Saint Quentin stage),
      187–189
   1986 (Nanterre-Sceaux stage), 185–187
   1986 (Nantes time trial), 191–194
   1986 (Nantes-Futuroscope stage), 195–197
   1986 (Nîmes-Gap stage), 219–220, 221
   1986 (opening-week stages), 189–190
   1986 (Pau-Superbagnères stage), 208–212
   1986 (Puy de Dôme stage), 260–261
   1986 (*Rolling Stone* coverage of), 199–200
   1986 (Saint-Étienne time trial), 255–260

1986 (stage 6), 191

1986 (Villard de Lans–Saint-Étienne stage), 250–

1989, 270, 275–276

1990, 270

1998, 276

2003, 276

2009, 276–277

2011, 278–279

debate over best ever, 275–279

and Hinault, 39–43, 44, 46–48

Hinault's confrontation with protester (2009), 115–116

Hinault's performance in 1982, 87

increased commercialization of, 40–41

Köchli and (1968), 110, 111

"Ray-Bans crash" (1985), 145–147

Van Impe's victory, 35

See also Goddet, Jacques; Lévitan, Félix

Tour de l'Avenir, 70, 73–74, 110, 196

Tour de l'Oise, 64

Tour de Romandie, 110

Tour of America, 93, 186

Tour of Flanders, 59

Tour of Lombardy, 126

Tour of Switzerland, 180

1986, 166–167, 169

Ullrich, Jan, 276

Union Cycliste Internationale (UCI), 60, 61

Valence d'Agen, France, 15–18, 19, 78

Vallet, Bernard, 21, 78, 229

Van der Poel, Adri, 97

Van Der Velde, Johan, 190

Van Impe, Lucien, 18, 32

at Dauphiné Libéré (1977), 36, 38

Tour de France victory, 35

Van Poppel, Jean-Paul, 190

Vanderaerden, Eric, 159

Verschuere, Pol, 187

Verses, Shelley, 185–186

on Hinault, 140, 217, 226–228

on Köchli's opposition to doping, 138

on LeMond, 227

on working for cycling team as a woman (1980s), 139–140

La Vie Claire team, 1, 2, 6, 101–106

interaction among Köchli, Hinault, and Tapie, 118

jersey design, 118–119

LeMond contract, 132–133

1986 training camp, 162–165

team for 1986 Tour de France, 157–159

and Tour de France (1986), 187–189, 267

See also Hinault, Bernard; Köchli, Paul; LeMond, Greg; Tapie, Bernard

Vigneron, Alain, 178, 261

Voeckler, Thomas, 278–279

Vuelta a España, 39–40, 59

1983, 89

1984, 202

Webb, Graham, 110

Who Is Bernard Tapie?, 175–176

Wilcockson, John, 67

Wilmann, Jostein, 46

Winterberg, Guido

and Tour de France (1986), 178–179, 188, 220, 218, 222, 277

and Tour de France (1986, Alpe d'Huez stage), 239–240

Yates, Sean, 21, 22, 146n.

Zenovich, Marina, 175

Zimmermann, Urs, 6

on LeMond, 234

novel by, 234n.

opposition to doping, 271

reaction to this book, 280–282

and Tour de France (1986), 189, 208, 210, 212, 218, 222, 280–281

and Tour de France (1986, Alpe d'Huez stage), 237–243, 246, 247

and Tour de France (1986, Bayonne-Pau stage), 203, 204, 233–234

and Tour de France (1986, Gap-Col du Granon), 231–235

and Tour de France (1986, Saint-Étienne time trial), 258

and Tour de France (1986, Villard de Lans–Saint-Étienne stage), 250–251

Zoetemelk, Joop, 36, 43, 44, 46, 50

and Tour De France (1986), 209

Zubeldia, Haimar, 277

ABOUT THE AUTHOR

Richard Moore is a freelance journalist and author. His first book, *In Search of Robert Millar*, won Best Biography at the 2008 British Sports Book Award. His second book, *Heroes, Villains and Velodromes*, was long-listed for the William Hill Sports Book of the Year. He writes on cycling and sport and is a regular contributor to the *Guardian*, Sky Sports, and the *Scotsman*. He is also a former racing cyclist who represented Scotland at the 1998 Commonwealth Games.